Changing Jobs

third edition

A Handbook for Lawyers in the New Millennium

Heidi McNeil Staudenmaier
Editor

Contributing Editors:
Bradley Abbas
Toya Cook-Haley
Diane L. Drain
Tracy S. Essig
Timothy R. Hyland
Maureen P. Kane
Jeffrey R. Simmons
Consuelo Ohanesian
David E. Vieweg

Defending Liberty
Pursuing Justice

Law Practice Management Section
American Bar Association

Commitment to Quality: The Law Practice Management Section is committed to quality in our publications. Our authors and editors are experienced practitioners in their fields. Prior to publication, the contents of all our books are rigorously reviewed by the LPM Publishing Board and outside experts to ensure the highest quality product and presentation. Because we are committed to serving our readers' needs, we welcome your feedback on how we can improve future editions of this book. We invite you to fill out and return the comment card at the back of this book.

Cover design by Laura Jacobson for Seven Rays, Inc.

© 1999 American Bar Association. All rights reserved.
Printed in the United States of America.

Library of Congress Catalog Card Number 99-65978
ISBN 1-57073-739-8

03 02 01 00 99   5 4 3 2 1

Discounts are available for books ordered in bulk. Special consideration is given to state bars, CLE programs, and other bar-related organizations. Inquire at Book Publishing, American Bar Association, 750 N. Lake Shore Drive, Chicago, Illinois 60611.

TABLE OF CONTENTS

Acknowledgments . . . . **xiii**

Introduction . . . . **xv**
Heidi McNeil Staudenmaier

PART I
Career Planning Strategies   **1**

Chapter 1
Career Changing in the New Millennium 3
Bruce Tulgan
    Profound Changes in the Economy 3
    Forces Shaping the Workplace of the Future 4
    The New Career Paradigm 6
    Think Outside the Box About Your Career Options 6
    Reinvent Your Role Where You Are Working Now. 7
    Leave Without Really Leaving 7
    Start Your Own Business 7
    Conclusion 7

Chapter 2
Career Self-Assessment 8
Maureen Provost Ryan
    The Goals and Benefits of Self-Assessment 8
    Career Self-Assessment: How to Do It. 9
    Skills Identification. 9
    Knowledge Areas 11
    Values 12
    Settings. 14
    Holland Code 16

Pulling It All Together 16
Conclusion. 17

Chapter 3
Personality Factors and Career Choice **18**
Dr. Larry Richard
Jung's Theory of Psychological Types 19
Extraversion versus Introversion 20
Sensing versus Intuition 21
Thinking versus Feeling 22
Judging versus Perceiving 23
Overview. 25

Chapter 4
Looking for More Career Satisfaction?
Use Your Whole Brain **26**
Dr. Janina C. Latack
A Whole-Brain Approach to Increasing Career Satisfaction 27
The Left-Brain Approach to Increasing Career Satisfaction 28
Is It the Job or Is It the Career?. 29
The Elusive Quest for Balance. 30
Identifying and Prioritizing Career Satisfaction Factors 33
The Right-Brain Approach to Increasing Career Satisfaction 34
Conclusion. 36

Chapter 5
Market Assessment: Translating Your Skills
to the Changing Profession **37**
Dr. Abbie Willard
Career Changes in the Law 37
Trends in the Market 39
Translating Your Skills to the Changing Profession 40

Chapter 6
How to Change Jobs If You Want To or Have To **42**
David S. Machlowitz
Warning Signs. 44
How to Prepare 45
Picking Up the Pieces. 46
Conclusion. 47

PART II
Career Identification   **49**

Chapter 7
Effective Job-Search Techniques and Strategies **51**
Michael J. K. Schiumo
Strategy 1—Focus and Plan 51
Strategy 2—Informational Interviews 52
Strategy 3—Allocate Your Time Properly 52
Strategy 4—Devote Your Full Effort 54
Strategy 5—Develop a Good Support Network 55
Seven Steps in a Successful Legal Job Search Campaign 55

Chapter 8
Networking **56**
Kathleen Brady
What Is Networking? 56
It Is Not Reasonable to Expect a Job Will Be Handed to You! 56
What If I Have No Contacts? 57
Strategies for Approaching Contacts 58
The Letter 58
The Telephone Call 58
The Informational Interview: Setting the Agenda 59
The Follow-Up 61
Overcoming the Fear of Being Labeled a "User" 62

Chapter 9
Using the Internet **63**
Erik J. Heels and Richard P. Klau
Applying for the Job You Want 63
Posting on the Web 66
Law-Specific Online Resources 67
Law Firm Web Sites 69
Discussion Lists 70
Topic-Specific Lists 71

Chapter 10
How to Use Your Law School's Office of Career Services **72**
Hillary Mantis
Services 72
Programs 73
Technology 74
Resources 74

Job Listings 74
Newsletters 74
Handouts and Regional Law Firm Lists 75
Books and Periodicals 75
Online Services 75
What Law School Offices of Career Services Do Not Offer. 75
Where to Look for Further Information 76

Chapter 11
Using Third-Party Intermediaries. **77**
Carol M. Kanarek
Legal Search Firms 77
Career Counselors 80
Outplacement Consultants. 82
Conclusion. 83

Chapter 12
How to Use the Bar Association as a Career Resource **84**
Brenda M. Thomas
Newsletters and Periodicals 84
Membership Directory 85
Legal Placement Services and Job Banks 85
Bar Web Sites 86
American Bar Association Division for Bar Services 86
You Can Work for a Bar Association 87
Jobs for Bar Staff. 87
Legal Organizations with Web Sites 88

Chapter 13
Career Opportunities for Minorities **96**
Suzanne Baer
Londell McMillan
Vanessa Davila
Networks and Mentors: You Never Know Who Is Going to Help You . . 96
Dealing with a Highly Competitive Work Environment 97
Career Advice from Minority Lawyers. 98
Choosing an Environment Where You Can Be at Your Best 99
Recruitment Opportunities and Professional Networks 100

PART III
Getting the Offer   **103**

Chapter 14
Writing an Effective Resume **105**
Pat Bowers Thomas
Description of a Resume 105

Different Uses of a Resume 105
Limitations of a Resume 106
Preparation of the Resume 107
General Rules 108
The First-Draft Components 109
The Visual Effect 111
The Examples 112
The Law Firm Resume 116
The Corporate Resume 119
The Law Firm Resume 123
The Corporate Resume 129
The Critical Eye 133
Comprehensive Addenda and the Resume Package 133
Testing Your Audience 134
Delivering Your Resume 135
Keep Your Resume Alive 136

Chapter 15

The Cover Letter **138**

Deborah Howard

Preparation 138
Self-Inventory 138
Develop a Target List 139
Research on Employers 139
Drafting the Letter 139
Opening Paragraph 139
Tailor Each Letter 141
Out-of-Town Employers 141
Why the Employer Should Be Interested in You 142
Crossover Applications 142
What to Leave Out 143
What Else to Remember 143
Closing Paragraph 143

Chapter 16

Interviewing Techniques **144**

Michael K. Magness
Carolyn M. Wehmann

Preparing for the Interview 144
The Initial Interview: Screening 146
The Follow-Up Interview: Selecting 147
Final Tips on Interviewing Strategies 149
Dos and Don'ts of Interviewing 150

Chapter 17
Negotiating Salary and Benefits **152**
Laura J. Hagen
    Overview 152
    Basic Compensation Schemes 152
    Law Firm Associates 153
    Negotiating Status 154
    Partner Compensation 154
    Book of Business 155
    In-House Compensation 156
    Preparing to Negotiate: The Rules 157
    The Negotiation 158
    Conclusion 158

Chapter 18
Making the "Right" Career Decision **159**
Robert A. Major, Jr.
    Short-Term Goals 159
    Long-Term Goals 160
    Factors Affecting Goal Attainment 162
    Research: Knowledge Is Power 163
    Making Job Selection Comport with Goals 164

PART IV
Career Options   **165**

Chapter 19
Practice Areas **167**
Brion A. Bickerton
    Predicting the Emerging Practice Areas 168
    Hot Practice Areas of the 1980s and Early 1990s—A Prologue 169
    Predicting the Hot Practice Areas for the New Millennium 170

Chapter 20
Geographic Areas **173**
Marcia Pennington Shannon
    Factor 1: Assess Your Motivations 173
    Factor 2: The Marketability of Your Practice Area 174
    Factor 3: Economic Climate of the Area 175
    Current Economic Trends 176
    Factor 4: Professional Development 177
    Factor 5: Personal Considerations That Affect You Professionally 177
    Ten Steps to an Effective Long-Distance Job Search—A Checklist 178
    Beyond the Obvious 179

The International Job Search 180
Resume Preparation 180
Finding the Job 181
Due Diligence 181
Some Additional Thoughts 181
Appendix A: Considering a Geographic Move: A Worksheet 182
Appendix B: State Bar Information 182
Appendix C: Creating the Practice Development Plan 192

Chapter 21
Law Firms **194**
Sandra O'Briant
Evolution of Today's Law Firms 194
Marketability 195
Size of Law Firms and Mergers 197
Law Firm Culture in the New Millennium 198

Chapter 22
Flying Solo **200**
Donna M. Ballman
Confessions of a Daredevil 200
Fear of Flying 200
Fear of Fleeing 200
Stalls in the Air 201
Stalls on the Ground 201
Touch and Go—Preparing to Solo 202
Touch and Go—Preparing to Go Solo 202
Solo Practice 202
Solo Flying 203
What It's Like to Go for It 203
Conclusion—Go for It 205

Chapter 23
Corporations **206**
H. Ward Classen
Finding an In-House Position 206
The Nature of In-House Positions 206
Identifying the Job Opportunity 207
Preparing for the Interview 208
The Interview 208
Receiving an Offer and Negotiating the Deal 209
Beginning Your Career 211
Mapping Your Career 211
Conclusion 212

Chapter 24
Federal Agencies **213**
Marilyn Tucker
    The Advertising of Lawyer Positions 214
    Target Your Federal Job Search. 216
    Legislative/Policy Positions 218
    Law-Related Positions 218
    Where the Jobs Are and Will Be 219
    Federal Employment and Future Marketability 220
    The Job of Getting a Job in the Federal Government 221
    An Aggressive Approach 222
    Timing Issues. 224
    The New Lateral Lawyer Recruitment Program, Department of Justice 225
    Compensation 226
    Career Advancement 227
    Advantages of Federal Legal Practice 227
    Capitol Hill 229
    Lawyer Positions on the Hill 230
    Job Search Techniques. 233
    Advantages and Disadvantages 237
    Federal Agencies and Capitol Hill—Resource List. 238

Chapter 25
The Judgeships **241**
Honorable Rebecca Albrecht
    What Skills Should a Judge Have?. 241
    What Are the "Costs" of a Judicial Career? 242
    Advantages of Being a Judge. 242
    The Judicial Selection Process in the State Court System 243
    The Federal Court System 244
    Becoming a Judge 245

Chapter 26
Judicial Administration, Staff Lawyers, and Law Clerks 246
A. Appellate Staff Lawyers **246**
Daniel P. Schaack
    What Staff Lawyers Do 247
    Pros and Cons of the Job 247
    Getting a Staff Lawyer Position 248
B. Law Clerks **249**
Sylvia J. Lett
    Which Court Is Right for You? 250
    The Application Process 250
    The Interview Process. 252
    Some Final Thoughts 252

Chapter 27
The Public Interest Market **254**
Alexa Shabecoff
C.A.Webb
    The Benefits of Public Interest Work 254
    Financial Considerations 255
    The Public Interest World: Finding Your Niche 256
    Public Defenders 257
    Nonprofit Public Interest Organizations 258
    Client-Oriented/Direct-Service Organizations 258
    Policy-Oriented Organizations 258
    Private Public Interest Firms 259
    International 259
    Legal Services/Legal Aid 260
    Creating Your Own Job: Fellowships and Entrepreneurial Grants 261
    Making Yourself Marketable 262
    Conclusion 262

Chapter 28
Teaching Law **263**
Gary A. Munneke
    Opportunities in Teaching 263
    Work 265
    Qualifications 266
    Pay and Benefits 267
    Finding a Job 268
    Conclusion 268

Chapter 29
Part-Time, Temporary, and Contract Employment **270**
Shelley Wallace
    Overview 270
    Part-Time, Temporary, and Contract Employment 271
    Alternative Working Arrangements Defined 271
    Corporate Law Departments 272
    Law Firms 272
    Alternative Work Arrangements: Circumstances and Opportunities . . 273
    Pursuing the Opportunity 276
    The Alternative Career Path 277

Chapter 30
Creating an Ideal Law Practice in Conjunction with Your Home **281**
Diane L. Drain
    Is an Office in or Near Your Home Possible? 284
    Goals 284

Special Issues Related to On-Site Offices 286
Setting Up a Small Office in Conjunction with Your Home 286
Office Requirements 286
Clients 287
Client Management 288
Equipment 288
Personnel 289
Miscellaneous 290
Office Management 290
Final Thoughts 290

Chapter 31
Telecommuting **292**
Nicole Belson Goluboff

Telecommuting: When Going the Distance Means Staying at Home . . 292
The Advantages of Telework 292
Increased Productivity 293
Greater Efficiency 293
Better Work Product 294
Increased Available Work Time 294
A Better and Cheaper Recruitment Process and Lower Turnover Costs . 295
Reduced Overhead Potential 296
Dispelling Concerns 296

Chapter 32
Nontraditional Careers for Lawyers **298**
Deborah Arron

Why Change Careers? 299
Keys to Success in Making a Career Change 300
Should You Be Leaving the Law? 301
Transferable Skills Analysis 302
Representative Alternative Career Choices 303
Leaving the Law Behind 304
Getting the Job 304
Would Only a Loser Lawyer Want a Job Outside the Profession? 305
You Cannot Afford to Take This Job 305
We Do Not Want a Lawyer in This Job 306
You Will Quit As Soon As You Find a Job in the Law 306
Stepping Out of the Profession 307

Resource List **309**

Contributors **325**

Index **335**

ACKNOWLEDGMENTS

The first edition of *Changing Jobs: A Handbook for Lawyers* was published in 1988 by the Career Issues Committee of the American Bar Association Young Lawyers Division. As a result of the dramatic change in the economic condition of the legal market during the late 1980s and the early 1990s, an update was deemed necessary. *Changing Jobs: A Handbook for Lawyers for the 1990s* was prepared with the hope that it would remain viable for job changers throughout the decade.

Now, with the year 2000 looming, yet another edition was considered worthy of undertaking. *Changing Jobs: A Handbook for Lawyers in the New Millennium* was prepared with the same care and attention to the many changes in the legal profession as were confronted in the prior editions.

Numerous individuals contributed to the success of this book and deserve some recognition for their assistance and efforts. First and foremost, without the support and cooperation of the experts and professionals who generously donated their time to researching and writing their chapters, this book would not be possible.

Equally important in the process were the contributing editors, many of whom are active members of the Maricopa County Bar Association's joint Quality of Life Committee with the State Bar of Arizona. These individuals are Bradley Abbas, Diane L. Drain, Tracy S. Essig, Toya Cook Haley, Timothy R. Hyland, Maureen P. Kane, Consuelo M. Ohanesian, Jeffrey R. Simmons, and David E. Vieweg. The contributing editors were instrumental in brainstorming the new edition, securing authors, and editing the written product submitted by the authors. Jeff, Brad, Dave, and Tim deserve special thanks for assuming—without complaint—"extra" burdens during the process. Beverly Loder of the ABA Law Practice Management Section publishing staff and Gary Munneke, Law Practice Management Section Chair for 1998–1999, also were extremely helpful, and their participation was crucial throughout the process.

Special kudos and thanks to my secretary, Valerie Corral, and to Arlene Cocco of the word processing department at my law firm, who were responsible for typing, revising, and proofing the various chapter drafts. Their hard work and efforts were invaluable. My law firm of Snell & Wilmer also deserves special mention for permitting me to take on this project and utilize firm resources and personnel.

Last, but certainly not least, I continually remain grateful to Bill, my husband of ten years. He supported me throughout the last edition and this recent edition, without complaint (even when it meant taking over more than his fair share of the duties for our three-year-old daughter, Kathleen). I thank him for enthusiastically supporting my numerous bar activities over the years at the local, state, and national levels. None of my bar work would be possible without his encouragement and support.

Heidi McNeil Staudenmaier
President (1999–2000)
Maricopa County Bar Association
Phoenix, Arizona

Introduction

Introduction

Heidi McNeil Staudenmaier

Ch-ch-ch-ch-changes
(Turn and face the stranger)
ch-ch-changes
— David Bowie, "Changes"

While much has stayed the same, there also have been many changes since the last edition of this book in the early 1990s. From a personal perspective, I remain the rarity among lawyers graduating from law schools since the early 1980s. I am still at the same law firm that I joined upon graduation in 1985—the same firm where I was a summer associate (although we were simply referred to as "law clerks" back then). And, while I may check the "grass is greener on the other side" concept from time to time—which I recommend that everyone undertake on a periodic basis no matter how satisfied you are with your job—I continue to conclude that I am in the right place.

Once again, I will use my husband to exemplify reality in the legal profession. When the last book was published, he was on job no. 3 since graduating from law school in 1987 (not including a one-year federal clerkship). Since that time, he has changed jobs yet again, returning to private practice after enjoying six years as in-house counsel for a major utility company. His changes have come about for various reasons, with the latest being motivated by an opportunity to work with a noted expert in his chosen area of practice, although there certainly was risk involved in making the change.

My career has not been devoid of change, however. In July 1996, my husband and I were blessed with our daughter, Kathleen, who is now an active and precocious toddler. After her arrival, I realized how important it is to balance work and family. Consequently, I have changed my work habits to help strike this balance. Telecommuting, e-mail, and the Internet have helped lawyers like me spend more time at home, yet continue to provide timely and quality service to clients.

Whatever the reason, lawyers continue to change jobs with regularity. Indeed, the late 1990s saw a boom in lateral hiring by law firms across the country: entire practice groups moved firms or highly sought-after specialists or rainmakers were "cherry picked" and enticed to pull up stakes for greener pastures. The statistics still show that most lawyers change jobs at least once (and these days, even more frequently) during their first ten years of practice.

Changing Jobs: A Handbook for Lawyers in the New Millennium is an update of the prior edition, but you will find many new chapters that were not even contemplated as truly workable for the legal profession until recently. For example, we have included chapters on using the Internet for career changing; telecommuting; and creating an ideal law practice based in your home. We also have added a chapter on negotiating salary and benefits in response to the lateral hiring trend. Additionally, we have included information on international job hunting.

This handbook is intended to assist lawyers—regardless of their age or years in practice—contemplating a change in legal positions or exiting the legal business entirely. The Maricopa County Bar Association's Quality of Life Committee (which was a joint effort with the State Bar of Arizona) enlisted the gracious assistance of over thirty experts in the fields of career planning and placement for lawyers to write this third edition. We hope that this book will remain a viable resource for job changers into the year 2000 and beyond.

Part I of the book begins with an overview of job changing in the new millennium, followed by strategies and techniques for successful career planning. Again, the key question you must first ask: Do you *really, really* want to be a lawyer, or do you want to do something else? The answers are found through chapters dealing with self-assessment, personality factors, market assessment, involuntary change, and finding more satisfaction with your current career.

Part II focuses on how to go about the job search. Chapters include job-search planning, networking and resources such as the Internet, law school career services offices, third-party intermediaries, bar associations, and other informational sources.

The fundamental skills required of a successful job hunter are explored in Part III. Topics covered include effective resume writing, cover letters, interviewing techniques, negotiating salary and benefits, and making the "right" decision once the offer is extended.

Part IV provides detailed analyses of employment opportunities for experienced lawyers within various public sector and private sector practice settings. Separate chapters are devoted to substantive practice areas ("what's hot, what's not"), geographic areas (including international job hunting), private practice in law firms, going solo, corporations, government, judgeships, judicial administration (including appellate staff attorneys and law clerks), teaching, legal aid, legal services and public interest, part-time/contract work, in-home law practice, and telecommuting. And for those lawyers who find that perhaps law is not quite what they wanted after all, the final chapter addresses nontraditional careers for lawyers.

The book concludes with a comprehensive bibliography of career-planning and job-finding resources.

No matter what changes you are contemplating, we hope that the tips and guidelines offered by the experts in this book will assist your career-change process. More important, by reading this book you will have the confidence that whatever the future holds with respect to your legal career, you have carefully planned a road map to long-lasting satisfaction.

PART I

Career Planning Strategies

CHAPTER 1

Career Changing in the New Millennium

Bruce Tulgan

I was a lawyer for 428 days, and then, five years ago at the age of twenty-six, I retired. After going straight through twenty years of school and then choosing a job with a big law firm in New York City, I realized that the career path I was trying to follow was outdated. As you think about the issue of changing jobs for lawyers, ask yourself if you, too, have been pursuing an obsolete career path. Changing jobs in the workplace of the past was a very different proposition than changing jobs in the workplace of the new millennium and beyond.

Profound Changes in the Economy

We are living through the most profound changes in the economy since the Industrial Revolution. Technology, globalization, and the accelerating pace of change have yielded chaotic markets, fierce competition, and unpredictable staffing needs; the relationship between employers and employees has been fundamentally reshaped. The fastest growing forms of work in today's economy are temporary work, leased work, outsourced work, consulting, and small to midsized business entrepreneurship (fueled largely by the booms in temping, leasing, outsourcing, and consulting).

All of these trends are freeing work from the confines of the old-fashioned "job," where you would go to work every day to the same organization in the same building during the same hours and perform the same tasks and responsibilities in the same position for a stable chain of command. In this system you could pay your dues and climb the ladder. The old-fashioned job and the career path that went along with it were perfectly designed for the industrial economy, and the system worked very well for more than a hundred years. No more.

The transformation in the economy is affecting lawyers at all levels: you probably have clients that are downsizing, restructuring, and reengineering, or perhaps you are working in-house at an organization that is going through some or all of these convulsions. So far, very few law firms have engaged in the kind of radical workplace conversions that are occurring in most industries; however, the changes under way in large accounting and consulting firms—including in some cases discarding the partnership structure—suggest that similar moves may soon be visited upon the legal profession.

Forces Shaping the Workplace of the Future

It is important to note the seven most powerful forces of change shaping the new working world:

1. Reengineering

Companies in almost every industry are wholly redesigning the way work gets done. Old-fashioned departments are being dissolved. People and resources are being reorganized along product and service lines and in ad hoc teams formed to address immediate needs. Long-standing work systems are being dismantled and refashioned to improve flexibility, efficiency, and effectiveness. For example, much of the document handling that has been a mainstay for so many lawyers will be streamlined with new technologies; thus, much less time and energy will be required for this task than in the past.

2. Restructuring

As business leaders reinvent work processes, organizational hierarchies are being leveled. Multiple layers of management are being eliminated. In their place are fluid, cross-trained teams, tackling whatever work needs to be done. There is no room for "deadwood" at any level. While many workers are eliminated, those who remain as part of smaller core groups of permanent employees have more work to do than ever before, and these core employees must be prepared to perform a wide range of tasks from one day to the next. This trend presents a direct threat to the traditional partnership system that is still used in most law firms.

3. Technology

Because of advances in technology, traditional boundaries are blurring—roles and tasks that used to be quite separate seem to be overlapping. It's no longer clear who is supposed to do what. It makes a lot less sense today for the senior partner in a law firm to have a secretary type letters ("dictated but not read"), when the partner has a computer sitting right on her desk. Filing is no longer a full-time job when most files are stored electronically in a local area network (LAN) and can be retrieved with the press of a button. Most offices will still need support workers, but their role is transforming, as is the role of the lawyer.

4. Knowledge Work

Selling knowledge used to be the special province of lawyers, doctors, architects, accountants, and others in the traditional professions. Not anymore. In the post–information revolution economy, market leaders in every industry will be the organizations that know how to employ knowledge workers—those who routinely leverage information and knowledge—at every level. The knowledge and ideas of any employee can quickly become product and service innovations that shake up markets and keep an organization on the cutting edge. No matter where you work, no matter what you are doing, you have to upgrade and diversify your skills and knowledge continually. You cannot rest long on your legal training, nor can you be satisfied with the traditional opportunities for continuing education.

5. Diversity

Although our society has made important strides toward workplace diversity over the past several decades, employers increasingly must accommodate the changing face of the American workforce: women, people of color, people with alternative sexual preferences, people with disabilities, people of all ages, non-English-language speakers, and others across the demographic map. By the middle of the next century, Americans who belong to racial and ethnic minority groups will outnumber non-Hispanic whites. Blacks, Asians, Native Americans, and Hispanics, alone, will attain a collective majority in the United States shortly after the year 2050. The wide range of life experiences, perspectives, preferences, values, and styles of this diverse workforce is radically rewriting even the most basic expectations about ways of doing business. So use your particular qualities to contribute to the reshaping of the legal profession. Understand what sets you apart from the crowd and how your difference might make you better prepared to understand, engage, or maximize a particular client or practice area.

6. Globalization

Multinational corporations have been pushing for globalization for decades. Advances in communications and transportation technologies have removed one barrier after another to international trade. With the dramatic geopolitical changes in the 1990s—the opening of Eastern Europe, the passage of the North American Free Trade Agreement (NAFTA), the General Agreement on Tariff and Trade (GATT), and the consolidation of the European Economic Community, to name a few big ones—few barriers remain. The doors have been blown off the hinges: almost anyone today can buy from foreign suppliers, manufacturers, wholesalers, and retailers; sell to foreign companies and foreign consumers; tap into existing markets or open new markets, start up foreign ventures, take over and reinvigorate existing business entities. So globalize yourself. Travel abroad and learn a language, a culture, and a foreign city. When you return home, you will be better equipped to help a law firm establish a global practice or to help clients do business in global markets.

7. Virtual Workplace

The traditional boundaries of the workplace and the workday are fast dissolving. You no longer have to go to a building to go to work, especially if you are doing most of your research on Lexis-Nexis or Westlaw, writing briefs, or preparing other documents; your client does not have to know that you are sitting by the pool when you call. With cell phones, laptop computers, and modems, you can do most legal work almost anywhere and anytime, as long as you have a power source. With global time differences to accommodate and round-the-clock service to provide, you can no longer afford to work nine to five. I am sure most lawyers have already done plenty of work from airports, hotel rooms, and offices at home. Many people today are working in executive suites rented by their companies far from company headquarters or in offices shared with colleagues because no one spends enough time in the office consistently enough to justify assigning one person per work space (an arrangement called "hoteling"). If you take full advantage of telecommuting, flexible schedules, and virtual office technology, you will probably end up doing a lot more work, under more convenient circumstances, and you will also have more time to devote to your personal life.

The New Career Paradigm

In response to all of these changes, a new career paradigm is emerging. Especially among those with high levels of education, training, and marketable skills—like lawyers—people are starting to see themselves as free agents. As sole proprietors of their skills and the ability to add value, these free agents are moving seamlessly from one new opportunity to the next. They think of their employers as "clients," create each job as a series of projects, and cash out their career investments regularly, often so they can reassess and renegotiate.

In the workplace of the past, the frequent job changer was labeled a "job hopper" and was often viewed with suspicion by many potential employers. Seniority was king, so the best strategy for most people was to stay in the same organization for as long as possible, to make a long-term investment and wait for the big pay-off. But in today's economy success will not be defined by where you stand in relation to the hierarchy of a particular law firm, corporation, or any other established institution that might employ you. Security will come from options rather than from commitments, from mobility rather than stability.

Stop thinking about moving from one good job to another and start thinking about your career in a whole new way. Position yourself as a free agent and focus on the key strategies that will guarantee your success in the workplace of the future. Be a voracious learner and keep building your skills and knowledge to forestall obsolescence. Anchor yourself to individuals instead of institutions. Look everywhere for new opportunities to add value and sell your way into those challenges. Work hard, but avoid burnout. Keep moving your life toward balance every day; take care of yourself because *you* are the only career asset that you can really count on.

Think Outside the Box About Your Career Options

Once you start thinking "outside the box," you will identify new opportunities to add value almost everywhere you look, more than you can possibly handle—some as a practicing lawyer, some not. Consider three outside-the-box options:

Reinvent Your Role Where You Are Working Now

There may be plenty of opportunities to change jobs within the law firm or legal department where you are now working. Work for multiple partners or senior lawyers within the organization—do not be content to work for just one boss. Work in several practice areas at once, so you will not be pigeon-holed. Juggle as many different matters as you can. Keep your eye out for projects to which you would like to be assigned: when your work schedule opens up, approach the lawyer in charge with a specific proposal for the role you would like to play in the project.

Leave Without Really Leaving

Short of moving to a entirely new job in a new organization, consider leaving your current position . . . without really leaving. You may be able to leave your full-time position but still add value as a part-time employee, flex-timer, or telecommuter. Perhaps you are well liked by certain partners or senior lawyers; you have a special rapport with certain clients; you have become quite familiar with particular matters; you have honed your skills in a specific practice area. These are assets that most law firms and legal departments will not want to lose.

Start Your Own Business

If you want to be your own boss, you can always hang out a shingle and go into private law practice. But just because you are a lawyer does not mean that is your only entrepreneurial option, or necessarily even your best option. The most successful entrepreneurs are starting businesses in emerging fields such as new media or businesses that flow from product and service innovations, so they do not have to contend with established competitors who already have more skills, knowledge, and experience over and above their existing customer base and cash flow. Consider merging a creative, nonlegal business concept with your experience and skill as a lawyer, and you may find yourself launching an innovative law practice. Perhaps you will revolutionize a whole practice area or invent a new one.

Conclusion

You will have endless options and plenty of mobility as long as you are willing to think outside the box about your career options and to reinvent yourself on an ongoing basis. As a lawyer, your level of knowledge and skill puts you in a very strong position. People like you will be in great demand in almost every industry for the foreseeable future, and not necessarily solely as practicing lawyers. Let me be among the first to welcome you to the workplace of the future. Do not be alarmed. It is going to be fine. It might even be fun.

CHAPTER 2

Career Self-Assessment

Maureen Provost Ryan

Whatever your dream job, identifying it may help you move toward it.
Robert O. Snelling, Sr.

Confronted with the necessity of a job hunt, candidates are advised by counselors to employ creative introspection and to assess the past thoughtfully in order to plan well for the future. Career self-assessment provides a road map that helps guide you to a desirable destination; without the destination or the map, you can become lost or sidetracked. Job searches are more efficient when the candidate has a clear sense of direction and purpose, and the resulting job is likely to be more satisfying. Morale is improved when your work is in sync with your values, skills, goals, and sense of higher purpose.

The Goals and Benefits of Self-Assessment

Introspection leads to insight, and insight leads to action and commitment. By engaging in self-assessment you can formalize the introspective process necessary to extract specific information and employ it usefully.

Career self-assessment guides the job seeker to articulate and define the following: accomplishments and achievements; motivated, functional, and transferable skills and success patterns (including legal and other skills); personality traits and style; work values, preferred working conditions, and the extent to which the current job fits these criteria; lifestyle needs (including geographic preference); interest areas and areas of expertise, which include compelling topics, causes to address, and problems to be solved; and potential professional or personal weaknesses to overcome.

You can achieve the following results through the self-assessment process:

- Clarification of objectives and articulation of goals
- Increased self-confidence

8

- Ability to describe and market oneself in an interview
- Ability to evaluate employment options informed by needs and desires
- Ability to create employment opportunities
- Sense of being in control by designing one's future
- A more efficient and focused job search
- Renewed enthusiasm with a positive expectation of the future

The self-assessment process allows you to shift from the posture of a passive victim to that of a powerful, efficacious person. For experienced lawyers, midcareer analysis and introspection provide an opportunity for realignment and redirection into more suitable employment.

Richard Bolles—the author of *What Color Is Your Parachute?*—advises the job seeker to identify the following factors as part of the process of identifying the ideal job:

1. Physical setting, including the geographic location that you prefer;
2. Salary level you expect to attain;
3. Tasks that are appealing to you;
4. Information you enjoy handling;
5. Issues that are satisfying and problems you enjoy solving;
6. Intangible aspects of a job, such as the emotional climate, working relationships among colleagues and the organizational culture that is compatible with your philosophy and values; and
7. Kinds of clients you prefer.

Career Self-Assessment: How to Do It

Various exercises can be used to assist law students and lawyers in their self-assessment process. Several such exercises appear throughout this chapter. Copy these pages and complete the questions. You may wish to work with a career consultant to process your findings and arrive at some decisions. He or she may utilize a variety of methods to assemble your profile, ranging from formal personality and career testing, to card-sort processes, to paper-and-pencil exercises. Some job seekers work through their goal clarification process with a friend or fellow job seeker. Contact your law school career services office—they provide counseling and information on a wide variety of topics free of charge to students and alumni.

Skills Identification

One of the most important aspects of the career-planning process is the identification of your most enjoyable skills, or success pattern (Exercises 1–3). Begin by cataloging the key events in your earlier life. To collect data about your past, you could write a narrative autobiography or utilize the shorter process described in this chapter.

Checklists also can provide an easy and effective means of self-analysis. Bolles's *What Color Is Your Parachute?* and *The Quick Job Hunt Map* list hundreds of skills and suggest that the job seeker indicate the number of times that these skills were utilized for each of the seven accomplishment stories being analyzed. The success pattern emerges very clearly through this exercise.

Skills are best evaluated in terms of your ability *and* the amount of satisfaction the use of the skill provides. Dory Hollander in *The Doom Loop System* asserts that some skills are enjoyable to use and others have either ceased to be or never were enjoyable to use. Therefore, a person may be good at something, even highly proficient, but no longer enjoys using this skill. Thus, once a list of skills has been developed, you should classify each one as enjoyable or no longer enjoyable and analyze the extent to which you are motivated to develop it further. Hollander believes that growth in one's career comes from developing skills in areas that are enjoyable but in which proficiency has not as yet been achieved. The doom loop occurs when a professional feels caught in a job that requires the use of skills that no longer are enjoyable or that one does not have.

EXERCISE 1: An Overview of the Key Events of Your Life

Draw four columns on a piece of paper. In the first column, make a vertical list of the five-year increments contained in your life span. Across the top of each of the remaining columns, write *Education, Work/Career,* and *Leisure.* For the duration of your life span, write down events in each of these areas, including the jobs you have held and the degrees you have attained at various schools. Examples might include winning a spelling bee or a science competition, being on a debate team or the Model UN, volunteering at a hospital, serving as an intern to a judge, learning a language, traveling abroad, arguing a case or participating in Moot Court, writing a thesis, working on a transaction, and so on.

EXERCISE 2: List of Accomplishments and Success Stories

List twenty accomplishments or achievements from your education, work/career, or leisure columns. Select the seven achievements that were most satisfying so that you can examine them more closely. For each, write a paragraph describing in detail the steps you took, from beginning to end, to achieve that satisfying result.

EXERCISE 3: What Are Your Transferable Skills?

List all the skills that were utilized for each of the seven achievement stories. Whenever possible, skills should be described in detailed phrases; avoid single-word entries. For example, "writing" is not nearly as descriptive as "writing performance manuals." A pattern should emerge from the seven stories. Which skills appear several times? Do some show up in every story? Each of us has hundreds of skills. Which skills do you consistently, characteristically, and happily utilize when faced with problems or challenges? The skills you have had the opportunity to practice have become competencies and proficiencies.

Knowledge Areas

Experience gained before, during, and after law school has allowed you to develop expertise in specific areas of the law or in dealing with the problems of certain types of people or organizations. Conduct an inventory of this experience (Exercises 4–6).

As a job seeker, you must consider whether you intend to stay in your current area(s) of practice or to shift to others. This shift might be achieved as easily as requesting new assignments or a change of practice area from your current employer. You may need to acquire additional training, such as pursuing an LL.M. degree or enrolling in continuing legal education (CLE) courses.

EXERCISE 4: In Which "Lawyer Skills" Are You Most Proficient?

In the first column below, indicate your level of proficiency on a scale of 1 to 5, with 1 as "not proficient," 3 as "average," and 5 as "excellent." In the second column, check those skills that you enjoy using and want to develop in your next position, regardless of how proficient you are now. (These skills were culled from the findings of the Harvard Career Paths Study, in which thirteen hundred lawyers identified traits necessary for success in the practice of law.)

Skill Level	Want to Develop?	Skill Clusters
_____	_____	Analytical abilities
_____	_____	Writing, legal drafting
_____	_____	Research, fact gathering, legal research
_____	_____	Oral advocacy, public speaking
_____	_____	Mediation
_____	_____	Negotiation
_____	_____	Adversarial skills
_____	_____	Business planning
_____	_____	Strategy formulation
_____	_____	Financial management, financial analysis
_____	_____	Assembling, structuring deals
_____	_____	Interviewing, client counseling
_____	_____	Management, manage complex tasks
_____	_____	Staff management, manage people
_____	_____	Business development, marketing
_____	_____	Client relations, client communications
_____	_____	Ability to build networks, networking
_____	_____	Productivity, work well under pressure
_____	_____	Quality control, attention to detail

_____	_____	Solve problems creatively
_____	_____	Commitment, drive, willing to put in long hours
_____	_____	Good judgment, common sense
_____	_____	Get along with colleagues, team player, good political judgment
_____	_____	Leadership
_____	_____	Ability to inspire confidence

EXERCISE 5: What Do You Want Your Work to Be About?

In which areas of practice do you have experience at present? Which do you find interesting? In which do you hope to continue to develop expertise?

What law-related and non-law-related interests do you have? What are the causes about which you feel most strongly? As a clue, consider the articles you stop to read in newspapers and magazines. What is the subject matter of the books you read? What seminars do you attend or wish you had the time to attend?

EXERCISE 6: What Do Your Billing Records Reveal About Your Experience?

Review the last few years of your billing or other work records to determine the types of work you have done in each practice area. Make an outline organized by practice area with the details of the experience you have in each area. On what types of transactions did you work? On behalf of what types of clients? How substantial were the amounts of money involved? If you are a litigator, what types of litigation were involved; what were the issues and the tasks required? What was the result for the client? What types of documents did you draft or work on? On which transactions or procedures did you work?

This research will be invaluable when you are marketing yourself to prospective employers. This document (called a "Summary of Experience") will describe the work you can do, the problems you can solve, and the projects that can be given to you immediately because of the nature of your experience.

Values

Another area you need to explore is values, which are also referred to as motivators, satisfiers, or "anchors" (Exercises 7–9). You can examine how past jobs and the present or last positions have been satisfying or unsatisfying, in an effort to compile a profile of factors to seek in the next position and factors to avoid.

EXERCISE 7: What Factors Are Crucial for Your Job Satisfaction?

Consider each item separately and rate each, with A as "very important," B as "moderately important," and C as "not very important."

_____	Achievement	_____	Pleasant surroundings
_____	Advancement	_____	Pleasure and fun
_____	Affiliation	_____	Prestige, status
_____	Authority/Power	_____	Public or client contact
_____	Autonomy/Independence	_____	Reasonable hours
_____	Being needed	_____	Recognition
_____	Boss you respect	_____	Respect
_____	Challenge	_____	Responsibility
_____	Competition	_____	Results of work seen
_____	Control	_____	Reward
_____	Creativity	_____	Salary
_____	Direct impact	_____	Stability
_____	Discovering new things	_____	Self-development
_____	Ethics/morality	_____	Self-expression
_____	Excellence	_____	Service
_____	Excitement	_____	Structured environment
_____	Improving the world	_____	Training
_____	Influencing people, leadership	_____	Traveling
_____	Intellectual stimulation	_____	Variety of work
_____	Interesting work	_____	Working alone
_____	Interpersonal relationships	_____	Working on teams
_____	Job security	_____	Other:
_____	Mentoring	_____	Other:

EXERCISE 8: How Happy Are You in Your Present Job?

Using the results of the previous exercise, list your top ten values down the left-hand column of a page. Across the top, list all the positions you have held thus far and, in doing so, create a grid for analysis. At the intersection of each job and each value, assign a 1–5 point score, 1 for "not satisfied" and 5 for "very satisfied." Finally, add the scores in each column to arrive at a total score for each of your past jobs.

To what extent does your present or most recent job satisfy your most important values? Which past jobs were more satisfying and why? Which factors are so important to you that you will be certain that they are present in your next job?

For instance, a job seeker might discover that he or she so valued having a boss he or she could respect, autonomy, and challenge that without these factors he or she would be miserable. These priorities will enlighten his or her evaluation of future opportunities, and the absence of these important values may explain the mismatch experienced in past jobs.

EXERCISE 9: What Did You Like and Dislike About Your Past Jobs?

List all jobs you have held since high school, including volunteer jobs and internships. For each position, list the aspects you liked and did not like.

What factors do you want to include in your next and future positions? Which factors do you want to avoid? Which factors are the most important contributors to your job satisfaction?

Settings

Exercise 10 asks the candidate to select appealing types of organizations in which to work. Preferences for work setting are related to values and suggest possible target employers, especially when cross-referenced with areas of practice in which the job seeker has interest or expertise. For example, if a lawyer is interested in pursuing elder law in the government, a hospital, a corporation, or a nonprofit organization, he or she would think, What kinds of jobs exist in each of these settings in the area of elder law? The answers to this question will generate a list of possible job titles in these settings to be researched.

Opportunities are plentiful as lawyers work in a variety of both traditional and nontraditional settings, ranging from law firms, corporate legal departments, accounting firms, prosecutorial offices, government and public-interest agencies, and the judicial system. Researching these options is covered in subsequent chapters of this volume.

EXERCISE 10: Where Might Your Talents Be Used?

Which of the following would be appealing settings in which to work? (Check all that apply, then place them in order by their desirability.)

_____   Accounting firm

_____   Advertising agency

_____   Bar association (national, state, or local)

_____   Community organization

_____   Consulting firm

_____   Continuing legal education provider

_____   Corporation

_____   Educational institution (law or graduate school, college or university, secondary school)

_____   Entertainment industry

_____   Entrepreneurial start-up

_____   Financial institution (bank, credit union, savings and loan)

_____   Government (federal, state, or local)

_____   Hospital

_____   Investment bank

_____   Insurance company

_____ Labor union

_____ Law firm

_____ Library or bookstore

_____ Lobbying organization

_____ Military

_____ Nonprofit organization

_____ Political organization

_____ Prepaid legal plan

_____ Private foundation

_____ Publishing house

_____ Trade association

_____ Transit company

_____ Trust company

_____ Other: _____

Place a check mark next to all types of organizations for which you have already worked. A lawyer considering building a practice might also use this exercise to decide which types of clients he or she would like to have.

EXERCISE 11: What Brings Out the Best in You?

Select several instances when you felt you did your *best* work, when you were proud of your results, everything seemed to go well, and obstacles were handled without difficulty.

Analyze these instances for the common themes that run throughout the skills and personality traits you have that contributed to the achievement of the goal, the reasons that you were inspired to do your best work, and the factors in the environment that enabled you to perform to this standard of excellence.

What are the implications for the type of work or projects you should seek out in the future? How can this information be used to describe you to a prospective employer in an interview?

EXERCISE 12: What Would Your Ideal Job Be Like?

Imagine that it is five years from now and you are reporting for work in a job for which you are very well-suited and in which you experience a great deal of satisfaction.

How long is your commute? If you go to an office, how do you get there? What type of setting are you in? Is it formal or informal? How are you and your coworkers dressed? Do you work in a team, alone, or both? How much time do you spend in and out of the office? What hours do you keep? What relationship do you have with your supervisor (if you have one)?

What types of clients do you have and what types of problems do you solve for them? How much pressure do you experience? What are the particular satisfactions of this work?

Holland Code

Finally, a fundamental aspect of style assessment is the mesh between your personality and the types of jobs to which you are drawn. The Holland classification system organizes jobs and people by themes and attempts to maximize the fit between people and careers. It is based on an assumption that there are six types of people and six types of jobs and that people are naturally drawn to jobs in which they could be themselves, use their strengths, and be surrounded by like-minded individuals. Various methods are used by career counselors to determine an individual's Holland Code, including card sorts and the Strong Interest Inventory. The six themes are *social, enterprising, artistic, investigative, realistic,* and *conventional.*

Lawyers often score as artistic, enterprising, and social. Holland noted that *artistic* types possess innovating, intuitive abilities and like to work in unstructured situations using imagination and creativity. They describe themselves as independent, unconventional, original, and intense. It is common to find a lawyer who in his or her life had strong interests in other types of artistic pursuits (e.g., the fine or performing arts) or who originally trained in an enterprise field (e.g., accounting or business). Those lawyers who have strong interests in areas other than artistic may experience restlessness or dissatisfaction in a traditional associate's role.

The Holland Code for a lawyer may indicate the area of practice for which he or she will be best suited. Artistic types communicate through words, visual images, or music. Do you, the lawyer, want to be a creative person? Or will you find it satisfying to have creative people as clients? If you want more artistic activity in your life, can the present job be expanded to include such activities or can your leisure pursuits more actively include artistic activities?

Enterprising lawyers will enjoy building a practice and counseling clients on the full range of problems encountered by businesses and corporations. Because of their strong leadership skills, they may enjoy the role of in-house corporate counsel, especially if they have the opportunity to participate in business decision making.

If your style as a lawyer is *social,* the importance of helping, counseling, and protecting the interests of individuals and families will be satisfying. These lawyers will actively seek out pro bono assignments to augment their work experience. If your score indicates that *investigative* is your style, scientifically based practice areas will be suitable, for instance, patent, environmental, medical malpractice, and health-law careers.

Conventional lawyers, because of their love of detail, will be drawn to financial, tax, and accounting matters. They will not mind the detail required in discovery and may be excellent at litigation-support projects.

If a lawyer has *realistic* preferences, he or she may enjoy work that allows time outside the office, such as environmental or construction law.

Pulling It All Together

To synthesize the results of your self-analysis into a coherent statement of immediate and long-range goals and objectives, you should, as a job seeker, consider enlisting the support of a career counselor, friend, or fellow job seeker. Job-search support groups are often available through bar associations, law schools, and other groups; these might be suitable settings in which to explore your options and generate possibilities.

One effective technique is to arrange the key factors on board using self-adhesive note papers. Note all findings, one key factor per note. Arrange them and rearrange them in clusters on the board to see how the whole picture fits together. This also helps you visualize the alternatives through making creative combinations. Show the board to a counselor, adviser, or friend, and brainstorm the possible jobs that would fit the criteria.

Consider whether your current job can be redesigned or changed in some way to better fit your strengths, preferences, and goals. Can projects be taken on that allow for development in the direction desired?

Stating your career objective in fifteen or fewer words will allow those who want to assist you or hire you understand what you are trying to accomplish. A suggested format would be as follows:

"I want to work as a _____ in a setting such as

_____ using my knowledge, skills, and expertise in

the area(s) of _____ on behalf of the following

[types of clients] _____."

Conclusion

The paradox of the job search is that you must simultaneously be focused on and open to possibilities. Too often, when you are a job candidate you feel at the mercy of a bad job market. You suspect that job satisfaction is a luxury and that you need to take just any job rather than the "right" job. The experience of looking for a new position can provide you with a valuable opportunity not only to reassess your career path, but also to explore your positive qualities, strengths, and potential. By conducting a thorough analysis of the past you can begin to chart your path to a more satisfying future. As you synthesize your findings you will be able to honor your preferences and your strengths as you step confidently into the future. As a job seeker, you must design your transformation, not merely survive it.

CHAPTER 3

Personality Factors
and Career Choice

Dr. Larry Richard

Finding job satisfaction in the practice of law has become a greater challenge during the past few years. With increasing time pressures, declining civility, and an increase in assembly-line legal work, many of your colleagues are facing difficulty finding a work environment in which they are able to enjoy the practice of law.

In order to find true work satisfaction, though, you have to do more than simply avoid an unpleasant work environment. What is needed is a thorough understanding of how your own personality fits key aspects of the job you select. The better the fit between your personality and your job, the greater the likelihood that you will experience job satisfaction.

A simple example suffices: a lawyer with a warm, nurturing personality and a high need for intimacy is more likely to report job satisfaction in a firm with an open, informal, and friendly "culture" and less likely to report job satisfaction in a firm with a more impersonal, austere, "eat what you kill" atmosphere.

Many lawyers wishing to change jobs make the common mistake of asking the wrong questions. For example, the first thing that many lawyers want to know is, What's out there? The individual hopes that he or she can discover an existing position that offers more satisfaction than the current job. However, it rarely works this way. A much better question to ask first is, What's my own personal career identity? If you can identify your unique personality needs, and begin to understand how deeply they affect your work satisfaction, you will be in a much better position to then turn your attention to the marketplace. Even more to the point, you will be better equipped to understand the specific features of jobs that might suit you. The principle that makes this possible is called the Job-Person Fit Theory.

Put simply, the Job-Person Fit Theory holds that the higher the degree of congruence or "fit" between an individual's overall career identity and the

18

demands of the job, the more likely it is that the individual will experience a higher level of job satisfaction. There are five critical elements of your overall career identity—your values, psychological needs, communication style, motivated skills, and career interests. Each one of these can be analyzed to determine whether there is a good fit between you and the job.

In this chapter I focus on the third component of career identity—your communication style. When I work with an individual, I often start with this component. Once you understand your communication style, you not only gain information about your job-person fit, but other side benefits as well. First, you will gain an understanding of how people think and behave in different ways. This knowledge can be valuable in guiding your approach to subsequent job interviews. Second, you will gain a new vocabulary that makes it easier to talk about all the other career components.

In this chapter we look at the system of personality—Carl Jung's Theory of Psychological Types—on which the Myers-Briggs Type Indicator (MBTI) is based. I review the MBTI categories and explain how lawyers score on them. I then relate this information to issues of job-person fit. Through this discussion, keep in mind that there is a danger in relying on just one career assessment tool when making a significant career decision, so be sure you read the following information about the MBTI in the context that I have provided above.

It is important to remember that the well-known and widely used MBTI is a formal professional tool and can be administered only by a licensed psychologist or someone specifically trained and certified to do so. This latter group includes many career counselors, placement officials, guidance counselors, therapists, and others. To find a qualified professional, check with your local law school placement office or university counseling center. You may also contact the Center for Applications of Psychological Type, Inc., a nonprofit agency in Gainesville, Florida (1-800-777-CAPT). They will be able to provide the name of a qualified counselor in your area.

Jung's Theory of Psychological Types

Carl Jung, the Swiss psychoanalyst, developed an insightful system of personality classification based on the idea that much of the patterned, habitual behavior of people can be explained by their preferences on four scales:[1]

Extraversion versus Introversion[2]
Sensing versus Intuition
Thinking versus Feeling
Judgment versus Perception

Jung conceived of each scale as a dichotomy. He reasoned that although everyone utilizes both sides of a given scale on a regular basis, over time each individual develops a psychological comfort for one side in favor of the other. The preferred side thus tends to have greater influence over a person's thoughts and behavior and eventually forms recognizable personality patterns. Preferences tend to be stable, long-term, and pervasive.

The MBTI reports one's preferences in the form of a letter score (E or I, for example) for each of the four scales, along with a numerical score that indicates how strong a score is.[3]

Each person maintains an independent preference on each of the four scales. For example, I prefer Extraversion over Introversion, Intuition over Sensing, Feeling over Thinking, and Perception over Judgment. Collectively, these four preferences constitute one's MBTI "type." I would thus be said to prefer the Extraverted Intuitive Feeling Perception type, or ENFP. (The "N" is used to designate Intuition so as not to confuse it with Introversion, which also begins with an "I".) There are sixteen such combinations possible in the MBTI system:

ISTJ	ISFJ	INFJ	INTJ
ISTP	ISFP	INFP	INTP
ESTP	ESFP	ENFP	ENTP
ESTJ	ESFJ	ENFJ	ENTJ

FIGURE 3.1

We can look at the four MBTI scales to understand more clearly the differences they represent:

Extraversion versus Introversion

This scale measures one's preferred source of psychological energy. People who prefer Extraversion are energized by the world outside their psyche, or by stimuli coming from outside the self. People who prefer Introversion are energized by their inner world, or by stimuli from inner thoughts, feelings, and sensations.

Extraverts are more likely to be gregarious, to enjoy client contact, and to prefer discussing a legal matter more than writing about it. They may tend to think out loud, and they do this more to clarify their own thoughts than to engage in meaningful conversation. They may positively enjoy the rainmaking process, are more likely to join clubs and bar associations, and will prefer breadth and variety in their work.

Introverts, on the other hand, tend to be more reserved, prefer working alone or in one-on-one relationships, and enjoy analyzing and writing about a legal issue. Their thinking is usually done silently, to themselves. They tend to prefer concentrating on a topic in depth, thinking it through and reflecting on it. The same events that an extravert finds exciting and energizing—parties, crowds, fast-breaking events—may be experienced by an Introvert as overstimulating, "too much," or simply not enjoyable.

In the United States, extraverts constitute a clear majority among the general population. Approximately 75 percent of all men and women prefer Extraversion. However, my own study showed that among lawyers, 56 percent prefer Introversion.[4] Also, unlike the general population, there is a gender difference: 58 percent of male lawyers prefer Introversion, as do 51 percent of female lawyers.

Despite the fact that more introverts are attracted to law, both male and female extravert lawyers report slightly higher job satisfaction than their introvert counterparts. We do not really know why this is so, but one explanation might be that introverted lawyers may grow weary of extensive client contact. Another possibility is that extraverts tend to report greater job satisfaction in surveys in general.

This particular personality trait can influence your comfort level in the office environment. Strong introverts can feel really out of place in a boisterous, high energy extraverted office. While less common, the opposite can be true for extraverts. If you are thinking about accepting a particular job offer, spend some time in the office of your potential employer and pay attention to energy.

It was indicated above that 56 percent of all lawyers prefer introversion. The remaining 44 percent prefer Extraversion. In my research, three legal specialty areas were found to attract significantly more extraverts: torts and insurance; litigation; and labor law (53 percent of all labor lawyers preferred Extraversion.) If you have a strong preference for Extraversion, you may consider exploring these fields. Work setting can also be important. My study also found that over 64 percent of all government lawyers in the study preferred Introversion.

Sensing versus Intuition

This scale measures how you gather information. Sensors are more comfortable with concrete, specific, factual data—the kinds of information you get from your five senses. Intuitives are more comfortable with abstract, impressionistic, or theoretical information—the kinds of information you get from your sixth sense. Sensors usually prefer low ambiguity, well-defined tasks, and a no-nonsense approach to work. Intuitives thrive on creativity, imagining what could be, and finding meaning behind the data.

This scale is highly correlated with many kinds of occupational choices. For example, more sensors than intuitives are attracted to the fields of engineering, bookkeeping, chemistry, and budget analysis. More intuitives than sensors are attracted to the fields of philosophy, psychotherapy, the fine arts—and law. While 70 percent of all men and women in the United States exhibit a sensory approach, 56 percent of all lawyers choose intuition in this scale. Thus, a higher proportion of lawyers choose Intuition than do persons in the general population.

Typical tasks in the early years of law practice are more suited to Sensing than the use of Intuition. Much of the work assigned to a young associate in the early years of practice is tilted toward the Sensing side of the scale—research on individual points of law, drafting and reviewing documents, combing through transcripts of depositions and answers to interrogatories, and so on. As a lawyer's career advances, more responsibility is likely to be conferred upon him or her, leading ultimately to "big picture" case responsibilities and dealing with the larger issues.

If you are a sensor, you most likely have some affinity for Intuition as well. Lawyers who prefer Sensing to the exclusion of Intuition are in a small minority. If you fall into this minority, your best path is to develop an expertise in a particular substantive area, preferably one with low ambiguity. Regulatory and code-based practice areas such as tax, securities, and many administrative law specialties will feel much more natural to the strong sensor. If you are comfortable with both Sensing and Intuition, most areas of law will fit. And if your preference for Intuition is strong, be patient and choose a practice area that will expose you to conceptual issues or one in which gray areas abound.

As mentioned above, 56 percent of all lawyers prefer Intuition. The remaining 44 percent prefer Sensing. My research has identified three legal specialty areas that attract more than their fair share of sensors: general practice (54 percent), real estate (57 percent), and tax/trusts/estates (57 percent). Likewise, three practice areas attracted a disproportionate number of lawyers who prefer Intuition: criminal law (64 percent), labor law (67 percent), and litigation (65 percent). While none of these figures is overwhelmingly tilted in one direction, the trend is clear. If you have a strong Sensing or Intuition preference, you may wish to explore one of the six practice areas above.

Your choice of a work setting may also be influenced by your preference on the Sensing versus Intuition scale. In my study, two settings attracted a disproportionate number persons who chose Intuition: judicial clerkships (78 percent) and legal aid and public defender offices (74 percent). This makes sense—most clerkships offer the promise of dealing with legal jurisprudence, the kinds of conceptual and philosophical issues that intuitives find appealing. Sensors prefer more practical objectives and thus are more likely to look for a first job that allows them to roll up their sleeves and get to work as a lawyer, such as a position in a traditional law firm. Lawyers who choose to work in poverty law possibly do so out of a motivation to achieve some philosophical end. It makes sense that intuitives would be attracted to such types of practice.

Similarly, it makes sense that 75 percent of the military lawyers in my study preferred Sensing. Other studies of military officers have found a preponderance of Sensing types among them.

Thinking versus Feeling

This scale describes two very different modes of decision making. Thinkers rely on logic and objective analysis to reach their conclusions. They may have strong feelings about the thing to be decided, but they usually make a conscious attempt to put those feelings aside and not allow them to influence their thinking.

Feelers, on the other hand, use a more personal, subjective strategy. Typical questions that a feeler might ask of himself or herself include, Do I like X? or Do I want X?

Thinkers have a greater tendency to be critical. They also tend to receive criticism from others as mere data, while feelers allow the emotions in along with the data, a practice that leads them to have their feelings bruised more easily. Because of this, feelers also tend to pay more attention to maintenance behaviors—harmonizing, avoiding conflict, paying compliments, and the like.

Thinkers are attracted to the realm of the mind. Ask a thinker, Why did you go into law? and you'll most likely hear the words "intellectual challenge" in the answer. Ask a feeler the same question, and you may hear answers that include the phrases, "to help people" or "to promote social justice."

The Thinking-Feeling scale is the only one that is distributed differently for men and women in the general population. Roughly 60 percent of all men prefer Thinking as compared to 35 percent of all women. The Thinking preference is one of the hallmarks of the legal profession. In my study, 66 percent of all women lawyers and 81 percent of all men lawyers preferred Thinking to Feeling.

Also in my study, thinker lawyers had a slightly higher level of job satisfaction than feeler lawyers. But it should also be noted that despite the minority status of feelers in the profession, many of them have found satisfaction.

No one knows why feelers have been able to find nearly equal levels of satisfaction in what is clearly a thinker profession. Possibly it is because they choose work environments or substantive areas wisely. For example, nearly 44 percent of the lawyers working for legal aid or public defender offices were feelers, compared to lawyers as a whole, of whom only 24 percent prefer Feeling.

Among female lawyers, according to my research, 34 percent prefer Feeling to Thinking on this scale. I found two legal specialties that attract greater proportions of Feeling women: labor law (44 percent Feeling vs. 56 percent Thinking) and litigation (41 percent Feeling vs. 59 percent Thinking). For lawyers who prefer Feeling, litigation can be a two-edged sword: it holds the promise of effecting social change (a value for many feelers), but it also represents the area of the law with perhaps the highest level of ongoing interpersonal conflict (a situation most feelers disdain).

Only 19 percent of all male lawyers prefer Feeling. My study found three legal specialties that attract greater proportions of men who select Feeling: general practice, criminal law, and matrimonial law, all of which attracted 28 percent male feelers and 72 percent male thinkers.

Lawyers with a Thinking preference—male and female alike—have found job satisfaction in nearly every legal specialty imaginable.

Judging versus Perceiving

This scale measures one's style in dealing with tasks and people. This scale is the most readily recognizable in others. Persons who prefer Judging prefer a life that is planned, decisive, and orderly. Those who prefer Perceiving prefer a life that is open ended and spontaneous. Judgers like to have control; perceivers like to keep their options open.

In order to maintain control, judgers tend to employ one or more of the following strategies: doing only one thing at a time; completing assignments in an orderly and timely manner so as to avoid the last-minute rush; keeping small manageable lists of things to do and methodically checking off completed items; making decisions at the earliest possible opportunity, without waiting for all information; scheduling time carefully and giving a great deal of respect to that schedule; keeping a neat desk; and planning for all possible contingencies in advance.

Perceivers like to keep their options open, and they do so by employing one or more of the following strategies: juggling many tasks, often doing more than one at a time; "playing it by ear"; making many lengthy lists (and sometimes losing them); putting off decisions in order to gather more complete information; maintaining piles in their office, any of which can be worked on; acting spontaneously; avoiding committing themselves to plans until the last minute; and enjoying surprises.

My study found that a higher proportion of lawyers prefer Judging (63 percent) compared to the general public (55 percent). Moreover, judger lawyers tend to have stronger numerical scores on the Judging scale than they do on the other three MBTI scales. In other words, many lawyers identify quite strongly with the Judging traits described above. It makes sense that a profession that has many deadlines and requires a great deal of organizational skills from its practitioners would attract more people with a personality trait that favors these kinds of skills.

Not only is the Judging trait more prevalent among persons in the legal profession, but those who have this trait enjoy greater job satisfaction as well, according my study. Less than 20 percent of all judger lawyers reported job dissatisfaction, compared to over 25 percent of all lawyers.

What strategies can you adopt if you have a strong Perceiving preference? I fall into this category and made the difficult choice to leave the law after ten years of practice. It was a good decision for me, but is certainly not the only option available.

The only work setting to which significantly more perceivers are attracted is legal aid and public defender offices: 57 percent of the lawyers in these specialties prefer Perceiving compared to 37 percent of all lawyers. If this type of work appeals to you for other reasons, you may find that your Perceiving preference fits right in.

In terms of practice areas, labor lawyers reported more perceivers than any other area (47 percent compared to 37 percent of all lawyers). Other areas with somewhat more perceivers than judgers include criminal law (43 percent), general practice (42 percent), and litigation (42 percent). As with the Feeling realm, perceivers in litigation are using a two-edged sword. The play-it-by-ear style of the perceiver is well suited to coping with the fast-breaking changes in circumstances quite common to litigation; this provides the perceiver with satisfaction. But many perceivers also tend to be a bit on the disorganized side, and the consequences of this can be more harsh and immediate in litigation than perhaps any other legal specialty.

The best advice for a lawyer with a strong perceiver preference is to surround himself with support staff—secretaries, paralegals, and so on—who have a Judging preference. Then count on them to help you out in the areas in which you are weakest. This strategy can enable even the strongest perceiver to find increased satisfaction in the law.

Overview

Perhaps the most important finding of my research is that it is possible for lawyers of every kind of MBTI preference to find job satisfaction. There was no single MBTI preference, and all of the sixteen MBTI types contained more satisfied lawyers than dissatisfied lawyers.

Although this chapter has focused on job satisfaction, one added benefit of learning about your Myers-Briggs type preferences is worth noting. A true understanding of typological differences can be a valuable tool in understanding others in the workplace and becoming more effective in communicating with them. An underlying premise of the MBTI is that all of the different styles of behavior are legitimate, and no single style is better or worse than any other. By truly understanding type preferences, you can gain a deeper understanding and appreciation for others who think and act differently than you do.

You should also be aware that several other key personality variables influence your job satisfaction besides your MBTI preferences: personal values (helping people, status, security, fun, etc.), psychological needs (need for control, inclusion, intimacy, achievement, etc.), motivated skills (writing, analyzing, persuading, etc.), and career interests (technology, health care, real estate, international trade, etc.). The more of these you pay attention to in formulating your job search, the more likely you are to achieve job satisfaction. Your local library or bookstore is full of excellent self-help books that cover most of these areas. Also, any good career counselor can help you identify your key personality traits and fit them to the job.

Finally, keep in mind that a job is just the first step in a career. Career satisfaction requires job satisfaction plus a clear game plan for the long term. Those who formulate long-term career goals and put them in writing are more likely to achieve what they want.

Notes

1. Jung explicitly identified three dichotomies. The fourth, Judgment versus Perception, was added by the developers of the MBTI, Katherine Briggs and Isabel Myers, since it was implicit in Jung's theory.

2. In Jungian and Myers-Briggs literature, it is customary to spell "Extraversion" with an "a" in contrast to the spelling "extroversion," which is used in standard American English.

3. Orthodox MBTI theory holds that the numerical score indicates how clear or certain one is of one's preference for the particular side of the dichotomy, and that it does not indicate the strength of the score. How could it, since we are theoretically dealing with a dichotomy and not a continuum? This point is the subject of much scholarly debate within the academic world, and in fact, the assertion that type is dichotomous is one of the vulnerable points of Jungian theory. In actual practice, most laypersons and many counselors treat the numerical score as a strength score, as in "He has a strong preference for Extraversion" or "She has a mild preference for Intuition."

4. My doctoral dissertation involved using the MBTI to understand the personality factor/career choice intersection among U.S. lawyers. I examined N lawyers, n males and n females over a period of X years. (See Resources for a more complete citation of this study.)

CHAPTER 4

Looking for More Career Satisfaction? Use Your Whole Brain

Dr. Janina C. Latack

Even a cursory review of recent books, articles, and Internet sites targeted at lawyers identifies continuing concern about career dissatisfaction and the on-going debate on the reasons for it. In fact, a poll that appeared in *The California Lawyer* estimated that 70 percent of lawyers would choose a new career if they could and 73 percent of them did not want their children to become lawyers. Lawyers, however, do not have exclusive rights to career angst. The continued interest in career dissatisfaction among professionals and managers is reflected in book titles such as *How to Switch Careers: The Professional Step-by-Step Guide* and articles such as "Why Do People Quit? Because They Can," which occupied nearly a full page in a recent issue of the *New York Times*. Clearly, career dissatisfaction haunts other groups as well.

Lawyers, however, have a career identity that intensifies their concern about dissatisfaction. Two major factors that underlie this intense concern are the investment that lawyers have made in their careers, and the fact that many of them ended up in law by default.

First, lawyers invest a great deal monetarily in becoming a lawyer. Moreover, most lawyers invest a great deal psychologically in being lawyers. They are personally identified with law—being a lawyer constitutes a huge portion of who each is as a human being in the world. After all, society views law as a profession similar to medicine or the clergy. People enter the profession with the expectation of a lifelong commitment and many see it as a calling. As one lawyer put it, "I've known since the age of five that I wanted to be a lawyer."

In contrast, many other lawyers chose the profession by default. When it came time to declare a major in college, prelaw was their "fallback" choice. If no other career choice emerged, or if you graduated and still lacked a specific career focus, you could always go to law school provided you were smart enough. Commonly, young people hear this advice: "Go into law because a law degree prepares you do to so many things—you can use it in so many different fields." However, this advice fuels the assumption that a law degree is excellent background for just about any job and may result in a young person postponing decisive career commitments.

It is true that law school and law practice provide broad training in what are referred to by career consultants as "transferable skills"—skills that can be applied to many other jobs besides that of a lawyer. Such skills include researching, analyzing, logical decision making, interviewing, synthesizing complex data into clear, nontechnical explanations, giving powerful presentations, and so on.

However, if you wish to transfer out of law into a new career field, you still require a clear picture of what you want to do. Those who entered law by default may not yet know what they want to do if law is not satisfying. Those who are strongly invested in their lawyer identity see the potential costs of a career switch as extremely high. Thus, the theoretical transferability of lawyering skills to another field is problematic, and many lawyers perceive themselves as having few desirable alternatives outside the law profession. Although the list of law-related career options that do not involve practicing law is fairly extensive, proportionately they represent a small number of opportunities relative to positions that involve responsibilities associated with a practicing lawyer. As a result, the desire to find satisfaction with law as a career choice is intense.

If you feel there is room for improvement in your career satisfaction, what do you do? How do you increase your career satisfaction? This chapter invites you to apply a "whole-brain approach." This approach will help you tap all of your powers—both analytical and intuitive—as you seek to improve your career satisfaction. It will also maximize the probability that actions you take to increase your satisfaction will be based on a comprehensive, creative process. Throughout you will find ideas, quotes, and advice from your fellow lawyers who are satisfied with their law careers.

A Whole-Brain Approach to Increasing Career Satisfaction

The whole-brain approach is rooted in research on brain physiology. Researchers have studied the different information processing capabilities of regions in the brain, giving rise to publicity about left-brain and right-brain thinking patterns. Although findings have been oversimplified, the left-brain/right-brain distinction has become a popular symbol for describing two different processes through which people may tackle dilemmas and create solutions. The left-brain thinking pattern focuses on logical analysis while the right-brain pattern is more visual, auditory, and intuitive. According to Maki Arao, writing in a Japanese industrial magazine, "What allows human beings to solve problems in the real world full of contradictory and incomplete information is the balance between the left-brain thinking pattern, which pursues matching of knowledge and the right-brain thinking pattern, which processes indefiniteness with guesses or intuition."

Obviously, lawyers emphasize the left-brain, analytical approach in their work—investigating facts that can be verified and used to draw logical conclusions that can be defended. That is, however, only one side of the equation for deriving career satisfaction. The other side of the equation addresses right-brain processes as well. As exemplified by an explosion of books on finding deeper sense of purpose at work, the right-brain approach focuses on vision and spirituality. *True Work: The Sacred Dimension of Earning a Living* and *The Job Hunter's Spiritual Companion* are just two of the titles that indicate the interest in a more visionary, intuitive approach to finding career satisfaction.

Although spirituality and intuition may not be the focus of hall talk at many law firms, the desire for more personal meaning at and connection to work has prompted dissatisfied professionals to take a more reflective approach in their search for career satisfaction. They recognize that resolving their malaise demands more than proposing flextime, managing the number of cases taken on, telecommuting, or developing a new legal niche or specialty. It calls for nothing less than a review of their lives up to now and a personal quest for what they want out of their lives going forward. This viewpoint gives strong attention to processes like visualization and meditation as vehicles for inner guidance in the search for purpose in life.

The answers to questions such as, What am I doing here? What's the purpose I am to fulfill in my life? Why am I taking up space on the planet anyway? are unlikely to be generated from data and logical analysis alone. Moreover, if one gives any weight to predictions about the upheaval that will accompany the millennium—including the uncertain global economic and environmental future and Y2K disaster scenarios—then fundamental reinventions of the way work is performed are imminent. Knowing how to develop answers to soul-searching questions makes it more likely that you will be able to define or redefine what career satisfaction means as you move forward. A clear sense of how to find individual purpose will give you a mechanism to help you navigate the predicted transitions.

Thus, a thorough approach to increasing career satisfaction would tap both the left-brain, logical analysis of data and the right-brain, intuitive forward-looking process to arrive at an understanding of what career satisfaction means to you and how to find more of it in your life.

The Left-Brain Approach to Increasing Career Satisfaction

As a departure point for the left-brain, analytical approach, we can define career satisfaction. First, a career can be defined in an external sense—the sum total of your work-related experiences, or what is on your resume. It can also be defined in an internal sense. Professionals like lawyers have an internal definition of career—performing work with which they psychologically identify.

Satisfaction is typically defined by organizational behavior theorists as a discrepancy—the gap between "what is" and "what should be." What should be is rooted in our desires and needs and in our expectations—that is, what we want *and* what we expect. We may be dissatisfied because we are not getting what we want. And we may be dissatisfied when something we expect does not occur. The more our unmet expectations gap is related to something we want very much, the more dissatisfied we are.

But as the Rolling Stones have admonished, "You can't always get what you want. . . . But if you try sometimes, you just might find you get what you need." Accordingly, some theorists have defined satisfaction in terms of how well our needs are met. We may want many things. But if our needs are not met, that is when dissatisfaction becomes serious.

According to Robert Glasser, in *Control Theory: A New Explanation of How We Control Our Lives*, we can distill our needs to five basic requirements: the need to survive and reproduce, the need to belong, the need for power, the need for freedom, and the need for fun. The list below provides one tool for analyzing your level of job satisfaction and you can use it to see how your career rates.

- *Need to survive and reproduce.* In a career context, this translates to feeling secure, having a sense that your work has lasting value, and being able to pass along to others your knowledge, including teaching and mentoring younger people. How do you feel about your security? How do you feel about what you are passing on to others including less experienced coworkers and clients?
- *Need to belong.* At work, this need is met through experiences of camaraderie, support, and teamwork. Are you included in ways you want to be? Do you feel accepted and supported as a lawyer and as a person?
- *Need for power.* We need to have influence, to be able to see our influence over processes and end results at work. Do you have a sense of your positive impact? Do your views carry weight in the way you want them to?
- *Need for freedom.* This is reflected in a need to be free to do your work in the way you think is best. Are you satisfied with the latitude you have at work? Are you able to be creative in ways that you want?
- *Need for fun.* This is obviously one need that is also met quite often outside the job. However, most people have a need to have fun at work as well. Is fun part of your career? Is there enough fun and joy overall as you think about your career?

As a professional, you expect these needs to be met at work to a considerable extent. If these basic needs are not met, you are likely to feel dissatisfied with your career. To do your analysis, make a more specific, individualized list of your vision of "what should be" under each of these five categories and compare it with "what is" in your career. This will give you a big picture view of your overall career satisfaction and suggest areas for improvement.

Is It the Job or Is It the Career?

It is useful to analyze whether your dissatisfaction is with the job you currently hold or more broadly with the career of law. Lawyers list many reasons why they feel dissatisfied:

- Quantity and quality of work
- Money
- Firm environment, collegiality, and culture
- Lawyer training and development

- Opportunities for advancement and job security
- Stability of the firm

As a first step in your analytical approach to career satisfaction, you need to determine if the factors listed above can be improved within your current firm. If this is the case, then your dissatisfaction may be with your current job and not the field of law as a career. Making a change will, therefore, close the gap between what is and what should be, and your career satisfaction will increase.

Making changes is critical. The longer your dissatisfaction persists, the greater the potential for your losing interest or getting stuck, which can set you on a path toward removal from your job.

The Elusive Quest for Balance

Something happens that transforms good lawyers into monsters. We're trained to be overachievers, but most of us can't keep pace with the Rolex-wristed and BMW-driven people in our lives. Much less find time to learn Java, sing the Messiah, and skydive. Balance and centering are much easier concepts to talk about than implement.

Jennifer Rose

You cannot analyze how to improve career satisfaction among lawyers without addressing the issue of balance. In fact, the quest for balance consumes many professionals today and is a major source of career dissatisfaction among lawyers and others. As Juliet Schor reported in *The Overworked American: The Unexpected Decline of Leisure,* we are now putting in an entire month more at work than we did twenty years ago. The pace of technology continues to accelerate at work, resulting in warp-speed expectations for response to faxes, e-mails, and pagers. Also, competition for clients continues to increase amid a labor market with too many lawyers, while billable-hours expectations rise. Simultaneously, dual-career families and, in many cases, dual-lawyer families are becoming more common. As a result, the pressures build in both work and personal life.

For lawyers and for many in the corporate world who enjoy their work, the *balance dilemma* can be captured this way:

I like what I do, I even love most of it—it's just that taken together, it's too big of a package, consumes too much of me. There's little left over. Little time. Little energy. The sheer volume seems overwhelming at times. In fact, most of the time. When I am able to reestablish a more balanced life, which is rare, my enthusiasm returns. To sum up, my career situation is, quite literally, too much of a good thing.

Lawyers also have no "exclusive rights" to the need for balance. Many professionals in business experience the same lack of balance—in light of mergers, downsizings, acquisitions, global competition, and so on. The issue is pervasive. One need only look at newspaper accounts of physicians as they struggle to adjust to the heavier patient loads that accompany managed care and the conversion of health care into a profit-making enterprise.

Is it the job or is it the career? To answer this question, first ask some others: If your life were more balanced, would you have the satisfaction you seek? If you could do exactly what you are doing, or most of it, and feel that you had time for a personal life, would you be happy? If you know the answer is yes, even without doing any analysis, and you are being as honest and as objective as you can, you might conclude that the dissatisfaction is more with your job, or job structure, than with your career.

Other questions come next: Is there a job that allows one to practice law with more balance? Can you restructure your current job—or yourself and the way you work—to achieve this balance? Your fellow lawyers suggest these strategies:

- *Develop a specialty.* You could specialize in an area where a smaller practice is allowed and lower revenue levels are accepted. Although this may leave you more vulnerable if client load drops, you can use the free time afforded by your specialty to scale back your lifestyle so you are less vulnerable if your income drops.
- *Opt to work part-time.* For many lawyers, "part-time" means thirty hours a week. Lately, some lawyers have proposed job-sharing. Expectations about the time frame for meeting partner requirements may be adjusted accordingly.
- *Consider becoming a contract lawyer.* With more concern about overhead, especially in smaller firms, the demand for contract lawyers is increasing. In this position, you can often choose the caseload you take. Consult *Practicing Law without Clients: Making a Living as a Freelance Lawyer,* the ABA book by David Robinson, as well as the recent book by Deborah Arron and Deborah Guyol, *The Complete Guide to Contract Lawyering.*
- *Accept reality.* "The reality of law practice is not often conducive to enjoyment, simply because much of what law does is either adversarial or nit-picky (and often both)," notes Thane Messinger, author of *The Lawyer's Jungle Book.* "Some are dissatisfied because they hold unrealistic expectations about a legal career." One lawyer advised, "You signed on for a highly competitive field, you worked hard in law school. It is what it is. Recognize you love it, warts and all."
- *Step back and think about what a good deal you have.* One lawyer exclaimed, "I'm from a small town in Kansas. I can't believe the life I have!"
- *Pay your dues and pace yourself.* Many lawyers believe that, early in a career, it is probably unrealistic to expect a balanced life. One lawyer noted: "It's a lifetime commitment and it's like a marathon—you have to pace yourself. After you have done your 'sprint' to begin your legal career, you can begin to take actions and communicate adjustments and changes you'd like to see within your firm."
- *Make your priorities clear; communicate, speak up.* A female equity partner in a large firm recounted her interview with the firm as she was just coming out of law school. At the time there was only one female partner in the firm, and she was single with no children. During the interview she blurted out, "What's your policy on maternity leave?" The reply came back, "We've never had the issue come up. We'll deal

with it later as it arises." She countered, "Well, it's really kind of important to me." On her way back home from the interview, she's thinking to herself, "Who am I? I don't even have a job offer!" Two weeks later, a partner called and offered her the job. He added, "Oh, by the way, we now have a maternity policy." And the policy was essentially that which was incorporated into the family leave legislation at a much later date. Another lawyer added, "Especially if you are with a smaller firm, you have to communicate your priorities to them. What's it worth to you?"

- *Boost your professionalism a notch.* There is widespread recognition of the negative image attributed to lawyers. Do your part to change that perception. Attend a bar association seminar on professionalism. Take the high road and when opposing counsel requests an extension—unless it genuinely disadvantages your client—grant it. Be active in a professional association. One lawyers' organization helped build a playground at a center for families of domestic violence. A lawyer who participated emphasized, "Activities like this help keep things in perspective."

- *Take responsibility for your professional development.* If you are interested in an area of law, read about it, locate training programs, and request to attend them. Even senior practitioners can retool; revive your interest. Ask for work when work is slow. Just as the rich get richer, the busy get busier. As you become more senior, develop your own business. Do not wait until you are drowning before you ask for help. Lack of control is frustrating, but you have more control than you think.

- *Explore alternative career tracks.* If approached properly, nonpartnership and nonequity partnerships can be attractive. Do not view them as booby prizes. If your firm does not have alternative tracks, develop a plan and present it to management, selling them on the benefits. If you are a partner, do not let ego or peer pressure keep you from exploring alternative career tracks in your firm, such as "of counsel" positions.

- *Learn to work smarter, not harder.* Ask the busiest, best-organized lawyers in your firm how they manage their time. Find out about techniques and software that can save you time. As you progress, look at delegating and learn how to do it effectively. Make more effective use of technology, especially for research and document preparation.

- *Get a life.* Do not look to work to meet all of your needs. Make time for community involvement, which might help with marketing; go to movies or do whatever you like to do; keep a sense of perspective about your work.

- *Surf the Web.* There are numerous websites that provide resources and information on how to address career satisfaction. Hundreds of sites exist that provide valuable articles and suggestions as well as e-mail addresses of other lawyers who are not only interested in this issue, but who have written about it. Many of these contributors have provided practical suggestions. Articles cover such topics as "Emotionally and Spiritually Health Career Choices," "Unlearning Dissatisfaction," "How Lawyers Can Increase Their Creativity," and "Your First Years as a Lawyer: An Owners Manual."

■ *Refer to "Life, Law and the Pursuit of Balance. A Lawyer's Guide to Quality of Life."* This book is devoted entirely to your problem. Select a short list of ideas from the suggestions contained in thirty-one chapters by lawyers and professional consultants. Develop a plan to implement those ideas that suit you.

The search for balance has commanded a considerable amount of attention in the study of lawyer career satisfaction. It is one of several important factors you must examine and understand if you wish to improve your career satisfaction. The next section shows you how to analyze and prioritize these factors.

Identifying and Prioritizing Career Satisfaction Factors

Somewhere, for some reason, some unfortunate people have conjured up the idea that the perfect job exists. In the work world, the perfect job is a very self-destructive fantasy that leads to great discontent and job-hopping. . . . The closest you'll come to a perfect job is one that's a good fit for you.

Robert Dilenschneider,
The Critical 14 Years of Your Professional Life

Although this advice may be realistic, it is not an excuse for accepting career dissatisfaction where you live. If you are dissatisfied with your career but have made no conscious choice to address it systematically, then you have decided to *stay dissatisfied.* For a comprehensive solution for your dissatisfaction, you need to answer one important question: *Who are you and what do you want?* Although suggestions from others about changes they have made in their jobs are very useful, determining what will work for you is a highly individual decision. You must apply your own criteria for evaluating whether or not what others have done will solve your problem.

To identify what changes in your current job are necessary improve your career satisfaction, you undertake much the same analysis as you would if you were looking for another job. You want to find or create another job within your firm or to recreate your job situation to improve career satisfaction.

The analytical approach has been well captured in numerous books on career management. An excellent example of the analytical approach is found in *How to Create a Picture of Your Ideal Job or Next Career* by Richard Bolles, who has been the most recommended author on how to find career satisfaction. He notes, "In order to hunt for your ideal job or even something close to your ideal job, you must have a picture of it in your head. The clearer the picture, the easier it will be to hunt for it." In other words, unless you know what your ideal job is, you do not know what to try changing about your current situation and where you are willing to compromise.

Bolles lists the following factors and insists that you create prioritized lists in each category:

■ Favorite kinds of things you like to work with
■ Favorite kinds of information you like to work with

- Favorite kinds of people you like to work with
- Favorite rewards at work
- Favorite spiritual or emotional setting
- Favorite outcomes, immediate and long-range
- Favorite physical setting
- Favorite transferable skills and style of working

Bolles advocates talking with people as a crucial next step. Based on the insights you gain from defining what you want, you can frame conversations with others at your current workplace and elsewhere to gather ideas and support as well as to assess the feasibility of making changes that lead to a closer fit with your ideal job picture.

For example, one lawyer is very clear that he values working with people in his local community and with bar associations at various levels. He has requested and gained support from the partners at his firm so that some of his energy can go to those professional activities he enjoys in addition to work that generates revenue directly. His firm accepts that he contributes less measurably in billable hours, but acknowledges that his visibility has value for referrals and public image. He noted, "Some firms even give monetary credit for service but this is rare. Lawyers do more community service than any other profession but they don't get credit for it because their image is tarnished by the adversarial nature of the legal system."

The left-brain approach reminds us, *"best" is the enemy of "better."* Avoid analysis paralysis. Some people get stuck in the search for the right or best decision. Decisions about how to improve your job satisfaction will come more easily if you realize you cannot make a "right" decision in the sense of fixing things permanently—similarly, you cannot make a "wrong" decision in the sense of messing things up permanently for your career, short of committing some heinous act! Sometimes, it is more important to act after considering some alternatives and then to make more corrections later if need be. After all, you know people who have made what appeared to be bad decisions or experienced failures, disasters even, only to find out later these experiences took them ultimately to much better situations.

The Right-Brain Approach to Increasing Career Satisfaction

We live in a time of great upheaval, turmoil and uncertainty. In the midst of the confusion, many of us struggle to stay connected and contribute in positive ways in our work. In these moments, we most need a deep understanding of our purpose and direction in life. Without this wayfinding beacon or vision, pulling us forward on our intended path, we may wander aimlessly, feeling empty and lost.

Ernest Schloss and Janina Latack,
Discovering and Living Your Vision Workshop

The basic concept behind the right-brain approach to increasing career satisfaction is that this quest is inseparable from the quest for a sense of purpose and a meaningful life. Both quests are accomplished by tapping a deeper level of consciousness not readily accessible to the analytical, rational mind. The creative processes at the core of this approach are intuition, visualization, meditation, and reflection, which help identify your personal strengths and the skills that *must* be used in fulfilling your life's purpose.

When people allow themselves to meditate and to dream about ideals and visions they truly desire for their lives and work, they attain clarity about actions to take and choices to make that will improve their lives and work and be of service to others. They even rest more comfortably with less than ideal circumstances, because they have a clearer sense of what they ultimately want to create in their lives.

Although some guidance regarding the visionary approach can be found in books, many people find it useful to pursue the right-brain approach by combining individual reading, reflection, and meditation with group experiences, such as discussions or workshops with others who are similarly inclined.

Here are ways to utilize your right brain to increase your career satisfaction:

- *Personal visioning.* Create quiet time for visualization and reflection so you can develop a personal vision of your life's purpose. Whether fuzzy or clear, whether it consists of a page of clearly written words, or just phrases strung together, clear pictures or vague images, devote time to the larger picture of what you want your life to be about. The fundamental goal here is to allow the answers to appear from a deeply internal place—your heart, soul, and unconscious mind that is uncensored by your conscious mind with all the training, prohibitions, and restrictions we learn as we go through life.
- *Distill from your personal vision, a personal mission or work focus.* What is your mission in the work that you do? A personal vision is broad, encompassing all aspects of your life, while a work mission is more focused on career.
- *Identify your unique gifts and align them with your work.* Unique gifts consist of your personal strengths and skills, distilled from your life experiences that you see as your most satisfying accomplishments. Often, because of the visualizations and reflections, people focus on experiences that highlight skills that may not emerge from the more rational, analytical approach alone. Your skills and gifts may take you beyond law as you are now practicing it.
- *Link strengths and skills to your vision and personal mission.* How will you use your strengths and skills to reorient your law career in the direction that takes you more toward your vision? For example, if you like conducting small group meetings and your vision includes greater collegiality in your firm, you might volunteer to plan a retreat that would address this issue and creative ways to improve it in your firm.
- *Design and commit to actions that move you closer to your vision.* What are you going to do in the next week, next month, next six months to move you closer to living your vision? What day-to-day actions can you incorporate so you start living your vision now? For example, one lawyer who wished to improve collegiality identified a partner who, based on a previous conversation, might be receptive to discussing how to achieve that goal. He made an appointment for lunch with that individual to discuss ideas. He reported, "Even if it

does not lead to major change, just by doing this one act, I'm closer to my vision of how things should be."

- *Create a supportive structure.* It is critical to address the issue of how to create a supportive structure. Without colleagues and friends who are on a similar path, many people flounder as they try to sustain momentum. What structures can you put in place to keep you moving toward your vision?

- *Change your outlook.* As Jennifer Rose put it in her article, "The Times They Are A-Changin'," which appeared in the ABA publication *The Compleat Lawyer*, "The only solution is do what we love and love what we do. And find peace in ourselves for doing it." Making a conscious choice not only to pay attention to the rewarding aspects of your law career but also to accept those aspects you find less fulfilling, can increase your overall sense of satisfaction with your career.

- *Develop flexibility. Blow with the wind, stick it out through the bad times:* As one lawyer said, "The folks I see who are dissatisfied are the ones who, when something doesn't go their way, they can't discard it. You need to say, 'Well, maybe their way is better.'" This quote is from an equity partner in a very large, prestigious firm who leaves at 4:30 p.m. several days a week to take her children to swim practice and who rarely works on weekends.

- *Make a priority out of your relationships with the people you work with and for.* Lawyer and executive coach Scott Hunter argues that in order to resolve the crisis created by competition for a shrinking pie of legal work, lawyers must move toward healthy relationships in the work environment. Relationships—meaningful interactions with others— are at the heart of satisfaction and accomplishment for clients, partners, lawyers, and staff.

Conclusion

Clearly, the search for more career satisfaction is a partnership between the left-brain (analytical) and the right-brain (visionary) processes. It is also a partnership between lawyers and their employers. Although it is up to individual lawyers to work through who they are and what they want and then to take action, it is also up to firms to recognize that resolving the career satisfaction dilemma has enormous implications for the bottom line and for firm and individual prosperity. One lawyer commented, "Firms need to be more flexible and, just like lawyers, they need to recognize you can't have it all— more and more profitability, billable hours requirements increasing from eighteen hundred to two thousand, and a high quality of life for their lawyers and staff. Quality of life is very difficult to achieve in a workplace driven by unreasonable expectations."

Finally, one lawyer, who had hung in there and worked hard to effect some changes to improve his satisfaction, had this to say: "Keep believing in yourself and keep your eyes wide open. Serendipity plays a much bigger part in all of this than you would like!" This is a piece of advice that deserves a place in your memory and is well worth passing on to others.

CHAPTER 5

Market Assessment: Translating Your Skills to the Changing Profession

Dr. Abbie Willard

Although career counselors and consultants appropriately focus considerable attention on self-analysis, few job seekers take the necessary second step in this process and devote similar scrutiny to the external forces that will affect each individual's job search. Self-assessment requires concentration on the attitudes, experiences and goals of the individual in search of a new job. In contrast, a market assessment—if it is to be relevant to an individual's career goals—must focus on the forces, patterns, and trends that set the parameters in which an individual job search occurs.

The marketplace of today, in which the lawyer must broker skills and experiences to make a job change, is very different from the legal marketplace of both yesterday and tomorrow. As executives, managers, consultants, futurists, and even lawyers agree, the one constant in the late twentieth and early twenty-first centuries is change. To understand this marketplace and assess its effect on the individual job seeker, you must examine recent trends and changes in the world of law practice. Then, you must turn your attention to what those trends and changes mean to you in your search for a new job.

Career Changes in the Law

Relatively little is known about the career paths of lawyers. While anecdotal information abounds, no systematic national investigation of the patterns and trajectories in lawyers' careers has been undertaken. However, early in 1998, the National Association for Law Placement Foundation for Research and Education published a study (*Keeping the Keepers: Strategies for Associate Retention in Times of Attrition*) in which career moves of lawyers in the private sector were examined.

The study was undertaken in two phases. In Phase I, more than 150 law firms reported comprehensive quantitative data on the retention status of more than 10,000 associates hired into law firms with 25 or more lawyers during the tumultuous years from 1988 to 1996. The responding firms were relatively equally distributed among five different firm sizes: 2–25 lawyers, 26–50 lawyers, 51–100 lawyers, 101–250 lawyers, and over 251 lawyers. This phase of the study revealed some interesting patterns. In the aggregate, a surprisingly large number of beginning associates, nearly one in eleven (9.2 percent), left their first employer within one year. The attrition rate nearly doubled over each of the next two years, with 43 percent of new lawyers departing their first employer within three years.

In Phase II of the study, anecdotal information about experiences in the legal marketplace and with types of employers was elicited. To obtain the qualitative complement to the quantitative data, thirteen focus groups involving more that eighty lawyers three to five years out of law school were conducted in four major metropolitan centers: Atlanta, Chicago, New York City, and San Francisco. A skilled focus group facilitator conducted a scripted group session in which numerous employment settings, expectations, and market forces were discussed.

The findings from these focus group encounters are amazingly similar across geographical boundaries and types of employers. The size of employer and the location did not seem to change the generalizable findings. Five of these findings are important to the market assessment for any lawyer anticipating a job change:

- While many individuals chose an employer initially because of salary or status, these factors quickly faded in importance as lawyers became more concerned about a search for personal and professional satisfaction.
- The importance of people and practice areas were the two most determinative considerations in the decision-making process to accept employment.
- Information provided during the recruitment process to potential lawyer hires frequently failed to emphasize the characteristics and benefits most often cited by the job changer as desirable. These include collegial relationships among the lawyers, financial benefits beyond salary, and substantial early inclusion in management and client matters.
- Access to partnership in the private practice setting is no longer an incentive for many lawyers to stay in an otherwise unsatisfying environment or to seek employment elsewhere.
- Lawyers report that the market provides ample opportunities to consider job changes, but that many of them approach a change as an opportunity to alter their lifestyle rather than change their job or garner a higher salary. In fact, many respondents indicated that they had or would take a reduction in pay in order to have a chance at life outside the office.

Although these summaries are only a partial sample of the important findings in this study, they are extremely valuable to an individual job changer's assessment of personal and lifestyle satisfaction as important variables in any equation of marketplace forces. On any scale, when you attempt to balance personal and professional satisfaction with economic trends and workplace patterns, you find that satisfaction weighs—for most experienced job changers—more heavily in a decision to make a job change (and in which direction) than do economic factors.

Trends in the Market

Law as a profession and legal practice as a job are changing with dramatic speed. Six trends are worth consideration by any potential job changer who wants to factor into a job search the patterns and forces that are shaping the way lawyers do what they do:

- *Multinationalism* in legal matters is rapidly becoming the rule rather than the exception in the scope of legal matters handled by many lawyers. This multinationalism can be seen in the number of lawyers, the types of matters, and the jurisdictional questions of many client and case management needs regardless of the type, size, and location of the employer. State government entities as well as federal, small firms as well as large, and public-sector lawyers as well as those associated with private firms all confront with increasing frequency a problem or an issue with multinational dimensions.

- *Globalization* is a force that has changed the way law is practiced. Earlier in the twentieth century, international law was a relatively narrow domain inhabited by a few large, private firms that held closely the clients who occasionally brought them matters of cross-border trade, business, banking, or treaty issues. The global marketplace for all goods and services has created an environment in which public- and private-sector lawyers in all developed nations must consider a wide variety of national and cultural ramifications beyond the legal issues and the rule of law.

- *Interdisciplinary cooperation* is becoming an important principle in the delivery of legal services to governmental, corporate, small business, and individual clients. In reaction to the economic downturn of the early 1990s, many private law practices began to diversify. That diversification laid the groundwork for the multidisciplinary partnerships of the late twentieth and early twenty-first centuries—partnerships that transcend the traditional bounds of legal practice and include accountants, urban planners, business managers, social scientists, and consultants. This pattern translates to both structural and personal differences in the experience of being a lawyer. In increasing numbers, firms are inhabited by lawyers working in teams with nonlawyer professionals. Family law practitioners work with social psychologist, litigators learn from communication and linguistic specialists, and their counterparts at the international business table work with consultants and transactional analysts. Lawyers themselves now rarely progress through a career without some form of training or familiarization in a field previously considered to be only distantly related to the practice of law.

■ *Competition,* once only discussed with hushed tones among members of the private bar, is now a hallmark of how lawyers—from solo practitioners to large firms with offices around the world—position themselves for business. That same need for a competitive spirit transcends the bounds of traditional legal practice as lawyers find themselves vying for clients and work with accounting firms, consulting firms, and the entire financial services industry. As the boundaries for who does what work for which clients continue to blur, this pattern promises to become more pervasive.

■ *Technology* will begin to come of age as a force for every type of workplace, including the one inhabited by lawyers. Web-based technologies in particular will make the access to information both immediate and global. Futurists tell us that shortly after the turn of the century there will be access to any information, any virtual reality, any computer model for any problem, and to human tutors or information specialists on any subject anywhere in the world. And all of this will be accessible instantly to anyone who can push a computer key. The pervasiveness of this and related technologies will make professionals electronic commuters in a twenty-four-hour workplace.

■ *Practice areas* in law have through the decades waxed and waned with cultural, social, and economic trends. Some twentieth-century booms will undoubtedly become twenty-first-century busts. As change escalates, so will the need for generalists with skills that transcend particular specialties in the law. Law as a profession has evolved throughout U.S. history as a reflection of the social and demographic characteristics of the age. Given this pattern, law practice opportunities will mirror what life looks like—more diverse, multi-cultural, multinational, interdisciplinary, and faster paced than ever before. Specialty areas will most certainly include technology and information access, the legal needs of an aging population and rapidly advancing health care delivery systems, the environmental concerns of a burgeoning world population, and workplace issues of professionals not bound by twentieth-century concepts of space and time.

Translating Your Skills to the Changing Profession

With such dramatic changes occurring in the marketplace and multiplying into the next century, how should the individual job seeker adjust his or her approach to the market? A five-step process is helpful:

■ *Reflect on the past.* What skill, role, or function has allowed you to excel and to experience job satisfaction?

■ *Visualize the future.* Identify the setting and job description you would like for your work life. How is this different from or similar to your present job?

■ *Build on the present.* Examine the general and specific requirements of jobs for which you are most marketable, given your experience, education, work attitudes, and goals. Arrange your current educational, training, and life experiences to provide bridges to your future goals.

- *Develop a package.* This includes your resume, a cover letter, and an interview style that markets you in a way most appealing to the type of employer with the type of work setting that you seek.
- *Make contact.* Establish a strategy, schedule, and timetable for initial communication with the people who might be a contact point in a specific type of employment setting. Follow up each lead or initial contact. The intensity of this marketplace requires a comparable personal intensity and commitment.

This five-step process is useful no matter what market segment you choose for your search. Initially, at least, consider all of the major traditional market segments open to lawyers: private firms, public interest organizations, corporations, financial services, government entities, and consulting concerns. If none of these is appealing, look beyond them to the quasi-legal and nonlegal marketplaces, which are as numerous and broad as are categories in a dictionary of occupational titles. Interdisciplinary opportunities, occupational titles, and job combinations as well as career paths are evolving rapidly in this marketplace. The boundaries between traditional disciplines and professional opportunities are rapidly disappearing.

Your task as a job seeker is to know not only the forces, patterns, and trends in the market that have been discussed, but also your own strengths and weaknesses that will determine just where in that market you will find the best fit. Approach the marketplace with an awareness of the forces that are constantly shaping and changing it: globalization, multinationalism, interdisciplinary cooperation, competition, and technology. In short, base the way you market yourself on an integration of your individual self-analysis and your awareness of current market trends. In that way, a market assessment will allow you to set realistic professional goals and move toward personal satisfaction.

CHAPTER 6

How to Change Jobs If You Want To or Have To

David S. Machlowitz

Last year I attended my twenty-fifth-year law school reunion, and my classmates each spoke briefly about their career paths since graduation. Most striking to me was that virtually no one was working at the same job he or she had upon graduation. In the generation before, it would have been very rare for a graduate to have worked in more than one or, at most, two places. Now, it is not unusual to have worked at five or more.

The reasons people gave for their transitions varied tremendously: "I got tired of billing so many hours"; "I wanted to join a national firm"; "I wanted to spend more time with my family"; "I wanted to go to a smaller firm and become part of management"; "I wanted to learn more about business." Many of the reasons were stated with sorrow: "Our firm broke up"; "Our company was acquired"; "We had a major downsizing."

In short, more lawyers than ever before are making career transitions, voluntarily or involuntarily. Voluntary transitions are not only happier, they are generally much easier because there is no time or financial pressure. Nonetheless, all transitions require taking important steps:

- *Decide what you want:* Your chances of finding the right next job will increase dramatically if you think carefully about precisely what you are looking for. Change for the sake of change often results in temporary happiness.
- *Try to improve your current job:* Fellow general counsel or law firm partners often tell me that they have lost a lawyer they wanted to keep because he or she never gave them the chance to give them what they wanted, whether it was more international work, more trial experience, or a bigger office. If your discontent with your current position is based on a few clear issues, why take on the uncertainty of a new position (which will often have a hidden downside) instead of trying to improve your current job?

- *Take your time:* The best thing about voluntary departures is not feeling the pressure of having to find something before your money runs out or your resume has an embarrassing gap in it.
- *Do not jump too often:* The more transitions you have to explain during an interview, the less time you have to focus on your strengths and the more questions may be raised in the mind of the interviewer.
- *Leave with class:* Satisfying as it may be to tell the jerks who have been making your life miserable for years that you are delirious with glee at leaving them, it seldom pays to burn bridges. Your new job may not work out and you may soon need a reference—or they may be asked for a reference without your knowing about it.
- *Exercise extra care with clients:* Nothing turns a previously amicable departure into thermonuclear war faster than the suspicion that a departing lawyer is trying to take away clients. Review Bar rules and partnership agreements and assume that any conversations or correspondence you have with any clients will be reported to (and frequently distorted by) the firm.
- *Maintain your work quality:* You owe it to your colleagues to do the caliber of work you are proud of until you walk out the door. If your employer starts making unreasonable demands, however, say so politely but firmly.

Unfortunately, far from all transitions are voluntary.

"Two weeks ago, I had a great job, a great salary, and a performance review that said I was headed for even greater things. Now, like dozens of other lawyers in my firm, all I've got is two months' severance, a student loan, a mortgage, and a draft of a resume." The speaker is one of the hundreds of lawyers laid off in recent years. Unfortunately, despite the current stock market boom, lawyer layoffs—from individuals not making partner to firms dissolving—remain a reality in the 1990s.

The psychological impact on the fired lawyers is often horrendous, especially because for so many this is the first setback after an unbroken string of successes in school. As one of them recalls, "It was devastating to my self-worth. Everyone else is going to work and you're not going to work. After a while, you wonder whether you're ever going to work again." The economic impact, of course, can be devastating as well, especially for those with student loans to repay and families to support. The days when associates from top firms could always land good jobs are long gone.

Is a layoff easier to take—or at least survive—if you are part of a two-income family? Not necessarily, says Debbie, a Los Angeles lawyer married to another lawyer: "Yes, we had two incomes, but we also had two sets of student loans. We had to have two cars, which our firms insisted be expensive enough to impress clients. We have to pay $17,000 a year of after-tax income to our child's care giver. So that we could see the baby more, we bought a home in the expensive area near our offices. When I was laid off, none of these expenses went away. We're eating into what savings we have now. If my husband is fired before I find a job, we're bankrupt."

What is behind the layoffs? At any one time, some aspects of business law—mergers and acquisitions in part of the 1980s, environmental law in the late 1990s—are slumping. Less work at a firm means either the same lawyers earn fewer dollars or fewer lawyers earn the same dollars. Years ago, most firms would have accepted fewer dollars (perhaps even enjoying the fewer hours worked) to save their colleagues' jobs. Now, such attitudes are unlikely.

As law firms grew, it became easier to fire partners and associates you barely knew. Today's business law climate incessantly emphasizes profits per partner. Avaricious headhunters encourage partners to jump ship for slightly more money. No one should doubt that firms are businesses and that nonperforming partners and associates should not have perpetual employment, but the late Judge Irving Kaufman of the U.S. Second Circuit Court of Appeals said that the then-current wave of firings in the 1980s was "a disgrace."

Michael Luskin had been a partner at New York's Gelberg & Abrams for two years when the senior partners dissolved the firm. Now a partner at Luskin & Stern, he looks back on the situation: "I worked hard for years to achieve my goal. It was very, very upsetting for me to watch a phenomenally successful firm—and my career—torn apart by small-minded people for no good reason."

He has advice for the newly employable lawyer: "I called everyone I knew, I spent at least four hours a day on the phone. Yes, you have to answer ads and see headhunters, but most of all call everyone on your Rolodex. You have to be disciplined about it. It was very gratifying that my friends—even people I had not seen in years—really helped me out. They set up interviews and made phone calls on my behalf. Now, I always help anyone who asks me."

And what about in-house lawyers? There have been some well-published instances of mass firings of corporate counsel—even of eliminating entire departments in perhaps illusory efforts to reduce expenses—and corporate hiring and salary freezes are common.

How can you tell when trouble is on the horizon? What can you do about it? First of all, do not panic, but do not just sit around, either. Head-hunter-turned-outplacer Carol Kanarek advises: "Find out what your true situation is before you do anything rash."

I can offer some practical pointers on identifying the warning signs of a layoff, preparing yourself for the layoff, and "picking up the pieces."

Warning Signs

There are many indications of an impending layoff. Some are readily apparent, while others are more difficult to discern:

- Have the firm's or company's revenues dropped? These days, many partners will not accept small drops in income to save associates' careers. Have competitors laid off lawyers recently? Once one firm takes the public-relations heat, others follow.
- Have partners left the firm? If a major rainmaker has left, disaster may be brewing. If service partners have been forced out, what hope is there for associates?

- Is the new CEO from a different city? Many New York Fortune 500 corporations spent tens of millions of dollars relocating to Connecticut to save their CEOs a fifty-mile commute. If the CEO is from five hundred miles away, watch out.
- Are merger discussions under way? "Redundant associates" will be fired before the handshake is concluded.
- Have salary increases been delayed or reduced? Next, entire salaries will be reduced—perhaps including yours. Have performance reviews been delayed? If profits are dropping, firms generally do not have good reviews to associates who soon will be terminated.
- Are partners spending unusual amounts of time in closed-door meetings? Are the firm's clients or the company's customers hurting? Are memos demanding a decrease in minor expenses circulating?
- Are bills being padded? Suicidal as it often is, firms often churn cases to raise cash, hoping that clients will not notice. Has hiring of new lawyers been reduced? The next step is firing of old lawyers.

How to Prepare

You can take several steps to prepare for a layoff:

- Increase your personal client base, which is the only real security in today's market.
- Develop a "hot" specialty, because being a "good litigator" or "solid generalist" is not enough any more.
- Step up your networking efforts.
- Be in touch with friends and acquaintances in the field so that your social connections are in good order in case you have to seek job market help. The later call will be less self-serving if your personal obligations have been kept up to date.
- Build your savings. Why have financial pressure added to professional pressure? Rely on liquid investments. Long-term stocks will not pay short-term rent.
- Try to get assignments from the most powerful potential mentors. They will be the ones making personnel decisions.
- Think about what you would like your next job to be and what would make you more likely to get it. Pick your future targets when you are not panicking.
- Talk to lawyers who have found new positions recently about what techniques worked for them. They have the most relevant advice.
- Update your resume. You want it ready to go before any positions are filled. Prepare different resumes that emphasize your different specialties.
- Draft a cover letter describing your strengths to possible new employers. This should be sitting in the drawer with your resumes.
- Get the names of any reputable headhunters in your area. The disreputable ones—and there are many—will find you.

Picking Up the Pieces

If you are laid off, you must be prepared to face the consequences.

- Negotiate as good a severance deal as you can. This means not only money, but access to a telephone, a secretary, and someone who will take messages. Find out what type of reference you will receive.
- Prepare psychologically for the change in the way people will treat you just before you leave the firm. The partners will be justifying their decision to fire you, and the associates may be afraid or embarrassed to associate with you. Being angry is natural and perhaps justified, but it will not help you. Redirect your rage into determination to find a new job.
- Let everyone know that you are looking (but not that you were fired). You never know from whom a lead will come. Ask people not only if they know of openings, but if they know of anyone who might know of openings. You may have only fifty contacts, but if each of them gives you only three more names, you have two hundred.
- Ask for help. None of us likes to beg, but your contacts' contacts will respond better to a call from them than a call from you. If you can ask a jury for $10 million in damages, or a seller to reduce his or her asking price, you can ask a friend for help.
- Contact associations. Your city and state bar associations and the local and national chapters of the American Corporate Counsel Association may maintain lists of openings. These organizations may also provide support groups and workshops on resume writing, interviewing, networking, and starting your own practice. Contact your law school or college alumni association for help. Alumni of your law firm might also lend a hand.
- Search for the right search firm. Be very selective about which recruiters you use, but if you find several who seem ethical and energetic, use them all. Do you think you are their only candidate? Just keep careful lists of who suggested which opening. Press them for more than job listings: you need comments on your resume, inside information about firms, and suggestions about how to discuss your firing with an interviewer. Follow up with recruiters monthly.
- Rely on a variety of job informants, and avoid dependence on headhunters, who are notoriously unresponsive to people more than four years out of law school. Be wary of "career counselors" or "outplacement consultants" that demand a fee up front and offer nothing but platitudes. If possible, contact desirable employers directly—not having a headhunter's fee attached to your hiring may help.
- Consider government positions. The work is often interesting and far more socially meaningful than private practice; the security is great; and you may learn a marketable specialty.
- Consider relocating. When Boston may be slumping Orlando may not be.
- Think about switching from outside counsel to in-house, or vice versa. A former client may have an opening. Or you can consult the

Directory of Corporate Counsel. If your in-house work is a specialty now in demand at law firms—such as international deals, employment, or patents—consider private practice.

■ Examine your life. Do you really want to be a lawyer? Being laid off may be the opportunity you need to start fresh.

■ Keep working no matter what. To stay solvent and keep from getting rusty, consider part-time work, pro bono projects, court-appointed cases, or temporary position. These activities might generate new contacts.

■ Stay visible. Use some of your time to line up speaking assignments or to write articles. It may pay off with a job or with clients later. It also breaks up the monotony of a repetitive job search, and it may boost your self-esteem.

■ Help your family cope. They are anxious, too. The impact on children can be especially severe.

■ Remember everyone who helps you and pay them back when you can.

■ Remember everyone who does not help you and pay them back, too.

Finally, do not jump at the first opportunity that knocks. Your hardest time actually may be when you are offered your first job following a layoff. If it is not what you want, think seriously about turning it down. Be realistic, but do not be desperate.

Conclusion

Making a successful voluntary transition requires careful planning and a cool head. Making a successful involuntary transition requires even more personal and professional resources, but despite the immediate emotional trauma of being laid off, it is certainly not the end of the world. It does not require passive acceptance—it requires an active campaign to secure another position.

PART II

Career Identification

CHAPTER 7

Effective Job-Search Techniques and Strategies

Michael J. K. Schiumo

The most persistent problem facing experienced lawyers conducting a job search for is the lack of structure to that process. This is exacerbated by the fact that most experienced lawyers seeking work are already employed in some capacity and that time spent on the job search is precious. This chapter, therefore, is an effort to impose some structure on what is too frequently a chaotic process. With this in mind, we must remember that there are five essential job-search strategies utilized by lawyers.

Strategy 1—Focus and Plan

Lawyers surveyed offer two types of advice to job changers:

1. *Assess yourself:* Spend *at least* half of your time planning, strategizing, and deciding what you really want to do.
2. *Assess your market:* Be a rifle, not a shotgun. Know your strengths and weaknesses, know your precise goal, put yourself in the shoes of a potential employer, and determine what factors will influence the hiring decision. Remember, being specific in what you want is not the same as holding out for the perfect job. So be reasonably flexible.

As a first step, you need to tally your accomplishments, your strengths, your shortcomings, what you like, and what you dislike. *Do not skip this step!* You must look within yourself before you can realistically examine various alternatives and possibilities. You must then assess the marketplace in order to draw a realistic map of your potential market and focus your efforts accordingly. Candidates who are unable to articulate their professional goals in some detail often lose out to other applicants who are more focused. If you are uncertain about what you are looking for or what you can offer, you can expect that the employer will be uncertain as well.

51

Strategy 2—Informational Interviews

The catch-22 of a job search is that you do not know what you are looking for because you do not know what is available. The only way to overcome this is to conduct informational interviews. Lawyers who have embraced informational interviews as a job search tool have found this technique to be exceedingly helpful not only in determining where to focus their energies, but also as a job search tool.

For example, you may decide that you want to move from private law practice to a corporate legal department because you desire more management responsibility and want more reasonable hours. Your first step should be to use your personal, alumni, and business contacts to seek out lawyers who hold positions in corporations. You need answers to important questions:

1. Are your assumptions about the working environment valid?
2. What are the possible roles for lawyers in corporations?
3. Which aspects of your background and experience would be of particular interest to a corporation?
4. What obstacles might you encounter and what strategies should you utilize to overcome those obstacles?

Informational interviews can also be used effectively as a way to educate yourself about a target market. For example, one lawyer who had been out of law school for twelve years had decided to pursue an advanced degree before moving to a new geographic area. She assumed her seniority would be an obstacle and that an advanced degree would improve her chances of locating a new position. She used informational interviews to test her hypothesis and called a few people in the city and practice area she had targeted. As a result, she discovered that her assumption about seniority level being a major impediment was not valid for that market and that an advanced degree would not improve her chances of getting a new position.

Strategy 3—Allocate Your Time Properly

Since you have only limited time to devote to a job search, you need to decide which sources will be most productive for you.

A recent survey examining how lawyers found jobs revealed the following:

- 68 percent found positions through personal contacts
- 16 percent found positions through published openings
- 11 percent found positions through search firms
- 5 percent found positions through mass mailings

The message is that the job seeker must distribute his or her time and energy wisely among various sources.

Ideally, 70 percent of your job-seeking time should be spent expanding your personal contact base. In addition, approximately 15 percent of your time should be devoted to locating and responding to job listings published on the Internet and in local newspapers, journals, government job listing services, bar associations, and your law school career planning office.

Mass mailings, while they do satisfy one's innate need for action, are one of the least effective methods for locating a position and should be viewed by you as a supplementary, not a primary, strategy. Search firms are worth at least a preliminary contact so that you can decide if their employer contacts are compatible with your background and interests. When dealing with a search firm remember that this is your career and do not let yourself be persuaded to accept a position that does not fit into your career goals.

Personal Contact Base

Many of the respondents to the survey told us how important networking was to them:

- "If possible, let as many people as you can know that you are in the market. Maintain frequent contact. I almost missed my new job opportunity by failing to stay in touch with a contact."
- "The time to make your contacts is before you need them. When the search starts, the guy with the fattest Rolodex wins."
- "Use every contact you've ever made to get an interview; if you do well in interviews, you can overcome any flaw in your credentials. The 'halo' effect is still alive and well."

Your personal contact base is an invaluable asset in any job search or career transition. Ignoring it means not utilizing one of your most beneficial resources. We all have our favorite stories on networking. In fact, one of my jobs was an indirect result of spending an evening in a hot tub in Palm Springs! As the saying goes, sometimes opportunities turn up where you least expect them. Luck is certainly involved, but networking puts you in a position to get lucky. As the statistics above starkly illustrate, very few people get a job by cranking out mass mailings and never leaving the house.

To find candidates for informational interviews, consider your law school's career planning office. In a dramatic change over the past fifteen years, career planning offices today spend much more of their time counseling alumni. After a counseling session in the career planning office, a counselor should be able to give you the names of several alumni in a particular practice area or particular geographic location who might be willing to speak with you.

Published Notices

Somewhat surprisingly, many lawyers find jobs by responding to published notices that advertise openings. Published notices are more common for job openings in government and in medium-sized to small law firms.

Many law schools are making their job listings available to alumni via the Internet. After receiving a supplied a password, the alumni are able to access listings at their own convenience. Since these listing are, by definition, "fresh," this is a dramatic improvement over the standard monthly alumni newsletters that most law schools have traditionally published.

A word about the Internet here. One of the most dramatic changes in society over the past five years has been the rise of the Internet. There has been a proliferation of Web sites geared toward job opportunities for lawyers, particularly experienced lawyers. Since search firms can become quite expensive for an employer, many employers will now list job opportunities on Web sites at no charge before employing a search firm. A recent visit to the career services portion of a law school's web site revealed over forty links to other career-related Web sites! Many are no-frills sites, while others are quite sophisticated and allow an individual to search by geographic locale, area of practice, or even salary. If you are a holdout against the Internet, let go. The use of the Internet for disseminating information about job opportunities has just begun. Surfing the net should be an essential aspect of every job search.

Search Firms
Search firms seem to play a slightly less prominent position in the legal marketplace as they have in the past. The survey results showed that most of the lawyers who successfully found a job through a legal search firm fit a certain profile:

1. Their earlier position had been with a large law firm.
2. They had been out of law school for two and a half to three years.
3. The new position they accepted was with a large law firm.

Be aware that all headhunters are not created equal. Some are better than others in keeping the applicants happiness in mind, but always remember that their motivation is based on making a deal and receiving a commission. Be you own watchdog in dealing with headhunters. If possible, get a referral from a friend or colleague who has had a pleasant and successful experience with a headhunter.

Successful job seekers can offer helpful advice about utilizing legal search firms: "Only deal with headhunters who are optimistic and willing to tell you specific actions they will take. . . . Do not let headhunters tell you (the job seeker) that you are too anything—too experienced, too specialized, too generalized."

Mass Mailing
Conducting mass mailings is the least effective of all job search strategies in today's legal, lateral job market. If you do try a mass mailing, remember to do your research so that you can target your resume and cover letter to the employer. Make sure you answer the question, What need do I fill for the employer?

Strategy 4—Devote Your Full Effort

Not surprisingly, studies have consistently illustrated that job seekers who devoted 80 percent or more of their time to looking for a new job were the most successful. The amount of effort expended in locating a new position is the most important factor in any job search campaign. This holds true for all levels of experience and seniority. The message, then, for all lawyers, is that once you have decided to make a job change, an all-out campaign is necessary in order to be successful. Set weekly goals so that you are able give the search some structure, and measure your progress in order to maintain momentum through an often-difficult process. Although it is not necessary, or recommended, that you quit your current full-time job in order to locate a new job, it is clear that once you have made the decision to look for new employment you should exert an all-out effort, and immediately utilize every strategy and resource available to you.

Strategy 5—Develop a Good Support Network

A job search is likely to fail nine out of ten times. The deck is stacked against us. With this in mind, it is extraordinarily important to develop a good support network.

One job seeker noted, "As is true of so many of life's transitions, the support of friends, family and mentors is a key in the job search process."

Another said that the "most important part of the job search is keeping a positive attitude and continuing to have self-confidence in the face of inevitable rejections. Every week do at least one job-search-related activity that is upbeat and reinforcing."

While the job search is statistically stacked against us, remember that statistics do not matter. In order to complete a successful job search, all you really need is one good job offer!

Seven Steps in a Successful Legal Job Search Campaign

1. Plan and focus. Spend at least half of your time up-front planning, strategizing, and deciding what you really want to do.
2. Begin your search by conducting informational interviews. Be specific when asking for advice. Never directly ask for a job.
3. Allocate your time appropriately among the various sources and strategies. Make the Internet an essential tool in your job search.
4. Network until you drop.
5. Get up and network some more!
6. Keep a written record of all of your efforts and make sure that you devote time and effort every week to your search. Never let the momentum stop.
7. Keep your spirits up by surrounding yourself with positive people.

CHAPTER 8

Networking

Kathleen Brady

What Is Networking?

Contacts are your single most valuable resource in the job search process, therefore, it is extremely important to master the art of networking.

Networking is simply meeting in person with professional and personal contacts and asking for ideas and advice on the ways your talents could best be used in the marketplace. Networking rests on the basic principle that business, jobs and careers are built on personal relationships; its true purpose is to get *information, advice,* and *referrals.*

Think about it. Networking occurs naturally in all areas of life. For example, when moving into a new neighborhood, you probably would not hesitate to ask your new neighbors for recommendations about dry cleaners, grocery stores, dentists, and so on. Or when planning a vacation you would not think twice about asking friends or family to recommend hotels and restaurants. In business it is common to ask colleagues to suggest accountants, bankers or computer systems. But for some reason, we hesitate to ask people we know about job opportunities.

It is important to understand what you can reasonably expect from relationships and what is outside those bounds. When networking to uncover job opportunities it is reasonable to expect the following:

- Information
- Referrals to others who can help you
- Feedback about resumes, cover letters, and approach
- Opportunities to test ideas and theories
- Assistance in formulating plans
- Moral support

It Is Not Reasonable to Expect a Job Will Be Handed to You!

Most of the people you will talk to will not know of many current job openings. If the only question you pose is, "Do you know of any openings?" you are likely to be told no. Worse, you have lost the opportunity to strengthen your relationship with your contact and gain some insight. Instead ask your contact what he or she does, and then ask about the opportunities related to their work and interests. Then you are likely to uncover information that will eventually generate job leads and preserve your relationships.

Countless books and articles have been written outlining networking techniques and gimmicks to coach readers. But you cannot be effective with empty techniques and gimmicks. You need to have a clear objective about what you are trying to accomplish before you visit anyone. *Think through your strategy first.* There should be no hidden agenda. You should simply be looking for information about where the jobs are. If you are playing the "advice and information game" when you really believe networking is nothing more than the back door route to a new position, you are being insincere, misleading, and in the end ineffective.

What If I Have No Contacts?

You might be thinking negatively: This is all well and good, but my problem is I do not *have* any contacts. Nonsense! Of course you do.

First, consider law school classmates and professors, college friends and family members, neighbors, former employers, colleagues and opponents, and bar association leaders. All of these people are contacts who may be able to assist you in your quest for information, advice, and referrals. Step 1 in the process is to review your personal address book and alumni directories with an eye toward who could be helpful.

Next, conduct library research. As a lawyer, you already possess the well-developed research skills needed to gather information. Effective research will help you identify people and organizations doing the type of work you want to do.

Finally, attend events! Go to professional association meetings, alumni reunions, church and synagogue events, weddings, and bar mitzvahs and work the room—that is, circulate comfortably and graciously through the gathering. People who genuinely enjoy others are the most successful at working a room. There is nothing calculated or manipulative about it because the process is based on mutual interests. Keep in mind what has brought this particular group of people together and why it is important for you to be there.

Introduce yourself: *Hi. I don't believe we've met. I'm Mary Smith.*

Proceed to tell them your connection to the event you are attending. You can continue the conversation by asking open-ended questions to learn about them. Your goal should be to meet and get to know people first; you can probe for information and openings later.

Keep in mind that you are completely responsible for what you bring into a room and for what you project onto other people. Dress like the confident professional that you are. Be positive and upbeat. Project a proud, confident image. If you look and act like a loser, that is how people will respond to you. If all you talk about is needing a job, people will run when they see you. Your goal should be for people to have a *pleasant, positive* experience of you. You want to make a strong first impression. You do not need to "close the deal" at this event; you simply need to create an opening to use later.

Strategies for Approaching Contacts

Whether your contacts are friends, people you have identified through library research, or those you have met attending events, it is important to use a well thought-out process when approaching them for assistance. An approach letter, followed by a phone call, informational interview, and thank-you note is most effective.

You must be able to clearly and succinctly explain why you are requesting a meeting. What do you hope to gain from meeting with your contact? Why have you chosen this particular person to contact over all of the other possibilities? What specifically do you want to find out? These types of questions will help you to clarify your objectives in networking and increase your chances of piquing interest in meeting you. You must be prepared to say more than "I am thinking of leaving my job and I was wondering if you know of any openings."

The Letter

Write a letter, then call, to ask for fifteen minutes of their time. Do not put pressure on the individual to find you a job or to interview you. That may be a long-term result, but when approaching a person, an informative conversation should be your objective:

Dear _____:

Mary Smith suggested that I contact you about my interest in career opportunities in [your interest in law]. I am a graduate of XYZ Law School with four years' experience in . . .

[Your next paragraph should tell something about your background. Include your prior work experience, current situation, skills, interests, academic history, connection to the geographic region, etc.]

As I venture into the job market, I hope to benefit from the experience and knowledge of others in the field who might advise me on opportunities for someone with my qualifications. I would appreciate the opportunity to meet with you for fifteen minutes for your guidance. I will call your office next week to see if we can schedule a meeting.

I look forward to discussing my plans with you.

Sincerely, [etc.]

Do not include your resume with this letter.

The Telephone Call

Nothing is more effective than a well-written cover letter followed promptly (five to seven days later) by a telephone call. Most job seekers never try to call decision-makers and even those who do try, do not try often enough. The telephone is the most underutilized tool available to the job seeker.

Hello, Mr./Ms. _____. This is Lyn Brown. I am calling at the suggestion of Mary Smith. I sent you a letter last week explaining . . . [re-
state the first paragraph of your letter]. I was wondering if you might
have fifteen minutes next Tuesday or Thursday to meet with me?

Naturally, if you have a personal relationship with a contact, a letter
may be too formal. Start with a telephone call. Go directly to the phone
and say:

- *To anyone you admire:* "You always seem to have good ideas."
- *To someone you have helped:* "We have helped each other in the past, so
  I am hoping you can help be now."
- *To a geographic contact:* "You have lived in this city for so long and
  know almost everyone."
- *To a socially active friend:* "You have so many friends, you probably
  hear about things before anyone."
- *To someone who works in your field:* "You've been working in the same
  type of job I am looking for, I am sure you have some idea how my
  skills might be viewed."
- *To a professor:* "You know better than anyone what kinds of jobs are
  open in this field."

Remember, you do not want to exert pressure on this person to find you
a job. You only want to explain the purpose of the meeting and articulate
how you believe your contact can be helpful. The objective is to unearth information about them and their job experience.

If the person seems hesitant to grant your request to meet, clearly state
that you are not looking for a job with them and that you are only looking for
advice and information. If you still meet resistance, try to conduct the informational interview over the phone. If even that feels uncomfortable, politely
bring the conversation to a close and than write a nice thank-you letter, again
stating your intended purpose. Mention your disappointment in not being
able to learn from the person's experience and ask to be remembered for future reference. Enclose your resume with this letter.

The Informational Interview: Setting the Agenda

Once you are in your contact's office, it is your responsibility to lead the conversation. You should be prepared to:

- Explain the purpose of the meeting.
- Show how your contact can be helpful.
- Present your background and skills to put the meeting in context.
- Ask questions to elicit the information you need.
- Give your contact a pleasant, positive experience of you.
- Get the names of others who could be helpful.
- Be considerate of the contact's time.

The purpose of the meeting is to determine how your talents could be
used in different settings, so it is important to do a good job presenting them.
The ability to communicate your qualifications to employers entails more

than just informing them of your technical competence. You must be able to illustrate that you have the requisite personal attributes—such as problem-solving abilities, analytical skills, assessment and planning experience—to perform the job. The examples you use to talk about your accomplishments should elucidate your thinking and problem-solving style. The more concrete and specific you are, the easier it will be for your contact to think of possibilities for you and to suggest additional people you should meet.

A common mistake people make during the networking and information-gathering stage is to use the meeting as a therapy session. You do not want to inspire guilt, pity, or dread. Your goal should be to make your contacts feel good about their ability to help you. It is important that you present yourself as positive, confident, and self-assured—not negative, needy, and desperate. Never make your contacts feel sorry for you or responsible for your situation. Do not scoff at their suggestions by saying, "I've tried that and it does not work." This may cause your contacts to doubt their ability to help you and to begin avoiding you. If you need to express anger, bitterness, anxiety, or other negative feelings, talk to the counselor at your law school's career service office or seek out a member of the clergy or a sympathetic friend before meeting with your contacts.

During your appointment you may want to cover the following issues:

1. The careers of the people you are visiting:
   - Their background
   - How their interest developed in this area
   - What they like best/least about their work
   - Their "career steps" (what former jobs they held, what they learned from each, how they progressed from one job to the next)
2. Advantages and disadvantages of work with:
   - That type of firm, agency or corporation
   - Their type of law practice
   - The geographical area
3. What your contacts' organization is like and how it operates:
   - Whom they supervise, and to whom they report
   - Performance expectations
   - Advancement opportunities
   - Future growth potential
4. What organizations such as theirs are looking for in an employee.
5. How to make yourself more attractive as a potential employee:
   - Suggestions on upgrading your resume
   - Tips on interviewing techniques
   - Ideas on additional educational and experiential qualifications you might pursue
   - Leads on where to go to find more information
   - Names of others in the field with whom you could speak
6. What specific job openings your contact thinks you should consider.

Once the contact gets to know you and you have asked questions about her career (showing genuine interest), it is her prerogative to offer further assistance. Toward the conclusion of your talk, her thoughts might naturally turn to what action she might take on your behalf.

Be sure to express gratitude for offers of assistance and take notes if the individual suggests that you contact colleagues. Ask if you may use her name when following up on this list. If your contact offers to send out your resumes for you or make calls on your behalf, make sure you arrange to get a list of those contacted so that you can take control of the follow-up process. Assuming responsibility for the follow-up process will allow your contact to experience you as efficient and conscientious.

Should your contact not offer assistance or additional names of people to call, you might gently ask if she could suggest names of individuals who could give you more information.

You may find that the fifteen minutes you asked for has stretched into a conversation lasting an hour or more. This usually occurs because the individual is flattered by being asked for advice and having the chance to act as a mentor. However, it is up to *you* to stick to the preset time limit. Let your contact take the initiative to extend the meeting, if she or he so desires.

People love to talk about themselves. This type of conversation tends to be very warm and animated, filled with goodwill. Even when they do not know of a specific job opening, your contacts are likely to keep you in mind when they do have one. Or, when a colleague is trying to fill a position, they may recommend you.

The Follow-Up

When you meet with people on your network list, take notes about the meeting. It would be helpful to start a file for each contact. Whether you choose a sophisticated computer software program or a simple 3 × 5 index card filing system, be sure to include the following:

- The contact's name (be sure you have the correct spelling)
- The date of the contact
- The results of the meeting
- Required follow-up and the timeframe
- The person who referred you
- Any personal information that may be helpful
- Your impressions of the person and the organization

The job-search process requires that you continually make phone calls, schedule appointments, write follow-up notes, contact new people, and generally keep the ball rolling. It is important to record the dates and times for each activity on a pocket calendar to remind you what needs to be done. This will help to organize your days, and organization will enable you to get more accomplished. Are there new books to read, new resources to consider, additional organizations to explore, new people to meet? Develop your plan of action based on this new information.

People who help you should be kept apprised as your job search progresses. If a lead they provide results in an interview, let them know. A note every two or three months to helpful contacts is appropriate. Remember, the way to get a response to any kind of marketing communication is to create multiple, positive impressions. *Your* job search may not be the most important thing on your contact's mind. If you can occasionally remind people that you are still looking, other opportunities may present themselves down the line.

Send a thank-you letter and let the contact know what specific follow-up actions you have planned. As a general rule, thank-you notes should be typed, particularly if you want to be formal or if you have terrible handwriting. Handwritten notes are fine if you have a personal relationship with the person or if the meeting was brief and informal.

It is appropriate to recontact people as you go through the process. New information may generate new questions. Additionally, your contact may be interested to learn some of the information you have uncovered.

Finally, after each informational interview, review your performance. Did you present your skills as effectively as possible? Did you craft your questions to elicit the information you needed? What could you have done better?

Overcoming the Fear of Being Labeled a "User"

Many people are hesitant about "using" people or asking for help. However, networking should be viewed as a communication process—exchanging and receiving advice and referrals about jobs. Many people these days consider it foolish *not* to use contacts, and those in a position to help you might even be insulted that they were not asked for assistance. People *like* to help others. It makes them feel good, powerful, and important. If you establish a specific and relevant basis for a meeting—asking for ideas, opinions, a reaction to your own thoughts—there is no reason for you to be turned down. Ask for something specific, something doable.

Since much of professional life operates on the "favor system," establish a reputation for being helpful. Pass along useful information or introduce contacts to people you have met along the way that could be helpful to them. Look for ways to build bridges. People will remember your thoughtfulness and will be likely to return the favor. Busy professionals understand the system, and they know that with just a little time and some guidance from *you* they can evaluate you for their own needs or those of their associates while still satisfying your request for information. Both you and the other person receive something. Therefore, do not feel guilty about approaching busy people for help; they will enjoy it and you will benefit by it. If you are doubtful, consider whether you would be willing to share your knowledge or give names to friends or business associates in order to be helpful.

The process of building and using networks should be a permanent aspect of your career, not just a technique you use for finding jobs and advancing your career. Keep in touch with people you meet. Drop them a note occasionally or send them an article you saw that made you think of them. When you do land a job, let your contacts know. Do not wait until you "need" something from them. Remember, it is important to develop, use, and nurture personal relationships on a daily basis.

CHAPTER 9

Using the Internet

Erik J. Heels

Richard P. Klau

You are changing jobs. You have access to the Internet. Do the two have anything to do with each other? Fortunately, the answer is yes. You can put your knowledge of the Net to good use. In fact, one of the most rapidly growing areas of information on the Internet has been job recruitment. Today, job seekers have more resources at their disposal than ever before. Between comprehensive databases of job announcements and industry-specific clearinghouses for new jobs, it is easier than ever to find the right job. In this chapter you will learn about the most effective ways to turn an Internet job announcement into a job offer. At the end of this chapter is a list of selected job-search Web sites of particular interest to lawyers and a brief description of what you can expect on those pages.

As the use of the Web increases in the legal profession, more and more law firms are using the Web to recruit lawyers, both new hires and lateral hires. Because there is no single, central place on the Internet that lists every law firm site or job opening, finding such information can be tedious. As a result, using law firm Web sites for hiring information is most helpful once you have narrowed your search by using some of the sites listed at the end of this chapter. The list is not intended to be exhaustive; it is merely representative. The list also contains sites not owned by individual law firms and sites for jobs in careers other than law.

Applying for the Job You Want

Finding the job listing you are interested in is the first step. The next steps are especially critical. In the days before the Internet, you applied for a job by printing your resume with a laser printer on heavy bond paper, including a cover letter, and hoping for the best. The nice printer, nice paper approach can be considered a standard in the job search process.

Unfortunately, many Internet users have failed to adopt similar standards for their efforts online. As a result, they come across as sloppy at best, and unprofessional at worst. Consider the following example of an e-mail sent by an applicant for a job at a law firm:

> Date: December 9, 1999 12:14PM–0500
> From: johnnyboy@aol.com
>
> To: recruiting@smithjones.com
> Subject: job
>
> Hi - I saw some info on your web site about a job. I attached my resume - let me know if you have qusetions. -John <file attachment: jrjres.doc>

Although the above e-mail is purely hypothetical, here are the common mistakes it illustrates:

The e-mail address.   Many job applicants prefer not to send e-mail from their work e-mail address. In general, this is a good idea, especially if you do not want your current employer to know that you are looking or to which companies you are talking. (Legally, it is well established that your employer has the right to read your e-mail. Though uncommon, it can happen, so you should practice discretion.) Since many individuals use America Online (http://www.aol.com/) from home, they rely on AOL's ability to send Internet e-mail.

Using AOL is not inherently a bad idea. But choose your address wisely: if you want to project a professional image, worthy of employment at a particular firm, do not start off on the wrong foot by having your first contact with the firm be as "johnnyboy."

Subject line.   Assume that the contact people who are reading and screening the incoming e-mail are receiving dozens, if not hundreds or thousands, of e-mails relating to the job openings at the firm. Many job descriptions that advertise e-mail addresses specify what to type in the subject line. They do this for a reason: in many cases, the screener is filtering all resumes to one mail folder. If you use a nonstandard subject line, the recipient will be forced to sort the e-mail manually. Already, you will be starting at a loss. (Indeed, at least one employer we have dealt with ignores any e-mail that fails to follow directions. So if you use the nonstandard subject line, your resume will not be read.)

With the subject line, as with the rest of the e-mail, pay attention to punctuation, grammar, and spelling. Capitalize words that should be capitalized, use proper punctuation, and check for misspelled words. When the goal is to stand out among hundreds of resumes, details count. And laziness will be obvious, as it is in the sample e-mail whose subject line reads just "job."

Message body.   It is shocking how casually many people treat e-mail. If you are applying for a job, your message body should be identical to the cover letter you would send in paper correspondence. Address the e-mail to the recipient (example: "Dear Ms. Robins:") and format the e-mail appropriately. Separate paragraphs, capitalize words, and conclude the letter properly. Instead of "-John" at the end, conclude with a paragraph thanking the person for his or her time, then sign off in a manner similar to a formal letter on paper:

> Regards,
> John Jackson
> 1424 Main Street
> Anytown, NY 11112
> (212) 555-4433

Because the tone is so casual (and so little attention is paid to the message itself), our writer failed to see the misspelling ("qusetion" instead of "question") in the e-mail: however, this is likely to catch the attention of whoever is reading the message.

Resume.   So far, we have addressed several mistakes and still have not discussed the resume. In the sample e-mail, John attached his resume (in Microsoft Word format) to his e-mail message. While most e-mail programs adhere to Internet standards with respect to attachments, this is still the most problematic area in sending e-mail. All too often, an attachment will get garbled in transit: either the sender's e-mail server improperly handled the attachment, or the recipient's server somehow botched the delivery and corrupted the file. Whatever the cause, the result is that recipients end up with the digital equivalent of garbage. And if they get garbage, they will not necessarily send you a follow-up e-mail to tell you about it. They will likely just throw it out and move on to those applicants whose resumes were readable.

At this stage, you have a few options. The first is to send a text version of your resume in the body of your e-mail. This is by far the most desirable option. It eliminates any chance for problems, assures that the recipient will view your resume without any confusion, and requires the least amount of effort on the recipient's end (thereby lessening the chance that an inadvertent mistake on your end will color the recipient's view of your resume). After all, the goal is to get your resume read; anything that gets in the way of that is just trouble for you. The downside to using text, of course, is that you lose the ability to control how the printed resume looks. This is a minor concession in most cases, as most employers are concerned with content and not presentation. In fact, many employers require that applicants send their resume in text-only format and as part of the message simply to avoid having to deal with the numerous problems that arise when using attachments.

To convert your resume to text, you may want to simply retype your resume. If you try to just save your formatted resume as a text file, you will likely see garbled text. You need to know some specifics when doing this: the standard line length for monospace (i.e., Courier font) text used by most e-mail programs is 80 characters. However, some programs insert hard returns at something less than 80 characters, which results in hard-to-read text. Avoid this problem by using just 70 characters per line. Once you have finished, send yourself a test message with the resume included. Did it go through smoothly? Are the lines formatted as you expected?

Users of many newer e-mail programs have the option of sending formatted e-mail. What they are really doing is sending e-mail as HTML (the same formatting language that is used for documents on the World Wide Web). The advantages to using formatted e-mail include the ability to use bold, italic, and other font enhancements, to control the layout of the page, and more. However, e-mail sent in this format is far from standard. If recipients do not have e-mail programs capable of displaying the formatting, they may see poorly formatted information; or worse, they will see nothing but gibberish. Unless you know that the recipient can view formatted e-mail, avoid it.

As a last resort, you may want to send your resume as an attachment. The pitfalls in this approach are many; there are numerous word processing formats in use today, and there is no guarantee that the program you are using is completely compatible with the version the recipient is using. A document that appears to be beautifully formatted on your computer may show up as disjointed paragraphs on another computer. If you are going to send an attachment, be sure to find out what word processing program and version the firm uses. Once you know that, you should be able to save your document in that program's format. (Of course, the translation between your program and theirs may not be smooth, which is another reason to avoid attachments.)

Encryption.   Discussions of the Internet almost always include concerns about security. Should you use encryption (a process of scrambling data so it is unreadable to all but the intended recipient) to safeguard your information? To encrypt a document, you will need to make sure that you and the recipient are using the same encryption program. (Popular encryption programs include PGP, or Pretty Good Privacy, as well as security-enabled versions of Microsoft Outlook and Netscape Communicator.)

The benefit to using encryption is that the underlying information is unreadable if intercepted or read by anyone other than the intended recipient. However, the implementation of encryption is far from widespread, and few users really understand how to use it. In all likelihood, you will not find many employers who are using PGP or other programs to protect their e-mail. If you are very concerned about someone intercepting your e-mail (or your employer reading it), find out if the recipient uses encryption. If so, make sure you know how to use the program first, then notify the recipient that you will be sending encrypted e-mail.

Posting on the Web

Some job applicants prefer to create their own home page on the Web and then post their resume on it. Any job applications can then be accompanied by your resume's URL (uniform resource locator); for example, http://home.aol.com/users/joe32/resume.html. There are several advantages to using the Web this way. First of all, you have greater control over the presentation of the resume. From an aesthetic point of view, this is certainly a benefit. More important, you can create hyperlinks to documents and organizations that are mentioned in the resume. For example, if you have published an article with a law review that publishes online, or if you clerked for a nonprofit organization that has a Web site, your resume can now make it simple for a potential employer to go to that information.

Another way to use the Web is to develop an authoritative resource on the practice area of your choice. For instance, one sole practitioner decided to develop a Web site dedicated to Internet-related legal issues. As more lawyers became interested in the legal ramifications of the Internet, many found this lawyer's site to be the most comprehensive resource of its kind. Before he knew it, he had become an authority who was frequently called for comments by journalists writing stories about the Internet and the law. He was able to leverage this notoriety into a job with a large firm. Your goal may not be to end up with a large firm, but the example is still a good one. You can get what you want by displaying your abilities rather than by trying to summarize them in a short resume that may not adequately explain your value to a firm.

Take advantage of today's door-opening electronic communications in your job search, no matter what type of job you want. Just remember to use all the tools at your disposal to get your application and resume noticed. Regardless of the medium used, your first communication with potential employers makes a lasting impression and could make the difference between getting an interview and staying stuck in a dead-end job. Good luck!

Law-Specific Online Resources

EmplawyerNet
http://www.emplawyernet.com/

The only possible conclusion one can draw from looking at the number of external links to EmplawyerNet (187) is that the site is the single best-kept secret on the Internet for lawyers looking for jobs. With more than seven thousand law jobs listed, EmplawyerNet is a gold mine compared to the nonspecific recruiting sites on the Internet. EmplawyerNet is a subscription-based service. As of 1999, lawyers pay around $10 per month, and law students, thanks to sponsorship from Lexis-Nexis, pay less. Subscribers can search EmplawyerNet's database of current job openings, view entries for legal recruiters by region, and participate in several online forums that allow EmplawyerNet members to interact.

Searching for a job is simple. Jobs can be located by region, practice area, type, and other categories. EmplawyerNet postings state the contact information and a brief job description. Members can send in resumes by fax or mail, and EmplawyerNet will scan them in and make them available to employers on request. Members of EmplawyerNet can establish a profile containing basic biographical information. EmplawyerNet allows subscribers to sign up for "Job Mail," a service that will e-mail you when jobs that match your profile are added to the system. The more information you enter about your abilities, the more likely it is that EmplawyerNet will find jobs that fit your criteria. The depth of information, quality of leads, and attention to detail make this an excellent site.

FindLaw Legal Classifieds
http://jobs.findlaw.com/

Click on "Attorneys" under "Legal Employment" and you will get a list (subdivided by state with total number of jobs listed) of all jobs available on the system. Jobs are also listed for summer clerks, law librarians, paralegals, and secretaries. The quality of information varies, from superficial (job title, contact info) to in-depth (description of responsibilities, contact info, Web address for further information). Navigation is easy (as it is with the rest of FindLaw's site), pages load quickly, and the content is quite current. Unlike other job sites, it costs nothing for employers to list here. We expect that Find-Law's list will become more heavily used as more employers find this free resource.

General Job Sites CareerWeb
http://www.cweb.com/

CareerWeb is an easy-to-use job search Web site. Users are invited to upload a copy of their resume. Once this is done, the resume is searchable by all potential employers. On the Internet, job seekers may very well hear from an employer before they contact the employer. The user's resume may be edited at any time to reflect changes, and when it is time to apply for a job listed on CareerWeb, the user can simply type in a resume number (every resume is given a unique ID number). CareerWeb takes care of the rest by sending the employer the resume and cover letter provided by the user. CareerWeb does not charge job seekers for the service, but employers pay a fee to list their job openings online. The overall interface is clean, allowing quick access to the job search process and easy maintenance of the online resume and cover letter.

Monster Board
http://www.monster.com/

Monster Board boasts one of the most comprehensive job search Web sites. Its value comes not just in its tens of thousands of job listings but in other services it provides. Most valuable is the "Jobba the Hunt" search agent, which will search all Monster Board job postings for keywords, locations and categories specified by the user. When it finds something that matches these criteria, "Jobba" will e-mail the user with the job listing. Looking for a job could not be easier. As with the other large recruiting Web sites, Monster Board does not charge job seekers a fee. Instead, it charges employers a fairly expensive fee. (In 1998, an employer profile and eight job postings cost $2,700.) Monster Board's popularity (it is visited by more than 2 million users a month) is at times a disadvantage; at peak times, users may not be able to edit their stored resumes or view their saved job searches. Because Monster Board breaks up legal listings ("Legal-Attorney," "Legal-Litigation Support," "Legal-Secretary," etc.), search results will not include extraneous listings. Overall, Monster Board provides an easy-to-use framework, powerful searching tools, and a frequently updated system.

CareerPath
http://www.careerpath.com/

CareerPath started in 1995 as a shared "help wanted" database for the *Boston Globe, New York Times, Washington Post* and *Los Angeles Times.* Over time, it has grown into an enormous database that contains the help wanted ads of more than sixty newspapers around the country. Updated weekly, CareerPath contains the full text of the ads that appear in each newspaper's classifieds each week. It is one of the most visited job sites on the Internet. CareerPath's strength is its nationwide coverage, and its weakness is its format. As with the classified ads in newspapers, the quality of help wanted ads varies considerably. However, CareerPath offers a significant benefit over its print counterpart: the ability to search the classifieds by keywords. Like newspaper categories, CareerPath's legal heading includes secretarial and paralegal jobs as well as lawyer listings. Using CareerPath will require slightly more work than some of its competitors, but its coverage is very broad.

Online Career Center
http://www.occ.com/

Online Career Center (OCC) is the granddaddy of Internet recruiting sites. It was the first on the block. This gives OCC a proven track record with employers. As a result, it has arguably the largest database of job openings on the Internet. Like its competition, OCC is employer supported and is free to job seekers. OCC's biggest drawback is its interface: the search options and search results are not as user-friendly as those for CareerWeb or Monster Board. Users are permitted to search by geography and keyword, but it may be difficult to narrow search results to the desired jobs. Overall, OCC is less useful for the law graduate than the other major sites listed above. It may be a better option for those with law degrees who are seeking an alternative career.

Law Firm Web Sites

Some law firms have their own Internet recruitment sites. We will describe briefly what you will find when you visit the sites listed below:

http://www.mckennacuneo.com/recruiting/home.html

McKenna & Cuneo, a government contracting firm in Washington, D.C., has offices all over the United States and two offices abroad. With more than 250 lawyers in the firm, the McKenna & Cuneo site gives both law students and current lawyers useful information about the firm in the hopes of prequalifying applicants. You will find a wealth of information on this page, including details about the summer associate program, the firm's pro bono commitment, and its training program. E-mail links are provided that allow the interested job hunter to contact the appropriate person.

http://www.sidley.com/about/students.html

Sidley & Austin, a large firm with primary offices in New York, Washington, D.C., Los Angeles, and Chicago, provides information primarily intended for law students on its recruiting page. The information includes detailed compensation information, interview and call-back procedures, and information about the firm's summer program.

http://www.kslaw.com/menu/recruit.htm

King & Spaulding, a national law firm with headquarters in Atlanta and offices in Houston, New York, and Washington, D.C., also provides a considerable amount of information for law students and lateral hires. E-mail addresses for contact people, information on how many associates will be hired, the firm's compensation plan, and a history of the firm are all included for the potential applicant to review.

Discussion Lists

Net-Lawyers

No discussion of networking on the Internet would be complete without a mention of Net-Lawyers, a moderated discussion list. Ostensibly geared toward lawyers using the Internet in their day-to-day practice, Net-Lawyers has hosted some lively discussions about ethics, emerging technologies and their effect on the practice of law, and developments in the law as they affect the Internet. Messages posted to Net-Lawyers will be seen by thousands of subscribers, many of whom are lawyers. More than one lawyer has found clients through postings made to Net-Lawyers, and many more have found help from fellow lawyers by asking questions. To subscribe to Net-Lawyers, send e-mail to listserv@peach.ease.lsoft.com with the command "subscribe Net-lawyers" in the body of the message. To view archives of the list (often a good idea when just subscribing or deciding whether or not to subscribe), visit the Net-lawyers archive on the Web at http://eva.dc.lsoft.com/Archives/net-lawyers.html

Law Jobs
http://www.legalminds.org/list/lawjobs-l/

If you want to subscribe to the lawjobs-l mailing list, you can send a message to listserv@lawlib.wuacc.edu with the following command in the body of your email message: subscribe lawjobs-l First_Name Last_Name

While the quality of the posts varies considerably (since this is an open list, anyone can post job announcements and/or replies to announcements), this is still a decent resource to use when evaluating what options are available to you. Using the URL above (LegalMinds is a free service of FindLaw), you can view an online archive of all posts to the list. This is an attractive option, as it allows you to see everything posted to the list without having to subscribe and deal with all of the e-mail being sent to your mailbox. You can also do keyword searches on the list using LegalMinds, which drastically reduces your search time and increases the likelihood that you will find something useful.

Topic-Specific Lists

If you are interested in obtaining a job in a particular practice area (e.g., intellectual property), you may want to consider joining a topic-specific discussion list. In most cases, many of the leading experts in the field will be participating in the forum, and once you have established your ability or interest, you may be able to draw on the connections of the group to find the right job for you. Approaching people in this way is far less intrusive than a cold phone call. You can expect generally positive results. Use LegalMinds (http://www.legalminds.org/) to browse a list of many law-related discussion sites and get a feel for what kind of dialogue you will find.

Everyone expects the use of the Internet to grow in all aspects of our society. Finding a job on the Internet is not only possible, it may in fact be the most efficient way for the busy job seeker to scan the marketplace efficiently and test how his or her expectations match what is available.

CHAPTER 10

How to Use Your Law School's Office of Career Services

Hillary Mantis

Most law students are familiar with their law school's career services office. Often, they have used the office to land their first jobs through on-campus or other recruitment programs. Or they have met with a career counselor at some point during their years in law school. What they may not realize, however, is that the office may provide many services to them after graduation.

Technology, as well as the ever-growing, ever-changing nature of the legal profession, has enabled law schools in recent years to expand their services to law graduates. Lawyers are changing jobs—and sometimes careers—much more often these days. Law schools have responded to this recent development by beefing up their existing services and offering several new programs designed specifically for alumni in career transition. What follows is an overview of services, programs, and resources offered to graduates by many law schools.

Services

Many law graduates are unaware that they can schedule individual appointments for career counseling with a counselor at their law school's office of career services. Most schools are not equipped to offer long-term counseling. However, even one appointment with a career counselor, which is generally free of charge, can provide valuable information, ideas, and a direction in which to start a career search. Generally, the individual must be a graduate of the law school to receive career counseling or other services.

For those having a hard time locating employment, the law school's office of career services often offers ongoing job-search support groups. Again, this service is free of charge and can be a useful source of job leads and other

72

information as well as emotional support. In addition to job-search support groups, career services will provide resume and cover letter advisement to any graduate of their schools in the job market. Many career services offices will provide this service by fax or e-mail, thus enabling graduates who no longer live in the area to use the service.

Several career services offices provide interview-skills workshops, mock interviews, and videotaped mock interviews as new services to graduates. Videotaped mock interviews, in which the career counselor conducts the interview and then critiques the subject, are especially useful. Often the office will provide the actual videotape, so that it can be reviewed at home before real workplace interviews.

Another service that has been expanded in recent years is the alumni job newsletter. Nearly every law school has created for its alumni a newsletter containing all of the job listings that it receives. It is e-mailed or sent by "snail mail" to alumni on request. Sometimes these are offered gratis or for a minimal charge. Most schools publish their newsletter either monthly or bimonthly. Job newsletters can contain a wealth of information and possible job leads, for many schools receive job listings from their alumni that are not published elsewhere. Many career offices also include job listings from local newspapers or job bulletins and report other relevant information, such as notices of upcoming local bar association programs. A number of law schools also trade their alumni job newsletters with other schools and keep the newsletters on file for alumni, thus giving their graduates access to job listings from other schools located in different geographic areas.

If a graduate is seeking employment in another city or geographic area, most law schools are able to arrange reciprocity for its graduates in that area for a limited duration (usually three months). Otherwise, a someone who did not graduate from the school generally will be prohibited from using that school's career center. If granted reciprocity, the graduate usually will have access to most of the resources that the school offers to its own graduates, including its job listings. In very competitive times, however, some schools curtail reciprocity, reserving all services for their own graduates.

Programs

Along with an increase in services to alumni, some law schools have developed programming for alumni in the job market. Among the new programs created are skills-training seminars, panels, and symposia. Topics have included networking, rainmaking, marketing skills, and how to become a solo practitioner. Some schools have instituted their own series of programs; other schools have joined efforts and offered combined programs for all law graduates of a group of schools in the same region. In addition to the informational value of such programs, many lawyers have found these programs to be excellent networking opportunities. Local area bar associations also have developed programs exclusively for lawyers in career transition. (See also Chapter 12 on bar association activities.)

Many career services offices have similarly developed networking and other types of receptions jointly with their schools' office of alumni affairs. Increasingly, these two law school departments have been working together to help their alumni. Recent graduates should take advantage of these "home court" opportunities, because alumni often are willing to help fellow graduates.

Technology

Because of advances in technology, law schools can offer all alumni, whether located nearby or out of state, their alumni resources. Almost every law school in the country has a Web site with its own career-planning section. These Web sites often duplicate services to alumni that were previously available only by visiting the office in person. The Web sites often have links to other major sites that have job listings for lawyers. To find your law school's Web site, either call the school's career-planning or alumni office, or link to it through the National Association for Law Placement's (NALP) Web site (listed at the end of this chapter).

Resources

Every law school's office of career services contains a small library where students and graduates can research job opportunities. By utilizing the career library, the graduate has access to a multitude of resources. In light of the recent advances in technology, law schools also have been able to upgrade their resource libraries and offer many computerized online services. The available resources are described in further detail below.

Job Listings

Every law school has job listings that are published for its graduates. Often, these jobs are not published elsewhere, especially those sent in by other alumni. Almost every law school has now computerized its job listings and made them available on the Internet at the law school's Web site. Usually a password is required to access the listings of a particular school. If the graduate does not have a computer or is not geographically located near the law school, she should check the job listings in person on a weekly basis rather than waiting to receive the alumni job newsletter in the mail. These jobs often are filled very quickly.

Newsletters

Most law schools subscribe to weekly or monthly commercially prepared job newsletters with listings all over the country. Utilizing these newsletters can provide graduates with access to hundreds of job listings and saves the expense of an individual subscription. Often, these commercially prepared newsletters are compiled by taking job listings from local legal periodicals and condensing them. Although repetitive, looking at all of the newsletters will ensure that all of the bases are covered and no advertisements are missed.

Handouts and Regional Law Firm Lists

Many graduates do not realize that law school career services offices spend a lot of time compiling their own resources to give to their students and graduates. Most schools put together and distribute lists of state and regional law firms and in-house corporate legal departments. Law schools often provide many handouts relating to different steps in the job search, including résumé, cover letter guides, and other valuable information.

Books and Periodicals

In addition to these resources, career libraries often subscribe to many local and regional publications and to national legal periodicals such as the *National Law Journal, American Lawyer,* and the *Chronicle of Higher Education.* Many popular career and self-assessment books—such as *What Color Is Your Parachute?*—are also kept in career services libraries and may be borrowed rather than purchased.

Online Services

Perhaps the most important advance in recent years has been the arrival of the Martindale-Hubbell directory on Lexis and NALPLine on Westlaw. Both databases enable the user to manipulate the directories to create a very targeted mailing list. For example, on Lexis you can request of a list of personal injury firms with two to twelve lawyers practicing in New York City; the computer will generate it from Martindale-Hubbell. The list can further be narrowed by specifying firms with alumni from your own alma mater. NALPLine on Westlaw can be used in a similar manner and contains salary, recruitment, and other information compiled by NALP.

In addition to finding job listings through the law school's career planning Web site, many schools have extensive links to other useful sites that have job listings for lawyers

What Law School Offices of Career Services Do Not Offer

Just as graduates are often unaware of all the resources that their law schools offer, they misunderstand or have misconceptions about what a law school serving thousands of graduates *cannot* offer. Time and budget constraints do not allow law school career counselors to see graduates for long-term, in-depth vocational counseling. However, they can refer the alumni to a private career counselor and assist in finding one.

Law schools similarly cannot perform the same function as headhunters; therefore, they cannot actually conduct one-on-one placements. They can provide a list of recruiters in the area and can help determine if it is in the graduate's interest to consult a headhunter. (See also Chapter 11 on using third parties in your job search.)

Where to Look for Further Information

For further information or to obtain the name and address of the assistant dean or director of career services at a law school, contact:

The National Association for Law Placement
1666 Connecticut Avenue, Suite 450
Washington, DC 20009
(202) 667-1666

The National Association for Law Placement also can be found on the Internet at http://www.nalp.org/

CHAPTER 11

Using Third-Party
Intermediaries

Carol M. Kanarek

When a lawyer decides that it is time to change jobs, one of his or her first thoughts probably will be, "Is there someone out there who can make the process easier, faster, and less painful?" In some cases, the answer to that question is yes, but many lawyers have serious misconceptions about the role that various third parties—including legal search firms, career counselors, and outplacement consultants—can play in the career planning and job search process.

Legal Search Firms

Most lawyers know that legal search firms exist, yet few understand what these firms realistically can—and cannot—do for them. As of January 1998, there were over four hundred legal search firms in the United States, including sixty-five in California and seventy-nine in New York. That may sound like a large number, but the reality is that these firms provide access to fewer than 10 percent of all jobs for lawyers and significantly less than that during difficult economic times.

Search firms are used only by those private-sector employers (predominantly large law firms) that are seeking lawyers with very specific expertise whom they cannot easily recruit through advertising, word of mouth, law school alumni placement offices, and unsolicited resumes. Because there is no shortage of lawyers to fill most jobs, the vast majority of employers of lawyers—including most small law firms, many corporations, and virtually all governmental agencies, academic institutions, and nonprofit organizations—do not use search firms. The reason for this is simple: it is very expensive to hire lawyers this way. Most search firms work on a contingency basis, and charge employers a fee of between 20 and 30 percent of the initial annual compensation of any lawyer hired by the employer as a result of the search firm's introduction of that lawyer to that employer. Consequently, the employers most likely to use legal search firms are law firms and corporations who require lawyers with sophisticated commercial expertise and experience representing corporations or financial institutions in such matters as mergers and acquisitions, project finance, real estate, securities and other corporate or banking regulatory matters, products liability, tax, labor, ERISA, and bankruptcy. Most legal employers who represent individuals or small businesses do not use legal search firms, yet those constitute the vast majority of employers of lawyers in the United States.

If you are seeking a nonlegal position or wish to change to a new area of practice you should seek the advice of your law school's alumni placement advisor or a career counselor; a legal search firm is not likely to have an appropriate job for you. If you are looking for an equity partnership position in a law firm, you will probably need to demonstrate a proven ability to generate client billings in excess of three times your expected compensation, although in booming economic times partners with sophisticated transactional expertise may not always need portable business. There are also geographic limitations. Most legal employers in suburban and rural areas, as well as many in smaller urban areas, do not use search firms. States with significant numbers of legal employers who use search firms include California, Connecticut, the District of Columbia, Florida, Georgia, Illinois, Maryland, Massachusetts, Michigan, Minnesota, New Jersey, New York, North Carolina, Ohio, Pennsylvania, Tennessee, and Texas.

The ideal candidate for most legal search firms is a lawyer with experience representing large corporations or financial institutions who is looking for a position practicing law with a firm that represents similar clients or with a corporation or financial institution. Many legal search firms only have positions with large law firms (or branch offices or small firm "spin-offs" of large law firms), as large law firms constitute the vast majority of employers who use search firms. Law firm experience is generally preferred, although many large corporations that use search firms now request candidates who have experience in both a large law firm and a corporation, and some law firms will accept candidates who have specialized governmental experience (e.g., the Securities and Exchange Commission or a U.S. attorney's office). Most positions listed with search firms require expertise at a level typically found in second- to fifth-year litigators, and second- to tenth-year transactional lawyers, although there are certainly exceptions to that general rule. By a ratio of about twenty to one, jobs listed by corporations with search firms require general corporate, transactional, or regulatory—as opposed to litigation—experience, with the exception of litigation-intensive companies, which may list positions with search firms for litigators with insurance, securities, employment, or product liability experience. Many employers who list jobs with search firms specify that candidates must have graduated from "national" law schools, and/or must have high grade point averages. Legal search firms do not establish these parameters; employers do. It is simply a matter of supply and demand.

So what does all of this mean to you? Above all, it means that if you have tried in vain to interest legal search firms in working with you, you are certainly not alone, and you should not take it personally. At least 90 percent of all lawyers are in the same position. Second, it means that you should have a fairly clear idea of what you are looking for before you make an appointment to meet with a legal search firm. Search firms are not career counselors, and you should not forget that the only way in which they make money is by finding suitable lawyers to meet the specific needs of their employer clients.

Once you have decided that you are both qualified for and interested in the types of positions that legal search firms usually have available, you are faced with the question of which firm or firms to use. Bear in mind that not all legal search firms are headhunters (i.e., telephone solicitors). You may miss a search firm that will give you a great deal of personal attention with respect to such critical matters as your resume and interviewing strategies if you limit your prospective choices to those firms that contact you directly.

Consult a list of legal search firms so that you have some idea of the universe that you are dealing with. *American Lawyer* includes a comprehensive pullout, "Directory of Legal Recruiters," in its January/February issue each year. Other legal publications also print this information periodically. If you do not have access to a directory, your law school's career services office should. The career services director may also be able to make some specific recommendations to you, as may your friends and colleagues. Many can point you in the right direction—or warn you of search firms to avoid.

In most instances, you will probably be best served by selecting a search firm in the geographic area where you intend to practice. The reason for this is simple: a search firm can develop closer relationships with local employers than it can with employers in other cities where contact is limited to mail, telephone, and fax.

When dealing with a search firm, always use your good judgment. If you feel that a search firm representative is obnoxious or pushy, the employers to which he or she wishes to submit your resume will probably think so, too. In some instances, that can mean the difference between being granted an interview and have your resume "circularly filed." This may be particularly true if your credentials and experience are marginal for a particular position; in such a case, a strong professional relationship between the search firm and the employer may be necessary in order to "sell" you as a candidate. Different styles appeal to different people, but you should always be wary of a search firm that engages in any of the following practices:

- *Using bait and switch tactics.* The search firm lures you in with the promise of a "dream job" and then tries to sell you on something completely different.
- *"Bad-mouthing" your current employer.* This is not only unprofessional, it is also designed to put you in a state of mind conducive to accepting the first job offer that comes along.
- *Name dropping.* A search firm that betrays someone else's confidence probably will not respect yours, either.
- *Requesting a resume without a meeting.* If the search firm is not interested in meeting you in person, how can it sell you effectively to its client employers? (An in-person meeting with the search firm is particularly

important if you believe that you are more impressive in person than on paper).

In addition, a search firm should never submit your resume to any employer without your authorization; nor should it send your resume to any employer from which it does not have a current job listing for someone at your level of experience in your specific area of practice. If a search firm representative seems to know little or nothing about the positions that allegedly are available (other than that they are "great jobs"), think twice about handing over your resume. Another search firm with the same job listing may have closer ties to the employer that will enable them to provide you with more-specific information so that you can sell yourself better in the interview. An intelligent legal search consultant can help you—and himself or herself as well, since the search firm makes money only if you get a job—by providing you with the following assistance that will enable you to receive more interviews and job offers:

- *Reviewing and, if necessary, revising your resume.* You may need to highlight the aspects of your experience that will be of greatest interest to a prospective employer. In some instances it may be useful to prepare several versions of your resume.
- *Supplying background information on prospective employers and available positions.* This should include both objective data (e.g., description of practice; history of the practice group; salary; expected billable hours, etc.) and subjective observations.
- *Suggesting effective interviewing strategies.* This can be especially valuable for lawyers whose most recent job interviews were during law school, because the interviewing process generally is quite different for experienced lawyers than it is for law students.
- *Helping to ease the transition to your new job.* This can range from suggesting ways to deal with, and obtain references from, your current employer to assisting in negotiating time off between jobs.

Career Counselors

Career counselors have very little in common with legal search firms, yet many lawyers mistakenly believe that they provide the same services. The most fundamental difference between them is that career counselors do not provide direct access to specific jobs, while legal search firms are exclusively focused on finding lawyers to fill their employer clients' job orders. The primary role of a career counselor is to guide you through the process of career planning—including self-assessment and market assessment—with the goal of helping you to identify career options that will be both satisfying and realistic. A career counselor also can assist in the job search process by providing guidance in resume and cover letter writing, networking strategies, and interviewing techniques.

When you work with a career counselor, you are the client and you pay the fee. Consequently, you should perform the "due diligence" necessary to satisfy yourself that the counselor's approach is compatible with your particular needs and objectives. Career counselors are not employment agencies, and you should be wary of any counseling service that lures you in with vague promises of "high-level contacts" and then charges a large fee for what is essentially a mass-mailing service.

Many career counselors place a strong emphasis on interests, skills, and values clarification. These counselors may use one or more of a variety of tools, including the Myers-Briggs Type Indicator, the Strong Interest Inventory, and various other self-assessment exercises. The interpretation of these exercises may help you determine what careers and work settings are most likely to give you satisfaction (see Chapter 3 on personality factors). Counselors who are strongly oriented toward this aspect of the career-planning process may be particularly appropriate for lawyers who are unhappy in the practice of law, but unsure about where to turn next.

A career counselor also can guide you through the process of market analysis. This is the "real world" half of the career-planning equation, and it is very important. Without it, you might formulate a career objective that is theoretically satisfying, but also totally unrealistic. The goal of market analysis is to gather as much specific information as possible about the jobs or careers that the self-analysis process identified as being potentially of interest to you, so that you can decide whether and how to pursue them.

The career counselor can show you strategies for networking and obtaining informational interviews that can help you collect this information. For this phase of the career-planning process it can be particularly useful to work with a career counselor who has extensive experience with lawyers. In the larger cities there are career counselors who specialize in "lawyers in transition." Your local bar association or law school career services office can help you identify counselors in your geographic area who have the background and experience that may be most useful to you.

Once you have completed the career-planning process (self-analysis plus market analysis), you might proceed directly to the job-search process. In some cases, however, additional education or experience may be needed; in other cases, you may decide to stay in your current position to acquire additional skills or save some money before embarking on a new career path. When you are ready to begin the job search, a career counselor can provide advice regarding the most effective ways to communicate with, and sell your credentials to, potential employers. A career counselor also can provide assistance with regard to many other matters, including difficult questions in interviews, salary negotiations, and reference checks.

Some lawyers only want or need assistance with the nuts and bolts of the job change process: resume preparation, cover letter writing, and/or interview skills. If this is the case for you, look for a career counselor who will bill you by the hour or by the task. If you are looking at a new legal position, make sure that the counselor has specific experience working with lawyers. This is important for both substantive and stylistic reasons. You will need someone who can assist you in describing your experience—both on your resume and in interviews—in ways that will be meaningful and attractive to other lawyers and who can help you to draft a resume and cover letter that will be free of the jargon that most legal employers find annoying. If the career counselor offers a generic, "one size fits all" cover letter, seek assistance elsewhere. Similarly, if you are looking to change a particular nonlegal career, look for a career counselor who has specific knowledge about your desired new career, so that he or she can help you to emphasize those aspects of your legal training and experience that are relevant to the new job you are seeking.

Outplacement Consultants

Outplacement assistance, long a staple in corporate America, is now a part of the lawyers' severance packages of many law firms, too. An outplacement consultant performs essentially the same functions as a career counselor, although time constraints often dictate that the focus be on rapidly securing new employment that will not be inconsistent with the lawyer's long-term goals. The fee for the outplacement assistance is paid by the employer who is asking the lawyer to leave. Many law firms—especially during booming economic times—only provide such assistance upon request; if you think it might be helpful to you, be sure to request it if you are told to find new employment.

The outplacement consultant is not involved in establishing the terms of the lawyer's severance, and conversations between the lawyer and the consultant should be strictly confidential. (However, you should make sure that this is the case in your first meeting with the consultant.) In some instances, the lawyer may wish to have the outplacement consultant discuss a particular issue with his or her employer, but such conversations would take place only at the lawyer's request.

Assistance provided by an outplacement consultant typically covers a range of areas: analyzing the needs of prospective employers, creating a network of contacts who can provide information about the legal job market in general as well as information about specific opportunities, drafting resumes and cover letters, practicing interview strategies, and negotiating the terms of employment.

An outplacement consultant can be of tremendous aid in helping you to find a new job, particularly if the counselor has direct knowledge of the specifics of the legal job market that is relevant to you. The consultant can offer information on which practice areas are in demand and which types of legal employers are currently hiring. He or she also can provide access to periodicals and Web sites with relevant job listings.

Equally important, the consultant can help the lawyer create a network of contacts and give advice on informational interviewing and computer-assisted search. All of these can yield data about prospective employers that lawyers can use during interviews to distinguish themselves positively from other applicants.

An outplacement consultant who understands the mind-set of legal employers can help the lawyer draft a customized cover letter that demonstrates an awareness of the bottom-line concerns of the law firms and companies to which the lawyer is applying. The consultant can also provide guidelines to senior associates and partners for the preparation of detailed experience summaries and practice development plans.

Effective interviewing is vital to the job changing process. The outplacement counselor can help to identify the probable questions and concerns that a particular employer may have regarding the lawyer's background and experience; he or she may also propose an effective strategy for addressing those issues.

A lawyer who is under time pressure to leave his or her current job is particularly vulnerable to accepting a position that may not be appropriate. Unlike the lawyer's employer or a legal search firm, the outplacement consultant does not have a personal stake, financial or otherwise, in the lawyer's decision to accept or reject a particular job offer. As a third party who is both knowledgeable and unbiased, the consultant is uniquely situated to assist the lawyer in researching prospective employers and to help negotiate salary and other terms of employment.

In addition to providing an overall framework for the job search, the outplacement consultant can help the lawyer respond to the questions and crisis that inevitably arise on a day-to-day basis. The consultant is someone with whom the lawyer can speak freely, without fear of personal or professional repercussions.

Conclusion

Finding a new job is seldom an easy undertaking, and the ultimate responsibility for most of the work that it entails rests with the lawyer who desires to make the move. In appropriate circumstances, however, third parties can be of significant assistance in navigating the uncharted waters of the legal employment world.

CHAPTER 12

How to Use the Bar Association as a Career Resource

Brenda M. Thomas

Looking for work? Look no further. Your local bar association may be the best place to begin your job search. The bar association is not only a clearinghouse for information on jobs in the legal community, but also a potential place of employment. Surprisingly, many lawyers do not realize the wealth of information that is available for the asking at their local bar association.

Bar associations are a repository for information on local and national legal issues, professional development, legislation, and civic activities impacting the legal profession. This information comes in a variety of forms, including bar publications, law journals, newsletters and magazines, Web sites, and continuing legal education seminar materials, as well as from volunteer activities. Your bar association may also have job placement and lawyer referral services, host social events, and provide professional networking opportunities through service on bar committees, sections, and leadership development forums. Although some activities are limited to members, participation in many others is unrestricted, which is intended to help recruit prospective members.

Bar services vary widely depending on the size of the legal community, size of the staff, and fiscal resources. Nonetheless joining a bar association can only enhance your employment prospects. Bar membership represents a relatively small investment of time and money for a great return. The following is an overview of bar resources and how to use them to your best advantage.

Newsletters and Periodicals

The quickest way to find out what is happening at the bar association is to stop by and peruse the publications on hand. The bar association membership newsletter or magazine will typically highlight the full range of bar services and member benefits offered. These publications can be an excellent source of information on local and national job opportunities. Consult the classified section for current job listings. You will find that many law firms and corporations routinely place advertisements in the state and local bar newsletters, in addition to local business journals, because they prefer to use publications with the largest lawyer readership. The newsletter will also contain a calendar of events featuring upcoming functions and seminars. Networking at bar-sponsored events will allow you to meet, firsthand, outstanding members of the bench and bar. Leading firms often produce the most active bar volunteers.

Membership Directory

The membership directory is a quick and handy reference to the demographic makeup, names, and addresses of local lawyers and law firms. Order a copy or simply refer to one at the local law library. You will find information on judges, the courts, and legislative officials. Pictorial directories can also help you familiarize yourself with specific lawyers, firms, and judges before a job interview or court appearance. The directory is also a great marketing tool for lawyers new to the community who wish to promote a practice or specialty. Lawyers who are considering relocation will find local lawyers listed in the directory who can answer questions about the quality of life, cost of living, cost of running a law office, and areas of law in demand in the community. These are all factors that should be carefully considered before making a strategic career move.

The bar directory will usually contain advertisements of vendors who cater to the legal community. As a bar member you can obtain discounts on all kinds of goods and services that are not available to the general public. You may receive discounts on office supplies and equipment, travel and rental cars, phone service, and insurance, including professional liability, health, long-term care, and disability insurance to name a few. Professional legal placement services can help you if you are looking for temporary or contract work. These vendors can help a lawyer make the transition to a new geographic location or employer and are usually familiar with the areas of law in demand.

Legal Placement Services and Job Banks

Check to see if the bar association in your community has a legal placement service or job bank. Legal placement services are typically staffed by bar employees or run by independent companies through a cooperative arrangement with the bar. Placement services provide career listings for lawyers, legal secretaries, paralegals, receptionists, word processors, and other law office support staff.[1] The fee for the service is usually charged to the employer, and may be a flat fee or percentage of the annual salary for the position. The advantage of using a placement service is that such services usually have more-extensive listings than the local papers. Placement services treat inquiries as confidential. They may also permit you to ask general questions about the employer or position not described in an ad. The disadvantage is that some employers consider the cost of placement services prohibitive and thus prefer to screen their own applicants. Some public employers post notices in city and government offices. These employers are more likely to provide listings to universities and bar associations that will post or publish job notices at no charge.

Some bar associations do not place or screen applicants but maintain a computerized or hard copy file of job listings. You may have to join the bar to obtain access to these listings, as job listings are usually restricted to members only. Your use may also require some nominal charge for the cost of photocopying notices or job applications.

Bar Web Sites

With the advent of the Internet, bar technology has grown in leaps and bounds. This has had a profound effect on bar communications and services. Many bar associations have established Web sites and communicate with their members via e-mail in addition to broadcast fax and direct mail. Some have established listservs and other methods to survey members on desired programs and services. Web sites typically contain a membership roster, calendar of events, lists of participating committees, sections, and divisions, online docketing, local statutes and ethics rules, lawyer referral service roster, classifieds, calendar of seminar offerings, and current events. The American Bar Association maintains an extensive list of legal organizations with Web sites. The list is regularly updated and features state, local, specialty, and international bar associations and legal organization Web sites (see list of legal organizations with Web sites at conclusion of this chapter). The Internet is the fastest and cheapest way to access bar resources, and it can be a discreet tool for job seekers that want to look before they leap.

American Bar Association Division for Bar Services

The American Bar Association (ABA), the largest bar association in the United States, is a particularly rich source of information for both new and established practitioners. The range of educational and career services it offers is staggering. The key is to learn about the full range of services and to target those that best suit your professional needs. The staff at the ABA Division for Bar Services is helpful and thorough. They can answer any questions you may have about ABA services generally, including information on jobs within the ABA. Check to see if your local bar Web site is linked to the ABA or contact the ABA Network directly. The American Law Institute–American Bar Association (ALI-ABA) Committee on Continuing Legal Education contains an extensive repertoire of continuing education materials, including audiotapes, videotapes, books, periodicals, and live telecasts for lawyers seeking to expand professional skills.[2]

You Can Work for a Bar Association

If you are no longer interested in practicing law, but are still interested in the legal profession, you should seriously consider working with a bar association. Although a legal education is not required, it can certainly enhance your ability to understand the objectives of the bar association. It is no coincidence that many bar directors and staff practiced law earlier in their careers. More important, there are literally thousands of bar associations and legal organizations across the country staffed by lawyers and nonlawyers alike. The legal community is diverse, the work is challenging, and the salaries are competitive. The National Association of Bar Executives (NABE) of the American Bar Association annually publishes a compensation survey that compares prevailing wages for bar jobs throughout the United States.

Before you apply for employment with a bar association, you should first learn about it. Visit the bar association and attend a meeting or bar function to develop a sense of the association's culture and activities. If the bar is located in another jurisdiction refer to the bar's membership directory or obtain a copy of the latest *ABA State and Local Bar Directory.* This handy publication is updated three or four times a year and lists demographic information about bar associations across the country. The directory contains information only on bar associations with at least three hundred members. It also includes each bar's annual budget, number of board members and term of office, size of staff, number of members, number of sections and committees and percentage of nondues income. This information will help you determine whether the bar association is popular and thriving within the legal community. The *ABA State and Local Bar Directory* lists the names and addresses of the executive director, president, and president-elect of each bar association in case you would like to contact them directly to supplement the information contained in the directory. It also contains the names and numbers for ABA Division for Bar Services staff persons.

Jobs for Bar Staff

Jobs at the bar vary widely depending on the fiscal resources of the bar and size of the legal community. Many bar associations belong to the National Association of Bar Executives, which is administered by the ABA. Each year the ABA publishes the *NABE Membership Directory,* which contains the names and addresses, dues structure, membership size, and key personnel at participating bar associations. The ABA recently released *Job Descriptions for Bar Association Staff,* available through ALI-ABA. Although this publication is primarily intended for use by bar executives, it contains a sampling of 150 detailed job descriptions obtained from bar associations across the country. The types of jobs are too numerous to include here, but fall generally within the categories listed below:

- Administrative/secretarial/clerical
- Assistant/associate executive director
- Executive director

- Executive administration
- Fundraising/development
- Divisions/sections/committees
- Finance administration
- General counsel
- Government relations/legislation
- Information systems/technology
- Lawyer referral service
- Legal services/pro bono
- Local bar liaisons
- Meetings management
- Membership
- Continuing legal education
- Communications
- Publications/media relations
- Law-related education
- Lawyer assistance programs

Generally speaking, the smaller the bar association, the more "hats" the staff wears. At a small bar association you will be required to cross-train on multiple job functions. Larger bar associations can afford to segregate job functions due to greater resources and membership demand. If you take the time to determine which bar association opportunities best suit your professional objectives, both you and the organization can prosper from the union. Bar association work is rewarding and challenging due to the myriad social and economic factors that affect the legal profession each day. Skilled bar staff can help lawyers meet the challenge of change within the profession while maintaining professional goals and quality of life. Most important, the bar association is a great place to meet talented and interesting people in the legal profession and your community.

Legal Organizations with Web Sites

State Bar Associations

Alabama State Bar
http://www.alabar.org/

Alaska Bar Assn.
http://www.alaskabar.org/

State Bar of Arizona
http://www.azbar.org/

Arkansas Bar Assn.
http://www.arkbar.com/

State Bar of California
http://www.calbar.org/

Colorado Bar Assn.
http://www.cobar.org/

Connecticut Bar Assn.
http://www.ctbar.org/

Delaware State Bar Assn.
http://www.dsba.org/

Bar Assn. of the District of Columbia
http://www.badc.org/

District of Columbia Bar
http://www.dcbar.org/

Florida Bar
http://www.flabar.org/

State Bar of Georgia
http://www.gabar.org/

State Bar of Georgia
Computer Law Section
http://www.computerbar.org/

State Bar of Georgia
Intellectual Property Law Section
ga_bar/frame7.htm

Hawaii State Bar Assn.
http://www.hsba.org/

Illinois State Bar Assn.
http://www.illinoisbar.org/

Indiana State Bar Assn.
http://www.iquest.net/isba/

Iowa State Bar Assn.
http://www.iowabar.org/

Kansas Bar Assn.
http://www.ksbar.org/

Kentucky Bar Assn.
http://www.kybar.org/

Louisiana State Bar Assn.
http://www.lsba.org/

Maine State Bar Assn.
http://www.mainebar.org/

Maryland State Bar Assn.
http://www.msba.org/

Massachusetts Bar Assn.
http://www.massbar.org/

State Bar of Michigan
http://www.michbar.org/

State Bar of Michigan
Probate and Estate Planning Section
http://www.umich.edu/icle/
sections/probate/index.htm

Minnesota State Bar Assn.
http://www.mnbar.org/

Mississippi Bar
http://www.msbar.org/

Missouri Bar
http://www.mobar.org/

State Bar of Montana
http://www.montanabar.org/

State Bar of Nebraska
http://www.nebar.com/

State Bar of New Mexico
http://www.nmbar.org/

State Bar of Nevada
http://www.nvbar.org/

New Hampshire Bar Assn.
http://www.nhbar.org/

New Jersey State Bar Assn.
http://www.njsba.com/

New Jersey State Bar Foundation
http://www.njsbf.com/

New York State Bar Assn.
http://www.nysba.org/

North Carolina Bar Assn.
http://www.barlinc.org/

Ohio State Bar Assn.
http://www.ohiobar.org/

Oregon State Bar
http://www.osbar.org/

Pennsylvania Bar Assn.
http://www.pabar.org/

Rhode Island Bar Assn.
http://www.ribar.com/

South Carolina Bar
http://www.scbar.org/

State Bar of South Dakota
http://www.sdbar.org/

Tennessee Bar Assn.
http://www.tba.org/

State Bar of Texas
http://www.texasbar.com/

State Bar of Texas, Computer
Law Section
http://www.sbot.org/

Utah State Bar
http://www.utahbar.org/

Vermont Bar Assn.
http://www.vtbar.org/

Virginia Bar Assn.
http://www.vba.org/

Virginia State Bar
http://www.vsb.org/

Washington State Bar Assn.
http://www.wsba.org/

West Virginia State Bar
http://www.wvbar.org/

State Bar of Wisconsin
http://www.wisbar.org/

Wyoming State Bar Assn.
http://www.wyomingbar.org/

Local Bar Associations

Mobile Bar Assn. (AL)
http://www.gulfmall.com/
mobilebar/

Alameda County Bar Assn. (CA)
http://www.acbanet.org/

Beverly Hills Bar Assn. (CA)
http://www.bhba.org/

Contra Costa County Bar Assn. (CA)
http://www.cccba.org/

Los Angeles County Bar Assn. (CA)
http://www.lacba.org/

Lawyers Club of Los Angeles (CA)
http://www.sidebar.com/lawyers

Lawyers Club of San Diego (CA)
http://www.lawyersclubsandiego.
com/

Marin County Bar Assn. (CA)
http://www.marinbar.com/

Orange County Bar Assn. (CA)
http://www.ocbar.org/

Palo Alto Area Bar Assn. (CA)
http://www.lawscape.com/paaba/
index.html

Queens Bench Bar Assn. (CA)
http://www.queensbench.org/

*Sacramento County Bar Assn. (CA)
http://www.sacbar.org/

San Bernardino County
Bar Assn. (CA)
http://www.website1.com/sbcba/

San Diego County Bar Assn. (CA)
http://www.sdcba.org/

Bar Assn. of San Francisco (CA)
http://www.sfbar.org/

San Fernando Valley Bar Assn. (CA)
http://www.sfvba.org/

San Mateo County Bar Assn. (CA)
http://first-webmaster.com/
smcba/index.html

Southwest Riverside County
Bar Assn. (CA)
http://www.lawrefcom/assoc/
9b.html

Sunnyvale-Cupertino Bar Assn. (CA)
http://www.lawscape.com/
suncupbar/

Ventura County Bar Assn. (CA)
http://www.vcba.org/

Boulder County Bar Assn. (CO)
http://www.boulder-bar.org/

San Luis Valley Bar Assn. (CO)
http://www.courts.state.co.us/12th/
bar/bar.htm

Greater Danbury Bar Assn. (CT)
http://www.thecommon.com/
dba.htm

Broward County Bar Assn. (FL)
http://www.browardbar.org/

Clearwater Bar Assn. (FL)
http://www.clwbar.org/

Orange County Bar Assn. (FL)
http://www.obar.org/

Atlanta Bar Assn. (GA)
http://www.atlantabar.org/

Cobb County Bar Assn. (GA)
http://www.kuesterlaw.com/cobb/

Decatur Bar Assn. (GA)
http://www.decaturbar.org/

Champaign County Bar Assn. (IL)
http://www.ccba.org/

Chicago Bar Assn. (IL)
http://www.chicagobar.org/

DuPage County Bar Assn. (IL)
http://www.dcba.org/

Louisville Bar Assn. (KY)
http://www.legalnetwork.net/lba/
index.html

Baton Rouge Bar Assn. (LA)
http://www.brba.org/

Anne Arundel Bar Assn. (MD)
http://www.aabar.org/

Baltimore County Bar Assn. (MD)
http://www.bcba.org/

Prince George's County
Bar Assn. (MD)
http://www.mdlaw.net/pgbar.htm

Boston Bar Assn. (MA)
http://www.bostonbar.org/

Grand Rapids Bar Assn. (MI)
http://www.grbar.org/

Oakland County Bar Assn. (MI)
http://www.ocba.org/

Washtenaw County Bar Assn. (MI)
http://www.lawtech.com/wcba

Hennepin County Bar Assn. (MN)
http://www.hcba.org/

Bar Assn. of Metropolitan
St. Louis (MO)
http://bamsl.org/

SASFIRM Section-Solo & Small
Firm Practitioners (MO)
http://bamsl.org/sasfirm/

Essex County Bar Assn. (NJ)
http://www.essexbar.com/

Albany County Bar Assn. (NY)
http://www.web-ex.com/acba

Assn. of the Bar of the City
of New York (NY)
http://www.abcny.org/

Brooklyn Bar Assn. (NY)
http://www.bklynbar.org/

Dutchess County Bar Assn. (NY)
http://www.mhv.net/-dcba/
dcba3.htm

Bar Assn. of Erie County (NY)
http://www.eriebar.org/

Greene County Bar Assn. (NY)
http://members.aol.com/dewoodin/
gcba/ gcba.htm

Bar Assn. of Nassau County (NY)
http://www.nassaubar.org/

Onondaga County Bar Assn. (NY)
http://www.onbar.org/

Queens County Bar Assn. (NY)
http://www.infoshop.com/qcba

Suffolk County Bar Assn. (NY)
http://www.scba.org/

Akron Bar Assn. (OH)
http://www.akronbar.org/

Cleveland Bar Assn. (OH)
http://www.clevelandbar.org/

Columbus Bar Assn. (OH)
http://www.cbalaw.org/

Toledo Bar Assn. (OH)
http://www.toledobarassoc.com/

Allegheny County Bar Assn. (PA)
http://www.acba.org/

Delaware County Bar Assn. (PA)
http://www.delcobar.org/

Erie County Bar Assn. (PA)
http://www.erie.net/-ecba

Lancaster Bar Assn. (PA)
http://www.lancasterbar.org/

Montgomery Bar Assn. (PA)
http://www.montgomerybar.org/

Philadelphia Bar Assn. (PA)
http://www.philabar.org/

Chattanooga Bar Assn. (TN)
http://www.cbal00.org/

Knoxville Bar Assn. (TN)
http://www.knoxbar.org

Memphis Bar Assn. (TN)
http://www.memphisbar.org/

Nashville Bar Assn. (TN)
http://www.nashbar.org/

Brazoria County Bar Assn. (TX)
http://www.mastnet.net/brazco/
bar/legal.htm

Dallas Bar Assn. (TX)
http://www.dallasbar.com/

Dallas Bar Assn., International
Law Section (TX)
http://www.obeliskcom.com/intlaw

Houston Bar Assn. (TX)
http://www.hba.org/

Travis County Bar Assn. (TX)
http://cust2.iamerica.net/tcba

King County Bar Assn. (WA)
http://www.owt.com/kcba/

*Spokane County Bar Assn. (WA)
http://www.spokanebar.org/

Tacoma Pierce County
Bar Assn. (WA)
http://www.co.pierce.wa.us

Whatcom County Bar Assn. (WA)
http://www.viewit.com/
WhatcomBar/

Specialty Bar and Other Legal Organizations

Academy of Florida Trial Lawyers
http://www.aftl.org/

ALI-ABA Committee on Continuing
Legal Education
http://www.ali-aba.org/

American Assn. of Law Libraries
http://www.aallnet.org/

American Bar Assn.
http://www.abanet.org/

American College of Trust
and Estate Counsel (ACTEC)
http://www.actec.org/

American Corporate Counsel Assn.
http://www.acca.com/

American Health Lawyers Assn.
http://www.healthlawyers.org/

American Immigration
Lawyers Assn.
http://www.alia.org/

American Inns of Court Foundation
http://www.innsofcourt.org/

American Intellectual Property
Law Assn.
http://www.aipla.org/

American Judicature Society
http://www.ajs.org/

American Society
of Corporate Secretaries
http://www.ascs.org/

Asian American Bar Assn.
of Michigan
http://www.icle.org/lawyers/
aso-asia.htm

Asian Pacific American Bar Assn.
of the Greater Washington DC Area
http://free.mrc.net/-apaba

Assn. for Continuing
Legal Education
http://www.aclea.org/

Assn. of Federal Defense Attorneys
http://www.afda.org/

Assn. of Legal Administrators
http://www.alanet.org/

Assn. of Pretrial Professionals
in Florida
http://www.appf.org/

Assn. of Trial Lawyers of America
http://www.atlanet.com/

Atlanta Legal Aid Society
http://www.law.emory.edu/PI/
ALAS/

Atlanta Volunteer
Lawyers Foundation
http://www.law.emory.edu/PI/
AVLF

Bar Assn. of National Lawyers
http://www.nationlaw.org/

Bay Area Lawyers for Individual
Area Freedom
http://www.balif.org/

Bexar County Women's
Bar Assn. (TX)
http://www.netxpress.com/-bcwba

Black Women Lawyers Assn.
of Greater Chicago, Inc.
http://ourworld.compuserve.com/
homepages/bwla

Boulder Criminal Defense Bar (CO)
http://www.members.aol.com/
bcrimdb/index.html

Charles Houston Bar Assn. (CA)
http://www.charleshouston.org/

Colorado Criminal Defense Bar
http://www.ccdb.org/

Colorado Women's Bar Assn.
http://www.cwba.org/

Commercial Law League of America
http://www.clla.org/

Consumer Attorneys of California
http://www.caoc.com/index.html

Corporate Bar Assn.
http://www.corporatebar.org/

Cyberspace Bar Assn.
http://www.cyberbar.net

D. Augustus Straker Bar Assn. (MI)
http://www.icle.org/lawyers/
aso-stra.htm

Federal Bar Assn.
http://www.fedbar.org/

Federal Communications Bar Assn.
http://www.fcba.org/

Federal Magistrate Judges Assn.
http://www.fedjudge.org/

First Amendment Lawyers Assn.
http://www.fala.org/

Georgia Assn. of Criminal
Defense Lawyers
http://www.gacdl.org/

Georgia Assn. for Women Lawyers
http://www.law.emory.edu/
GAWL/gawl.htm

Hispanic National Bar Assn.
http://www.incacorp.com/hnba

Inter-American Bar Assn.
http://www.erols.com/iaba

Inter-Pacific Bar Assn.
http://www.ipba.org/

International Trade Commission Trial
Lawyers Assn.
http://www.itctla.org/

Internet Bar Assn.
http://www.lawyers.org/

Italian American Lawyers Assn.
http://www.iala.lawzone.com/

Kansas Trial Lawyers Assn.
http://www.ink.org/public/ktla

Lawyer-Pilots Bar Assn.
http://www.lpba.org/

Louisiana Young Lawyers
http://www.younglawyers.org/

Maine Trial Lawyers Assn.
http://www.mtla.org/

Minnesota Women Lawyers
http://www.mwlawyers.org/

National Academy of Elder
Law Attorneys
http://www.naela.com/

National Asian Pacific American
Bar Assn.
http://www.napaba.org/

National Assn. of Bar Executives
http://www.abanet.org/barserv/
nabe.html

National Assn. of Bond Lawyers
http://www.nabl.org/

National Assn. of College
and University Attorneys
http://www.nacua.org/

National Assn. of Legal Assistants
http://www.nala.org/

National Assn. of Legal Secretaries
http://www.nals.org/

National Assn.
of Patent Practitioners
http://www.napp.org/

National Assn. for Public
Interest Law
http://www.napil.org/

National Bar Assn.
http://www.melanet.com/

National Employment Lawyers Assn.
http://www.nela.org/

National Federation
of Paralegal Assn.
http://www.paralegals.org/

National Law Firm Marketing Assn.
http://www.nalfma.org/

National Lawyers Assn.
http://www.nla.org/

National Lesbian and Gay Law Assn.
http://www.nlgla.org/

National Organization
of Bar Counsel
http://www.nobc.org/

New Jersey Institute for Continuing
Legal Education
http://www.njicle.com/

New Jersey Lawyer Newspaper
http://www.njlnews.com/

New York State Defenders Assn.
http://www.nysda.org/

New York Trial Lawyers Assn.

http://www.nystla.org/

Pennsylvania Bar Institute
http://www.pbi.org/

Philadelphia Trial Lawyers Assn.
http://www.philatla.org/

Queens Women's Bar Assn.
http://www.wbasny.org/
queens.htm

Tennessee Assn. of Criminal
Defense Lawyers
http://www.tncrimlaw.com/

Texas Young Lawyers Assn.
http://www.tyla.com/

Women's Bar Assn. of DC
http://www.wbadc.org/

Women's Bar Assn. of Massachusetts
http://www.1weekly.com/wba.htm

Women's Bar Assn. of the State
of New York
http://www.wbasny.org/

International Bar Associations

Australian Plaintiff Lawyers Assn.
http://www.apla.com/

Canadian Bar Assn.
http://www.algonquinc.on.ca/cba

Federation of Law Societies
of Canada
http://www.flsc.ca

Finnish Bar Assn.
http://www.asianajajat.fi

International Assn.
of Constitutional Law
http://www.eur.nl

International Assn.
of Korean Lawyers
http://www.napaba.org/iak/

International Bar Assn.
http://www.ibanet.org/

Law Society of England and Wales
http://www.lawsoc.org/.uk

Law Society of New South Wales
http://lawsocnsw.asn.au

Law Society of Western Australia
http://www.lawsocietywa.asn.au

Manitoba Bar Assn.
http://www.mblawyers.org/

New South Wales Bar Assn.
http://www.fl.asn.au/nsw-bar

Ontario Trial Lawyers Assn.
http://www.otla.com/

Turkish Bar Assn.
http://www.avukat.com/
tbb-eng.htm

Ukranian American Bar Assn.
http://www.brama.com/uaba

Victorian Bar (Melbourne, Australia)
http://www.ozemail.com.au/
-vicbar

Notes

1. For example the Cincinnati Bar Association (CBA) Legal Placement Service offers full- and part-time placements exclusively to CBA members. The service is confidential and features a ninety-day refund policy and screening and skill testing of all law office support applicants.

2. For a complete bibliography, call 1-800-CLE-NEWS or, on the Internet, see http://www.ali-aba.org/ and request the 1997 *ALI-ABA Report*.

CHAPTER 13

Career Opportunities for Minorities

Suzanne Baer

Londell McMillan

Vanessa Davila

In general, it has been more difficult for minority lawyers to find equal opportunity in the legal profession. For this reason, affirmative action programs were initially instituted. Although all doors may not yet be open, the playing field has begun to level, and changes are visible. Minority lawyers have worked their way into every arena of the profession, from the bench to the academy.

Today's minority lawyer, whether Hispanic, African-American, Asian, or Native American, has more opportunities to succeed in the legal profession than in the past. The magnitude of the change is demonstrated by the increased numbers of minority lawyers who have moved into positions of influence and who will help shape a profession that promotes fairness in career opportunities for all lawyers. Nonetheless, even when one is "qualified," success is not always obtainable because obstacles to opportunity remain. However, if you can see success as being ready for the struggle, if you can see limitations as temporary deficits to be overcome, if you subscribe to the concept that most everything can in fact be learned, you are well on your way to building a successful career.

But first, how do you learn what you need to know, and how do you get where you want to go? Two paths are through networks and the use of mentors.

Networks and Mentors: You Never Know Who Is Going to Help You

Networking is the art and science of cultivating connections. First, you begin with a recognition of and support for others: *What goes around, comes around.*

These are a critical factors in attracting attention and support for yourself. As you cultivate connections, you are always in a learning mode and developing your interpersonal skills and leadership opportunities. Here are just a few reasons minority lawyers credit networks as critical in building their careers:

- Networks provided them with reliable sources of practical information.
- Networks assured them of a "choir" of affirmation.
- Networks helped them maintain a true sense of self-worth and self-esteem.
- Networks bolstered their confidence in the face of the obstacles, prejudices, and inequities they encountered.

For minority lawyers to succeed in the legal profession, they must build networks of relationships beyond their own ethnicity. Coalitions between different minority group members and effective relationships with nonminority lawyers are essential. Minorities who already enjoy success in the mainstream workplace have developed a capacity to see beyond race while simultaneously understanding the politics of race dynamics. We all need to remember that fundamentally what really makes us alike is that we all are different.

When you start out as a practicing lawyer, make friends with everybody. You never know who is going to be able to lend a helping hand in the future. Minority lawyers are increasingly able to move into areas where they were not previously seen . To accelerate this process, it is in your interest, and in that of the profession, to attend panel discussions, continuing legal education (CLE) programs, and bar association meetings whenever possible. Join committees; run for office. Find out what steps were taken by others who opened new specializations to minority lawyers.

Young lawyers working in law firms and aspiring to succeed in the firm environment should not underestimate the need to acquire client development skills early on. In today's law firms, providing excellent service to clients is not enough. lawyers that rise to and remain in partnership levels at firms are those who are able to bring clients, and therefore additional revenue, to the firm. Specialized publications, CLE, and networking conferences are available to help lawyers overcome the barriers faced by minorities in client development. (See listing of Recruitment Opportunities and Professional Networks at end of this chapter.)

Dealing with a Highly Competitive Work Environment

Meeting the challenge of building and promoting a career in the twenty-first century will depend on your flexibility and willingness to develop new skills to meet labor market changes. Law practices will have to respond even more rapidly to the requirements of global business. The present-day corporate world is leaner and less predictable than it used to be. Corporations, business owners, and individuals are demanding lower costs, increased efficiency, and improved customer service from all their service providers, including their lawyers.

Now, more than ever, minority lawyers should learn how to promote their credentials, their leadership experience, and their uniqueness. Examples of these are specialized educational courses or degree programs, a second language, a familiarity with a specific culture, travel experience, or governmental or political experience. A by-product of this competitive environment is the fact that many lawyers today are succeeding in alternative careers, such as human resources, banking, governmental relations, and many others.

The political world has already begun to meet the demand for improved racial and gender balance in appointed and elected officials. Lawyers must be active, committed participants in civic, social, and professional organizations. This activity will position them to benefit from new opportunities as the legal profession changes to meet the reality of a diverse workforce.

Career Advice from Minority Lawyers

When people look back at their career paths, frequently there is greater insight and understanding of the choices and decisions made along the way. We asked minority lawyers to look backward, especially along these lines:

- What were your three most successful career-development decisions?
- If applicable, what were the three most effective methods you used to make a transition from one job to the next?
- How do you feel the present conditions and trends in today's public and private marketplace affect the types of career strategies minority lawyers should pursue?

These minority lawyers had a lot to say. Here are some of their noteworthy responses:

- When you start out in law practice, make friends with everybody. Everyone can help you.
- Get involved in politics. Politics is the center of power. Campaign for candidates in the political party of your choice. Being political helps you get places.
- Maintain involvement in community organizations. To be truly successful you have to be able to step out of the comfort of your own community, as well as work in it.
- Network with experienced minority lawyers because you need those who have been through it to tell you how they made it.
- The best way to learn what to do is to watch people who excel at what you want to do.

Additional advice includes the following:

- *On the subject of a career in teaching law, minorities opt out and do not even apply for faculty positions.* It is a myth that you must have only perfect credentials, law review experience, a prestigious clerkship, et al. You have to make your interest in law teaching known to a lot of people. Many law schools are looking for minority faulty. Start by calling faculty where you went to law school to find out about the process.
- *Wisdom from a prosecutor.* Work to set yourself apart. Go out of your way to find new responsibilities. Keep growing, learning, and seeking new responsibilities. Do more than you need to do to prepare a case

and more than others do. Research every case meticulously. The time you put in, the extra lengths you go to—that is how you stand out.

- *Toot your own horn.* Minorities have to learn more about promoting themselves. If you do not know how to get known, start by watching a known commodity in your workplace—see what he or she does, and learn when and how to do it for yourself.
- *Look for a mobility model.* When you meet minority lawyers who have moved from one job to another, find out how they got there. Break it down a step at a time—what did they join, whom did they know, how did they develop their expertise?
- *Build your most visible skills.* Law is advocacy in organized, persuasive, clear language and writing. Remember, writers are made, not born. Some tips on continuing to develop your writing talent include get on a bar association committee and volunteer to write a report; write an article or even a letter to the editor and get it published; write a long letter to a judge about a trial issue that interests you; write a memo on a current legal issue; get on CLE panels; keep a file of speeches. Build an impressive writing portfolio.

There is consensus among the minority lawyers we talked to about the three most effective career strategies:

- Seek out mentors and role models. Become active in bar associations for friendship and networking.
- Keep developing new skills.
- Your career plan must have a focus, but you cannot plan every step. Take risks and be alert to unplanned opportunities.

Choosing an Environment Where You Can Be at Your Best

Imagine coming across this law firm in the National Association for Law Placement's *Annual Directory of Legal Employers:*

> 245 partners, 47 are lawyers of color and 138 partners are women. The firm's managing partner is an African-American female, the hiring partner is a white female, the Associate Committee Chair is a Hispanic male.

You get the point! While you will not find a twenty-first century law firm like this yet, here are some touchstones for you to consider when choosing the environment where you can be at your best. If possible, speak with minority lawyers in the organization before accepting an employment offer and ask them to evaluate their experience and perception of the environment. Some important questions to ask are:

- Do you believe your work is consistent with and as challenging as assignments given to white peers?
- What do minority lawyers report about communication and feedback in the organization?
- Do you feel you are continually required to demonstrate your competence?

- Have minorities advanced in the organization recently to senior levels of management?
- What do minority lawyers report about being mentored; are they recommended for professional association committees and CLE presentations? Are there minorities at senior levels of the organization to assist you?

A growing number of legal organizations have undertaken an assessment and cultural analysis of their work environment. The use of a consultant to assist an organization in the retention and advancement of a diverse workforce demonstrates a serious commitment to the inclusion of minorities. Management consultants have advised Fortune 500 corporations since the early 1970s on how to create cultural environments that increase retention and promotion of minorities and women. Legal employers in the new millennium have begun to acknowledge the need for, and value of, this process.

A review of some important indices of commitment to workforce diversity include the following:

1. Frequent performance evaluations and communication of expectations at early stages in the lawyer's employment;
2. A carefully monitored work assignment system;
3. Attention to, and quality of, training;
4. An infrastructure of support for new lawyers, that is, advisers and mentors;
5. A "safe" place in the organizational structure for addressing problems without fear of reprisal;
6. Employer participation in programs to foster diversity, such as bar association or school sponsored minority clerkships, minority hiring from regional law schools, participation in minority job fairs, lateral hiring of minority lawyers, support of minority-focused community activities, joint venture projects with minority-owned law firms, and inclusion of minority vendors.

Recruitment Opportunities and Professional Networks

American Bar Association
Commission on Opportunities for Minorities in the Profession
750 North Lake Shore Drive
Chicago, IL 60611
(312) 988-5667
http://www.abanet.org/

Publications of the ABA Commission on Opportunities for Minorities in the Profession:

The Minority In-House Counsel Directory
Group Directory
Directory of Minority Partners in Majority/Corporate Law Firms
National Directory of Minority Bar Associations

Programs of the ABA Commission on Opportunities for Minorities in the Profession:

Minority Counsel Program
Multicultural Women Attorneys Network
Minority In-House Counsel Group

Publication of the ABA Judicial Division, Task Force on Opportunities for Minorities:

Directory of Minority Judges of the U.S.

Minorities in the Profession Committee
American Bar Association
Young Lawyers Division
750 North Lake Shore Drive
Chicago, IL 60611
(312) 988-5611

American Indian Bar Association
Kirke Kickingbird, Native American Legal Resource Center
Oklahoma City University Law School
2501 Blackwelder, Suite 209
Oklahoma, OK 73106
(405) 521-5188

National Asian Pacific American Bar Association
Nancy Choi, Executive Director
1717 Pennsylvania Avenue, N.W., Suite 500
Washington DC 20006
(202) 974-1030
http://www.napaba.org/

Hispanic National Bar Association
National Headquarters
P.O. Box 66105
Washington DC 20035
(202) 293-1507
http://www.hnba.com/

National Bar Association
John Crump, Executive Director
1225 11th Street, N.W.
Washington DC 20001-4217
(202) 842-3900
http://www.nationalbar.org/

National Association for Law Placement
1666 Connecticut Avenue, Suite 325
Washington, DC 20009-1039
(202) 667-1666
http://www.nalp.org/

Directory of Minority Programs
All Things Being Equal (Videotape and Discussion Guide)
(Many other relevant publications listed in Web site)

The following bar associations and city and state groups of law firms have signed Statements of Goals to increase minority representation in the profession:

Association of the Bar of the City of New York
Boston Law Firm Group
Chicago Bar Association
Connecticut Law Firm Group
Colorado Law Firms
Dallas Bar Association
District of Columbia Conference on Opportunities for Minorities
  in the Legal Professions
Houston Law Firms
Los Angeles County Bar
Maricopa County Bar Association (Phoenix)
New Jersey Law Firm Group
San Antonio Law Firms
San Francisco Bar Association
State Bar of Arizona
State Bar of Texas
Tarrant County Law Firms (Fort Worth, Texas)
Travis County Law Firms (Austin, Texas)

PART III

Getting the Offer

CHAPTER 14

Writing an Effective Resume

Pat Bowers Thomas

A lawyer's resume is perhaps his or her single most important career advancement tool; therefore, its content, structure, and mode of presentation need to be perfected. A quick glance at a resume frequently determines whether a particular candidate is worthy of further evaluation and an initial interview. Therefore, you must be prepared to devote substantial thought, time, and energy to creating a resume that distinguishes you from the crowd.

Description of a Resume

In this age of digital communication, we find that the hard-copy resume is still the document most employers want to see. It has, however, evolved beyond a conventional chronological outline. Ideally, it is a well-organized and concise, yet thorough, presentation that emphasizes a lawyer's growth and development. The language in a resume should speak to experienced lawyers and human resources professionals. The resume should be constructed in a format that allows readers to find quickly the information that they consider key to a specific employment slot.

Your resume should be drafted strategically, taking into consideration each potential employer's particularized criteria in conjunction with your experience and agenda. You should highlight the parallels between the two by identifying specific accomplishments in your academic and professional endeavors. Effective resumes focus on the substantive nature of your practice, detail the various types of work product produced, describe the levels of responsibility that you have achieved, and identify your experience with specific types of clients and industries.

Different Uses of a Resume

In this chapter, three fictitious lawyers will be discussed: Dale S. Technical, a very junior lawyer with a scientific/technical focus; John Q. Corporate, a midlevel corporate lawyer; and Sarah M. Litigator, a senior litigation lawyer. As an exercise, we will create resumes for these lawyers. We will begin with initial drafts and then explore the format and style changes necessary to tailor certain of the resumes for separate positions—one with a law firm and one with a corporation.

Even if your practice specialty is not covered in one of these examples, you should be able to draw parallels to your substantive focus. These examples should enable you to construct resumes for all types of employment situations.

Limitations of a Resume

A number of misconceptions must be dispelled before we can begin the process of drafting and tailoring a resume.

Misconception 1: "More is better" or "less is better."   While it often has been a rule of thumb that the length of a resume should be one page for every seven to ten years of practice, this generalized rule is harmful if your finished product does not highlight your significant accomplishments in an effective manner or if it constitutes a laundry list of every legal matter you have touched since beginning law school. Finding the happy medium between being verbose and being laconic is a more important guideline than restricting information to a predetermined number of pages.

Misconception 2: By carefully crafting a resume, you can hide (1) frequent job changes, (2) lack of experience, and (3) poor academics.   A lawyer's resume should, at a minimum, contain all legal positions held since graduation from law school and set forth any practice breaks or sabbaticals longer than six months. Omitted legal employment information is usually uncovered—typically with less-than-favorable results.

Your resume should be designed to put your best foot forward and in the process emphasize your short-term and long-term career goals. Therefore, it is counterproductive to exaggerate your experience or embellish your academics with insignificant activities. If you feel pressure to do this, then return to your career planning and redirect your efforts toward more compatible and realistic goals (see Chapters 2 and 3).

Misconception 3: A resume should begin with an "objective" section stating your career goals.   While there are two schools of thought on this topic, each with plausible arguments, the information found in an objective section usually should be included in a cover letter, not in the resume itself.

Misconception 4: Salary information should be included on a resume.   Preserve your flexibility and privacy. You must gain enough information on a particular employment opportunity to compare it with your current position. Typically this comparison cannot be made before completing several stages of the interview process; therefore, you should not include a salary history on your resume. If you are predisposed toward sharing your salary information, you may choose to provide a desired salary range in your cover letter when applicable.

Misconception 5: Employers' addresses and telephone numbers should be included on each employment entry.   Do not give away the store. Once an employer has interviewed you, reference checking can begin at the appropriate and mutually agreed-upon time.

Preparation of the Resume

Evaluating Your Experiences

In earlier chapters, you learned how to identify your career motivational attitudes, work ethics, and the current marketplace. Now you are ready to consider these elements in conjunction with your substantive experience and academic performance. Prioritize your experience, keeping in mind your career goals. Identify your work by the percentage of time you have spent in each substantive area. List levels of responsibility reached for each type of work product and the types of clients for whom you performed these services.

Targeting Your Audience

Decide what experience and academic achievements should be emphasized by learning as much as possible about a particular employment opportunity. This information may be gained from friends or school alumni working for that employer, an attorney recruiter, your law school placement office, articles in legal magazines, and the like. In analyzing a position, consider the following:

- What substantive knowledge and skills will be required? Are there any additional practice areas that will help place you in the top 10 percent of candidates? Has the prospective employer given subtle or not-so-subtle clues as to the expertise sought (e.g., the size of projects or dollar amounts involved in those projects) to indicate the complexity of the experience required?
- What productivity requirements and added levels of drive are needed to receive promotions within the organization?
- What value does the organization place on intelligence, creativity, and leadership?
- Who will be your superior? What support do they expect from you? Who will your peers be? What are the profiles of these people?
- What percentage of time will you spend interacting with people outside your legal group? Who are they?
- What oral and written skills are required? Does the position require management skills?
- What is the culture and personal style of this employer and its employees? Are its lawyers known to be aggressive or reserved, formal or casual, strictly focused on the practice of law or active in diverse community and other interests?

Each time you consider a different opportunity, reevaluate and revise your resume in light of that employer's position specifications as well as less obvious requirements relating to the client's culture.

General Rules

When creating your resume, you should follow certain guidelines:

- A resume should contain enough information to encourage a personal meeting, but not so much information that the curiosity of the reader dissipates.
- Consider your audience. For example, if you are applying for a job in the United States, nationally recognized employers need no introduction on a resume. Local or regional employers may need identifying information on the resume when you apply for positions in other areas of the country. However, provide identifying information for all employers when applying outside the United States. Identifying factors can include size or number of lawyers, industry or practice focus, and former affiliations. For example:

  YOUNG & RESTLESS, Anytown, USA
  (Thirty-lawyer litigation boutique spin-off from O'Great & Powerful in 1985)

  CORPORATION POWERFUL, Anytown, USA
  (Fortune 500 company developing electrical products for the medical, telecommunications, and transportation fields)

- Unless you are currently unemployed, the body of information relating to your current position should be written in the present tense. All too frequently, lawyers who are job searching have psychologically departed from their position and thus refer in the past tense to their present employment situation.
- Place any related information together under one heading so that all accomplishments in one academic or employment setting are tied together. For instance, if you wrote for Law Review during law school, include this information with your law school entry, not your publications section.
- Leave out information that is unnecessary, is assumed, or has become irrelevant. Be careful with this. For instance, it is not assumed that more senior lawyers working on complex matters perform all levels of less complex work below the experience listed.
- The telephone numbers on your resume should place a caller in direct contact with you or allow him or her to leave a private message. Do not needlessly jeopardize your current employment situation.
- The reader of a resume will not necessarily know the status of your present employment; therefore, mark directly on the resume that this is a confidential submission.

The First-Draft Components

For any writer, committing pen to paper is difficult. When developing a re-sume, you must remember that your first draft will be just that—an initial step in the process. Try to include as much information as possible, organiz-ing each section chronologically. Then, put your first draft aside for a rest and plan to evaluate it with a critical eye another day.

Education

Academic achievements and leadership qualities have long been key indica-tors for employers regarding potential intelligence and commitment. Com-petitiveness, selectivity, and performance standards of a highly regarded ed-ucational institution suggest greater intelligence and excellence of the applicant just by reason of association. Moreover, some law firms give extra weight to an applicant's association with such institutions, viewing them as potential "peer breeding grounds" for future client development. Graduates from the "top twenty" or first-tier law schools who achieve Order of the Coif status and become editors of their school's Law Review are coveted for their stellar academics. However, being one of the top five graduates from a midtier school may carry equal or more weight than graduating at the top 20–33 percent of the class from a first-tier school. Impressive extracurricular activities often imply productivity and commitment. Earning a degree while working or raising a family may have much the same effect, particularly if coupled with a strong record.

Begin your academic history with college, continuing through postgrad-uate studies. Generally, you should not include high school unless, for exam-ple, you attended a special school in Switzerland for more than a year and now are applying to an employer where that cultural and academic experi-ence may be important.

While high class standing (the top 20 percent or above) should always be included in this section, you can drop your SAT and LSAT scores once you have become a member of the bar and practiced for 12 months.

Employment Experience

As is true with academic accomplishments, a high value is placed on prior associations with easily recognized and highly regarded employers. These former employers afford a "shorthand" reference to the type of training that you have received and the complexity of matters that have been available to you at your level of practice. Less easily recognized employers can be en-hanced by a short description that piques the reader's curiosity and encour-age investigation during an interview.

Within the legal community, great value is placed on job stability as well as on steady progression in level of responsibility. Employers tend to use a critical eye in this section to evaluate your level of commitment, loyalty, moti-vation, initiative, job performance, and intelligence. Obviously, individuals dealing with more complex matters than expected for their level of experi-ence are seen as having higher potential value. Be cautious, however, not to overplay the complexities of your work at the expense of the necessary basics. Corporate employers and smaller firms become leery of candidates who perform only "headline-making" work. They often need employees who are willing to work in the trenches.

Employers appreciate detail regarding your work, including substantive expertise, client and industry interaction, roles and responsibilities, and interpersonal effectiveness. Employers also may gain insight into your commitment through information regarding your nonbillable legal responsibilities and management or supervisory roles. Again, remember to prioritize your experience in light of the audience you are targeting.

For a number of lawyers, law is a second or continued career following employment after undergraduate schooling. If this is your situation, establish separate sections on your resume to deal with legal and nonlegal experience. Determine the amount of detail necessary regarding your nonlegal experience by evaluating its correlation to your legal employment.

Memberships, Certifications, Affiliations, and Activities

Prominently display your bar memberships. If bar admission in a particular state is considered difficult and selective, indicate the year that you passed the exam. Passing the bar on the first sitting in a state such as California, where there is no reciprocity, is considered a strong indication of intellectual achievement. Registration to practice before the U.S. Patent & Trademark Office, particularly when earned during the same year as a state bar membership, is another example of highly valued certification.

Affiliations with large organizations should be detailed to identify participation in specific sections and committees that have an easily identifiable value to your career plan. For instance, simply listing membership in the ABA is far less useful than an environmental lawyer adding: *Member, Natural Resources, Energy & Environmental Law Section: Special Committee on Environmental Crimes.* Personal interest entries also may assist in identifying your diversifications. Entries such as *Women's Lawyers Caucus, Secretary of Regional Activities* and *Member, Native American Indian Bar Association* give the reader a more complete picture of your background and interests.

Community activities may be important to a potential employer. They can indicate diverse interests, social responsibility, and beneficial business contacts as well as geographic ties and stability. Maturity and strong organizational skills are often inferred from significant responsibilities within these organizations.

There is much debate concerning inclusion of leisure activities and personal information. When submitting a resume to a potential employer, determine whether inclusion of this information will indicate a cultural fit within the organization. When you do include this information, keep it short. Here are some commonly held perceptions of employers regarding certain leisure activities:

- Sports—fit, may be a team player, competitive, self-disciplined
- Cultural activities—diversity, intellectual breadth
- Travel—adaptability to different regions and cultures, curiosity

Listing too many activities, however, may be viewed as a lack of commitment to your career.

In today's global economy, the ability to conduct business in another language often distinguishes a candidate from the pack. Many of today's employers are evaluating the international implications of their businesses. Include your language capabilities on your resume if you have at least conversational proficiency. Be sure to list the specific level of your proficiency in each language.

The Visual Effect

How you present your resume is almost as important as the facts presented. Because you are a professional, look professional. Visually, your resume should be clean, with easy-to-read type. Important information should be highlighted. The page should be organized so that readers easily can find the information that you feel is essential to their evaluation of your candidacy.

Remember, an individual who regularly screens numerous resumes spends approximately *five to ten seconds* glancing over each resume. At least 80 percent of the resumes are disqualified on this first glance. Be sure you put your best foot forward, leaving a favorable impression.

Because you initially are developing a resume that meets the needs of potential employers in general and then tailoring it for specific submission, you should utilize a computer and laser printer to create your resume. Resumes should be regularly updated; store this information on a diskette for future revisions.

Appearance

Several factors contribute to the attractiveness of a resume:

- *Quality paper.* Select a neutral (white, cream, beige, pale gray, etc.) paper in 20- to 24-pound weight. The paper should feel neither heavy nor flimsy. Paper with too deep a grain or "tooth" tends to break up the print (broken letters) and does not fold well when placed in an envelope. Test the paper by printing a sheet with a laser printer and folding the paper. Taking the time to test paper will yield subtle benefits in the long run. If you are submitting your information directly to an employer, purchase envelopes to match the paper.
- *Print.* Use compatible typefaces and sizes and print in black ink. You may choose to have a print shop typeset your resume or to use the flexibility of computer software and letter-quality printers. Word processing programs have a variety of typefaces—usually called fonts—available. To give you an example of the possibilities varied fonts provide, the individual resume examples that follow use different fonts (see Figures 14.1–14.10). Typewriter copy and dot-matrix prints are not acceptable.
- *Reproduction.* If you decide to produce a single hard copy of your resume and photocopy originals as needed, be sure you produce clean, sharp, and evenly aligned copies. If you fax your resume at the request of an employer, mail a hard copy on the same day as a backup.

Layout

Choose a layout style that assists the employer in rapidly finding your key qualifications:

- The text should include adequate margins and tabulations to create clean lines and "white" space sufficient to produce visual balance, both vertically and horizontally, on every page. Your name, address, and telephone information is always at the top of the first page. Second pages should be marked clearly with your name.
- The print should be bolded, underlined, or italicized to highlight significant information and to organize the page.
- The length of a particular employment or academic entry should be proportional to the level of experience and importance that it represents.

Organization

Decide what information should be most visible and the order in which it should be presented. Generally, very junior lawyers and new graduates should provide academic information first. As attorneys become more senior, it often is appropriate to place legal experience as the first entry on the resume.

You must objectively determine how your resume will fare in the brief-glance test. This evaluation involves critically reading it quickly left to right, top to bottom. Generally, a resume screener spends the most time glancing from top to bottom along the left half of the resume, so put key information there. Also, be sure the information near the end of your resume remains interesting; otherwise, shorten your resume.

Here are some examples of how to address employers' hiring criteria through strategic organization of information:

- Does the employer seek stability? If you are not a job hopper, then list your employment dates first in the left-hand margin (in chronological order).
- Is the employer looking for identifiable training from "name" employers? Assuming you have had such employers, list them first in the left-hand margin.
- Will this employer seek a candidate who has held certain positions with increasing levels of responsibility? List your positions first followed by your employers.
- Is your overall experience most important to this employer? If so, summarize your experience before giving an employment history.

The Examples

You are now ready to see these ideas put to work. Three fictional lawyers have made a first draft of their resumes and have given them the brief-glance test. We now turn to perfect their work. While there are numerous layouts and structures of resumes, the following examples should illustrate the important guidelines you must follow to compose a resume tailored to your needs.

Candidate 1: Dale S. Technical

Dale's search involves potential employers that will be most interested in candidates who have had specific job positions, levels of increasing responsibility, well-regarded employers, and technical knowledge. The layout and organization of the resume shown in Figure 14.1 (the first draft) does not address these employer interests first, while the improved resume in Figure 14.2 does.

In the second resume, boldface and capitalization was added in order to emphasize the most important information. Less obvious are the changes in the headings (*Education, Other Professional Experience,* and *Languages*); the organization and visual appearance of similar elements are made uniform. Additionally, the method of listing employment dates was made uniform ("1989 to 1993" changed to "1989–1993"). States were consistently abbreviated rather than spelled out when identifying the location of employment. Admissions information was corrected to represent the complete and correct organizational name.

Dale worked her way through school as an engineer; therefore, she attended classes in both the day and night divisions; she has made the work-and-school combination more apparent by adding *Day & Evening Divisions* to her law school entry. She spent her last year of law school in Palo Alto, a hotbed of computer-related activity, where the reader may presume she studied under prominent intellectual property/patent professors. This information has been added to the law school entry to further emphasize her computer studies and training. A sophisticated screener often will highlight such information for investigation during an interview.

Dale took the state bar in July and the patent bar in August following graduation from law school. Passing both on the first sitting and within two months is a significant accomplishment. Therefore, this accomplishment is featured in the *Admissions* section.

The specific technical direction of Dale's practice (electronics), the types of applications the work encompasses, and the fact that it involves domestic and foreign filings have all been added to the text of the current employment setting (*Legal Experience*). The copy has been changed to the present tense (she has not left this position).

Note the increase in the amount of space devoted to Dale's current position when comparing versions 1 and 2 of her resume. This was done to define subtly the balance between her legal and technical experience. Added to this section was Dale's work as a patent agent for the firm while in law school. This rounded out the chronology of her work experience, further solidifying her strong focus and work ethic.

Dale is a recent graduate of law school, having worked for ten years as an engineer before beginning her legal education. This experience is specifically applicable in her patent practice so these prelaw employment entries have been included also.

The patent field, as in many of today's substantive practices, frequently utilizes foreign language skills. Therefore, Dale's foreign languages are listed in anticipation of their value to a potential employer.

The work telephone number was removed as a contact point because it is not a direct dial and, therefore, not sufficiently confidential.

FIGURE 14.1

Dale S. Technical Resume—Version One

```
DALE S. TECHNICAL
444 W. 4th Street                          Home (299) 555-6666
Midwest, IL 50505                          Office (299) 557-7000


EDUCATION:
            The Midwest University, Chicago, IL
            J.D.,1997, Top 15%
            Member, Midwest Computer & High Technology Law
            Journal
                1995-96

            University of the Midwest, Duluth, Minnesota
            M.S., 1987, Electrical Engineering

            Polytechnic State, Milwaukee, WI
            S.B., 1986, Electrical Engineering


ADMISSIONS: IL 1997
            Registered to practice before the United
                States Patent and Trademark office


LEGAL EXPERIENCE:
            Prosecution, Application & Infringement
            Chicago, IL
            Associate 1997 - present. Work involved patent
            prosecution, validity and infringement
            studies, licensing and negotiation; and client
            counseling.


Other Professional Experience

            Magic Corporation, Chicago, IL
            Engineering Manager 1993 to 1996. Managed a
            team of twelve engineers involved in the
            development of computer-aided design software
            tools. Position involved budget proposals and
            allocation for the financing for the
            development of new applications for company
            products.

            EFZ Systems Company, Palo Alto, California
            Design Engineer 1989 - 1993. Programmed
            computers to develop tools for designing
            integrated circuits. Designed computer-aided
            engineering software for engineering work
            stations.

            Computer Corporation, Palo Alto, CA
            Engineer 1987 -89. Designed programs and
            databases.


Languages: Japanese, Chinese (Cantonese), and Russian
```

FIGURE 14.2

Dale S. Technical Resume—Version Two

DALE S. TECHNICAL

444 W. 4th Street
Midwest, Illinois 50505
Home: (299) 555-6666

EDUCATION: **THE MIDWEST UNIVERSITY**   1997
(Spent 3rd year at Palo Alto Law School, Silicon Valley, CA)   Chicago, IL
J.D., Top 15% (Day & Evening Divisions)
Member, Midwest Computer & High Technology Law Journal, 1995–96

UNIVERSITY OF THE MIDWEST   1987
M.S. in Electrical Engineering   Duluth, MN

POLYTECHNIC STATE   1986
S.B. in Electrical Engineering   Milwaukee, WI

ADMISSIONS: State Bar of Illinois, 1997
Registered to practice before the United States Patent and Trademark Office, December 1997

LEGAL EXPERIENCE:

Patent Associate   1997–Present
PROSECUTION, APPLICATION & INFRINGEMENT   Chicago, IL

Preparation and prosecution of U.S. and foreign applications specializing in electronics covering computers, digital and analog circuits and systems, signal processing and architecture, semiconductors, and software architecture; validity and infringement studies; licensing and negotiation; client counseling. Clients range from independent to multinational corporations.

Patent Agent   Summer 1996

OTHER PROFESSIONAL EXPERIENCE:

Engineering Manager   1993–1996
MAGIC CORPORATION   Chicago, IL

Managed a team of twelve engineers involved in the development of computer-aided design software tools. Position involved budget proposals and allocation for the financing for the development of new applications for company products.

Design Engineer   1989–1993
EFZ SYSTEMS COMPANY   Palo Alto, CA

Programmed computers to develop tools for designing integrated circuits. Designed computer-aided engineering software for engineering work stations.

Engineer   1987–1989
COMPUTER CORP   Palo Alto, CA

Designed programs and databases.

LANGUAGES: Japanese, Chinese (Cantonese), and Russian

*Submitted in confidence. Do not contact present
or former employers without prior approval of Dale S. Technical.*

Candidate 2: John Q. Corporate

John is a midlevel associate with stellar academics, broad corporate transactional experience, and employment stability. This very basic information is lost in his first draft (see Figure 14.3), which fails to differentiate between the amount of information given for his various academic, employment, and leisure entries. In addition, the flat format and lack of emphasis in the type style may cause this resume to be disqualified before it has been fully read.

The Law Firm Resume

Look at Figure 14.4 for a solution. After reading this chapter, John developed this resume for potential law firm employers.

John decided that law firms would be most interested in employment stability and the "valued associate" connotation that it implies. Next, he felt that they would look for "name or selective" employers and academic institutions, followed by depth of experience in corporate practice. He chose a format that emphasized these elements in declining order of priority—that is, date, employer, and experience.

With his solid employment credentials, John felt comfortable organizing his resume so that his work experience came before academic achievements. He added considerable information to his law firm experience by detailing the breadth of his practice and his focus specialties, levels of responsibility, types of clients, client contacts, and firm activities. He included his summer clerkship to underscore his commitment to the firm; he also wished to signal the firm's investment in his training and their selection of him as an associate. He eliminated first-person expression ("I") because it may cause a candidate to be viewed as self-centered and limited in his or her ability to be a team player and dedicated member of an organization.

To attend undergraduate and law school, John depended on scholarships and worked odd jobs between class schedules, experiences he grouped under *Various Jobs*. This positioning gained him resume space while supporting the inference of being a hard worker, intelligent, and down to earth.

The value of John's work experiences is reinforced by his academic entries. These entries also indicate good writing skills (law journal) and good communication and rapport with people (being elected president of Quest Hall).

John did not want three short sections at the bottom of his resume out of concern for diluting the importance of each, so he chose to place his bar memberships directly above his work experience. This provides the necessary information without modifying the strength and structure of this resume format.

Associates know that client-development skills are an important prerequisite to making partner. John specifically included speaking before a group of potential clients in the *Activities* section to emphasize his potential talents in knowing how, when, and where to develop business.

John also included very specific information regarding his language skills as a "plus factor" in his candidacy. His personal information was

FIGURE 14.3

John Q. Corporate—First-Draft Resume

```
JOHN Q. CORPORATE
456 Trial Lane
Tireless, New York 12345
Home (212) 123-4567
Office (212) 765-4321
```

Education
    Johnson High School   1985
    (high honors)

    QSU, BA   1989

    Stellar Law School, J.D.   1993

Employment

    Tireless County Road Corporation   July – Oct 1985
    Construction Worker

    New York Grocery   Summer 1986
    Store Clerk

    KHRT Radio   March 1989 – July
                             1990

    Program Assistant Researcher

    Law Offices of Herman Lawyer   Jan 1991 – June 1991
    Law Intern

    Apple, Bean, Carrot & Frye   Summer 1991
    Summer Clerk

    O'Great & Powerful   Summer 1992
    Summer associate: legal research and drafted memoranda
    and pleadings.

    Whye, Nott, Merge & Achoir   Summer 1992
    Summer associate

    O'Great & Powerful   Sept 1993 – present
    I am an Associate practicing in the Corporate Department
    with an emphasis on mergers and acquisitions,
    securities, and general corporate law. Member of the
    Hiring Committee.

Personal

    Born: January 1, 1968 New York Plains, NY
    Single. Enjoy skiing, wines, chess, and the classics.

FIGURE 14.4

John Q. Corporate—Law Firm Resume

JOHN Q. CORPORATE

456 Trial Lane
Tireless, New York 12345
Home (212) 123-4567
Office (212) 765-4321

Bar Member: New York (1993), District of Columbia (1994)

EXPERIENCE
Legal:

Sept 1993– Present	**O'GREAT & POWERFUL,** New York, New York *Corporate Associate.* Practice sixty percent of time with the Corporations Department, with an emphasis on mergers and acquisitions, securities, and general corporate law. Leading role on a variety of transactions for clients ranging from emerging companies to Fortune 250 companies. Senior associate responsible for all aspects of transactions, including drafting and negotiating documents, overseeing due diligence and handling closings. Primary client contact for ongoing general corporate work. In addition, broad experience in financial regulatory matters, real estate loans, environmental compliance and land-use, and corporate workouts and restructuring. Member of the firm's Associate Hiring Committee for both law school graduates and lateral associates. (May–July 1992, *Summer Associate*)
July–Sept 1992	**WHYE, NOTT, MERGE & ACHOIR,** Washington, D.C. *Summer Associate.* Split summer clerking with the firm and current employer. Received permanent offer of employment.
May–Sept 1991	**APPLE, BEAN, CARROT & FRYE,** Chicago, Illinois *Summer Clerk.*

Other:

July 1985– April 1990	**VARIOUS JOBS** During undergraduate, worked in order to earn 60% of the money needed to finance QSU and first year of law school. These jobs included working as a grocery store clerk, a construction worker, and an assistant program researcher for a local radio station. Became employed full-time by the radio station to write editorials on the effect of national news items on local citizens.

EDUCATION

1993	**STELLAR LAW SCHOOL,** New York, New York *Juris Doctor,* Top 11% (24/200) Publications Editor, Stellar Corporations Law Journal Attorney's Scholarship 1992–1993
1989	**QSU,** Quest, New York *Bachelor of Arts, summa cum laude* Dual Major: English and Communications President, Quest Hall 1987–1988

ACTIVITIES   Speaker, New York Association of General Counsel (NYGC) Program: "The Effect of M&A on Executive Compensation"
Member, American Bar Association Business Law Section: Subcommittee on Securities Regulation

LANGUAGES   Fluent French, conversational Japanese

*Submitted in confidence. Do not contact present or
former employers without prior approval of J.Q. Corporate*

omitted because it was not essential to this firm-oriented resume; its exclusion neatly kept the resume length to one page.

Because John has been practicing for less than seven years, it may be difficult to provide enough concrete examples of his responsibilities and duties to distinguish him from the other top 20 percent of applicants for the position. To remedy this, an addendum was added to his resume entitled *Representative Corporate Experience* (see Figure 14.5). This type of information can be organized chronologically or by substantive subspecialties, as in John's addendum.

In brief sentences, John has described a specific project for a client, giving the size of the deal, the type of work, his responsibilities, and the type of client. Clients may be referred to by name or generically. These projects are organized on one page by substantive groupings, for example, *Securities Offerings, Mergers & Acquisitions,* and *General Corporate.*

This addendum is a very useful tool. While the basic details on your resume may not change so rapidly, the specific projects that you work on and the level of responsibility that you have at work changes more frequently. New projects often require exploration into new legal issues and corresponding substantive work. Therefore, the addendum becomes a simple method for updating your resume more frequently.

It is a healthy practice to keep an up-to-date sampling of recent work projects. For each project you feel is significant (whether a favorite project or one that gave you difficulty), write a summary that includes:

- The nature of the project (size, type of client, people involved, etc.)
- Your role in the project (substantive responsibilities, level of autonomy, and team interaction, including to whom you reported and whom you supervised)
- The outcome of the project (what this project produced for the client, what could have been improved, what the project did for you and your career)

Take these summaries and capsulize them to create brief descriptions such as those in John's addendum. Save your more-lengthy summaries to review in preparation for interviews.

The Corporate Resume

Figure 14.6 is an example of John's resume recrafted for submission to a corporation. Corporations often value managerial and interpersonal skills, business knowledge, the ability to interact effectively with nonlegal individuals, and an ability to identify with corporate goals on the same level as legal expertise. Also, they evaluate the size of your current employer's organization and your specific team setting. Many are interested in your ability to do work as a "generalist," including the breadth of your knowledge of different legal areas and your familiarity with, and capacity for, the more mundane day-to-day legal work found in-house.

In light of these considerations, to pinpoint John's experience, information that will be important to a corporation has been "bulleted." Furthermore,

FIGURE 14.5

John Q. Corporate—Addendum to Law Firm Resume

JOHN Q. CORPORATE

REPRESENTATIVE CORPORATE EXPERIENCE

CORPORATE FINANCE AND SECURITIES

- Participated in preparation of registration statements and other documents for public offerings of common stock and collateralized mortgage obligations for ABC Mortgage Company and its subsidiaries. Prepared stock option plans and agreements and related registration statements.

- Represented The Underwriters, Inc., in the $11 million common stock offering of Corporateronix, Inc.

- Represented Securities Brokerage House as underwriter for the public offering of ABC Company, Inc. common stock. Conducted due diligence review, drafted S-11 registration statement and prospectus, and prepared closing documents. Assisted in drafting correspondence with the NASD and NYSE.

- Represented Major Oil & Gas Company in the sale of 23,000,000 shares of common stock (largest equity offering in 1993). Drafted S-3 registration statement and closing documents. Assisted in drafting correspondence with the NASD and NYSE.

MERGERS & ACQUISITIONS

- Represented Patt Industries, Inc., in its $7 billion merger into a subsidiary of The Industry Corporation, a subsidiary of Major Corporation, Inc.

- Represented purchaser in acquisition of major food company. Conducted due diligence review, drafted stock purchase agreement and letter of intent, and assisted in drafting financing commitment letter.

- Represented parent company in sale of assets of two aerospace divisions and stock sale of a defense-related subsidiary. Assisted in drafting asset purchase and stock purchase agreements. Drafted ancillary documents, including assignment agreements, schedules for agreements, non-compete agreements, guaranties and indemnity agreements. Prepared reasoned opinion regarding Section 271 of Delaware General Corporations Law.

GENERAL CORPORATE

- Prepared employment and consulting agreements and negotiated shareholders' agreement and related documents for formation of joint venture for MB Corporation.

- Represented ABC Corporation in changing their state of domicile.

- Represented The Maritime Corporation in its recapitalization.

- Negotiated and drafted the $400 million contract between ABC Telecommunications and Ye Grande Manufacturer to design and build a telecommunications satellite for the Latin American region.

FIGURE 14.6

John Q. Corporate—Corporate Resume

JOHN Q. CORPORATE
456 Trial Lane
Tireless, New York 12345
Home (212) 123-4567
Office (212) 765-4321

Bar Member: New York (1993), District of Columbia (1994)

EXPERIENCE
Legal:

Sept 1993
To Present

O'GREAT & POWERFUL, New York, New York
Corporate Associate at a national law firm with over 400 attorneys.

- Serve as issuers' and underwriters' counsel in public securities offerings. Responsibilities include preparing registration statements and coordinating regulatory filings.

- Frequently act as outside general counsel on wide variety of issues including general corporate, employment, real estate, environmental compliance and land-use for the three largest subsidiaries of a national chemical company.

- Counsel clients in antitrust matters and deal with the provisions of the Robinson Patman Act and the Clayton Act including predatory and discriminatory pricing issues and Hart-Scott-Rodino filings.

- Active in various mergers and acquisitions including serving as principal attorney for a worldwide media company in connection with asset purchase of going concern. Evaluate litigation matters as part of acquisition-related due diligence.

- Representation of three middle-market companies in workouts and restructuring.

- Senior associate responsible for overseeing junior associates on due diligence and research matters on large transactions. Personally draft and negotiate significant documents, and handle closing details.

- Administrative responsibilities for firm in the interviewing and hiring of law school graduates and lateral associates.

- Summer Associate, May–July 1992

July to
Sept 1992

WHYE, NOTT, MERGE & ACHOIR, Washington, D.C.
Summer Associate. Split summer clerking with this firm and current employer. Received permanent offer of employment.

May to
Sept 1985

APPLE, BEAN, CARROT & FRYE, Chicago, Illinois
Summer Clerk.

FIGURE 14.6

John Q. Corporate—Corporate Resume, continued

JOHN Q. CORPORATE
Resume—Page Two

Other:

July 1985 to **VARIOUS JOBS**
April 1990   During undergraduate, worked in order to earn 60% of the money needed
to finance QSU and first year of law school. These jobs included working as
a grocery store clerk, a construction worker, and an assistant program
researcher for a local radio station. Became employed full-time by the radio
station to write editorials on the effect of national news items on local
citizens.

EDUCATION

1993   **STELLAR LAW SCHOOL,** New York, New York
Juris Doctor, Top 11% (24/200)
Publications Editor, *Stellar Corporations Law Journal*
Attorney's Scholarship 1992–1993

1989   **QSU,** Quest, New York
Bachelor of Arts, summa cum laude
Dual Major: English and Communications
President, Quest Hall 1987–88

ACTIVITIES   Speaker, New York Association of General Counsel (NYGC) Program:
"The Effect of M&A on Executive Compensation"
Member, American Bar Association Business Law Section:
Subcommittee on Securities Regulation
Vice President, Big Brothers of Greater New York

LANGUAGES   Fluent French, conversational Japanese

PERSONAL   Single. Enjoy skiing, chess, and renovating old houses.

Submitted in confidence. Do not contact present
or former employers without prior approval of J.Q. Corporate.

John's resume has been personalized, to a degree, for submission to corporations in the telecommunications and media industries. In determining what information to include and the order of presentation, John reviewed his law firm resume information, addendum information, and experiences that he had originally thought less important given his limited years of practice when applying to law firms. Please note that even though there has been an informational and format change on John's resume for submission to corporations, he may still want to consider including the addendum from his law firm resume to further define his expertise.

John included the *Various Jobs* entry from his law firm resume in this corporate resume to reveal his work experience with nonlawyers, his ability to roll up his sleeves and work hard, and his early interest in media and communications. The experience with the radio station exposed John to some of the day-to-day operations of a sector of the industry that he is now seeking to join.

John added *Personal* information to highlight his "well-rounded" lifestyle and to point to his geographic stability. Furthermore, by stating that he is single, he hopes to imply flexibility because many of the positions he seeks involve significant travel. Family-oriented candidates tend to project maturity and dependability. John hopes to convey these traits by adding his participation in Big Brothers.

Candidate 3: Sarah M. Litigator

Sarah is a seasoned litigation lawyer who has worked in a variety of settings. She has represented corporate clients in private practice, as well as having been an in-house counsel utilizing outside counsel. She has been a servicer of other lawyers' clients as well as a rainmaker. She has worked in government and has had significant trial experience.

Sarah's experience presents the challenge of consolidating years of experience into a meaningful resume. Her varied employment settings and transitions need to be shown in a fashion that leads the reader to conclude that there has been a continuity of practice and expertise that could have been gained only through such employment movement.

Figure 14.7 is Sarah's first attempt at a resume. While it contains much valuable information, it requires the reader to comb carefully through each employment description before gaining a clear picture of Sarah's value. With typically five to ten seconds to screen a resume, the reader is not likely to find this resume useful.

The Law Firm Resume

Sarah's second attempt at a resume, with its primary focus on law firm employers (Figure 14.8), summarizes her expertise in a brief opening paragraph. This legal experience is followed by her chronological employment history.

After reading an overview of her work experience, Sarah decided that potential employers would be interested in which organizations employed her, followed by specific practice experience for each employer. Although

FIGURE 14.7

Sarah M. Litigator—First-Draft Resume

SARAH M. LITIGATOR

5 Beach Way   (110) 543-6789
Ocean, CA 54321   E-Mail: SML@TFB&S.org

EMPLOYMENT

1989-Present   **Time, Fore, Business & Strength,** San Diego & Los
                Angeles, CA
                (Small & Dynamic merged with TFB&S in June 1995)
                Chair, Trial & Appellate Practice Group 1994 - Present

                In 1989, joined Small & Dynamic to develop white
                collar crime trial practice as well as acting as chief
                trial counsel on other major complex corporate and
                business litigation. By 1994, had developed
                significant business and expanded trial practice into
                a group of 10 partners and 20 associates emphasizing
                white collar crime, labor & employment, securities,
                environmental, intellectual property, and insurance
                coverage.

                Personal practice focus as first-chair litigator in
                white collar crime, securities fraud (including class
                actions and shareholder derivative matters), directors
                & officers issues, and RICO as well as general
                litigation advice as part of a "general counsel"
                relationship with firm clients.

                Over 20 first-chair and jury trials in both state and
                federal courts as well as several appellate and
                administrative appearances.

1985-1989   **Major Corporation,** Cincinnati, OH
                Litigation Counsel. Responsibilities included managing
                litigation for the corporation and its subsidiaries,
                reviewing and drafting commercial contracts, and
                providing legal support on a wide range of marketing
                issues.

1983-1985   **Large & Powerful,** Los Angeles, CA
                Associate. Business litigation experience in a variety
                of civil matters including RICO, contract,
                construction, product liability, and antitrust as well
                as white collar crime. Exposure to all aspects of
                trial and appellate litigation. Direct contact with
                several major clients of the firm.

1980-1983   **U.S. Attorney's Office,** Los Angeles, CA
                Assistant Attorney, Member, Special Prosecutions Unit

                Involved in prosecution of major white collar criminal
                cases, including obstruction of justice, commodities
                fraud and investment fraud.

1978-1979   **Honorable Charles F. Justice, III, Senior Judge,**
                United States Court of Appeals for the Second Circuit
                Judicial Clerk.

Summer 1977   **Large & Powerful,** Los Angeles, CA
                Law Clerk.

Summer 1976   **Public Counsel,** Los Angeles, CA
                Law Clerk on Housing Fraud Project.

FIGURE 14.7

Sarah M. Litigator—First-Draft Resume, continued

SARAH M. LITIGATOR
Resume—Page Two

Education

1975	**Delaware/Washington Law School,** Washington, D.C.
	LL.M. in Securities Law

1973   **UCSB School of Law,** Sacramento, CA
          J.D., Top 20%
          Law Review Articles Editor
          Honors Moot Court Competition
          Voluntary Defenders Program

1970   **The Woman's College,** Boston, MA
          A.B., Political Science
          Phi Beta Kappa

          Graduate Institute of International Studies,
            Geneva, Switzerland, 1968–1970

ADMITTED   California, 1973; New York 1974; Ohio, 1980
           United States Supreme Court
           Courts of Appeal for the Federal, Second, Fifth, Seventh
             and Ninth Circuits
           All District Courts in California, New York and Ohio

*Submitted in Confidence. Do not contact present
or former employers without prior approval of S.M. Litigator*

FIGURE 14.8

Sarah M. Litigator—Law Firm Resume

SARAH M. LITIGATOR
5 Beach Way
Ocean, California 54321
Office (110) 543-6789
E-Mail: SMLit505@internet.com

LEGAL EXPERIENCE

Trial attorney with twenty years of experience focusing on civil and criminal litigation in federal, state and appellate courts. Lead Counsel in over 40 court and jury trials involving RICO, white collar crime, contracts, antitrust, directors' and officers' liability issues, and securities fraud including class actions and shareholders derivative matters . Have supervised up to thirty attorneys and acted as outside general counsel to clients regarding litigation advice.

EMPLOYMENT HISTORY

TIME, FORE, BUSINESS & STRENGTH; 1989–Present   Los Angeles, CA
(Small & Dynamic merged with this Firm in June 1995)   San Diego, CA

Chair, Trial & Appellate Practice Group since 1994; *Partner* beginning 1991.

Substantive Experience:
- White collar crime, securities, Directors & Officers issues and RICO for domestic and international clients ranging from middle market to Fortune 500 companies and wealthy individuals. Case value ranged from $75,000 to $4 million.
- Advise clients on business matters relating to contracts, agreements and other business relationships.
- Administrative hearing experience before the Securities & Exchange Commission and Federal Trade Commission.
- Have appeared in international arbitrations and matters before the International Trade Commission.

Management Experience:
- Chair, Trial & Appellate Practice Group, 1994 to present. Established Small & Dynamic's white collar crime practice in 1989, growing the practice into a broad based trial practice group in Los Angeles and San Diego. Group now numbers 30 attorneys and 12 legal assistants.
- San Diego Office opening. One of three attorneys who staffed the Firm's San Diego office during its first year of operation in 1996. Responsibilities included the recruitment of attorneys and paralegals for the office.
- Partner in charge of coordinating and administering firm's basic and advanced trial and litigation training programs, 1995–present.

MAJOR CORPORATION; 1985–1989   Cincinnati, OH
($4 billion holding company involved in the manufacture and sale of financial products)

Litigation Counsel. Responsibilities included managing the litigation for the corporation and its subsidiaries including first-chair responsibility for a $7 million breach of contract action, reviewing and drafting commercial contracts, and providing legal support on a wide range of marketing issues.

FIGURE 14.8

Sarah M. Litigator—Law Firm Resume, continued

Sarah M. Litigator
Resume—Page Two

LARGE & POWERFUL; 1983–1985   Los Angeles, CA
(400 attorney international firm)

Associate in the business litigation and trial practice. Exposure to all aspects of trial and appellate litigation. Direct contact with clients and responsibility for a complex litigation matters including a case involving securities fraud for firm client, Major Corporation.

Summer Law Clerk, 1977

UNITED STATES ATTORNEY'S OFFICE; 1980–1983   Los Angeles, CA
Special Prosecutions Unit

Assistant U.S. Attorney involved in prosecution of major white collar criminal cases, including obstruction of justice, commodities fraud and investment fraud.

HONORABLE CHARLES F. JUSTICE, III; 1978–1979   New York, NY
Senior Judge, U.S. Court of Appeals for the Second Circuit

Judicial Clerk.

PUBLIC COUNSEL; Summer 1976   Los Angeles, CA
(Pro bono interest law firm)

Summer Intern working on housing fraud litigation.

EDUCATION

DELAWARE/WASHINGTON LAW SCHOOL; 1980   Washington, D.C.
LL.M. in Securities Law

UCMB SCHOOL OF LAW; 1978   Los Angeles, CA
J.D., Top 20%
Law Review Articles Editor
Honors Moot Court Competition
Voluntary Defenders Program

THE WOMAN'S COLLEGE; 1975   Boston, MA
A.B., Political Science
Phi Beta Kappa
President, College Debate Team

Graduate Institute of International Studies, Geneva, Switzerland, 1974–1975

ADMITTED

California, 1978, New York, 1979; Ohio 1985
United States Supreme Court; Courts of Appeal for the Federal, Second, Fifth, Seventh, and Ninth Circuit
All District Courts in California, New York, and Ohio

LANGUAGES

Fluent in French, conversational in Spanish

Submitted in confidence. Do not contact present or
former employers without prior approval of S.M. Litigator.

Sarah had moved in and out of the law firm environment, she was elected to partnership, an important indication of her value to the firm, and became chair of her practice section. Therefore, Sarah included her titles immediately below the employer's identity.

Visually, this establishes the layout and organization of the resume. The grouping titles, *Legal Experience, Employment History,* and *Education,* have been centered on the page. After the *Legal Experience* summary, Sarah provides a detailed description of her accomplishments in each employment setting. For each employer, she balances the visual prominence of the employer's name with her employment title. Sarah remained at each position a respectable period of time; she wanted to provide this information without complicating the layout or confusing the priorities that she had chosen. These dates are less prominent when they follow the name of an employer. Sarah established a far-right column showing her ability to work in a variety of geographic locales. She felt this was a potential asset to a firm with a national client base.

The organization and layout of the information to be contained in the description of Sarah's current employment experience presents a challenge. She has both substantive and management responsibilities. She began with a smaller firm that merged into a larger entity. While her initial focus was on white-collar crime, she expanded into other areas of litigation. She established a new office for the firm, working in two of its geographic locations. She became a successful rainmaker as well as a servicer of firm clients. With her increasing levels of success and responsibility, her title has changed several times. Sarah has been effective in the training of young lawyers.

The solution to the organizational challenge presented by Sarah's breadth of experience is to simplify the presentation of the information by using a layout that creates categories of accomplishment.

First, the merger of her prior law firm into her current law firm is identified in conjunction with the name of the merged entity. Then, her experience is broken down into bulleted highlights under *Substantive Experience* and *Management Experience.* Because Sarah felt it would clutter the resume and would be explained during an interview, she omitted her title, Of Counsel, for her first two years of employment with Time, Fore, Business & Strength.

This format successfully conveys information and leaves an overall impression of Sarah's commitment to the success of her practice and the successful growth of the firm.

Prior to joining the Time, Fore firm, Sarah spent several years as litigation counsel for Major Corporation. For her application to law firm employers, Major Corporation was defined by giving information regarding the type of entity, its financial strength, and the nature of the products it produces. This information provides a point of reference concerning the potential complexities of the work Sarah performed for the corporation.

To maintain a unified format, a definition for Large & Powerful was included. The nature of Sarah's work as an associate for the firm was further clarified by emphasizing that she expanded into civil litigation after leaving the U.S. Attorney's Office. Also, the link is provided between her work with Large & Powerful as an associate and her eventual employment with Major Corporation; Sarah stated in the description of her work as an associate with Large & Powerful that she represented Major Corporation in a securities fraud case.

To clarify relationships and to provide an early recognition of her potential legal skills, Sarah's summer clerkship with Large & Powerful is included in this entry. Judicial clerkships, particularly for a superior or Supreme Court judge, are valued by employers as indicators of intelligence, strong training on legal issues before the court, and as a strengthener of writing skills. For Sarah, her clerkship solidifies the screener's understanding of her early training and a recognition of her potential beyond the indications of her law school class standing.

Sarah's work at Public Counsel is included to identify her early commitment to pro bono work. The remainder of Sarah's employment and her education entries have been adjusted to comply with the selected layout.

Sarah spent one-and-one-half years studying abroad during college. This is included with the Woman's College because it was viewed and credited by that institution as similar to a junior year abroad.

Sarah's state bar memberships have been organized chronologically. Language proficiency can be viewed unexpectedly as a necessary asset. Sarah has maintained her conversational and written proficiency in two languages, so they are therefore included on her resume.

Sarah has included her personal e-mail address at home. While she feels that she has control over her e-mail at work, she recognizes that it is employer owned – even if she erases e-mails, a ghost image is left on the employer's server. She prefers to have a higher degree of privacy and choose the time when her employer becomes aware of her search. (For more on the Internet, see Chapter 9.)

Trial lawyers often are measured by their effectiveness in court. Sarah developed *Significant Litigation Matters* (see Figure 14.9), an addendum to Figures 14.8 and 14.10, for such an evaluation as well as for reasons similar to those of Candidate 2, John Q. Corporate.

This addition to Sarah's resume is developed chronologically—separated by *Federal and State Court* actions, *Arbitrations,* and *Administrative Hearings.* A very brief sketch is provided to assist in creating such a page. Each entry should include the title for the action, the side represented, the location of the action, the substantive issues involved, the outcome of the proceedings, and whether any further action was taken.

The Corporate Resume

Sarah may want to consider certain in-house opportunities. Figure 14.10 is a resume designed to meet these needs. The *Legal Experience* statement was modified to help hold the interest of a corporate employer by highlighting her work experience in a variety of settings.

More detail was given to her responsibilities as Litigation Counsel for Major Corporation. This experience is delineated by bullets targeting central duties and responsibilities.

FIGURE 14.9

Sarah M. Litigator—Addendum

SARAH M. LITIGATOR

SIGNIFICANT LITIGATION MATTERS

Note: <u>Double underline</u> identifies the client represented in each case.

Federal and State Court

1993   Publications, Inc., v. <u>Major Corporation</u>, USDC, ND Cal (Thomas, P.)
          Securities fraud, and antitrust case involving alleged Preliminary injunction
          sought by plaintiff denied. Currently on appeal to the Ninth Circuit.

1992   <u>Domestic Learning</u> v. The Broker-Dealer Inc.
          Multi-million dollar action for breach of fiduciary duty and negligence against
          defendant broker. Preliminary injunction granted.

Arbitrations

1991–1992 Court appointed chair of arbitration tribunal in In the Matter of Arbitration of
           The Houseproduct Group, Ltd and Conglomerate Corporation, San Diego
           Superior Court No. 0597459.

Administrative Hearings

1990   Lead counsel in major Title VII administrative class action in which a federal
          agency was found to have intentionally discriminated against a nationwide
          class of upper-level gay and lesbian employees.

1992   Counsel in trial of FTC trade regulation case in the health care industry, FTC
          Dkt No. 9100.

FIGURE 14.10

Sarah M. Litigator—Corporate Resume

SARAH M. LITIGATOR
5 Beach Way
Ocean, California 54321
Office (110) 543-6789
E-Mail: SMLit505@internet.com

LEGAL EXPERIENCE

Civil and criminal litigation attorney with twenty years' experience working in corporate, private practice, and government settings. Lead counsel in federal, state, and appellate courts in over 40 court and jury trial including RICO, white-collar crime, contracts, antitrust, directors' and officers' liability issues, and securities fraud including class actions and shareholders derivative matters. Have supervised up to thirty attorneys and acted as outside general counsel to clients regarding litigation advice.

EMPLOYMENT HISTORY

TIME, FORE, BUSINESS & STRENGTH; 1989–Present   Los Angeles, CA
(Small & Dynamic merged with this Firm in June 1995)   San Diego, CA

Chair, Trial & Appellate Practice Group since 1994; *Partner* beginning 1991.

Substantive Experience:

- White collar crime, securities, Directors & Officers issues and RICO for domestic and international clients ranging from middle market to Fortune 500 companies and wealthy individuals. Case value ranged from $75,000 to $4 million.

- Advise clients on business matters relating to contracts, agreements and other business relationships.

- Administrative hearing experience before the Securities & Exchange Commission and Federal Trade Commission.

- Have appeared in international arbitrations and matters before the International Trade Commission.

Management Experience:

- Chair, Trial & Appellate Practice Group, 1994 to present. Established Small & Dynamic's white collar crime practice in 1989, growing the practice into a broad based trial practice group in Los Angeles and San Diego. Group now numbers 30 attorneys and 12 legal assistants.

- San Diego Office opening. One of three attorneys who staffed the Firm's San Diego office during its first year of operation in 1996. Responsibilities included the recruitment of attorneys and paralegals for the office.

- Partner in charge of coordinating and administering firm's basic and advanced trial and litigation training programs, 1995–present.

MAJOR CORPORATION; 1985–1989   Cincinnati, OH
($4 billion holding company involved in the manufacture and sale of financial products)

Litigation Counsel. Responsibilities included:

- Litigation Management - Managed fifty percent of the litigation for the corporation and its subsidiaries with primary responsibility for the Check Printing for division.
- Hands-on-Litigation - Lead Counsel responsibility for a $7 million breach of contract action.
- Commercial Contracts - Sole responsibility for reviewing and drafting commercial contracts for division of company that previously had significant litigation claims.
- Marketing - Provided legal support on a wide range of critical marketing and sales issues.

FIGURE 14.10

Sarah M. Litigator—Corporate Resume, continued

Sarah M. Litigator
Resume—Page Two

LARGE & POWERFUL; 1983–1985   Los Angeles, CA
(400 attorney international firm)

Associate in the business litigation and trial practice. Exposure to all aspects of trial and appellate litigation. Direct contact with clients and responsibility for a complex litigation matters including a case involving securities fraud for firm client, Major Corporation.

Summer Law Clerk, 1977

UNITED STATES ATTORNEY'S OFFICE; 1980–1983   Los Angeles, CA
Special Prosecutions Unit

Assistant U.S. Attorney involved in prosecution of major white collar criminal cases, including obstruction of justice, commodities fraud and investment fraud.

HONORABLE CHARLES F. JUSTICE, III; 1978–1979   New York, NY
Senior Judge, U.S. Court of Appeals for the Second Circuit

Judicial Clerk.

PUBLIC COUNSEL; Summer 1976   Los Angeles, CA
(Pro bono interest law firm)

Summer Intern working on housing fraud litigation.

EDUCATION

DELAWARE/WASHINGTON LAW SCHOOL; 1980   Washington, D.C.
LL.M. in Securities Law

UCMB SCHOOL OF LAW; 1978   Los Angeles, CA
J.D., Top 20%
Law Review Articles Editor
Honors Moot Court Competition
Voluntary Defenders Program

THE WOMAN'S COLLEGE; 1975   Boston, MA
A.B., Political Science
Phi Beta Kappa
President, College Debate Team

Graduate Institute of International Studies, Geneva, Switzerland, 1974–1975

ADMITTED

California, 1978, New York, 1979; Ohio 1985
United States Supreme Court; Courts of Appeal for the Federal, Second, Fifth, Seventh, and Ninth Circuit
All District Courts in California, New York, and Ohio

LANGUAGES

Fluent in French, conversational in Spanish

Submitted in confidence. Do not contact present or
former employers without prior approval of S.M. Litigator.

For the most part, little else has been changed on this resume from the resume in Figure 14.8. Many of the layout and organization choices made for her law firm resume work well on a corporate resume for similar reasons. Sarah has the option of including her addendum *Significant Litigation Matters* with the submission of this resume. This document can be rearranged and other cases can be added to illustrate Sarah's experience in a particular industry or to highlight her experience relative to the requirements of a potential employer.

The Critical Eye

No matter what particular formats you use or targets you develop, some general rules apply to all resumes.

Once you have printed your resume, put it away for at least twenty-four hours. When you return to your resume, review it with a critical eye:

- How clean, neat, and professional does it appear?
- What do you notice first, second, and third? Do these items reflect your personal agenda and what you understand to be the crucial elements for the targeted employer?
- Does the resume convey what you like to do and what you know how to do?
- Can a screener determine how your experience is relevant to the employer?
- Is the potential employer likely to see you as an asset? Can the potential employer see what you have done for someone else?
- Does the potential employer have enough information to evaluate your past choices and transitions?
- Can the potential employer see that you are a problem solver?
- Is the potential employer given significant clues about your personal style and people skills?
- Is the layout consistent?
- Are there *any* typographical errors?
- What, if anything, is missing?

Comprehensive Addenda and the Resume Package

Often, there is information that you feel should be included, but is too lengthy. Or you may be uncertain about its importance to an employer, but the information is important to you. Quite often, information such as speeches and publications fall into these categories. If this information is too lengthy to include on your resume and you want to provide it to a potential employer, then consider creating a separate page for it.

Depending on the position that you seek and the prevailing culture of that particular employer, you may want to include certain items with your resume submission:

- *School transcripts.* The less experienced the lawyer, the more often these are necessary. Include them on an initial resume submission only if they are an academic asset. Usually, law school transcripts are sufficient; however, undergraduate transcripts are useful if the degree earned has a direct application to your legal practice (e.g., B.S. Technical). Postgraduate and advanced legal degrees may have similar applications. Plan to keep an official copy of all school transcripts in a safe place where you easily can retrieve them. Today, more and more employers require your official transcripts prior to processing your initial application for employment or before extending a formal offer. It often takes months to receive additional official transcripts from a school, so plan ahead.
- *Writing samples.* This is a wonderful demonstration of your written work product. While a prospective employer may request a writing sample when you submit a resume (as in a newspaper advertisement), you may voluntarily choose to submit one to emphasize experience in a particular area or offset some of your weaker credentials (for instance, they want top 10 percent and you are top 25 percent). Such submissions should be purely your own work, e.g., research, analysis, organization, and writing. If this is not the case, include a careful explanation of the contribution of others. Each submission should be no longer than 15 pages, demonstrating your clear and concise analytical thinking and your ability to communicate persuasively and effectively. All samples should be cleansed to ensure the confidentiality of the work product.
- *References and recommendations.* You should be prepared to provide three professional references and three personal references. One of the professional references should include a superior at your current place of employment. Because of the exposure this creates with your current employer, it is often best to hold back references until the potential employer has placed an offer on the table. If you have left a position unexpectedly, a letter of recommendation may help correct a perceived blemish on an otherwise strong resume.

Testing Your Audience

Locate individuals who can view your resume with a critical eye while maintaining the confidentiality of your search. A review by a third party who will not eventually be one of your search targets is an essential proofreading step. Qualified evaluators for this process may be a law school placement director, a lawyer friend who is part of the hiring team at work, a friend who works in the field that you are targeting for your search, or an attorney recruiter. Recruiters review and help write hundreds of resumes per month. Recruiters who are members of the National Association of Legal Search Consultants (NALSC) are especially helpful because they have years of experience with resumes and recruitment issues and are bound by the NALSC Code of Ethics which ensures confidentiality for you.

Provide these people with a thumbnail summary of the type of position that you are seeking. Ask them to evaluate your resume for that purpose as well as to provide you with general observations and questions arising from the resume. Ask them to be very diligent with their critique, particularly regarding the content and visual impact of your resume. Once they have taken the time to give you particularized input, take their comments seriously and make adjustments to your resume where necessary.

Delivering Your Resume

If you are conducting your search without the assistance of an attorney recruiter, you need to consider the pros and cons of the various methods of delivering your resume. The tactile experience and appearance of a hard copy resume on good rag paper sends a subtle message of quality to any recipient. Therefore, the best method of delivering your resume continues to be this traditional hard copy form. The delivery can be accomplished through the U.S. Postal Service, courier service, or personal hand delivery. While this last method may have benefits, be sure you employ it only when it will not be perceived as intrusive or inappropriate.

When time is of the essence for a particular job search or for a specific position, use of a facsimile machine or e-mail may be appropriate. In these situations, it is a good practice to mark your cover letter and/or resume *"Sent Via _____ and Mail"* (insert *Facsimile* and indicate fax number or insert *E-mail* and indicate e-mail address), then, send a hard copy as a back-up. You should weigh the reduced confidentiality of faxed resumes; they often are transmitted into central mail departments where they are amassed and eventually hand delivered to the intended recipient.

E-mail, while widely used, requires some technical adeptness and luck in compatibility when using the attachment feature to provide your resume with the e-mailed cover letter. Unfortunately, all too often a portion of the information is lost to garble or the formatting is lost when there is not full compatibilty, thereby introducing unnecessary imperfections in your resume. Too often a potential candidate is not informed of this mishap, and the hiring authority moves on to the next potential candidate. Hiring personnel and recruiters regularly complain that resumes transmitted via e-mail are difficult to read, if not illegible. With this is mind, do your best to perfect your transmittal techniques (see Chapter 9) and never rely on a facsimile or e-mail as your sole method of resume delivery.

If your e-mail is connected to your employer's server, a copy of all transmissions typically remains on the central server even after you have erased messages and documents from your screen. Weigh carefully the confidentiality risks, keeping in mind a realistic time frame needed to secure a new position. The immediacy of your needs may not outweigh the actual potential for your exposure.

Chapter 9 deals with the Internet in greater detail, however, let's review some creative ways to turn it into an effective resume delivery tool.

The Internet has provided an additional method of delivering your resume, the personal Web site. When confidentiality is not at issue, this method may be effective. This "electronic resume" looks much the same as the resumes created in this chapter. However, to be most effective, hyperlinks should be utilized. For example, have your Web site set up so that clicking on a high-lighted keyword such as **"securities offerings"** delivers the reader to samples of work you have completed in this area. If you are sophisticated enough, you may have the reader click on a reference to a particular employer to jump to that employer's Web site. This can help the reader learn more about the business of the employer in conjunction with the candidate's work, allowing a more informed comparison between the candidate's past experience and the present job opening.

If and when the skill to develop such a site is mastered, there are a number of issues to confront with the electronic resume Web site. The number of Web sites on the Internet is growing at such a rapid pace that, in many instances, you may be quite fortunate to have someone visit your Web site. If you have decided to develop an electronic resume Web site, then add to your plan the development of a customized "spider" that will collect potential readers and deliver them to your Web site. (This search engine alternative is called a "spider" because spiders "crawl" the Web, searching the Web on your behalf, mapping areas that the search engines miss, collecting the information you want and converting it into a database. Spiders can collect, for instance, e-mail addresses, resumes, personal home pages, job listings from a multitude of locations and, if you choose, refer these collected locations to your electronic resume Web site.) Through this vehicle, you can proactively use the Internet.

Remember, the Internet is merely a tool to help get your resume recognized by hiring authorities. Do not overdo your presentation on the Net. You have approximately 30 seconds to grab the attention of a visitor. Again, the Web site, like a paper resume, should pique their interest enough to motivate an interview; it should not replace, preclude or undermine the interview. Additionally, by placing your resume electronically on a Web site, you should be aware that you are sending a message not only of availability, but also that your current employer either is likely aware of your search or that you are presently unemployed.

In short, take care to deliver your resume with the same care and attention you have used during its development.

Keep Your Resume Alive

Your resume allows you to focus on your career goals and achievements and to share that focus with others. It is a flexible marketing document that can become your ticket to an interview. It is a two-dimensional portrait of you and your academic and professional experiences. As such, it changes as you do. It is not a static career tool. Revise and tailor your resume to meet specific opportunities. Keep the lines of layout clean and the organization simple, yet ensure that the information is appropriately detailed, relevant, and delivered in a way that sparks the reader's interest. Be sure it is an exemplar of your intelligence, your contributions, and your energy. Then, be prepared to be as dynamic, organized, and informative in person when you are called for an interview.

CHAPTER 15

The Cover Letter

Deborah Howard

A cover letter is an important part of your job search arsenal. It is your first chance to make a favorable impression on a potential employer. It is also the first sample of your writing that most employers will see, so it is important that your cover letter be well written. A well-written letter can persuade a potential employer to invite you for an interview; a poorly written one may end your chances for the position before the employer even reads your resume.

When you write a cover letter, you have an opportunity to give a potential employer information about who you are and why you are worth hiring. To be effective, it must help an employer realize what is unique about you so that your application will stand out in a large stack of other applications. Time spent writing a quality cover letter is well worth the effort.

Preparation

Writing an effective cover letter takes preparation and effort. Good cover letters are the product of time spent in thought. Self-assessment is a prerequisite to being able to tell an employer what it is that makes you special and unique. Before you can convince an employer that you are special and unique, you must know what it is about yourself that makes you so. You must know who you are and try to put a piece of yourself in your cover letter. You must also think about what you are looking for in a job and find a way to express that in your letter.

Self-Inventory

Take some time to put together an inventory of your strengths, skills, and qualities. Think about adjectives that describe you. Also think about activities in which you have performed well, whether these are papers you have written, cases or projects you have worked on, ideas you have developed, even sports you have played. Detail the experiences you have had and the specific classes in which you have excelled. Then determine what skills those activities incorporate, such as the ability to write well, to organize, to be a team player, to take initiative, and so on. Focus on how those experiences have affected you and what they reflect about you. Take note of what expertise your classes represent. This exercise should serve not only to give you information about yourself that can be incorporated into a cover letter, but also to strengthen your self-esteem and confidence. If you do not believe in yourself, it is hard to convince others that they ought to.

Once you have developed your inventory, synthesize this information into a paragraph detailing who you are and why you are special. This paragraph can then be adapted and tailored for each potential employer to whom you apply.

Develop a Target List

Your next task is to develop a target list of potential employers. This, too, involves time and effort. Spend some time determining your interests. Knowing the area of law or practice in which you are interested can help you to decide on the types of employers to whom you should or should not apply. Once you are able to focus your search, it is easier to develop a target list. If you have two or more areas in which you are interested, there is nothing wrong with developing two or more different target lists.

Research on Employers

Once you have developed a target list, obtain enough information about each employer to draft a cover letter in which you can articulate your interest. This may require some research, which can take the form of speaking with current and former employees of the employer, looking up the employers in various directories, such as the *Martindale-Hubbell Directories* and the *NALP Directory of Legal Employers,* and conducting research online using the Internet. (For more detailed information about conducting research on employers, see Chapters 5, 7, and 8.)

Drafting the Letter

Now that you have completed your preparation by doing a personal inventory of yourself and by conducting research to obtain information about employers, you are ready to write your letter. See Figure 15.1 for an example of the cover letter format.

Opening Paragraph

Your opening paragraph informs the employer why you are writing to them. When applicable, mention the name of the person who referred you to this employer. If you are responding to an advertisement, mention the advertisement and the specific position to which you are applying, since an organization can be advertising for more than one position at a time.

FIGURE 15.1

Sample Cover Letter Format

Address
Date

Contact Name
Contact Title
Organization Name
Address

Dear Mr./Ms._____:

Opening Paragraph: Statement of Objective. State why you are writing to this person/organization.

Qualifications and Statement of Interests Paragraph: Statement of Your Qualifications and Why You Are Interested in This Organization. State why the organization should hire you; tell the employer why you are special and unique and how you will fit the employer's needs; describe your skills, experience, qualifications and strengths; explain what about the organization is of interest to you.

Closing Paragraph: Closing Statement. Close with a reminder of your interest and your willingness to be available at the employer's convenience for further discussion.

Sincerely,

Signature

Printed Name

Tailor Each Letter

Every cover letter you write should be tailored to a particular employer. Writing an identical letter to each employer, while an especially easy method in this age of merge mailings, is not an effective one. The best way to make a positive impression is to avoid sending out "cold" cover letters (letters to people with whom you have no contact); it is better to send "warm" cover letters (letters to people suggested to you by other people). A letter that starts with "I am writing to you at the suggestion of Mr. So-and-So" will get more attention than one that starts with "I am responding to your ad in the *New York Times*." The best way to develop a target list for warm letters is to engage in networking. (See Chapter 8 for more information on networking.)

If you do not have the name of a mutual contact to use and must write a cold cover letter, whenever possible, address your cover letter to a specific person—the contact person listed in an advertisement, the person to whom you were referred, the hiring partner, or the recruitment coordinator. Starting a letter with "Dear Sir or Madam" is a clear sign of a mass-mailed form cover letter.

To further tailor your cover letter, you not only have to know about yourself, you also have to know about the employer to whom you are writing. The more you know about the employer, the more personalized your cover letter will be. Your letter should articulate why you are interested in working for this particular employer. To do so, you need to have information about the kind of work the employer does. This is where your research comes into play.

Employers do not react favorably to receiving a cover letter that demonstrates an applicant's ignorance about their organization. For example, if the employer to whom you are writing is a law firm that specializes in tax litigation, a cover letter in which you discuss your experience and interest in admiralty law will make a very bad impression. Similarly, a letter to a legal aid organization that focuses on your prosecution experience, but does not mention your advocacy skills and your desire to provide defendants with representation, will make a less than favorable impression.

On the other hand, if you are writing to a firm that specializes in bankruptcy law, a cover letter that discusses your internship with a bankruptcy judge and the bankruptcy-related courses you have taken is likely to be viewed favorably. Employers should not feel that they are just one of hundreds of employers to whom you are applying. A cover letter that sounds sincere and well-thought-out will always make a better impression than a rote-sounding form letter for a mass mailing.

Out-of-Town Employers

If you are writing to an out-of-town employer, let the employer know why you are interested in that particular geographic area. You may, for example, have ties that are related to family, bar membership, or your intention to take the bar. Employers are wary of interviewing someone from out of town unless it is clear they are serious about relocating. Be sure that you have sufficiently demonstrated that your interest in the employer's geographic area is more than a passing one. If you plan to be in the employer's city, let them know when you intend to be there. The fact that you will be in town may lead some employers to grant you an interview.

Why the Employer Should Be Interested in You

After you have informed the employer of the reasons you are interested in them, state why they should be interested in you. This is where the time you invested in your personal inventory pays off. Tell employers about yourself. Sell yourself! Point out any special qualifications, strengths, experience or other skills that you may have and demonstrate to employers how these skills, strengths, and qualities will be of use to them.

Sell yourself to each particular employer. Try to determine what the employer values in an employee and point out how you fit the bill. If you are applying to an organization in which lawyers carry a large caseload and work under short deadlines, let the employer know that you are hardworking and can handle pressure well. If you are responding to an advertisement, do not regurgitate the wording of the advertisement; paraphrase the ad and indicate how you meet its stated requirements.

When writing to a small law firm, for example, you may stress your independence and your ability to take initiative and work on your own. When writing to a public interest employer, on the other hand, you may stress your commitment to public interest work and describe specific experiences that demonstrate such a commitment.

In addition to focusing on your skills, strengths, and qualities, highlight any relevant work experiences and course work. Tell an employer who specializes in tax work about the A+ you received in taxation. Let an employer who specializes in environmental law know about your experience working for the Environmental Protection Agency. Ensure that your letter is tailored to meet the needs of the particular employer to whom you are applying.

Crossover Applications

A strong cover letter is especially important for lawyers attempting to cross over to a different area of practice or to a nonlegal position. Do not forget about your *transferable skills* in making such an application. Transferable skills are skills you have developed in one context that can be put to use in a different context. For example, skills developed in a legal setting that are applicable to a nonlegal position (or vice versa).

Do not expect an employer to recognize your transferable skills simply by reviewing your resume. You must use your cover letter to make the connection explicit. For example, if you worked as a banker before (or during) law school, highlight the skills you developed as a banker that would be applicable in a corporate legal setting. Similarly, if you are a corporate lawyer applying for a nonlegal business position, emphasize the business skills you have developed in your practice. Or, if you are a real estate lawyer wishing to switch into the bankruptcy area, focus on your work in real estate financial restructurings. And, if you have been out of work but have been active as a volunteer, discuss the projects you have worked on and point out the skills you have developed as a result. In this way, your cover letter helps you market the skills you have that are likely to be of interest to a potential employer.

What to Leave Out

Just as important as what to include in a cover letter is what you should leave out. A cover letter is not the place to bring up anything damaging or anything that weakens your application by making you appear less attractive as a candidate. For example, do not state that you are interested in working for an employer because you feel the experience will strengthen your existing skills. Do not lead an employer to think that any of your skills need strengthening.

A cover letter is your opportunity to sell yourself and present yourself in the most positive light possible. Thus, if your law school grades were not good, do not attempt to explain this in your cover letter. Or, if you were laid off, the cover letter is not the place to bring up this fact. This kind of information, which requires explanation, is better left for an interview than a cover letter. Including such information may prevent you from getting an interview at all.

What Else to Remember

It is important to remember that your cover letter is the first sample of your writing that a potential employer sees. To the employer, your cover letter is a demonstration of the quality of legal work you are able to perform. It must, therefore, be as well written as possible. Write in a logical, smooth manner with appropriate transitions and do not include any irrelevant information. If your cover letter is not well written, an employer will assume your legal writing skills are not adequate. Similarly, if it contains any typographical or grammatical errors, an employer will assume your legal work is careless. Thus, before mailing any cover letter, proofread it carefully and have someone else read it over as well.

Closing Paragraph

End your cover letter stating the action you plan to take or the action you would like the employer to take. Do not, however, make a statement that indicates that you assume you will be granted an interview. This can be viewed as presumptuous. Rather, you can state that you plan to contact the employer in a week or so to follow up, or that you look forward to hearing from the employer.

A cover letter is an important tool in the job search process. Take the time to make it as effective as possible.

CHAPTER 16

Interviewing Techniques

Michael K. Magness
Carolyn M. Wehmann

Preparing for the Interview

Successful interviewees have one very attractive trait in common: they have spent considerable time planning their career strategy, and it shows. Lawyers are impressed by interviewees who know what they seek in a legal employer and what they want from their careers. You should follow closely the career planning steps outlined in Parts I and II of this book. You must carefully choose how and where you wish to use your talents—and to what type of employer you wish to commit your energy and your future—before you interview with prospective employers.

When preparing for interviews, learn certain key facts about the employer: size, major practice areas and important current work matters, the identity of notable partners or senior lawyers and their notable achievements, and policies that govern the management and training of junior lawyers. You should also try to obtain information about other employers in the same city (or practice area) considered their "competitors." Your knowledge of each employer will be clearer if you have a sense of the local or regional market. It also will be easier to formulate questions if you can develop a broad perspective on each of your potential employers.

Another helpful way to prepare for interviews is to search out people you believe to be knowledgeable about the employers with whom you plan to interview. Law school career-planning offices often have on file written statements from students or graduates describing their employment experiences. You also will find your classmates, colleagues, and law professors eager to offer their opinions on any number of "facts" about the employers that you are considering. A word of caution, however: Critical employment decisions should not be based on the advice of those notorious twins, myth

144

and innuendo. When making a career choice, try to rule out any information that you suspect is based on hearsay, based on short-term (or no direct) work experience at the employer's office, too outdated to be relevant today, or information that is based on a single negative incident that may color the speaker's ability to offer a balanced view. Instead, to help counteract the effect of biased personal advice, you should obtain information from *as many different sources as possible,* measuring the value of each against your own criteria for evaluating each of your employment options.

Formulating questions to use in the interview is another helpful preparation exercise. You will be able to project a relaxed, confident demeanor if you have prepared thoughtfully for your conversation with interviewers. Obviously, you will want to avoid creating the impression that you have a "canned act" to perform. Your prepared questions should be designed to elicit two kinds of information: (1) elaboration on the employer's practice, lawyers' current (and past) work matters, working style and lifestyle, and other issues that are particularly important to you in making your career choice; and (2) a variety of insights into individual lawyers' experiences that will help you predict what your own work experience might be like. In addition to your set of general interview questions, you will want to prepare questions relating specifically to each employer.

There are several other reasons for preparing your interview questions in advance. Very often, *interviewers* will not be well prepared. If the interviewer begins by asking, "What can I tell you about my firm?" you will have your set of questions ready. Sometimes, awkward pauses will disrupt the flow of your interview, or you might find that the interviewer is not given to easy conversation. In these situations, a series of prepared questions can save the day and spare your nerves.

You should spend a considerable amount of time thinking about the kinds of questions that *you* will be asked so that you can prepare the general answers that you will use in interviews. Not all of these themes can be listed here, but the sampling below should help you become comfortable discussing a whole range of facts:

- Your past academic and work experiences
- Your legal abilities, career goals, and your career and life choices thus far
- Your achievements and your failures
- Your strong points and the areas you have worked to improve
- The personal qualities and skills that you use to get your work done effectively

If you take time to think about your education and work experiences in retrospect, and if you can articulate realistic career goals, your answers to interviewers' questions about your past performance will flow quite naturally. If you have formulated in advance your answers to difficult questions, you will be less vulnerable to unanticipated questions or the stress questions some interviewers like to use.

The Initial Interview: Screening

The initial interview is a critical meeting. As a result of this meeting, the applicant and the employer each make a decision about whether to pursue their interests in each other. You must be ready to seize this opportunity by preparing good questions and thoughtful, honest answers to the questions that you think an interviewer may ask during an initial interview.

The initial interview is the time to ask good, to-the-point questions that will clarify specifics of the employer's practice, the work of junior lawyers, and any other information that is basic to your decision to pursue (or not pursue) your initial interest in that employer. A trained interviewer will allow you only five to ten minutes to ask questions, but inexperienced interviewers often will leave the interview—and the questioning—entirely up to you. When you have an opportunity to ask questions, *ask your specific question first*; if time permits, you also can use several of the general questions you will ask of all interviewers. Above all, your questions must be appropriate to an initial interview; they should convey your interest in, enthusiasm for, and knowledge of the employer's practice. This is not the time to ask when salary levels will be increased.

Your answers to questions, like your prepared questions, should be to the point, revealing your preparation for the interview and your enthusiasm for working with a particular employer. An articulate presentation is important, so pause and take time to think before you respond to important questions about your experiences and goals. Remember, the way you feel about your accomplishments will be as apparent to interviewers as the quality of those accomplishments. If you take time to prepare fully, you will be able to project a positive image of yourself in interviews instead of an unfocused or apologetic one.

Once you have prepared yourself for interviews, you will need to practice another skill: listening. Active listening means being on the alert for information from the interviewer that answers your basic questions about the employer. This information will provide you with the keys to asking additional probing questions during the interview. Lazy listeners lose critical information. They miss opportunities to hear about issues that are at the root of the specific questions that they have asked.

Because you can listen four times faster than a person normally speaks, you will be able to measure what the interviewer is saying against what you believe to be true about the employer. Good listening allows you to *test your various hypotheses* about the employment situation that he or she describes. Are your basic needs for a certain type of practice, work style, and lifestyle likely to be met? Listen carefully, for at the end of the interview you must ask, "Does this opportunity interest me? What about this job/employer/interviewer intrigues me? Is this a place where I will feel comfortable and be free to develop to my full potential?" As you take note of (and verify) the facts the interviewer shares during an initial interview, you also should *listen to the attitudes expressed* below the surface of the interviewer's sales pitch. After the interview, you will have to ascertain what the limitations of this opportunity may be and what reservations the interviewer conveyed. By listening and carefully interjecting questions during the interview, you will be able to elicit and investigate a wide variety of facts and subjective information on which to base your decision: Should you pursue your initial interest in the employer if you are considered further?

Of course, the goal of the initial interview is to make a good—and lasting—impression. You want to be invited for another series of follow-up interviews with other lawyers at the employer's office. To make a good impression and avoid the pitfalls of initial interviews, you must prepare to take an active (but not aggressive) role in the process. Here are the top five avoidable pitfalls:

1. General lack of knowledge about or interest expressed in the employer
2. Failure to convey more information than is outlined on your resume
3. Failure to make a lasting impression on the interviewer
4. Lack of attention to the serious business purpose of the initial interview
5. Failure to demonstrate that you meet the employer's minimum standards for intellectual capability, motivation, and positive personal qualities

The Follow-Up Interview: Selecting

Follow-up interviews provide an opportunity for you to fine-tune your initial decisions about suitable employers. During these follow-up interviews, you and the employer will be asking more-probing questions to determine how good your mutual fit is likely to be. While all of the strategies of initial interviewing also apply to the follow-up interview, some important differences do exist, both in terms of the types of questions you should prepare to ask (and be asked) and the interpersonal skills you need to use to set the tone for this kind of interview. These differences relate to the fact that the balance of power shifts toward you, the well-qualified candidate, during follow-up interviews. Up to this point, you have had to do most of the "selling"; as your interviews progress, however, you and your prospective employer are on more equal ground. If you have choices to make among employers, you will be selecting the best opportunity as well as continuing to sell yourself. Employers can be expected to do more selling than they did initially, but they also will be asking for more in-depth information to ascertain the chemistry (or fit) between them and you.

What questions are appropriate for follow-up interviews? Ask the questions about the employer's substantive practice that you wanted to ask but could not fit into your initial interview, and ask the work style/lifestyle questions that you might have misinterpreted in the initial interview, such as how matters are staffed and how young lawyers are supervised, trained, evaluated, and otherwise developed as they move up the ladder. Take care, though, about asking specific questions about billable hours, parenting leaves, or flextime unless these matters are critical to your selection of an employer. These questions are best discussed when an offer is in hand.

Because you will be meeting a number of additional individuals in the follow-up setting, you can feel perfectly comfortable asking the same questions of everyone you meet. The variety of their responses should paint a more accurate and intricate picture of the employer, the office environment, and the people who have chosen to work there.

There are three types of questions you can expect to answer in follow-up interviews. Unfortunately, the first type is the one most often encountered and, from your perspective, the least useful: the screening of your resume and credentials—your grades and basic work experience—that already took place during your initial interview. Too many follow-up interviewers cling to this type because they do not know what else is important or how to get at the deeper, more-subjective criteria, such as your motivation and the personal qualities and skills that indicate your potential to perform well on the job. Be prepared to discuss, with limitless patience, the same facts that got you through the initial interview.

The second type of question is intended to reveal the substantive knowledge, interest, and experience you have in a particular field or fields of law. You should be meeting lawyers in your areas of interest or practice at this follow-up stage of interviewing, and they will be curious about what your experiences have been and whether you will fit the particular needs that they have. This line of questioning offers you an opportunity (which may not have existed in the initial interview) to reveal your knowledge, experience, and intellectual qualities, and to illustrate the many, varied connections between your interests and experiences and the employer's needs. Again, it is important to prepare for these interviews. You should be comfortable fielding almost any question relating to your legal expertise and career interests.

The last type of question deals with your motivation and personal qualities. These are questions for which you should prepare carefully. It would be unfortunate to miss getting an offer because you appeared unmotivated to do an employer's work and instead were preoccupied with a discussion of the employer's benefit plan. Often an interviewee will misjudge the level of motivation that the employer expects and will lose out because he or she seems either too disengaged or too aggressive during the interview. Lawyers who use follow-up interviews effectively will spend quite a lot of time asking probing questions in this area to determine your potential fit. Your answers, therefore, must candidly articulate your strengths, thoughtfulness, and seriousness, and they should characterize you as a "good risk." You must know yourself and what you are looking for in any employer to answer these questions honestly and positively.

Good listening skills are as much in order during your follow-up interview as they were during the initial interview. If you fail to hear what various interviewers tell you about their own original perceptions about the employer, the aspects of their practice that differed from their expectations, and what still interests them about their career, you run the risk of making a career decision based only on your *initial* impressions. Furthermore, if you find yourself talking with interviewers who are delirious with joy about their experiences working shoulder to shoulder with their comrades around the clock, and if these individuals are not much like you in a variety of subjective areas, failing to listen may mean that you will be working shoulder to shoulder with a lot of smart, motivated people you do not like very well. The bottom line is: Pay attention to what the people you will be working with say about the day-to-day work they do, their career goals, and what else they have time for in their professional lives. Listen!

In short, if you want to improve your chances of getting an offer, start out by being prepared, then practice your interviewing skills so that your questions and answers will flow smoothly. Sell yourself by illustrating the motivation and personal qualities that will make you a desirable colleague. Be well informed about the employer and know why you have accepted the invitation for follow-up interviews. You will often be asked for those reasons. If you can, convey your commitment to your work, but balance that seriousness with a sense of humor. At the end of the interview, lawyers will ask themselves, "Is this someone I will trust to take over an assignment for me? Is this someone with whom I look forward to working, on a personal level, especially in stressful situations?"

Final Tips on Interviewing Strategies

The most common reasons given by interviewers for rejecting candidates are as follows:

- The candidate did not indicate a strong interest in the employer or was not knowledgeable about the position available.
- The candidate did not make a convincing connection between his or her knowledge and experience and the employer's needs.
- The candidate was not memorable, either in terms of resume credentials or personal presence during the interview.

If you are prepared for an interview, you should be comfortable with what you are selling. *There are no shortcuts* to taking time to assess your strengths and weaknesses, to determine your needs, and to plan a career strategy if you want to succeed in presenting yourself effectively during interviews.

You will occasionally encounter difficult questions during interviews. These can be divided into two categories: questions that you find difficult to answer because they probe areas about which you are uncomfortable and questions that are inappropriate (or illegal) for the purposes of an employment interview.

The answer to dealing with difficult questions is prepare, prepare, *prepare!* You, more than anyone else, can best anticipate the employment questions that you will find difficult to answer. During your self-assessment, focus on the sensitive areas in your background and think about ways to respond in a positive, confident fashion. You want to give thoughtful, candid answers to difficult questions. If your answers appear to be canned, rehearsed, or superficial, the interviewer may continue to question you in these sensitive areas and you may not be able to move on to a discussion of your positive selling points.

Inappropriate questions often cause the greatest amount of concern because you will be unwilling to answer these questions, but equally unwilling to forego an employment opportunity by walking out of the interview. I encourage you not to interview with "a chip on your shoulder." Often inappropriate questions indicate thoughtlessness or personal biases on the part of the interviewer, but do not necessarily reflect the views of the employer as an organization. If a question or the interview situation is blatantly discriminatory (such as sexual harassment), you may decide to excuse yourself and pursue the matter directly with the employer. In most other situations, providing a forthright answer indicates that you are aware that the question is inappropriate (or illegal) without alienating the interviewer in return. For example, you might respond to a question about your spouse's career plans by saying, "My (spouse) is willing to relocate if I decide to accept an offer of employment in (city). Is this an issue that (employer) will weigh in deciding whether to consider me further for this position?" Ultimately, you want to keep your options open and retain control of the situation. Then, if you receive an offer and are interested in the employer, you can and should raise the issue of inappropriate questioning before making a final decision.

Dos and Don'ts of Interviewing

To interview effectively you must:

- Prepare for the interview by assessing what the right career options are for you, including fields of law, cities, and lifestyle.
- Obtain information about the employer from as many sources as possible.
- Prepare questions and answers to use in interviews.
- Be prepared to meet different types of interviewers and learn to vary your interviewing style.
- Dress and act professionally to make a positive impression.
- Take control of the interview by knowing what you want from the experience.
- Remember the differences between initial and follow-up interviews.
- Ask thoughtful questions and provide thoughtful answers.
- Listen to the interviewer and gather information.
- Make a convincing but low-key sales pitch to assure that the interviewer will remember you and know why you are interested in the position.
- Maintain a professional demeanor during the interview, even in the face of questions that you find inappropriate.
- Keep your career goals firmly in mind, and do not be swayed by what the employer wants to sell you or by hearsay from others.

- Remember that the interview is a learning experience and a business opportunity, not a crisis situation.
- Relax and be confident. If you have done your homework, you will succeed in landing the job that will be right for you.

Successful interviewing is a skill that is developed by a combination of perception, preparation, and practice. If you can dedicate yourself to these tasks, you not only will succeed in landing a job, you will launch a productive and satisfying professional career.

CHAPTER 17

Negotiating Salary and Benefits

Laura J. Hagen

Overview

Just when we thought that we had seen the end of the excesses of the 1970s and 1980s, the legal market for lateral hires has exploded. The profession is placing increased emphasis on law as a business and on professional management in law firms; accordingly, increased attention is being paid to controlling costs. Nevertheless, law firms are being faced with a significant shortage of trained associates, especially in the transactional areas. This shortage has led to a frantic round of raises in compensation and "salary wars" by firms attempting to attract the best and brightest. Moreover, the market is showing differentiation in salary between different tiers of law firms: the more profitable are able to maintain higher salaries, while the less profitable fall behind. Corporations are also being challenged, as law firm salaries outstrip the ability of businesses to stay competitive.

In this volatile marketplace, it is more important than ever for the candidate to have a clear focus and the best, most current information available in order to negotiate a satisfactory compensation package.

Basic Compensation Schemes

Law firms are the major employers of lawyers (according to the American Bar Association's state surveys for 1997, over 975,000 lawyers are active and licensed). Corporations, however, increased their hiring of lawyers during the 1980s (according to the *Directory of Corporate Counsel*, 76,355 lawyers were employed by corporations in 1997–1998). You will face different concerns in negotiating a salary in each setting.

Law Firm Associates

Law firm salaries in the 1990s have become more differentiated, both from firm to firm and within a given law firm. Performance-based compensation systems have become the norm. In the past, most firms categorized lawyers by law school graduating class and compensated them accordingly. The progression was "lockstep," with raises given automatically each year at set variations between the classes. Lawyers within a class were treated equally, irrespective of the quality of their work, the number of hours they billed, or the amount of business they brought to the firm. In the years preceding partnership, each class received graduated raises as new associates joined the firm out of law school.

This lockstep system no longer describes the situation in the vast majority of firms. With increased competition, many firms evaluate lawyer performance in terms of quality of work, number of hours billed, and the intangibles a lawyer brings to the table. Lawyer compensation, once immune from discussion as well as scrutiny, is now more open to negotiation.

Any lawyer considering a move should investigate the target firm's compensation system for both partners and associates. At one extreme is the seniority-over-performance compensation of the lockstep system. At the other end is the "eat what you kill" system, in which individual practitioners are compensated on the basis of their particular billing rather than the performance of the firm as a whole. This can result in less collegiality and hamper the ability of the firm to think and act as a unit.

With the trend toward performance-based compensation, associates are subject to within-class compensation distinctions. Although pay for the first two or three years may be the same across the board, many firms now rank associates by performance and assign salaries accordingly. Thus, some firms have a high, low, and medium compensation designations within each class. Other compensation schemes, such as a base salary with a profit-sharing component or a base salary with a bonus calculated on the performance of the particular associate, the firm in general, or a combination of the two, are becoming more common. At the more senior associate levels, there may be a reward for bringing business to the firm.

You should understand the basic ranges of compensation at your target firm from the outset. Do not waste your time or the time of the employer in a firm where compensation ranges fall below those you find acceptable. If you are a lateral, or experienced lawyer, you must understand that many structural factors contribute to the ranges of compensation within a firm. Do not expect that a firm with a lower-than-acceptable compensation scheme will magically recognize your true value and produce an offer comparable to the salary in a different type of firm.

It is important to remember that the appropriate time to address specific compensation issues is when an offer is being contemplated or has been made. Some employers will not risk making you an offer unless they feel certain you will find the compensation acceptable. This is usually ascertained by discussing "hypothetical" packages. A lateral's leverage is the greatest before a move, and all compensation issues should be on the table for the negotiation. It is a mistake to accept a compensation package you believe is inappropriate with the expectation that it will all work out later. Nevertheless, compensation is a delicate issue, and the candidate must walk a thin line between negotiating an appropriate package and appearing to be overreaching. In the end, you must have confidence in the employer and in your senses of shared values.

Negotiating Status

When negotiating with a law firm, lawyers should consider two significant elements. One is the class within which the lawyer is placed. This often determines salary, or at least the range of salary that will be available to earn. The other is the designation of years to consideration for partnership status, an area in which there is little room for negotiation for laterals. Most firms demand at least a one- to two-year delay before considering a lateral for partnership. It may be in your best interests to divorce the consideration of the two issues and agree to be compensated within a class of graduation, but with a deferral for partnership consideration to a different class. Considerations that affect this decision include the need for exposure to various partners within the firm who will support the partnership decision, as well as the competitive composition of the classes. For example, if your class has five certain winners for partnership, you may be better off agreeing to a deferral.

Usually, a lawyer who is not already a partner cannot expect to gain that status in a lateral move. Whether a lawyer should accept an associate offer rather than demanding entry as a partner or a contract partner will be determined by his or her leverage in the marketplace. A lawyer with a practice area critical to the new firm may have the leverage to obtain the coveted "partner" designation. Another circumstance that may warrant the increase in title includes moving from a national firm to a more regional or local one. Often, a group head may be able to negotiate partnerships for key lieutenants as part of a package deal. A lateral must decide whether the title is deserved or required based on an analysis of all these factors. If you are moving, however, with the expectation that you will be bringing business, developing business, or building a department, you would be wise to view partner status as critical to the success of the venture. If these are the expectations you face, you should fight hard for the designation of a partner.

Partner Compensation

Partner compensation is generally determined as a share of the firm's profits, usually allocated as "points." At least a portion of this amount is usually paid out in advance throughout the year as a "draw" against year-end results of the firm. There are wide variations in compensation schemes, and it is important for a lateral to understand how compensation is determined in any firm being considered. It is critical to be slated at the appropriate level, as compensation that is too high or too low can be detrimental to integration in the new firm. Variables considered in determining partner compensation include hours billed and collected, generation of business, contributions to the firm (including management and training) and profitability of work (premiums collected or write-offs taken), technical contributions and importance of practice area, contributions to the profession, and seniority. In some firms, partners are grouped in classes by points assigned. Moving up or down depends upon an evaluation of your work and your contributions to the firm. Usually, this is viewed on a rolling basis so that consistent trends over a period of years rather than spikes or valleys in a particular year will govern compensation decisions.

A lateral must be clear about how compensation decisions are made in a firm, as these vary from a tightly controlled process determined by one or two key players to a free-for-all. A common system for determining allocation of profits is for each partner to write an annual review of his or her performance for the fiscal year and recommend action to a "compensation committee." In some firms, partners evaluate each other and state what they believe their peers should be taking home. At the other end of the scale are firms in which each partner is allocated a share of overhead and pays other firm lawyers a percentage for completing work. The partner retains the balance of his or her collections.

Income or contract partners are a hybrid category. They are usually held out to the world as "partners," but internally they may not share in profits or participate in management. They may be treated either as employees or partners for tax purposes. A lateral should be clear on the tax treatment of this category in the new firm, as well as on standards for advancement to equity partnership.

Financial concerns for a lateral partner include capital contributions, unfunded liabilities, and personal guarantees. Moving a book of business is always uncertain, and a lateral must be careful in making representations to a new firm. It is advisable to consult a lawyer with experience in the laws and ethical rules applicable to partners moving business from one firm to another. One must be particularly careful about not contacting clients until the current firm is advised. State law governs many issues involved and varies from jurisdiction to jurisdiction.

Book of Business

Valuing a book of business for negotiating purposes is inherently difficult because the client ultimately decides whether a matter will move with you or remain at your old firm. In arriving at your estimate, you should look at a three- to five-year history of your billings and understand any trends your numbers reveal. Work that you have originated will generally move with you unless it is an exceedingly complex matter in which lawyers in your old firm have been deeply involved; in such a case it may not be cost-effective for the client to move the work. Similarly, matters that are near conclusion may not move. A client's history with a firm may also influence whether the business moves or not. If there is a long history between the client and the firm, the business may not move even though the client has an excellent relationship with the handling lawyer. Similarly, a client with widespread relations in the firm may be reluctant to move the business. And even a client that is willing to move may ask for concessions as lawyers in the new firm are brought up to speed. These concessions can affect the value of the business, at least in the short term.

In valuing a book, you must carefully evaluate potential conflicts with the new firm. These can range from direct conflicts, such as the new firm representing parties openly averse to your client, to more indirect conflicts, such as the new firm representing within-industry competitors of your client. You must also carefully evaluate the billing rates at the new firm. Are they significantly higher? This might discourage the client from moving. As a lateral you must also evaluate the type of business you receive from a client: Is it steady and repetitive and likely to continue, or is it an infrequent relationship or a one-shot deal? If a lawyer is being hired for a particular expertise, where are the competitors who might have a chance at taking business away? Also, is the proposed firm comparable to or better than the old one, and will you be able to get the new firm on the "approved" list? It is better to be conservative in estimating your book than to overestimate and disappoint your new firm in your first year. One way to protect yourself is to estimate conservatively for negotiating your base compensation, but provide a method of sharing in the success of your practice if you exceed expectations (for example, a bonus consisting of a certain percentage of all billings in excess of a stated dollar amount). Valuing a book is an art rather than a science, and both sides must be prepared for the unexpected. This is why lateral moves must make long-term sense for both the candidate and the employer.

In-House Compensation

In corporate settings, compensation is both less complicated (the cash side) and more complicated (the benefits side). Salaries generally are set by the budget for the legal department that allows so many dollars for slots—and by the titles assigned to the slots—rather than based on years out of law school. For example, a general counsel may have a lawyer slot at a certain range of compensation into which he or she could place a lawyer within a wide range of years since law school graduation. Corporations are far less concerned with a candidate's year of graduation than with his or her substantive practice experience. The bonus is usually a much higher percentage of the total cash compensation in a corporation than in a law firm. Stock options also can become a significant part of the compensation package.

Corporate benefits often are more significant than those provided by law firms. The value of these benefits often can more than offset the lower cash component of compensation sometimes offered in the corporate setting. Although corporate salaries generally are lower than those offered in firms, there are other obvious trade-offs, such as escaping the pressure of the billable hour and the need to become a rainmaker. Other factors, such as enhanced health insurance or retirement benefits or miscellaneous perquisites such as telecommuting, flextime, casual dress, on-site childcare, or extra vacation time, may make a move worthwhile for a particular candidate. You should not view a corporation as a panacea, however, because success in a corporate law department requires many of the same skills needed in a law firm. Moreover, the edge in lifestyle previously thought to have been offered by corporations has lessened dramatically in recent years. Internal clients can be as demanding and the work as time-consuming as a law firm client base (see Chapter 23).

Preparing to Negotiate: The Rules

The cardinal rule of negotiating a salary in either context is "know thyself and thy market." Before negotiating, sit down and review your career in depth. Look at old time sheets, diaries, and reviews to refresh recollections as to all substantive areas of the law with which you have dealt. This will give you a better sense of your expertise and your value to potential employers.

In addition to assessing your own skills, you should review your salary history, including not only cash compensation, but health insurance, life insurance, pension, and profit sharing. This will give a range for what your skills should be worth in the marketplace. Examine your W-2s to see what has been included. If there are stock options or unvested pension plans, become familiar with vesting provisions. It would be foolish to begin a job search shortly before a major vesting anniversary. Take into consideration the timing of a move and its effect on lost bonus or payout for work brought to the firm.

Know your market! Know how your compensation ranks in relation to others within your organization. If it will appear out of line to a new employer, you should be able to explain that it was average or high for your past employer, and you should gather information about compensation in the market that you are investigating. This information is best gathered from peers and secondary sources, such as trade publication surveys or legal search consultants. In many cities, groups of associates compile salary surveys that can prove invaluable. When gathering salary information from others, do not put them on the spot by asking how much money they make. Rather, ask them how they would estimate the compensation value of a lawyer within a specific class and possessing certain skills. Be sure to ask them to make this estimation within their own organization and to share what they know about compensation in other environments. Most people are happy to discuss compensation in general terms when the question does not appear to be directed at their own compensation.

The third rule is know your employer. It will not do you any good to try to negotiate a "New York" salary in a law firm that has consistently been in the lower to middle range of salaries within its market. The ultimate salary is not only a reflection of the firm's interest in you, but also factors intrinsic to the firm, such as profitability. If you do not have sources within the firm, perhaps some of your classmates in other organizations have friends who will share this information with you.

Above all, know what you want. Before you go into your final set of interviews, have a clear idea of what compensation package would be acceptable to you. If there are any major issues (such as stock options you are about to lose and for which you would like to be compensated), be prepared to raise them at this time. Timing is of utmost importance in negotiations. Employers do not like to go down the road with a candidate and receive an ugly surprise at the end when the candidate says, "By the way, I'd like you to cover that $100,000 bonus I'm going to lose by moving in November instead of January."

The Negotiation

If working with a search consultant, be frank with the search consultant on what the bottom line *really* is. The consultant, an ally in this process, wants the transaction to be completed and can offer helpful advice, not only as to a particular offer, but how that offer fits into the marketplace.

Respond to an offer in a timely manner. Employers are justified in assuming that when the process gets to this point, everybody is serious. Do not attempt to collect offers only to bring them back to a current employer as a means of increasing your salary. If you move a negotiation to the point of receiving an offer, be prepared to consider this offer seriously. Most offers are made subject to references checking out, although some employers insist on checking references from former employers before proceeding. Be careful on this point. Do not allow a prospective employer to contact your current employer until you receive an acceptable or workable offer. Also, understand whether there are any contingencies to the offer. Is the offer subject to a physical, a drug test, or a psychological examination or will those be handled before you must provide references?

If dissatisfied with any elements of the offer, be prepared to sit down and discuss them. If you feel the offer is below market, say so—and present your reasons for believing so. If the employer is off the mark, he or she will appreciate being educated on this point. Remember that your negotiating power is never so high as right before you accept the offer, since presumably the employer wants you. Once you have accepted, the power balance shifts dramatically.

Make sure that the terms of the offer are clear and in writing. It is customary for employers to send an offer letter. If there is a contingent component of your compensation, be certain that the contingencies are spelled out. If it is a bonus, the provisions pertaining to when it is due and what factors will determine whether or what portion of the bonus you will receive should be clear. For instance, is your performance based on written reviews or the performance of the firm or company? Is it a combination of both? If you have reached an agreement regarding consideration for partnership, be certain that this is part of the letter. This avoids possible misunderstandings later, where parties other than the one with whom you negotiated may question what was promised to you.

Conclusion

You should negotiate from a position of strength, the strength that derives both from your knowledge of yourself and your skills and from your knowledge of the market and how the market values your skills. Recognize that this is a business relationship and that the best time to structure this relationship is before you accept the offer. Preparation for the negotiation process can turn what might be an awkward and stressful situation into a positive beginning to a new professional relationship.

CHAPTER 18

Making the "Right" Career Decision

Robert A. Major, Jr.

You have successfully assessed your career plans and strategies. Based on that planning, you have identified what you want to do and how to go about achieving it. But how do you choose between competing opportunities that closely, though not perfectly, match your goals? What is the right job?

In the mid-1990s, lawyers confronted with a contracting supply of jobs were forced to make compromises. Savvy job-seeking lawyers became smarter shoppers. As we reach the end of the decade and enter the new millennium, the job market has shifted dramatically as the demand for lawyers has increased. But the analysis that job seekers employ should remain roughly the same. Lawyers who become smarter job seekers will have an edge over the competition, especially for the most sought-after positions.

Short-Term Goals

Making the right career choice depends heavily on defining your goals and making honest appraisals of how your job prospects achieve them. Part I of this book details useful approaches to goal identification. Training, for example, is an issue that concerns new lawyers. Dissatisfaction with training is the single biggest complaint voiced by junior lawyers. If you feel that your training has not been what it should, access to more or better training will clearly be on your list of goals to pursue the next time around. You know that mere assurances and recruiting pitches by prospective employers are not enough. You will want to know what constitutes the training program, how the employer tracks a lawyer's progress and responds to the need for improvement in certain areas, how the training program has evolved over time, and how the other junior lawyers have graded their training.

Many job seekers are seeking more interesting work. This is a tricky area, because much of what lawyers do is simply not that interesting. This is especially the case with more-junior lawyers, who usually are assigned the less-complicated, more-routine (yes, boring) tasks, such as preparing initial drafts of contracts or pleadings or coordinating document productions. Lawyers who are dissatisfied or bored with their work often have the suspicion that they may have chosen the wrong profession; they may be right. Many lawyers want to practice in "exotic" fields such as entertainment or media law or something with an international bent. While certainly there are practitioners in these specialties, the need in these fields is relatively low and usually offered to more senior lawyers. The competition is fierce. In the international area, language skills (meaning fluency in speaking and writing, not simple conversational skills) have become virtually mandatory.

A third short-term goal is "resume" value. Some lawyers seek a change to upgrade their resumes. They want to work for a more prestigious firm or to switch to an in-house position. The analysis here really should relate to a long-term goal: How will "upgrading" my resume fit in with my ultimate game plan? You must analyze carefully why you want to make a change and consider the risks, and the benefits, involved. For example, with the market shift in the late 1990s, "prestigious" law firms are broadening their criteria for admission, reaching deeper into classes, and expanding the number of law schools they recruit from. This newfound opportunity, however, comes with risks. If the market shifts again and forces law firms to take a hard look at their associates, who will stay and who may be deemed expendable?

A fourth short-term goal is the desire or need to make more money. Unless the change represents a significant increase in compensation (25 to 30 percent), this is not a particularly good basis on which to make a move. You may be trading "down" in other areas (such as collegiality or working more hours to justify that higher pay scale). In-house opportunities, especially with emerging growth companies, have caught the fancy of many in the job market who eye the potential offered by stock option packages; however, what goes up may come down, so you might be giving up security for something far more speculative. How risk-positive can you afford to be?

Long-Term Goals

Long-term goals, not surprisingly, provide a far better basis on which to evaluate a job opportunity.

Partnership or its equivalent: Partnership (if a law firm) or a senior position commanding responsibility and professional stature (in other organizations) is the Holy Grail of law practice. Lawyers by nature are competitors who need to feel that they are advancing toward a goal. That goal for decades was law firm partnership. The late 1980s and 1990s proved that making partner is not for everyone. Law firm economics have now focused on awarding partnership to those who can bring in business. Law firm management committees have long memories; we are unlikely to see this trend reversed.

Partnership, however, remains for many lawyers a greatly desired goal. Lawyers seeking new jobs must be brutally honest with themselves about just how important it is to "make" partner. If partnership is important, then the statistics each law firm compiles on how many associates make partner (and who they are) will be indispensable in deciding whether that is the place for you. If the law firm has completed a National Association for Law Placement (NALP) form, these figures are readily available. If not, you should ask (discreetly) for them.

The attraction of going "in-house" has probably been the single biggest market shift in the late 1990s, boosting the popularity of in-house practice to unprecedented heights. The diminishing partnership "pie," the aversion to hustling for new clients, the desire for more free time, and the notion that working for a corporation will allow one to get involved in business are all factors that have lawyers in private practice polishing up their resumes. And the legal press has widely heralded the evolution of in-house legal departments from their previous "backwater" status to state-of-the-art entities that function as influential partners within the corporate structure. When you add the financial potential showcased by several well-publicized success stories, you have what amounts to a headlong rush to the corporate counsel ranks. As a result, competition for these positions—especially general counsel spots or counsel to dynamic emerging growth companies—has increased proportionately.

Geography: In times of high demand, lawyers have greater choice in specifying where they want to practice. Naturally, the great money and power centers—New York, Chicago, Houston, Washington, Boston, Los Angeles, and San Francisco—attract a large percentage of new lawyers. The excitement of "big firm" practice, fat salaries, and prestige all provide an irresistible lure to the big city. As lawyers mature, of course, their priorities change, and technology has allowed most professionals new flexibility in where and how they do their jobs. Lawyers accustomed to new flexibility in simple everyday matters, such as personal banking, want to adapt these technologies to other aspects of their lives. Lifestyle issues *matter:* people are attracted to law firms with a culture based on something other than money. They are opting for geographic areas where they can raise a family or simply enjoy a better standard of living themselves. No one, after all, seriously enjoys a two-hour commute.

When assessing your long-term goals, you must choose carefully where you want to practice. Do not underestimate the power of a spouse's attachment to your in-laws, or the deep-seated love you have for location-specific leisure activities such as skiing or fishing. Technology and economic shifts have dispersed the practice of law across the land—indeed, across the globe—with increasingly little dilution in the quality of practice.

Colleagues: Interviewing in law school is rather serendipitous in terms of selecting future colleagues. Law students tend to focus on institutional reputation and practice areas when choosing a law firm. A stint as a summer associate allows a closer look at individual lawyers (and vice versa), but the summer associate experience can differ markedly from the regular associate experience. Regardless, the shifting personnel in firms means that you never know who will be there by the time you join or make partner.

A chronic complaint among lawyers—both partners and associates—relates to interpersonal issues: "The firm isn't the one I joined when I was a summer associate." "I keep thinking, do I really want to be partners with these people?" The answer to this problem is twofold: deep introspection to determine just how important collegiality is to you and research into the potential employer to find out what kind of place it is and how the lawyers and staff relate to each other. The latter is exceedingly difficult. The best sources are former employees willing to be candid with you. But even this approach has its obvious flaws. These assessments are highly subjective. Besides, people change, especially with greater attention paid institutionally to difficult or idiosyncratic personalities.

Factors Affecting Goal Attainment

Certain overriding factors affect your selection of a job and the means to secure it. These factors are practicality, flexibility, and self-assessment.

Practicality: Practicality is essential to becoming the "smart-shopper" lawyer. One aspect of this is getting a sense of what kind of practice areas are in demand and molding yourself to fit that demand. Although law is becoming increasingly specialized, there always will be certain generic practice areas. People always will bring lawsuits, so there always will be litigators. People will always want their business affairs negotiated and documented, so there will always be business lawyers. Certain practice areas, however, have experienced decline. Maritime law, for example, has slowed down because of containerization and other methods of transporting goods. Environmental law, a darling of the job market in the early 1990s, has seen its popularity wax, then wane.

Geography is also a limiting factor, even with the broadening influence of technology. Lawyers who want to practice international law should not set their hearts on living in Dubuque, Iowa. Those with fluency in Chinese, for example, are better off on the West Coast than in the Southeast or Maine. Entertainment law is flourishing in Los Angeles and New York, not San Francisco or Washington, D.C. Practice in the life sciences area invariably is linked to places with preeminent research institutions.

Flexibility: Your skills should be broad enough to allow for cycles in practice areas. In the early 1990s, real estate across the country was significantly depressed, causing some anxious moments for practitioners in that field. Fortunately, most real estate lawyers had enough flexibility in their skills to respond. They became workout and restructuring lawyers. The cycle reversed itself in the late 1990s when real estate lawyers were in high demand. Unfortunately, relatively few had entered the field, so the market saw an acute shortage. You should be careful to widen your practice to be able to shift areas if your main interest area falls into decline.

Self-assessment: One advantage that experienced lawyers have over neophytes is the fact that practicing law no longer is theoretical study. Practitioners have a sense of what they like, and do not like, about their work. For example, a common complaint from litigators is that they are tired of the constant battle of litigation and disturbed by what they see as a waste of human and economic resources. After years of warring with opposing counsel, many have turned inward and discovered that they are happiest when they are conciliators. This self-discovery often is a bit late, because—as everyone knows—employers are pyramids; one's "marketability" tends to narrow with seniority. Thus, it is important to make these critical self-assessments that will guide your career choices as early in your work life as possible.

Another factor gaining importance in law firm practice is whether the lawyer is capable of attracting business, the "rainmaking" syndrome. The economics of law firm practice emphasize business development; lawyers come under pressure to bring in clients, especially as they mature. For many law firms, business development is the sine qua non of partnership. Lawyers should factor this into their self-assessments when evaluating whether a law firm practice is right for them.

Research: Knowledge Is Power

Knowledge also is crucial to making job shoppers into *smart* job shoppers. It is an enduring curiosity that lawyers who willingly commit hours to studying the most minute statutory or case law to prove a point will often rely on instinct and superficial research when deciding their own career choices.

The legal profession has been revolutionized in the past quarter century by the amount of information available on law firms and, to a lesser extent, other employers such as corporations. The *American Lawyer,* the *National Law Journal,* and the local legal and popular press have unlocked what previously were the sealed vaults closed to the public eye. Today's law firms, with their marketing directors and spokespersons, now rush to tell their story to anyone who will listen.

The story, of course, is always mixed. No institution is without its problems. This is particularly true in a profession with more than its share of prima donnas. The point is not to find a flawless firm or corporation. The point is to find an employer with fewer of the traits that you find most objectionable.

You can start with the printed materials prepared by the employer itself. These, naturally, tell the "party line," but they are useful starting points. If the employer is a law firm and has completed an NALP form, be sure to obtain one. This form contains important data on billable hours broken down between associates and partners, the number of partners promoted from the associate ranks, the number of laterals, associate compensation, pro bono policies, and much more.

Law firm brochures are of limited value, although exceptions do exist. More useful are the materials prepared by individual practice groups; be sure to ask if there is one for your practice area. The Internet has also become an increasingly popular and useful resource. Most employers have Web pages. A principal advantage of the Internet is that these sites are updated fairly often. For example, a law firm's web page usually has a more accurate count of its lawyers than Martindale-Hubbell.

Press reports and third parties are great sources of information. Be careful that information contained in press stories is current. Placement directors of local law schools and local headhunters usually are treasure troves of current information—if you can get them to talk to you.

Even better are lawyers formerly employed by the law firm or the company in which you are interested. You can identify them by comparing this year's Martindale-Hubbell with last year's. The local bar association will have their current addresses. Is it appropriate to ask former employees about what it was like at their former firm? Certainly. If your potential employer finds it appropriate to check your references, then you may—and should—do the same. Besides, it is in the employer's best interest to maximize the chances of a successful marriage.

Making Job Selection Comport with Goals

The following exercise is a simple way to identify how different job opportunities fare in comparison with each other.

The first step in the exercise is to list all the factors that are important to you. Location, compensation, the challenge of the work, your colleagues, potential for advancement, training, and "resume value" may be among the factors. The second step is to rate, on a 1-to-10 scale, just how important each of the factors is to you. For example, if you really do not care where you practice, as long as you make partner somewhere, location will score very low while potential for advancement will score very high. The third step is to rate each of your opportunities according to each category. Then it is a matter of doing the math and comparing the totals.

You may be surprised at the result. Many people end up changing the relative weights accorded each of the factors, if only by a point or two. The exercise helps them examine their priorities and the importance they attach to different factors. Changing the weighting also may indicate that the lawyer has a "gut" favorite deep down that should be the mathematical winner, but is not.

Your gut feelings are important. To sort them through, sit down with someone you really trust and who knows you very well. The best person is a friend or advisor who has no interest in the outcome other than a desire to see you happy. This person will be able to spot when you are fooling yourself, or at least when you are inappropriately allocating values to different factors. Tell this person about the process and your opinions, including honestly appraising the choices in front of you. Discuss the pros and cons and pay particular attention to the grid—especially if it did not produce the result you expected at the outset of the process. You will likely hear the right answer in the discussion, or you may know it in advance. The exercise will usually confirm it.

PART IV

Career Options

CHAPTER 19

Practice Areas

Brion A. Bickerton

In the early 1990s, the country was in the grips of a severe recession. The times are better now, but we learned a valuable lesson. There is no longer an unlimited amount of legal work to be shared among the mushrooming number of lawyers. As we enter the new millennium with approximately 1 million lawyers—one for every 250 people—there is more competition for less work. In short, the pieces of the pie are getting smaller and, in good times or bad and in every phase of their careers, lawyers should be evaluating the growth potential of their practice areas.

In an increasingly crowded and competitive legal field that receives thousands of new lawyers each year, many may find that their success and happiness will depend on their capacity to become experts in newly emerging fields. These lawyers will be able to capture a significant market share and establish a competitive lead. As the number of lawyers in the United States exceeds *1 million,* lawyers must become cognizant of emerging and dying areas of practice and then must plan to adjust their own interests accordingly.

Has the bull market of the later 1990s given lawyers any less reason to look over their shoulders and constantly evaluate the strength and weaknesses of their practice areas? *The short answer is no.*

Despite the very impressive revenue and profitability figures that the top corporate firms in America have been posting for the past three to four years (see the *American Lawyer*'s Annual Survey of America's 100 Highest Grossing Firms), countless lawyers are finding it hard to make a good living; they are struggling in their practice areas. Except for those who emerge from the top law schools, many graduates struggle to find their first good, full-time position. Senior lawyers who are displaced by corporate reorganizations or are squeezed out of their firms continue to find it difficult to secure promising opportunities. The supply of lawyers well exceeds demand and there is no end in sight to that dilemma.

As a result, the issue of identifying growing and dying practice areas is one that confronts the solo practitioner in Houston, the associate in a five-hundred-lawyer firm in New York City, and the partner in a ten-lawyer firm in St. Louis.

The need for the solo practitioner to identify a growing practice area should be self-evident. Associates in a five-hundred-lawyer New York firm should give this topic great thought as well, for it may have implications for developing a niche at the firm early on and securing a bid for partnership. If partnership is not a goal or becomes improbable, being in the right practice area should ease the transition into the next position. Partners in a firm should be evaluating potential growth areas of practice not only to keep their own practice base growing but also to target new practice areas for the firm in general.

Predicting the Emerging Practice Areas

Young lawyers in particular who are yet to be exposed to a wide range of practice areas first must identify the universe of opportunities. The following is a comprehensive outline of current major practice areas:

- Administrative
- Admiralty
- Advertising
- Agricultural law
- Alcoholic beverages
- Alternative dispute resolution
- Animal law
- Antitrust and trade regulation
- Appellate practice
- Art law
- Aviation and aerospace
- Bankruptcy
- Banks and banking
- Biotechnology
- Business law
- Children
- Civil rights
- Class actions
- Commercial law
- Commodities
- Communications and media
- Computers and software
- Constitutional law
- Consumer law
- Copyrights
- Criminal law
- Customs
- Domestic relations
- Education
- Elder law
- Election, campaign
- Employee benefits
- Energy
- Entertainment
- Environmental law
- Federal tax
- Fidelity and surety
- Finance
- Franchising
- General practice
- Government
- Health care
- Immigration
- Imports/exports
- Insurance
- Insurance defense
- Intellectual property
- International law
- Internet
- Investments
- Investment company
- Labor and employment
- Legal ethics
- Litigation
- Lobbying
- Medical malpractice

- Military law
- Mutual funds
- Natural resources
- Nonprofit and charitable
- Patents
- Personal injury
- Products liability
- Professional liability
- Public law
- Real estate
- Religious institutions
- Resorts and leisure
- Securities
- Security transactions
- Sports
- Taxation
- Telecommunications
- Trade
- Trademarks
- Transportation
- Trusts and estates
- UCC
- White-collar crime

Hot Practice Areas of the 1980s and Early 1990s—A Prologue

During the 1980s, the following hot practices emerged as hot: environmental law, real estate, corporate leverage buyouts, corporate mergers and acquisitions, syndications (real estate, equipment leasing, oil and gas), health care, employment litigation, patent litigation, and product liability (in particular, toxic torts such as asbestos cases and certain medical litigation). Some areas deflated, such as traditional labor, Occupational Safety and Health Administration (OSHA), and antitrust. Some areas died almost as soon as they developed, such as wage and price control.

During the recession of the early 1990s, it was no surprise to see bankruptcy and financial workout activity increase dramatically. General commercial litigation boomed, particularly in the areas of the country where the recession took its biggest toll. The failed banks, distressed real estate markets, and troubled corporations provided plenty of litigation work for all. Environmental practice was strong, and the intellectual property fields started to develop significant strength. Employment practices started to gain further strength, particularly in the aftermath of significant corporate downsizing.

Through the recovery and bull market periods of the mid-1990s and up to the present, the following areas of practice started to become hot: corporate securities, real estate investment trusts (REITs), antitrust, health care, intellectual property, real estate, employment, telecommunications, biotechnology, asset securitization, international, mergers and acquisitions, software and technology licensing, patent prosecution and litigation, and of course, Internet-related law.

While the emergence or deflation of some of these practice areas was predictable, other practice areas were either negatively or positively affected by less predictable market factors or legislative changes. Anyone following the Tax Reform Act of 1986 should have moved quickly out of syndication practice. The decline of traditional labor practice was the consequence of a predictable and long-term shift in American industry from smokestack industries to high technology and service industries that have been less susceptible to unionization.

The decline in the practice of many antitrust lawyers in the 1980s was to a degree the result of policy changes in the Reagan administration. While the shift in antitrust enforcement depended on a change in administration and was difficult to predict, anyone practicing in the area should have been sensitive to the fact that his or her practice area was vulnerable to such political changes. A more aggressive enforcement policy of the Clinton administration has resulted in significant increases in the antitrust field.

The environmental area of practice, after having grown substantially during the 1980s, has seen little growth in the last four to five years. A number of law firms have severely trimmed back the size of their environmental departments. Was the stagnation of this practice area predictable? To a large degree the lack of growth in the practice was a result of the decline in resources that the federal and state governments invested in enforcement activities. In addition, a number of the Superfund site cleanup activities came to resolution or completion.

Independent power project finance emerged as a new practice in the 1980s. The emergence of this field wholly depended on Congress passing legislation that opened up entry into the utility market. While previously the sole province of monopolistic utility companies, the power industry became the subject of extensive congressional focus. The result was the passage of a complex set of laws that allowed independent entities to develop power facilities and required the monopolistic public utility companies to purchase power from these entities. The new legislation spawned a whole new industry, and it is logical that lawyers would become extensively involved in a statutorily created enterprise. Who could have predicted such developments? Anyone knowledgeable about the industry.

The surge in REIT activity was very much a by-product of the hot stock market, as it became cheaper for investors to raise money in the equities markets.

Predicting the Hot Practice Areas for the New Millennium

How does one pinpoint growth areas of practice? Lawyers need, on a regular basis, to step back and assess societal trends and technological changes affecting industry. The writings of such futurists as John Nesbitt (*Megatrends*) and Alvin Toffler belong on your list of required reading. Do not ignore the larger forces that will ultimately dominate business.

Some of these forces are undeniable, such as the graying of the baby boom generation. Lawyers need to assess how such a trend will provide growth opportunities. Mutual fund lawyers, for example, are currently benefiting from this aging population trend. This is because the graying baby boom generation is finally reaching a stage in life where it must start planning for retirement. In recognition of this reality, the mutual fund industry has been aggressive in capturing retirement savings. As a result, the number of funds, and the number of lawyers servicing those funds, has exploded during the past five years.

The need for the baby boom generation to save for retirement is being fueled by corporate America's ongoing reduction of employee benefits: individuals increasingly must provide their own retirement nest eggs. This stripping away of pension benefits is itself a result of another larger trend at work—the globalization of industry. American industry has responded to the competitiveness of a wider, more demanding global marketplace. The graying of the baby boom generation is creating a demand for lawyers to provide services to the elderly (Medicare, Medicaid planning, asset protection, age discrimination, health care problems, and more).

Additional areas may be viewed as hot fields for the new millennium:

Internet law: Only the most technologically astute lawyer would have seen the commercial potential of the Internet, as it seized our economy overnight. Those who woke to its potential early enough grabbed the moment to become experts on the legal issues peculiar to the Internet. They are benefiting from that early entry into the field.

Intellectual property: The golden era of intellectual-property litigation was ushered in with the Reagan era when the Department of Justice reversed a long-standing policy of using antitrust laws against companies that refused to license patented technology. In addition to a need for patent lawyers with litigation skills, there will be continued strong demand for lawyers conversant enough with technologies to represent companies who continue to enter into joint ventures, research and development collaborations, and cross-licensing agreements.

International law: The number of international transactions will continue to grow substantially. Lawyers practicing in this general field will need to have core skills as corporate lawyers, but lawyers who have multicultural backgrounds and language skills will also be needed.

Elder care: As Ken Dychtwald points out in his book dealing with the aging of the population (*Age Wave,* Bantam Books, 1993), legal services for the elderly will have expanded vastly by the end of the millennium. These lawyers will be assisting the elderly with protection of their assets against Medicare, dealing with nursing homes and health care facilities, and euthanasia issues. One Texas lawyer has already responded to this reality by focusing on representing aggrieved patients in nursing home facilities who are victims of abuse. Her practice has skyrocketed.

Employment law: As *Fortune* magazine pointed out in its March 1993 issue dealing with the "new" unemployed in America, terminations and unemployment are a permanent phenomenon of traditional corporate America. This has resulted in significant increases in litigation for the labor force, including wrongful terminations and age discrimination complaints. All major law firms have groups of lawyers now dedicated to employment litigation cases. As predicted, the Americans with Disabilities Act greatly increased the number of job-related lawsuits (see *Forbes,* May 1993).

Health care: The health care industry can only grow larger as the baby boomers reach older age and face greater medical problems. The enormous pressure that those economic demands will place on society and on the health care industry will insure plenty of change and challenge for years to come. Whether or not a health care reform bill is enacted this decade, it is clear that health care will continue to be a major industry in the United States. With its range of regulations and its ability to affect all of our lives, health care promises to be an important practice area for lawyers.

In a broad discussion about job growth in its July 12, 1993 issue, *Fortune* magazine succinctly stated the new reality for lawyers and other professionals: "Aspiring managers and lawyers—along with those already in the workforce—will have to hone skills that set them apart from the crowd and take laser-like aim at areas where growth prospects are brightest." That statement will hold true for the legal profession well into the new millennium.

CHAPTER 20

Geographic Areas

Marcia Pennington Shannon

Remember the quote attributed to that famous baseball icon, Yogi Berra? *"You've got to be very careful if you don't know where you are going, because you might not get there."*

This quote applies to every job search, but especially one that includes a change in geographic location. No job search is without its challenges. And while stress and excitement are inherent in the job search process, these are multiplied when distance is included. Without thoughtful assessment and careful planning, you may feel that you are just spinning the proverbial wheels.

This chapter will focus on the factors to consider in planning for a long-distance job search, strategies to use in conducting the search, and some resources that can aid you in your research of geographic locations and employers. A discussion of an international job search is included.

The decision to move from one location to another is never an easy one, but it is especially difficult for someone who seeks to establish a legal career in another location. You must consider five factors as you make this important decision.

Factor 1: Assess Your Motivations

You must be able to answer the question, Why are you interested in this geographic location? Not only is it a question that you should ask yourself, but it will be asked by all employers in the prospective location. Why are you considering a move to another location? What are your connections to this region? Is this a lifestyle choice?

Consider the experience of one lawyer: "I spent many summer vacations on Cape Cod, loving every minute I was there, and longing for the time I'd return. Finally, I decided that I simply should live there, combining my professional career with a location where I felt so comfortable. It was an emotional decision. I forgot to explore several factors. First, what would it be like to live in a place that is so full of tourists during the summer? I would no longer be a tourist myself. Dealing with tourists, as opposed to being one, became irritating. But, even more so, the first winter was a real rude awakening."

Had this individual explored his motives for the move ahead of time, he might have realized that he needed to test his assumptions about living full-time, year-round in this particular location. Do some reality testing before committing to a geographic change. Depending upon your motivations, lawyers practicing in the considered geographic location might be excellent resources. The local Chamber of Commerce may also serve as a good source of information.

Factor 2: The Marketability of Your Practice Area

Is your current practice area marketable in the geographic location that you are considering? If it is not, are you willing to retool and to use your current skills and knowledge in a different practice area? Are you willing to accept a drop in your seniority level of your career? As you assess your marketability, consider how you will "sell" your experiences to potential employers. Consider the extent of your experiences, the industries about which you are knowledgeable, and the current clients who may be willing to follow you to a new firm, wherever it is. Is there a shortage of lawyers with your substantive knowledge in this specific geographic location?

Do you have "portables"? How might you convince your present clients that you can still service them from your new location? The new firm or location may offer your clients greater or more cost-effective services. As you think about the change, consider what resources or legal talents you might need in addition to your own to service your clients fully in your new location. In assessing a geographic location and a new firm, the question of whether your clients' needs can be met is an essential one. In addition, what will you do if your clients do not choose to follow you to your new practice? To whom will you refer them and what work will you need to accomplish on their cases before referring them to someone else?

Is your experience marketable to employers outside private law firms? What types of employers are located in this area? How might you market your experience to these employers?

Information about current practice area trends by region can be quite useful in assessing the marketability of your legal experience. In the latter half of the 1990s, lawyers' hiring has increased significantly nationwide from what was practiced during the early 1990s recession. This has been especially true in major cities for midlevel associates. It is important to remember that lawyer hiring is tied to economic cycles. When the economy is strong, there is an increased demand for corporate transactional, and other business-related practice areas. A weakened economy often increases the demand for litigators as the need for corporate lawyers wanes. While the future of the economy can be hard to read, a look at projected practice trends by geographic area will increase your ability to make an informed decision about a possible move.

Northeast and Middle Atlantic: Corporate transactional, mergers and acquisitions, structured finance, patent, securities, project finance, some litigation, and real estate are all active practice areas in this region.

Southeast: Corporate law, especially in the area of "deal making," banking/ finance, intellectual property, and real estate are mentioned often as growth practice areas in the Southeast.

Midwest: Corporations from all over the country, many of which are located in the Midwest, have shown an increase in hiring for their law departments. It appears that this trend will continue at a steady pace. In addition, corporate generalists, labor and employment lawyers, health care lawyers, commercial litigators, and patent lawyers have all found strong markets in the Midwest.

Rocky Mountain and Southwest: Intellectual property, commercial litigation, corporate transactional, environmental litigation, and real estate practice specialties are active areas in these regions.

West: Intellectual property, labor and employment, international, commercial litigation, and corporate finance lawyers will find active markets in the Western states.

Information on "hot" practice areas for a specific location can be attained by talking with search firms in the particular region, local bar associations, and representatives of law school career services offices. Perusing local legal publications and relevant Internet sites, particularly the classified advertisements for lawyers, is also a useful way to keep informed about practice area trends.

Factor 3: Economic Climate of the Area

From a professional standpoint, it is important to look at the economic factors of a new location. Will this new location enhance or diminish your legal career? Does the economic climate appear to be "friendly" toward your area or attractive to the type of clients that you will need? What, generally, is the job market for lawyers in this area? Where are lawyers employed? Is the economy strong and growing? If there is an economic downturn, how will this area be affected?

The following resources are helpful in attaining this type of information:

- Local Chamber of Commerce
- Business section of the local newspaper or a financial newspaper from the area
- *Money Magazine*'s list, "Best Places to Live in America"
- Internet sites for economic information such as the *Wall Street Journal* or the U.S. Department of Labor's Bureau of Labor Statistics

If you are considering pursuing employment with a law firm or starting your own practice in this area, begin to put together your practice development plan for building a practice. A significant part of your plan will include information about the economic factors and industry trends that lead you to believe that you can build a practice in your specialty. You should also include the business entities to which you will be marketing your legal services. As you begin to write your plan, you will be able to see specific gaps in your knowledge about the area. Your plan will be an effective tool to use with employers as you convince them to consider you for employment.

Types of economic data to be collected include the following:

- What is the economic climate in this area?
- What types of industries are the base of this area's economy?
- Is the economy diversified or based on one or two industries?
- What plans, if any, does this area have for economic growth? Is it attracting new business?
- What is the unemployment rate for this area?

Current Economic Trends

As you begin to do your research on an area's economy, you may find it useful to look at current and projected trends around the country.

Northeast and Middle Atlantic: Although certainly affected by the downturn of the early 1990s, this region appears to be slowly coming back, in large part because the region has diversified its economic bases. Particularly strong additions to the region include high-tech businesses, mutual fund operations, publishing, and finance. New York seems to have made the most rapid turnaround. New Jersey has seen a growth in small businesses and increase in start-ups. Companies specializing in software, banking, brokerage and other financial services, and biotechnology and other high-tech concerns have increased the economic strength of New England, particularly in the Boston area. Washington, D.C., and surrounding areas have become high-tech locations as well. Some economic forecasters point to Pittsburgh, Syracuse, and Boston as the "hot" cities in this region.

Southeast: Economic growth in the Southeast has been spurred by an increase in high-tech industries, services, and international trade. Many companies have relocated to the Southeast because of its lower costs of doing business. Florida, Georgia, and North Carolina have been particularly strong areas in this region, and North Carolina is growing as a banking center and, of course, the Research Triangle continues to expand the state's economic base. Virginia, too, has emerged as a strong center of computer communications companies. Florida has a variety of industries, including tourism, import/export, international banking, and biomedical technology.

Midwest: The Midwest has an assortment of industries—farming, manufacturing, environmental services, health care, and high technology. Economic forecasters see this region as having steady growth, with possible occasional downturns. Indiana, Nebraska, and Iowa are listed as having particularly good economic futures due to diversification, new emerging industries, and low unemployment. Toledo, Omaha, and Minneapolis/St. Paul are recommended as this region's particularly dynamic cities.

Rocky Mountain and Southwest: Economic forecasters warn that these regions may be headed for some economic downturns as we head into the new millennium. Currently, the economy is active due to the influx of high-tech and software companies over the past several years, continued status as top vacation and retirement locations, and growth in population. Colorado is home to many high-tech industries, financial concerns, and cable companies. New Mexico, in addition to its health care and defense industries, also has added high-tech jobs to its economy. Idaho is the center of an active semiconductor industry, along with business services, recreation, and government industries. Salt Lake City has particularly impressed economic experts as a sound, business-friendly, and growth-oriented city.

West: The economic forecast for this region is strong, with job prospects continuing to grow. California's economy has fully turned around with tourism and the entertainment industry topping the list of active industries in this state. Other factors playing into this economic base include the high-tech companies and a diverse manufacturing base. The rest of the region also seems to have a strong economic future. High-tech companies moving into the region have improved other industries, including real estate and construction. The area has also increased as a center for Far East trade. While the timber and aerospace industries that were formerly a significant base of this region's economy have greatly declined, new industries seem to be keeping the economy steady.

Factor 4: Professional Development

In considering a move to a new geographic location, you must explore opportunities for professional development. First and most important are the state bar admission requirements. Are you able to "motion" into it? Will you have to take another exam? Does this state have reciprocity? These are important questions for you and for your prospective employers, as well. Current state bar requirements and telephone numbers of their boards of examiners are included at the end of this chapter (Appendix B). Be sure to call the board of the state you have targeted for updated information.

You must also consider the availability of continuing legal education in your new locale. Are professional development courses for your practice area available nearby or will you have to travel to update your training? For example, a lawyer who moved his ERISA practice to another state found that all continuing education courses had to be taken in places at a great distance from his new location. In addition to your own specialty, are there other opportunities for professional development? Are the local bar associations active? Are there opportunities to develop your professional connections in the community? Your own career development is essential for your continued satisfaction with the practice of law.

Factor 5: Personal Considerations That Affect You Professionally

There are several personal issues that you may want to consider as you make the decision to relocate. First, what is the cost of living for this area? Is it comparable to your present location? What are salaries like for your profession? Being aware of the financial elements of a relocation is important; you must be prepared for any financial change that you may incur. Web sites that you will want to peruse for cost-of-living information include those of the *National Business Employment Weekly, Money Magazine*'s Cost-of-Living Calculator, U.S. Cost-of-Living Comparisons from DataMasters (see *http://www.dbm.com/jobguide/relocate.html* for links to these items).

Transportation issues should also be explored. How will you get to work? Is there public transportation? Is housing available near your target employer? Do people have to drive long commutes to get to work? Take the lawyer who moved to a new geographic location for lifestyle purposes only to find that she had to commute a minimum of 45 minutes in each direction, actually adding time to her work day.

Are cultural activities important to you? What is the availability of cultural outlets in this new location? Are there opportunities to pursue your hobbies and other nonwork activities? Do you need to find a family-friendly environment? Is housing readily available in neighborhoods where you will want to raise your children? What is the quality of the public school system? What is the availability of day care or other child care arrangements?

Are there career opportunities for your spouse or significant other in his or her field?

What is the climate like? Is this something that will bother you?

You may think of other considerations that will enhance or take away from your professional life, as well. Think about your own priorities and interests. If others are involved in this move, think about their priorities and interests. Does this new location meet those requirements?

Appendix A at the end of this chapter contains an organized worksheet to help you explore these factors. As you fill it out, you will be able to see where some of the gaps exist in your information and what information you may still need to collect to make a thoughtful decision.

Ten Steps to an Effective Long-Distance Job Search—A Checklist

You have completed all of your homework in terms of investigating the factors important in considering a change in geographic location. You have made your decision and you are ready to begin the job search. Where do you go from here?

1. Review your resume. Is it reader-friendly to employers in this particular location? Have you included your ties or connections to this location? Do you mention your knowledge of industries that are part of this area's economy? Is your bar admission status for this state included?
2. Research legal employers in this geographic area. Make a list of those employers with whom you would like to explore employment possibilities. How will you market yourself to them? Why should they consider someone who is not from their location?
3. Find out bar admission requirements of this state. If necessary, sign up for the next bar exam or collect relevant information to send to the state bar examiners.

4. Make a list of your contacts in this location.
5. Use your contacts as informational sources regarding strong practice areas in this location; local employers who might hire lawyers (both private practice and other options); economic information; personal considerations such as housing, school systems, and community activities. Your contacts can also help you with your job search. This demonstrates to employers that you do have connections to their location.
6. Locate and peruse job-listing resources. If useful, connect with local search firms.
7. If you are seeking employment with private law firms or will be starting your own practice, create a practice development plan. (See Appendix C at the conclusion of this chapter.)
8. It is very important to write strong cover letters that include your connections to a particular location, your reasons for relocating, your bar admission status, and, if known, when you will be in this location for interviewing purposes.
9. Set up visits to the location for interviews. Visiting a particular location for several days to participate in initial interviews can be quite effective for long-distance job hunters.
10. Consider other connections and sources of information:
    - Local bar associations
    - Local law schools (do not overlook the possibility that your school may have reciprocity with the career services office of law schools in your target location)
    - Alumni from your law school or your graduate or undergraduate institutions

The more connections you make, the more likely that you will hear about possible opportunities. Remember, most jobs are never advertised. The information about possible openings or potential employers comes from other people.

Beyond the Obvious

Sometimes securing a position in a new location requires a little creativity. Consider these further suggestions:

- Look at announcements by employers in local legal publications. Are there any law firms opening a new branch office in your city of interest?
- Is there a possibility that your present employer would find it worthwhile to open an office in the location you are considering? If you choose to approach them with this option, be sure to create a practice development plan first.
- Many relocated lawyers have started off in a new area by taking legal temporary or contract positions with local employers. Not only does this give the employer the opportunity to see you in action without making a full commitment, but it also allows you the ability to get to know the legal community in that area and to demonstrate your commitment to the new location.

- Are there any judges who need a law clerk? Yes, experienced lawyers are seeking and landing law clerk positions with judges. This option is particularly effective if you are not too far out of law school (usually no more than two to four years). Like the temporary or contract positions mentioned above, this gives you the opportunity to get to know the legal community as well as the particular location.

The International Job Search

An international job search poses different concerns for the job seeker than a search within the United States. In considering a move overseas, it is important to have a clear idea of where you want to be and what you want to do in a foreign country. According to the American Bar Association's *Careers in International Law,* opportunities fall under several different categories:

- Federal and state governments
- International organizations
- Contracting and consulting firms (includes law firms, accounting firms)
- Nonprofit and private voluntary organizations
- Multinational corporations
- Businesses and the travel industry
- Educational organizations
- Trade and professional associations
- Foundations
- Research organizations
- Entrepreneurs

The type of organization in which you seek employment will be dependent upon the type of legal work you want to do. For instance, are you interested in international policy? Seeking work with the federal government or an international organization such as the United Nations may best fit your goals. Do you want to do intellectual property work? A multinational corporation may be your target.

Have a clear idea of what type of work you want to do, the kinds of skills and experience you will bring to it, and your reasons for wanting to live overseas. International experience, such as traveling or living overseas, and language fluency are baseline requirements for most international positions. In addition, many international employers are seeking very specific skills and substantive knowledge. Occasionally, fluency in a particularly difficult or unusual language (for example, some of the Eastern European languages) may open up opportunities that otherwise would have been more difficult to pursue.

Resume Preparation

Foreign recruitment specialists are much more accepting of a multipage resume than their American counterparts. In fact, they are not satisfied with the typical one- or two-page resume and instead expect a three- or four-page vita that includes far more detail about your experience and education. Be sure to include any credentials from international institutions, particularly legal credentials. Language fluency must be stated accurately. If you say that you are fluent in a language, the interviewer will expect to conduct the interview in that language. Relevant undergraduate or graduate course work, such as economics or foreign policy, should also be highlighted. When describing your experiences, both volunteer and paid, emphasize skills, accomplishments, and responsibilities. Publications, speeches, and presentations can be important. Memberships, especially if they have an international flavor, should be noted. Also include extensive travel experience or other occasions when you have had the opportunity to experience other cultures. Some of the experiences you might list under this category are military experience, the Peace Corps, student exchange or study abroad programs, and international business contacts.

Finding the Job

Most international positions for lawyers are never advertised so your contacts make all the difference. It is important to network as much as possible in the international arena and to create as many new sources for possible information as possible. Most international organizations, law firms, companies, the federal government, and other organizations do most of their recruiting and hiring at their headquarters, often in the United States. Most hiring for legal positions overseas occurs in the District of Columbia, New York, Los Angeles, and San Francisco. In addition, executive search firms handle many legal placements in the foreign locations of corporations. Most of the search firms have headquarters in the United States. If you are looking in a particular country, however, it is useful to locate a local search firm in that market. They will probably have more local listings, while the larger U.S. search firms will tend to represent only the largest corporations.

Due Diligence

It is important to research the regulations in your selected locations regarding the practice of law. Each country will vary in who may practice and what credentials are required. Job descriptions in international corporations are often not as clearly defined as they are in the United States, so be certain exactly what the position entails. Employment laws vary dramatically throughout the world, as well, so be aware that interview questions that might be illegal in the here may be acceptable abroad.

Some Additional Thoughts

- The Central and East European Law Initiative (CEELI) of the American Bar Association provides opportunities for those who are interested in helping with legal education and judicial and bar reform in participating countries. These positions typically last for one year and have the support and structure of the ABA.
- If your firm has connections to any foreign law firms, you may be able to organize an exchange program. This short-term exchange,

usually not much longer than three to six months, can give you the experience of living overseas while making strong contacts that can be helpful in building your practice in the United States.

- Many international organizations will take volunteers. If you are in a position to work without compensation you may be able to move to the country of your choice and obtain experience that can be marketed to other organizations overseas.

Appendix A

Considering a Geographic Move: A Worksheet

1. What are my motivations for wanting a change in geographic location? What information do I need to make sure this move will meet my goals for changing locations? Have I tested my assumptions about the new location to make sure they are correct?
2. How marketable is my practice area in this location? Will I have to retool to a different practice area? What of my experience and skills are transferable to this legal marketplace? What will I sell to potential employers?
3. What is the economic climate of this location? Is it growing? What are the economic bases of this area? Do these bases enhance or detract from my practice area? Does this area have plans for further economic development, and if so, what are they?
4. What is my bar admission status here? Will I have to take another bar exam? Can I be admitted on motion? Do they have reciprocity? If I have to take another exam, when will the next one be given? What application materials do I need?
5. What are the continuing legal education requirements and opportunities in this location? Are there active local bar associations? Do the local bar associations provide professional development opportunities? Does this area have a strong legal community?
6. What is the cost of living in this new location and how does it compare with my present location? What are salaries like and how do they compare with my present salary?
7. What is the cultural flavor of this area? Will I be able to pursue my extracurricular activities here? Is this a place that I will want to raise my family? What is real estate like here? How will I commute to work? What are the schools like? What is the political climate in this area? What is the typical weather here?
8. Are there other factors that are important to me that I need to explore before deciding on this location?

Appendix B

State Bar Information

The following provides information on reciprocity of all of the state bars of the United States. It is advised that you call the state in which you have an interest to ensure that there have been no changes in the state's reciprocity policy since the compilation of this list.

Alabama State Bar Admissions Office
(334) 269-1515
Reciprocity
Acceptance of multistate bar examination (MBE) score: Applicants may transfer previous MBE score from another jurisdiction if a scaled score of 140 or higher was achieved within twenty months and if admitted to jurisdiction where exam was taken.
Admission on Motion: No; examination is required of all applicants.

Alaska Bar Association
(907) 272-7469
Reciprocity
Acceptance of MBE Score: No
Admission on Motion: May be admitted without exam if applicant has engaged in active practice of law five of seven years immediately preceding application and has passed written exam in reciprocal state. Must be a graduate of an ABA-accredited law school.

Arizona—Supreme Court of Arizona
Committee on Examinations
(602) 340-7295
Reciprocity
Acceptance of MBE Score: Arizona accepts an MBE scaled score from a concurrent exam only.
Admission on Motion: No; examination is required of all applicants.

Arkansas Board of Law Examiners
(501) 374-1855
Reciprocity
Acceptance of MBE Score: Will accept previous MBE score from another jurisdiction for up to three years or six consecutive exams.
Admission on motion: No; examination is required of all applicants.

California - Office of Admissions State Bar
(415) 561-8303
Reciprocity
Acceptance of MBE Score: No
Admission on Motion: No; examination is required of all applicants. Lawyers who have actively practiced four of the six years immediately preceding application may be eligible for lawyer exam.

Colorado Board of Law Examiners
(303) 893-8096
Reciprocity
Acceptance of MBE Score: No
Admission on Motion: Applicant must be a graduate of an ABA accredited law school and have practiced law for five of seven years immediately preceding application.

Connecticut Bar Examining Committee
(860) 568-3450

Reciprocity
Acceptance of MBE Score: Accepts MBE scaled scores from concurrent exam or any of the three previous exams.
Admission on Motion: Admission without exam if practiced law for five of seven years immediately preceding application. Applicant must be a graduate of an ABA accredited law school.

Delaware Board of Bar Examiners
(302) 658-7309

Reciprocity
Acceptance of MBE Score: No
Admission on Motion: No; examination is required of all applicants.

District of Columbia Committee on Admissions
(202) 879-2710

Reciprocity
Acceptance of MBE Score: May be admitted without exam if applicant received a scaled MBE score of 133 or higher on an exam upon which applicant was admitted in another jurisdiction within the last twenty-five months, achieved a scaled score of 75 or better on MPRE, and has a Juris Doctor from an ABA accredited law school. The twenty-five-month time limit begins to run from the date the exam was taken. An applicant who received an MBE scaled score of 133 or higher but was not admitted in that jurisdiction may waive the MBE score and take only the essay portion of the exam. An essay score of 133 will then be required to pass the essays.
Admission on Motion: Applicant who has been a member of another bar and in good standing for five years immediately preceding application may be admitted without exam.

Florida Board of Bar Examiners
(850) 487-1292

Reciprocity
Acceptance of MBE Score: No
Admission on Motion: No

Georgia Board of Bar Examiners
(404) 656-3490

Reciprocity
Acceptance of MBE Score: No
Admission on Motion: No

Hawaii Board of Bar Examiners
(808) 539-4977

Reciprocity
Acceptance of MBE Score: No
Admission on Motion: No

Idaho State Bar
(208) 334-4500

Reciprocity
Acceptance of MBE Score: Applicants may transfer previous MBE scaled score from another jurisdiction if taken within twenty-five months of the date of exam. (Board recommends transferred score be at least scaled score of 140.) Admission on Motion: No; examination is required of all applicants. Lawyers who have actively practiced five of seven years preceding application are not required to take MBE.

Illinois Board of Admissions to the Bar
(217) 522-5917

Reciprocity
Acceptance of MBE Score: Applicants may transfer previous MBE scaled score of at least 140 from another jurisdiction if from preceding two exams and applicant passed the bar exam in jurisdiction where MBE was taken. Applicants may not have MBE score transferred to Illinois from a concurrent exam.
Admission on Motion: Persons admitted to practice in a reciprocal jurisdiction who have been engaged in the active and continuous practice of law for at least five of the seven years prior to making application and who meet the educational requirements for admission on exam may be admitted on motion. Applicant must be a graduate of an ABA-accredited law school.

Indiana State Board of Law Examiners
(317) 232-2552

Reciprocity
Admission on Motion: May be admitted without exam. Conditional one-year licenses granted to applicants who have actively engaged in the practice of law five of seven years immediately preceding application and intend to practice predominantly in Indiana. After fifth consecutive renewal, admission becomes permanent.

Iowa Board of Law Examiners
(515) 281-5911

Reciprocity
Acceptance of MBE Score: Iowa accepts an MBE scaled score from another jurisdiction within previous two years.
Admission on Motion: May be admitted without exam. Must be an Iowa inhabitant or demonstrate a bona fide intention to establish an office for the practice of law in Iowa and have practiced five of seven years immediately preceding application.

Kansas—Attorney Admissions Kansas Judicial Center
(913) 296-8410

Reciprocity
Acceptance of MBE Score: Applicants may transfer MBE scaled score of 120 or higher from another jurisdiction if from a concurrent exam or received

within thirteen months prior to the current exam, provided that the applicant passed the entire exam in the transferring jurisdiction.
Admission on Motion: No

Kentucky Board of Examiners
(606) 246-2381

Reciprocity
Acceptance of MBE Score: Will accept MBE scaled score of 132 or higher received within the previous three years.
Admission on Motion: May be admitted without exam from states admitting lawyers from Kentucky without exam. Must have practiced five of seven years immediately preceding application. Must have qualifications sufficient to allow exam in Kentucky. Must be a graduate of an ABA-accredited law school.

Louisiana Committee on Bar Admissions
(504) 566-1600

Reciprocity
Admission on Motion: No

Maine Board of Bar Examiners
(207) 623-2464

Reciprocity
Acceptance of MBE Score: Applicants may transfer previous MBE scaled score from another jurisdiction. No specific score is required for transfer.
Admission on Motion: Examination required of all applicants. Lawyers who have achieved a scaled score of 155 on the MBE are eligible for a modified exam. Lawyers who have practiced for at least three years need only sit for the essay day of the exam.

Maryland Board of Law Examiners
(410) 514-7044

Reciprocity
Acceptance of MBE Score: Applicants may transfer MBE score of at least 140 from another jurisdiction if from concurrent exam or from the immediately preceding exam.
Admission on Motion: Out-of-state lawyer applicants required to take an essay exam on Maryland Civil/Criminal Practice & Procedure and Rules of Professional Conduct. Must have practiced law as a principal means of support in another jurisdiction for ten years, or five of the last ten years immediately preceding application, and must have been admitted by exam in another state. Applicants must have intent to practice in Maryland.

Massachusetts Board of Bar Examiners
(617) 482-4467

Reciprocity
Acceptance of MBE Score: Applicants may transfer actual raw MBE score from another jurisdiction only if from a concurrent exam.

Admission on Motion: May be eligible on motion. Must have been admitted in another jurisdiction for five years and have engaged in the practice or teaching of law since prior admission; must meet educational requirements; and must have passed MPRE.

Michigan Board of Law Examiners
(517) 334-6992

Reciprocity

Acceptance of MBE Score: Applicants may transfer previous MBE scaled score from another jurisdiction if within three years and from reciprocal state. Applicant must have passed entire bar exam of which MBE was part.

Admission on Motion: Applicant may be admitted without exam if intends to practice in Michigan, has practiced three of five years immediately preceding application, and is a graduate of an ABA-accredited law school.

Minnesota Board of Law Examiners
(612) 297-1800

Reciprocity

Acceptance of MBE Score: Applicant may be admitted on the basis of MBE scaled score received in the previous two years without further exam, provided that applicant received a scaled score of 145 or higher on the MBE, was successful on complete exam and was admitted in that jurisdiction. Subject to MPRE requirement.

Admission on Motion: Applicant may be admitted on motion if engaged in the practice of law for at least five of seven years preceding admission. Must be a graduate of an ABA-accredited law school.

Mississippi Board of Bar Admissions
(601) 354-6055

Reciprocity

Acceptance of MBE Score: Applicant may transfer MBE scaled score if attained within twenty months prior to Mississippi exam.

Admission on Motion: May be eligible for attorneys' exam. Must have practiced at least five years in a reciprocal state and establish office within thirty days of admission.

Missouri Board of Law Examiners
(573) 751-4144

Reciprocity

Acceptance of MBE Score: Applicant may transfer previous MBE scaled score if from past three exams, provided applicant is admitted and licensed in the jurisdiction in which the MBE was taken and attained a scaled score of at least 133.

Admission on Motion: Admission without exam possible if applicant has practiced five of last ten years in a jurisdiction admitting Missouri lawyers without exam. Applicant must be a graduate of an ABA-accredited law school.

Montana State Bar
(406) 442-7660

Reciprocity
Acceptance of MBE Score: Accepts previous score if at least 130 (scaled) and from within two years.
Admission on Motion: Applicant may petition for waiver of exam if graduate of an ABA accredited law school and has actively practiced for at least five years. Abbreviated exam may be ordered.

Nebraska State Bar Commission
(402) 475-7091

Reciprocity
Acceptance of MBE Score: Applicant may transfer previous MBE scaled score of at least 140 if attained within three years immediately preceding Nebraska exam.
Admission on Motion: Applicant may apply for admission without exam if applicant is a graduate of an ABA-accredited law school and has actively practiced law for five of seven years preceding application, or is a graduate of an ABA-accredited law school, has passed a bar exam equivalent to that of Nebraska, and was admitted to practice. Subject to MPRE requirements.

Nevada State Bar
(702) 382-2200

Reciprocity
Acceptance of MBE score: No
Admission on Motion: No

New Hampshire Supreme Court
(603) 271-2646

Reciprocity
Acceptance of MBE Score: No
Admission on motion: No

New Jersey Board of Bar Examiners
(609) 984-7783
Reciprocity
Acceptance of MBE Score: Applicant may transfer MBE scaled score from another jurisdiction if exam was taken concurrent to New Jersey essay exam.
Admission on Motion: No

New Mexico Board of Bar Examiners
(505) 271-9768

Reciprocity
Acceptance of MBE Score: No
Admission on Motion: No

New York State Board of Law Examiners
(518) 452-8700

Reciprocity

Acceptance of MBE Score: Applicant may transfer MBE score from a concurrent exam only.

Admission on Motion: May be admitted without exam from states admitting lawyers from New York without exam. Must have practice five of the last seven years and be a graduate of an ABA-accredited law school.

North Carolina Board of Law Examiners
(919) 828-4886

Reciprocity

Acceptance of MBE Score: No

Admission on Motion: May be admitted without exam from states admitting lawyers from North Carolina without exam. Application must be on file with the Board not less than six months prior to consideration of application. Applicant must be a graduate of an ABA-accredited law school, have actively practice law four of six years immediately preceding the filing of the application and have passed MPRE.

North Dakota State Board of Bar Examiners
(701) 328-4201

Reciprocity

Acceptance of MBE Score: May be admitted without exam based on MBE scaled score of 150 or higher within two years, provided admitted in jurisdiction in which MBE was taken. Must be a graduate of an ABA-accredited law school.

Admission on motion: May be admitted without exam. Must be an ABA-accredited law school graduate, a member of bar for five years preceding application, have practiced four of last five years and have forty-five hours CLE course work in last three years (three of the forty-five hours must be in the area of legal ethics).

Ohio Supreme Court
(614) 466-1528

Reciprocity

Acceptance of MBE Score: No

Admission on Motion: May apply for admission without exam. Must meet general admission requirements; be a graduate of an ABA-accredited law school; have passed a bar exam and been admitted in another jurisdiction; have actively practiced outside of Ohio on a full-time basis for five of last ten years; intend to actively practice in Ohio; have not failed the Ohio bar exam.

Oklahoma Board of Bar Examiners
(405) 524-2365

Reciprocity

Acceptance of MBE Score: Applicant may transfer MBE scaled score from concurrent exam only.

Admission on Motion: May be admitted without exam from states admitting lawyers from Oklahoma without exam. Must have practiced for five of seven years immediately preceding application and be a graduate of an ABA-accredited law school.

Oregon State Board of Bar Examiners
(503) 620-0222
Reciprocity
Acceptance of MBE Score: No
Admission on motion: No

Pennsylvania Board of Law Examiners
(717) 795-7270
Reciprocity
Acceptance of MBE Score: No
Admission on Motion: May be admitted without exam from states admitting lawyers from Pennsylvania without exam. Since admission in reciprocal state, must have practiced (including teaching in any of the accredited U.S. law schools) for at least five of seven years immediately preceding application. Must also be a graduate of an ABA-accredited law school.

Rhode Island Supreme Court
(401) 277-3272
Reciprocity
Acceptance of MBE Score: Applicant may transfer MBE scaled score from concurrent exam only.
Admission on Motion: Rhode Island does not provide for admission on motion. Exam is required of all applicants. If have practiced five of the ten years immediately preceding application, only Rhode Island essay exam required.

South Carolina Supreme Court
(803) 734-1080
Reciprocity
Acceptance of MBE Score: Applicant may transfer MBE scaled score from concurrent exam only.
Admission on Motion: No

South Dakota Board of Bar Examiners
(605) 773-4898
Reciprocity
Acceptance of MBE Score: Board may in its discretion accept MBE scaled score of 130 or higher if MBE taken within twenty-five months prior to next scheduled exam and if applicant passed the other jurisdiction's exam.
Admission on Motion: No

Tennessee Board of Law Examiners
(615) 741-3234

Reciprocity

Acceptance of MBE Score: No

Admission on motion: May be admitted from other states after five years of practice, has taken and passed an equivalent bar exam, and is otherwise qualified. Must have a present intent to actively practice law in Tennessee and be a graduate of an ABA-accredited law school.

Texas Board of Law Examiners
(512) 463-1621

Reciprocity

Acceptance of MBE Score: No

Admission on motion: May be admitted without exam if actively engaged in the practice of law for at least five of seven years immediately preceding application; have a Juris Doctor from an ABA-accredited law school; have an active license and have been a member in good standing at all times. If actively practiced three of five years and meet above requirements, of five of seven, but non-ABA graduate, may be eligible for short form exam.

Utah State Bar
(801) 531-9077

Reciprocity

Acceptance of MBE Score: Utah accepts an MBE score from a concurrent exam only.

Admission on Motion: Examination required of all applicants. Applicants who have been admitted for five years and practiced four of five years are eligible for one-day attorneys' essay exam.

Vermont Board of Bar Examiners
(802) 828-3281

Reciprocity

Acceptance of MBE Score: Applicant may transfer MBE scaled score of 135 or higher from another jurisdiction, provided that exam was taken within previous five years.

Admission on Motion: Applicant may be admitted without exam. Must have practiced five of ten years (or reciprocal state's time period if three years or more) immediately preceding application.

Virginia Board of Bar Examiners
(804) 786-7490

Reciprocity

Acceptance of MBE Score: No

Admission on Motion: Contact the Clerk's Office of the Supreme Court of Virginia at (804) 786-2251 for information on reciprocity or admission on motion.

Washington State Bar Association
(206) 727-8209
Reciprocity
Acceptance of MBE Score: The MBE is not used in Washington.
Admission on Motion: No

West Virginia Board of Law Examiners
(304) 558-7815
Reciprocity
Acceptance of MBE Score: Applicant may transfer MBE scaled score from a successful exam taken within thirteen months of present exam.
Admission on Motion: May be admitted without exam from jurisdictions with admission standards substantially equivalent to those of West Virginia. Applicant must have practiced for five of the seven years immediately preceding application, passed MPRE, and be a graduate of an ABA-accredited law school.

Wisconsin Board of Bar Examiners
(608) 266-9760
Reciprocity
Acceptance of MBE Score: Applicant may transfer MBE scaled score of 145 or higher achieved on exam taken within twenty-five months of present exam and part of successful exam.
Admission on Motion: May be admitted without exam from states that admit Wisconsin practicing lawyers without exam. Applicant must also satisfy originating jurisdiction's requirements for admission on motion.

Wyoming State Board of Law Examiners
(307) 632-9061
Reciprocity
Acceptance of MBE Score: Applicant may transfer MBE scaled score of 130 or higher achieved within three years of present exam.
Admission on Motion: May be admitted without exam if practiced five of preceding seven years, graduated from an ABA-accredited law school, and admitted in a jurisdiction admitting Wyoming lawyers without exam.

Appendix C

Creating the Practice Development Plan

If you are considering law firm employment, starting your own practice, or opening a branch office of your current firm in the new geographic location, and you are an experienced lawyer, you will want to create a practice development plan. The plan will underscore to employers your commitment to building a practice in the new area. It will also serve as your plan of action.

1. Review of your practice
   - Describe your practice and the practice of the potential firm (if known)

- Highlight some representative engagements indicative of your practice
- Define your target clients
2. Inventory of your professional achievements
   - List your professional achievements, highlighting the ones that might influence clients in sending you their legal matters
   - Describe the marketable aspects of your practice
3. Description of the market for your services
   - Review the market conditions in the new geographic location
   - Discuss the demand for your legal specialties specifically
   - Review the top competition for your target clients and why they might attract those clients
4. Description of the market for a branch office of your current firm (If you are considering presenting the idea of a branch office to your current employer, complete this section.)
   - Describe the practice of your current firm
   - Discuss the demand for the legal specialties of your current firm in the new geographic location
   - Review the top competition for the target clients of the branch office and why the firm might attract those clients
   - Highlight the advantages for your current employer of opening a branch office in the new location
5. Analysis of personal and firm marketing activities
   - If known, describe the marketing philosophy of the potential firm
   - Describe your personal marketing philosophy
   - Note all marketing activities that have been successful or those for which you anticipate success in the future
   - Identify marketing activities that you hope to undertake in the future
6. Statement of long-term goals
   - General long-term goals and specific objectives to achieve them (goals refer to long-term plans and hopes for your practice and objectives are steps to achieve them)
   - Specific long-term goals and objectives to achieve them
7. Timetable for implementation of the plan

CHAPTER 21

Law Firms

Sandra O'Briant

Evolution of Today's Law Firms

The hard lessons learned by law firms of all sizes in the economic recession of the late eighties and early nineties should not be forgotten. Law firms learned to concentrate on the bottom line, and the demand rose for increased associate *and* partner billable hours. Many major—usually large—law firms expanded into new geographic areas to compete with other law firms indigenous to the area. Not only did most firms have clients doing business in the new location, the branch offices of major firms also grew through the acquisition of local lawyers with portable practices. Consequently, all law firms revised and redefined their partnership agreements with a greater focus on the retention of rainmakers.

Many law firms reduced their ranks, eliminating deadwood or partners who were not bringing in clients. As a result, the whole notion of partnership and what it really means came into question. Associates were no longer assured of a lockstep path to partnership. Once they achieved partner, there were no assurances that they could remain without producing new business for the firm. Along with the usual associate reviews regarding quality of work and total billable hours, lawyers at every level began to be asked to develop business plans for client development in a shrinking market of available clients.

It was a buyer's market for businesses purchasing lawyers' time. Companies were no longer willing to pay for the training of inexperienced lawyers. They theorized that they received greater value by having more senior lawyers complete their work. The birth of "premium billing" was aided by law firms' incentive to increase the billable hours of lawyers who had a higher billing rate and for whom they had ostensibly invested so much in terms of training and client promotion. Companies hired fewer lawyers out of law school and relied heavily on hiring laterals with proven track records in specific areas of the law. In addition, the current surge in contract or temporary positions is tied to the rising cost of associates' salaries along with dwindling partnership opportunities. In the past, when firms needed extra help they hired more lawyers, heedless of whether their workload would inevitably lessen. Now that alternative is simply too expensive.

With the spotlight on premium billing, client retention and generation, and the increased emphasis on billable hours, senior associates and partners at many law firms became reluctant to delegate work to junior associates. This exacerbated the predicament of an already insecure rank and file. At its peak, the recession left many lawyers unwilling to explore opportunities at smaller and medium-sized firms. They perceived a certain level of security in numbers, even if they were not happy. Partners with a practice area such as real estate or securities law, both hard hit by the recession, saw the volume of their business decrease and decided to hold the line until their numbers went up.

The economy has improved but the legacy of these experiences remains. Lawyers are more mobile, and there are far fewer value judgments attached to this mobility than in the past. Most lawyers join their first law firm out of law school eager to learn their trade and excel at it. While they may hope to make a career at one firm, most realize that at least one move and probably more are in their future. The key is to remain challenged and enjoy forward movement in your career. It helps to think of yourself as part of an industry rather than simply a member of a specific organization within an industry. Therefore, you should always be aware of information networks, making contacts, and promoting yourself. With close observation, many lawyers are often keenly aware of a potential difficulty within their own firm before it grows to the point of affecting their own work.

For example, a junior or midlevel partner who knows there will never be the opportunity in his firm to run his own department or perhaps run the larger deals in the department may choose another firm offering such an arrangement. The senior associate whose prospects for partnership are dim or who perceives that partnership will not make much of a difference in her life may prefer another firm with a greater promise of upward mobility. A tragedy in the making is to spend eight years without significant client contact and to focus solely on billable hours. Your goal should be to develop skills that put you in situations that create client interaction. Insist on being given the work you need to grow professionally. Typically, you are ready to move when you feel you have reached your potential at your present law firm and you want to widen your base.

Marketability

Associates with one to seven years of experience who are considering their first lateral move should focus primarily on the four important factors at a prospective new firm.

Practice/client base: Everything that is important to your career springs from the strengths and weaknesses of your law firm's client base. The section at the end of this article delves a bit more into questions regarding practice.

Feedback/mentoring/training: This is the area where firms cheat young lawyers the most. Substantive feedback from partners and senior associates takes time, thought, and the firm's understanding that they have a vested interest in developing talent. Ask if the firm has a formal procedure for the development of younger lawyers, then ask associates at the firm for a report on the actual practices.

Level of responsibility: You do not want to be stuck in the library most of the time, nor do you want to be assigned the same little pieces of large deals repeatedly. Your responsibility for client matters should change and increase over time. Oftentimes, a lateral move insures that this will happen. Many firms are attempting to attract recruits and reduce attrition by providing associates with additional responsibility. For example, some large law firms known for megacases that are staffed to the hilt routinely bring in more modest matters to educate their junior associates.

Client contact: Ask how assignments are doled out and if associates are allowed to sit in on strategy meetings with the client. Will you be allowed to call the client or will the client be advised to follow up with you?

    For more-senior lawyers, those with seven or more years of experience, something tangible beyond specialized knowledge, creative ideas, innovative systems, or leadership ability is crucial to enhance mobility. Portable business is the tangible asset most law firms look for when evaluating a more senior lawyer. The amount and kind of business determine your range of lateral options. As a practical matter, this means that a lawyer with more than $500,000 in portable business can go to virtually any size law firm (certain geographic differences exist, of course, with less required in a smaller urban area and more in a larger urban area).

    In addition, although outstanding academic performance will serve you throughout your career, this will become less relevant as you mature in your practice. The lawyer who attended Brand X law school at night but who now has a portable practice in an area actively sought after in the current market, is likely to have more options than an Ivy League graduate with no portable business. The outstanding senior lawyer with no portable business will have fewer options, and those options will be very market dependent. For example, in an expanding economy where everyone is doing deals, new firms are established. Whether they are branches of existing firms or new firm startups, they create opportunity for more-senior lawyers. However, many of the problems that moved a more senior lawyer to seek change may still exist at a new firm. Thus a checklist of items you must consider if you wish to make a meaningful change is given at the end of this section.

    Overall, a lateral move for such an lawyer can be very positive if you ask the right questions up front and do your homework. The partner interviewing you may have made a lateral move to the same firm. Ask why he chose this firm and what he took into consideration. If he came up through the ranks, ask about the firm's experience with laterals: Are any of them partners? Are they on the executive committee or otherwise active in firm administration? Do not be afraid to stipulate your concerns or to negotiate. You are your own client when strategizing a career move, and a savvy potential employer will recognize and appreciate this.

The legal market is fluid, and so there are no hard and fast rules about which lawyers have the best prospects of finding new jobs, especially as you gain seniority. Most of the time the lawyers who want to leave are the ones in the most profitable specialities, especially if such contribution is not reflected in partner compensation. This may be a group or department who feel like they are carrying the burden of a hundred-lawyer firm.

Size of Law Firms and Mergers

Law firms have been the subject of the same merger mania that has occurred in other businesses. The dynamics influencing these new arrangements are the result of the economic forces described above and other considerations unique to law practice. Whether to address problems such as poor geographic reach, lack of practice area depth, and unanticipated market changes or to meet the needs of their fastest growing clients, many law firms have been changing their identities through mergers or by acquisition of practice groups. In general, lateral movement occurs in the following categories: boutique firm is acquired by large firm; group or department leaves one firm for another, usually larger, firm; individual partners leave a firm for another firm; large firm merges with another large firm (usually in different geographic locations); solo practitioners form an association.

Smaller firms may feel forced to grow to overcome a prejudice about perceived lack of depth. One school of thought is that firms must get bigger or die. It has been theorized that in the future the market will be dominated by a few giants: highly leveraged, full-service law firms with a Fortune 500 client base willing to pay a premium will control the bulk of the law business. In this scenario, law firm culture would vary little from one law office to another.

However, boutiques specializing in one particular area have proven to be equally profitable contenders. Many midsize firms claim there is still an abundance of blue chip work to do. Often, small and midsize firms do get involved in large transactions. This occurs in situations where they have long-term relationships with their clients, frequently dating back to when the clients themselves were not so big. In our current era of economic opportunity, venture capitalists, and emerging growth companies, this aspect of small and medium-sized law firms should not be ignored. Moreover, small firms prefer to hire lawyers who can handle cases with a minimum of supervision, thus creating ample room for the demonstration of partnership potential. Nevertheless, it is difficult to determine whether the partnership track is any easier at smaller firms. The primary variable affecting small-firm partnership growth is the size of the client base and the relative size of the partnership profit slices. The same considerations exist in a large law firm context; however, it often is easier to make partner in the earlier years of a smaller law firm. On the other hand, whereas some larger firms may have at one time been uninterested in smaller matters, they are now competing for a share of midsize and smaller deals and the kinds of clients that generate them, potentially offering a similar opportunity for partnership.

In reality, the mergers of the largest law firms or career changes of lawyers with multimillion dollar books of business have little to do with the majority of lawyers practicing across the country. Many are successful solo practitioners or partners in firms with fewer than ten lawyers. Still, these lawyers may be interested in broadening the scope of their practices or sharing management issues and overhead. Such lawyers sometimes form associations to address these concerns. Although not true partnerships, these associations are contractual relationships that provide many benefits to those involved. Increasingly, maturing lawyers in such practices are concerned about succession plans. This is a value-added aspect of working in a larger firm which is often taken for granted when hot young lawyers with portable practices decide to strike out on their own.

To summarize the discussion, consider the following advantages when moving from a smaller to a larger firm:

- More support for current matters
- Opportunities to work on bigger deals
- Referrals for covering your clients' work in other departments
- Long-term security (advisedly)
- Vacation coverage from colleagues and juniors
- Greater pool of persons for collegial relations

Moving from a bigger to a smaller firm has positive aspects, too:

- More control over practice
- Greater autonomy and influence in building the firm
- Fewer client conflicts
- More room for creativity (advisedly)
- Fewer colleagues, thus stronger friendship ties

Law Firm Culture in the New Millennium

As law firms grapple with the same economic pressures while simultaneously competing for the same business, the differences in law firm cultures become less distinct. In the final analysis, firm culture comfort depends on an individual's work style, lifestyle requirements, and career objectives. When considering a move to a law firm of any size the following parameters should be considered:

- Old clients still with firm since founding
- New areas of practice developed
- No overspecialization in one area
- Anticipated level of responsibility
- Lack of dependence on any one corporate client or area of legal work
- Growth in numbers of lawyers in most recent three-year span
- Promotion to partnership ranks of associates in same time span
- Age of partners with whom you will be working (reflects on transition of responsibility for major clients and governance in firm)
- Actions firm has taken to retain associates and partners
- Ease of recruiting

- Management style, or how decisions are made
- Reputation for collegiality
- Compensation issues

Primary consideration has been given to parameters surrounding a firm's client base, as well it should, since so much of a law firm's strength and weaknesses spring from this area. In addition, much attention has been given recently to the characteristics of successful rainmakers among lawyers. Here again the client is the focal point. Rainmakers are described as really caring about their clients, having an absolute commitment to client satisfaction, regarding clients as people with whom to develop relationships, knowing the client's industry, and always seeking to help the client achieve long-term business goals. When contemplating a lateral move a lawyer should evaluate a prospective new firm in much the same way as he would a new client. Establish a close relationship and find out everything you can about them.

CHAPTER 22

Flying Solo

Donna M. Ballman

Confessions of a Daredevil

When I was fifteen, I had two dreams. The first I had no doubt about: I would have my own law practice by the time I was thirty. The second was more wishful thinking: I would become a pilot. At the end of 1989, right after I turned thirty, I began making both dreams come true. Call me wild. This is the story of my progress in both adventures.

Fear of Flying

I began my flying lessons several months before I opened my own practice. I was bored with the same old routine in my firm and thought I needed some excitement. My life was stable and I was making more money than I felt I needed, so why not try something new?

My first lesson gave me little chance to be afraid. It was in the air, in the pilot's seat. Actually, it is amazingly like driver's education. The instructor is seated to the right of the student and has an identical set of controls. I had white knuckles but was comforted knowing that someone else was in control. When I got over my initial shock, I began to look around and feel the exhilaration of soaring slightly below the clouds. In my heart I did not believe that I had the courage to go it alone.

Fear of Fleeing

Shortly after I began my flying lessons, things started happening at my Miami law firm that made me examine the relative comfort of my existence. A big client left and refused to pay a large hunk of their fees. Half of the partners had broken off the year before, and now many associates were leaving. When I started we had twenty-five lawyers. That number now dropped to ten. The litigation department, to which I belonged, dropped from thirteen to four lawyers. We lost two other steady clients within a very short period of time.

I began to confess my worries to my best friend, who had started her own practice with a partner three years earlier. She put a bug in my ear: the tenant in the office space she sublet with her partner was about to move. They needed a new tenant. The terms could be flexible. They would refer all of their litigation to me. At first, I balked. I was not ready. I had only graduated from the University of Miami School of Law three years earlier. It was comforting to know that someone else was in control. I gave in to the school of thought that a young lawyer had to serve an apprenticeship for other lawyers, develop her own reliable client base, and become well known in the community before going solo. I knew people who had gone out on their own, but surely they were suicidal daredevils.

I began a somewhat frantic search for another job. After all, I was an experienced commercial litigator. Surely someone would snap me up. I did not believe then that I had the experience, the clients, or the courage to go it alone.

Stalls in the Air

The worst part about my first set of flying lessons was practicing stalls. Stalls are maneuvers that require the student pilot to point the airplane as straight up as possible, until the plane stalls and starts dropping rapidly. These maneuvers prepare you for making mistakes while landing or taking off. If you pull the plane's nose up too high on takeoff or landing, the plane will stall and you will not have time to think about what to do. You have to know how to respond instinctively.

No matter what I tried, I could not get stalls right. There was nothing in the world, other than the physical strength of my instructor, that could get me to point the plane up far enough to actually get it to stall. I knew in my heart that I would drop from the sky like a rock.

I got over my resistance by having a ground school lesson on aerodynamics. I was able to get over my fear only after my instructor proved to me beyond a doubt that the plane could not smack into the ground from 2,000 feet up without defying the laws of physics. The next time I went up, I performed my stalls without a fight.

Stalls on the Ground

The worst part about looking for a job was trying to be patient. It was the end of the calendar year and interviews were coming slowly. Nobody wanted to hire in November or December. I thought I had all the time in the world, but frustration was setting in. When I was a new law school graduate, in the top 10 percent and with Law Review on my resume, the large firms wanted me but I did not want them. Now that I had decided that my best, most stable bet was with the large firms, they did not want me. Nobody goes from small to large firms. Small is better, said the common wisdom.

Somehow, I could not seem to get my interviews right. The large firms all seemed the same. Would I be going from bad to worse? Was I really that miserable? Our year-end bonuses were withheld, first "just until the beginning of January," then indefinitely. The partners, who had never gotten along well, began sniping in front of the associates. Staff started to be laid off. Still, my friend was having a hard time convincing me to go solo. I had no clients that I thought would come with me. Surely I would never be able to bring in clients like my boss, the amazing rainmaker. After all, I was no daredevil.

I only started to become convinced about going solo when my friend and her partner mentioned that a client of theirs had a possible litigation matter. Would I at least have lunch with them? We had a pleasant lunch, and I discussed the client's problem with him. We hit it off. What would it take to get me to handle the case, he inquired. My friends were pleased. They had proven to me beyond a doubt that I could get clients. I went to lunch with the next potential client without a fight.

Touch and Go—Preparing to Solo

Once you show that you know your stalls, you have to learn to take off and land before you can solo. The practice exercise is called "touch and go." It is just as it sounds: you take off and land over and over until you get it right. You can solo only after you can do this exercise completely without help and without scaring the instructor.

I took it very slowly. I could only go to lessons once a week at best, so I was taking a long time to get it right. I enjoyed working the radio, but the instructor was too comforting and too "there" for me to not rely on her. So I took off and landed over and over again for weeks, until it was comfortable.

Touch and Go—Preparing to Go Solo

The Florida Bar does not have any prerequisites to going solo. There is no comfortable period of practice beforehand. The only person you can scare is yourself. I went to the library, got all the books, and did the calculations. I determined how much my expenses would be and how much I would need to bill to pay overhead and survive. I determined that, if I used my reasonable associate's hourly rate for the first year, I would only have to bill and collect four hours per day.

I gave my firm six weeks notice and began working three jobs. I began to wrap up my old practice, set up my new one, and do my own secretarial work for the new practice. I had to do everything at once. It had to be right the first time or else. I bought computers and programs, got supplies at a going-out-of-business sale, and borrowed and bought some furniture. I hired a part-time freelance secretary who would start in a few weeks. I started doing work for my new clients. It was nerve-racking, and there was no one to rely on but myself.

Solo Practice

I soloed in my law practice before I soloed flying. I held my open house on the first of March, and it was a whopping success. I invited all the lawyers, business people, politicians, and friends that I knew. Most of them came. My freelance secretary started working part-time that same day.

Being an employer changed my perspective on life. I took back almost everything I ever said about my former bosses. Suddenly I had no runners, copy people, paralegals, or any of the other services I was accustomed to. I bought a billing program and an accounting program for my computer to manage my administrative duties.

Just as everyone had told me, the clients came somehow; mostly through other female lawyers who were delighted that I had "broken free." I started to market my practice with some limited success by joining organizations and networking, writing articles, and doing a brief promotion with direct mail. I had no trouble billing my four hours a day, except that administrative duties took up much of the rest of my time.

I was free. I could come and go as I pleased, work the way I had always wanted, and abide by no rules but my own. In many ways I was under more stress, but it was a productive stress that came from being in control of my life.

Solo Flying

My first solo flight came about two months after I opened my new practice. My instructor asked me if I could come during the week because the airport was less crowded. I could, much to my own amazement, because there was nobody to tell me that I could not. It was clear when I went up; my first touch and go was fine. Then came the traffic and the cloud. I had to continue downwind of the airport because of traffic. The air traffic controller would tell me when to turn. I kept going farther and farther until I could no longer see the airport. A rain cloud was ahead and I must have veered to the left just a little. Finally air traffic control authorized me to turn. I turned toward the airport and all I could see was the rain cloud.

I assumed that the airport was somewhere ahead of me, so I flew straight ahead. I headed for the first runway I saw, then realized it was the wrong runway. I quickly turned and somehow got to the proper runway and landed. I had made it! It had been stressful, but now that I had passed the point of no return, it seemed easy.

What It's Like to Go for It

People always ask me what it is like to be on my own. I tell them it is scary, exhilarating, tedious, and exhausting all at the same time. It is scary because you have to be totally self-reliant and confident. Sometimes you have moments of fear and doubt. You wake up at four in the morning and think you have missed that big hearing or deadline, just like the old law school nightmares of missing an exam. If you go out on your own right out of school, you have to have the self-confidence of a superhero, because you are still learning the ropes. I waited until I got some experience and felt confident in my area of practice, which is what I would recommend to people who are thinking about soloing.

As a solo, you have to be very careful about "calendaring," and if you are sick on the day of a hearing, you have to hope for some understanding from opposing counsel and the judge. You do not always get that understanding, either. There was one case where I called the judge's office, too sick to come to the hearing. I asked to appear by telephone or to reschedule. The judge allowed neither. I asked opposing counsel to call me and reschedule. He went in ex parte and got the order he sought. Of course, I sought a rehearing and got it, but in the interim I had a bitter day of panic while being too sick to do anything about it.

Solo practice is exhilarating because your victories are your own. When I won my first solo jury trial, the victory was all that much sweeter knowing it was mine alone. The clients thank you, not the partner in charge of you. Then they recommend you to their friends. This is the highest compliment of all. When you get new clients, nothing can compare to the feeling that it was your hard work and success that brought them through the door.

The tedium in soloing comes from performing the boring administrative chores that you must do to keep the firm functioning. Billing, accounting, government forms, reports, and all the tasks once performed by an office manager now fall on you. On the brighter side, however, you know you will perform these tasks correctly the first time, as compared to being in a large firm where you are truly at the mercy of support staff.

Soloing is exhausting because you work all day and still have to find time to market your services. Your day is spent networking, turning out quality work, doing more networking, and doing all the other things to keep the firm operating. Somehow, you still need develop a life outside your firm. My free time used to be spent in politics, but now that I am a new mother I ask myself, What free time? However, I managed to connect my profession and my avocation by advising campaigns on election law. I have turned my avocation into a profession by writing a book on election law and acting as counsel to candidates on various legal issues. The point is, you can do what you love and make money if you are creative about it.

Once you start soloing, you begin to develop a reputation in your area of practice. My primary area of practice is employment litigation and discrimination. Once you become known, lawyers and people you never met will refer cases to you. Then the skill comes in separating out the cases you want from those that will be all work and no pay. I recommend that you pick areas of practice that are specialized so you have a niche. That way, general practitioners will not be afraid to send you cases because there is no risk that you will steal their clients. Do not be afraid to change your primary area of practice. I started out doing primarily commercial litigation, but found that I liked discrimination work and found it easier to get business in that area. You should market continually, from speaking engagements, to writing, to sending out press releases so that your reputation develops along with your expertise.

People say it is daring to go out on your own. I say it is daring to rely on a firm for your living in these days of economic recession and hardship. I know too many young lawyers who were thrown out of their jobs without any warning. The best person to rely on is you.

Conclusion—Go for It

My point is that in any endeavor there is a first time. The first step is always the hardest. In flying, I had a truly hair-raising experience with my first solo flight. I had to develop the confidence to know I would be all right up there; otherwise, my instructor would always have to be by my side.

Down on the ground it is exactly the same. It would have been easy to stay in the cozy cocoon of a law firm, always having a partner at my side. I would not have had to learn the ins and outs of the administrative side of the practice. Solo practice is scary, but the hardest part is that first flight on your own.

The thing you must do is to plan carefully. Know your first steps, then jump in. The key to success is overcoming that initial fear. I hope all budding soloists find out what it is like to be so busy that you turn down work. Trust me—as impossible as it seems, it happens to even the most tentative soloist.

CHAPTER 23

Corporations

H. Ward Classen

Finding an In-House Position

With their increased status and salaries, as well as the competitive nature of the practice of law in general, in-house legal positions are more desirable than ever. Often, however, lawyers seeking an in-house position find their search frustrating because they lack the necessary tools to complete their search successfully. This chapter will attempt to help those lawyers seeking an in-house position obtain their goal. While this chapter cannot guarantee employment, it will certainly place readers further ahead in their job search.

The Nature of In-House Positions

The nature of in-house legal positions varies widely depending upon the employer. Lawyers working in the nonprofit sector are often the sole lawyer for the employer or are one of a small group of in-house counsel. In a for-profit setting, the number of lawyers may range from one to more than five hundred. It is in the for-profit sector that the greatest number of opportunities lies. Corporate legal departments, however, are not immune to the cost cutting affecting corporations in general. In fact, a few but growing number of corporations have outsourced their legal departments, either by transferring in-house lawyers and work to an outside law firm or by creating their own "captive" law firm. Some corporations have actually recreated their in-house staff after outsourcing it. Furthermore, after an acquisition, the acquired company's lawyers are usually terminated. Consequently, there is a level of insecurity even in in-house legal work.

The major benefit of working in-house has traditionally been the freedom from billable hours. Customarily, in-house counsel have not billed their hours, although a growing number of in-house lawyers are having to account for their hours in some way. The other advantage of an in-house position is developing an in-depth relationship with the business people. Instead of having many clients, the in-house counsel has only one. One company, acting through its nonlegal employees, one business person. This personal relationship may span the lawyer's entire career instead of solely the duration of one project. Young lawyers will have the opportunity for significant client contact, which is usually not available with outside law firms until later in their careers. Today, hours for in-house lawyers are very comparable today to those worked by outside counsel. The days of nine-to-five jobs are long gone as in-house legal departments are forced to justify their existence in an ever cost-conscious world.

Identifying the Job Opportunity

Most in-house opportunities are not advertised because most corporations realize that there is a surplus of qualified lawyers who would like to move in-house for a variety of reasons. Furthermore, they are reluctant to pay a recruiter 30 percent of the lawyer's first-year salary when they can conduct the search themselves. Thus, the successful candidate will have to make the first steps in his or her search.

Usually the first step a corporation takes to fill a vacancy is to ask the existing in-house legal staff for references of friends and acquaintances who may be interested in the position. Another common means of seeking qualified candidates is to discuss the open position with outside counsel who may know a suitable lawyer. Filling a position through outside counsel is often mutually beneficial because the corporation is able to hire a lawyer who may already be familiar with the corporation, while the outside law firm strengthens its relationship with the corporation by placing one of its lawyers in the corporation's legal department. As such, a lawyer should informally contact those clients capable of supporting an in-house lawyer and ascertain their potential interest in hiring in-house counsel.

A few corporations advertise in the mass media, usually in local papers or the local law journal. They also may advertise in specialty journals; such as the Computer Law Association's *Bulletin* and the American Corporate Counsel Association's *ACCA Docket*.

ACCA also maintains a job bank for lawyers seeking in-house positions (see http://www.acca.com). A corporation may advertise vacancies in law school placement offices (and online job placement banks for some law schools). Responding to advertisements in the mass media or in law school placement offices has a low success rate because the positions may have already been filled, having been viewed by perhaps thousands of potential applicants. Advertising a position through the mass media is not favored by a corporation seeking to fill a position because the advertisement will often result in an overload of resumes and telephone calls from candidates.

Another tactic you may use to seek this kind of job is to contact in-house counsel you know and request an informational interview; you may also invite an in-house lawyer to lunch to discuss your job search. During this meeting you should indicate your interest in an in-house position and ask if there are any opportunities either in that lawyer's company or in other companies she knows. You may then approach that company and offer your resume.

Finally, be sure to contact local search firms and place your resume on file with them as well. While search firms normally make the majority of their placements in law firms, they usually have several openings in corporations.

In deciding where to seek employment, you should determine the local rules for practicing law. Some states require in-house counsel to be admitted to that state's bar. This may be a significant burden if you cannot waive in.

Preparing for the Interview

Once you have been selected for an interview, it is imperative to undertake the necessary research on the corporation and the interviewers themselves to demonstrate interest in the position. The best way to research the corporation is through its proxy, 10K, annual report, and Lexis/Nexis. If possible, conduct a Dunn & Bradstreet search to see if the corporation is financially stable. Be wary of a corporation in financial difficulty or one in a troubled industry.

Sources to research the legal department and its members are the corporate counsel listings in Martindale-Hubbell and Prentice Hall's *Guide to Corporate Counsel.* If possible, try to learn as much about the interviewers and their backgrounds. Attempt to determine their seniority within the legal department, their practice specialties, and their tenure with the corporation. The corporation's proxy statement will often give the general counsel's background as well as his compensation, which may be useful to you in salary negotiations.

The Interview

Asking the right questions in the interview will make you stand out from other potential applicants and will provide you with the opportunity to determine if the corporation and position are a good fit. Each corporation has its own culture, which can vary greatly, making the work experience exciting and challenging, or equal to a long prison sentence.

First, determine the nature of the position. Will the position be on the legal staff or on the contracts administration staff, a nonlegal function? Many companies employ contracts administrators who have legal degrees and are on the corporate staff but are not considered to be lawyers for the corporation or to be practicing law. This is usually not a rewarding career because the career path is limited by being outside the legal department. Furthermore, most corporations do not hire their contracts administrators when a vacancy occurs in the legal department. It is also necessary to determine the legal department's reporting structure and organization. Be wary of a corporation where the general counsel does not report to the president or CEO, as this is indicative of the legal department's lack of stature.

Find out whether the corporation's lawyers are consolidated at the corporate headquarters or are dispersed in the operating units, and determine the level of autonomy the position will require. Some corporations consolidate the legal department at the corporate headquarters, while others distribute the legal staff geographically throughout its operating units. Most lawyers enjoy the autonomy of working at the division/business unit level instead of the bureaucracy of a large legal department operated at the corporate headquarters. If the position is not in that lawyer's geographic location will he or she have to relocate? The geographic location of the legal department is an important consideration because the applicant's career path may be predicated on relocating.

Ask about the level of supervision that will be received. A junior lawyer may welcome greater supervision, while a more senior lawyer may value independence. Will you be able to work independently, directly with the business people? One of the greatest advantages of being in-house counsel is the access and interaction with the business people. Be sure to explore the nature of the position itself. Does it require a generalist or an individual with a depth of knowledge in a specific industry? Larger corporations have the luxury of a specialist, while small corporations desire someone who can handle almost all issues that arise.

Is there room for advancement? Will advancement arise from the growth of the company or is it tied to the promotion retirement of the candidate's potential boss? One who is determined to advance within the corporation should ask the interviewer to map the successful candidate's potential career path and the accompanying time frames. Explore whether the corporate culture is casual or formal. The corporate culture should match the applicant's. If the culture is staid and formal, a free spirit might find working at that company frustrating. Other people, especially lawyers leaving a large firm, may chafe working at an informal entrepreneurial corporation without a chain of command.

Ask why there is an opening. Is this a newly created position or did a member of the legal staff leave? If they left, what were the surrounding circumstances? Significant turnover in a legal department is reason for concern and should be explored in greater detail. Usually, it is indicative of poor compensation, a stagnant career path, or a lack of confidence in the corporation's future. If you are interested in performing pro bono work, determine the corporation's policy on such work. Given that corporations are focused on profit and are not in the legal business, outside bar activities and pro bono work are usually not encouraged or supported. Such work is usually allowed, however, in off hours.

Even though the potential employer may have a casual dress policy, wear formal business attire for the interview and always remember to write a thank-you note. A candidate should be careful, however, to avoid asking too many questions regarding compensation issues or becoming too aggressive in probing career path issues. It is best to go into greater detail after the candidate has received an offer from the employer.

Receiving an Offer and Negotiating the Deal

Once an offer is received, do not hesitate to negotiate its terms. Remember, however, that as an applicant negotiating with his future employer, it is imperative to be realistic and cordial.

Of primary concern to most employees is the cash compensation. Many organizations, such as Altman Weil Pensa and Abbott, Langer & Associates publish salary surveys for in-house counsel segmented for different geographic locations, the employer's industry, and seniority of the lawyer, so an applicant should be able to find a lot of valuable information. Look in the corporation's proxy to determine the general counsel's compensation. If interviewing for a senior position, an applicant may be able to gauge the appropriate salary based on the general counsel's compensation, as well as the appropriate type of benefits to seek. If there is wide disparity between the offer and the desired salary, the candidate should try to educate the employer about salary levels in the area. Often the employer may be unaware of rapid increases in salaries in the local job market. The candidate should also inquire as to bonus eligibility. Many lawyers are eligible for annual bonuses. If so, the lawyer should determine whether the bonus is based on the lawyer's performance, the company's performance, or a combination of both.

As an applicant, you should be sure to determine when your annual review will occur and when you will be eligible for a salary increase. Many companies grant raises to all employees on a set date, such as the first of each year. An employee hired midyear may not want to wait eighteen months before receiving a salary review; as such the parties should agree on when a salary review will occur. Look in the footnotes of the corporation's annual report addressing pension assumptions, because the corporation is required to project its annual percentage salary increase.

When accepting a position, it is best to make sure that a title has been agreed on and that it is included in the offer letter along with the lawyer's reporting relationship. The reporting structure should be clearly explained. While law firms usually have only two classes of lawyers, partner and nonpartner, corporations have many. Titles in corporations are very important because they are often used to determine the level of benefits provided to an employee, such as stock options and the ability to participate in deferred compensation plans. Titles may also determine who attends management meetings, which in turn provide the exposure to senior management necessary for advancement.

Many companies offer stock options to their employees. A new employee should determine the basis for their award and whether he will receive any. If he does not initially qualify, he should ask when he will or what he needs to do to qualify. He should determine the corporation's vacation, 401k, pension, and maternity policies. A new employee should not be afraid to ask for more vacation than the general policy because many corporations make exceptions for their lawyers. Depending on the level of seniority, one should inquire whether there are any country club or athletic club allowances. The more entrepreneurial the corporation, the more likely an employee is to receive stock options and nontraditional benefits, such as sabbaticals and the ability to work from home. Finally, determine whether employees are reimbursed for bar dues, professional organizations, and continuing legal education. In almost all cases they are with some limits.

Although it may seem awkward to ask so many questions, experience has shown that it is easier to get the answers to these questions before starting employment. Once the lawyer has begun his employment, an employer may not be motivated to respond as quickly or to negotiate. Finally, a new employee should make sure the offer letter includes all terms that have been agreed upon so that there is no misunderstanding later; this makes your position clear even if the person who negotiated on the corporation's behalf leaves the firm.

Beginning Your Career

First impressions are important when working at a corporation. You will be judged not only on your intellect but also on your ability to get along with other people and your willingness to work long hours to support the business team. Personality is often the most important factor for success. Business people want a cohesive team and do not appreciate individuals with large egos or overly critical work styles. In a corporation, lawyers are expected to operate in a support role and provide advice as needed. They do not, for the most part, lead the team, make the decisions, or receive the glory. Because business people have profit and loss responsibility, it is they who have the final decision-making authority. Lawyers should feel free to provide constructive criticism while also recognizing that business people have the ultimate business decision-making authority. Do not interfere unless they are undertaking an illegal or unethical act.

Some in-house lawyers have a habit of criticizing their clients and the risks the business may decide to take. This only serves to alienate the client and create ill will between the parties. In these situations the lawyer will become further removed from the business process and suffer a loss of status. The successful in-house counsel will support the business people in their business decisions, good or bad, and if they believe there is a better solution, will make suggestions in a positive manner.

Mapping Your Career

Once new employment has begun, you need to map your career path. The first step is to ascertain your long-term career goals. If you want to become the corporation's general counsel, determine what promotions will have to be received and how to receive them. For example, if your boss is only two years older than you, does she have to be promoted in order for you to be promoted? If your employer has distinct divisions, such as commercial, governmental, international, do you need to work in all three groups to become general counsel? Identify the business people who are rising stars or who are powerful and well respected, and try to work for them. In order to reach the senior levels of a corporation, a lawyer must have prolonged visibility and the support of the executive management team. This come only from working on high-level projects.

When a lawyer becomes confident in his or her position it is time to formulate a career path. In other words, what is your goal and where do you want to be at the end of your career? Depending on your aspirations, focus on different parts of career development. If the goal is to become general counsel, work with as many parts of the corporation as possible even though this may require extensive travel or relocation. Others may be satisfied with a stable position and be unwilling to make the personal sacrifices necessary to ascend the corporate ladder. Regardless of their career goals, every employee needs to assess continually their career to make sure they fulfill their career goals.

Conclusion

While an in-house position can be an exciting and challenging one it is not for everyone. I hope that this chapter has provided the insight necessary to obtain an in-house position. Best of luck in finding the position of your choice.

CHAPTER 24

Federal Agencies

Marilyn Tucker

The federal government employs approximately 25,350 lawyers and many others with law degrees who are employed in law-related or nonlegal positions. Nearly 45 percent (11,500) of these lawyers are concentrated in the Washington, D.C., area. During the past five years, the percentage of women in federal legal positions in the nation's capital increased from 42 percent to the current 47 percent. Nationally, women account for 38 percent of federal lawyers, which represents an increase of approximately 11 percent over the past decade.

Economic and political factors govern the number of lawyers hired annually by the federal government. During the 1997 fiscal year, the most recent year for which this information is available, 880 new full-time lawyers were hired, up from 660 in 1996, according to the Statistical Analysis and Services Division of the Office of Personnel Management (OPM). However, over the past decade there have been many fluctuations in the number of full-time lawyer positions available. For example, 1,654 new lawyers were hired in 1991, while two years later this number decreased dramatically to 582. At many agencies today, cutbacks have slowed lawyer hiring; in other agencies, like the Securities and Exchange Commission (SEC), there has been a greater than usual number of employment opportunities because of increased employee turnover. Although the economy has a direct impact on employment opportunities, lawyers are always being hired by the government, even while a freeze is on, while cutbacks are occurring, or when economic conditions are less than favorable. Job seekers, therefore, should not be discouraged by numbers alone.

An understanding of the employment patterns of federal lawyers, and which agencies provide the most likely opportunities for experienced lawyer applicants, will make the job-hunting task less daunting. According to Linda A. Cinciotta, director of the Office of Attorney Personnel Management, Department of Justice, of the total number of lawyers employed by the federal government, one-third work at the Department of Justice. Other federal

213

lawyers work for approximately sixty-four different agencies. The top ten agencies employ about 23,000 lawyers and twenty-seven agencies have more than a hundred lawyers on staff (see the list at the end of this chapter).

Lawyers, as part of the Excepted Service, are not rated by the OPM; rather lawyer recruitment and hiring is handled by individual federal agencies. This eliminates the bureaucratic red tape of the OPM rating process; however, it also means that there is no central information source on lawyer job vacancies. Consequently, a decision to seek legal employment with the federal government means checking with each agency of interest to determine its current needs and procedures. Often, applicants have difficulty obtaining such information, and the decentralized process can seem overwhelming and frustrating. Many prospective applicants do not know how to begin the process of seeking federal legal employment, and frequently are neither thorough nor aggressive when searching for opportunities.

The Advertising of Lawyer Positions

Because the OPM is not involved in lawyer hiring, job openings do not have to be advertised. Individual agencies have the authority to hire without justifying their selection to an outside oversight agency. Those government agencies with large lawyer populations often have separate offices for lawyer personnel recruitment; however, most of these offices are more involved in entry-level than experienced lawyer hiring.

Although it is not a requirement, some agencies regularly advertise lawyer openings, while others advertise only when very specialized and difficult-to-find experience is sought. In some agencies, when an opening becomes available, employees within the immediate division, as well as within other divisions of the same agency, are made aware of the opening. Also, some agencies mail job announcements to those federal agencies on their employee service mailing list.

A small number of federal agencies use vacancy announcements to advertise lawyer openings. Since vacancy announcements are used infrequently for advertising legal positions, many applicants overlook this valuable information source. Agencies that do use vacancy announcements, such as the U.S. Department of Agriculture, post announcements in their own personnel office and send them to other agencies and to law school career services offices. All vacancy announcements for legal positions will have a "905" occupational code designating a "lawyer" position—one in which the individual has a lawyer-client relationship with the agency. Jobs that directly draw upon legal skills, but that have been classified as legislative or law-related, will not have a "905" occupational code. Vacancy announcements also give the position title, location of the job, opening and closing dates for accepting applications, qualifications desired and required, and a position description. The position description section is highly detailed and, as a result, is the most helpful part of a vacancy announcement. Job seekers are able to use the specifics of the job description in tailoring a resume, completing a Standard Form 171, which is still in use, or the newer OF 612, and in planning an interview strategy. Thus, vacancy announcements should not be overlooked when seeking government legal employment.

Positions that are publicly advertised usually appear in the *National and Federal Legal Employment Report,* in *The Federal Career Opportunities Bulletin,* which is more general and not exclusively for legal positions, in *Legal Times,* the *Washington Post,* and in some law school alumni job bulletins. The Federal Bar Association (FBA) publishes the *Lawyer's Job Bulletin Board,* another source used by agencies to list lawyer positions. The FBA has an Internet address (*http://www.fedbar.org*) that provides more information on obtaining a subscription to the *Lawyer's Job Bulletin Board.* If very specialized experience is sought, positions are likely to be advertised in trade publications whose readers are prospective applicants and in periodicals such as the *Legal Times,* the *National Law Journal,* or on rare occasions, the *Wall Street Journal.*

In addition, there are now many sources of legal job information on the Internet. Most Web site databases list private sector positions, but there are also various sites that maintain information on opportunities in the government. For example, the federal government's human resources agency, the OPM, maintains an Internet site (http://www.opm.gov). This site provides one of the best online resources to access information on federal job opportunities quickly and without any cost to the job seeker. The site allows job seekers to search the database by selecting from a set of categories. For legal jobs, an individual can either conduct a search by inputting the field of interest and the preferred geographic location or by selecting a specific agency, which will bring up all positions currently available in that agency.

Two providers of legal research tools, Lexis-Nexis and Westlaw, also maintain information that is helpful in the job-search process. Lexis-Nexis has a database source available called the Career Center (*http://www.lexis-nexis.com/research*), which can be searched by selecting from different directories. It includes a great government directory that provides information about opportunities in federal agencies, Congress, and the judiciary. In order to search the database, individuals must acquire a sign-in code and password from their law school career services office (or contact them at the customer service line at 1-800-45-LEXIS for more information). In addition, Lexis-Nexis provides information on their Web site (*http://www.lexis-nexis.com*) that can be useful to individuals in the research process when targeting the federal job search.

Westlaw also maintains information available online regarding legal employment (http://www.westgroup.com). One of the resources available through this site, the *West Legal Directory,* can be used to retrieve information about the federal government as well as about specific firms, lawyers, and the judiciary. Many of the resources available in print such as the *United States Government Manual, The Federal Yellow Book, The Federal Regional Yellow Book,* and *The Congressional Yellow Book* are available through Westlaw's Web site. This allows job seekers to conduct research and to locate specific individuals whom they can contact in particular agencies or departments more quickly and efficiently.

Another source of online federal job information is provided by the Federal Research Service, Inc. (http://www.fedjobs.com). This service maintains an extensive, daily updated, database of job opportunities in the federal government. Listings of available legal positions are also available and can be accessed directly by conducting a search by category name. Although an individual may browse the Internet site for general information, in order to conduct a search, he or she must subscribe to the service for at least one month.

These are by no means the only resources available through the Internet. With the vast growth in information technology, more resources are constantly becoming available online that will make the research and job-seeking process more efficient and much less time-consuming. Many of the sources available in print will also provide an Internet Web site address that an individual may access. Because Web sites can be updated more quickly than paper publications, it is wise to check them for additional information.

Even after utilizing these possible sources of information, it is important to keep in mind that many lawyer positions are not advertised publicly. Thus job seekers who desire a legal career with the federal government should rely heavily on networking and making contacts.

Target Your Federal Job Search

The first thing you will need to do is to narrow down your "federal government legal position" job search. Begin by reading about and understanding the nature of the legal work done by each of the various agencies. Do not assume that general knowledge provides enough information about the legal work of the agencies to enable you to skip this important research step. Too often, opportunities are overlooked because job seekers take this attitude. Many job seekers, for example, believe that all positions with the Internal Revenue Service (IRS) require a background in tax. Although this is certainly true for most of the IRS divisions, one does not need a tax background to work in the Disclosure, Litigation, Criminal Tax, or General Legal Services divisions. Similarly, job seekers often assume that all positions at the Department of Justice (DOJ) are for those interested in litigation. This is also an incorrect assumption as there are numerous opportunities at DOJ for lawyers not interested in litigation. It is important, therefore, to do the background reading and not to assume that the name of an agency provides all of the required information. Lawyers, as job seekers, frequently base major career decisions on "hunches" and "assumptions." You would not advise a client to make important decisions without facts, and this decision is at least as important to you and your long-term career satisfaction.

A good way to begin is by reviewing the *U.S. Government Manual* for a broad overview of each federal agency and its mission. Two sources, *Federal Careers for Attorneys* and *Now Hiring: Government Jobs for Lawyers* (hereafter, *Now Hiring*), can be utilized to learn more about legal positions in the federal sector. *Federal Careers for Attorneys* has an excellent topical index that simplifies the task of identifying agencies and specific divisions within agencies in considering particular areas. For example, the "civil rights" topic in this index refers the reader to approximately thirty different divisions or sections of federal agencies that deal in some way with civil rights issues. These three sources should provide enough background for you to eliminate some agencies and determine which others are of interest. You will then be ready to develop a list of "target" agencies.

While focusing on agencies in which you have a particular interest, think also about geography. Although nearly half (approximately 11,500) of all federal lawyer positions are in the Washington, D.C. area, there are more than thirty federal agencies with regional, district, or field offices that use legal staff. The staffs of regional offices are small, and, as a result, it can be more difficult to obtain a legal position with a satellite office. Nevertheless, if your primary goal is to get a job with a specific agency—either because you have expertise you want to build upon or because you wish to begin acquiring expertise in a specific field—it is certainly worth considering several locations. Lawyer hiring is handled by the individual regional, district, or field offices—although there are some exceptions like the National Labor Relations Board, in which all lawyer hiring is handled through the central office in Washington.

In addition, a number of publications may be helpful in identifying possibilities outside the Washington area. One excellent resource mentioned earlier, *Federal Careers for Attorneys,* provides a geographical listing of federal agencies in each state that have legal staffs. Although some other publications do not limit their information to agencies with legal staffs, these resources are helpful information sources when considering federal employment. *The Federal Regional Yellow Book,* for example, is a semiannual publication covering federal government offices outside Washington. Another resource for identifying nationwide possibilities is *The Federal Yellow Book,* which identifies federal hiring offices throughout the country. While not comprehensive, the list below is intended to give you an idea of agencies with regional or satellite offices:

- Department of Agriculture
- Department of Defense
- Department of Education
- Department of Health and Human Services
- Department of Housing and Urban Development
- Department of Justice
- Department of Transportation
- Department of the Treasury
- Environmental Protection Agency
- Equal Employment Opportunity
- Federal Deposit Insurance Corporation
- Internal Revenue Service
- Postal Service
- Securities and Exchange Commission

Once you have narrowed your initial search to a few target agencies, check agency Web sites (see the list at the end of this chapter) to get further information and to determine if those agencies publish a brochure for prospective lawyers. Some Web sites even link the user to information about job openings specifically for lawyers. Recruitment brochures, though usually written specifically for new lawyers, contain information that is relevant to all lawyer applicants. Reading the brochures will help you determine to which sections, departments, or divisions of the agency you want to direct your application. Otherwise, if you apply to the agency as a whole and do not indicate a preference for particular departments, those individuals screening resumes will decide for you where to direct your application. The choice should be yours; it is, after all, your career.

Legislative/Policy Positions

Many positions which are sought by lawyers are legislative and policy-oriented and thus do not have the words "Attorney Advisor" or the 905 occupational code in the title. These positions are not part of the Excepted Service and as a result, there is a far more structured system for obtaining those opportunities. Individual applications are evaluated by Personnel and rated according to a very elaborate point system. Nonetheless, these evaluations are made based upon information provided by the applicant. How well individual applicants complete the appropriate forms and detail their relevant experience is very important in determining how high a ranking the applicant is given. Using the right buzz words, for example, is important in filling out the forms. Every phrase and clause, every function performed, every class attended, helps to add to the rating score and makes the applicant more competitive. Job seekers are well advised to spend the time working on a carefully crafted description of their background—a description that errs on the side of specificity. Remember, the burden of proof is on the job seeker! Consequently, applicants should talk ahead of time with people in the department/section of interest to get helpful hints, word choice considerations, and so on. While each step of the job search process is time-consuming, this is a step worthy of the time because only the credentials of the highest ranking candidates and those whose qualifications have been certified are sent to individual supervisors for consideration.

Law-Related Positions

There are many government jobs that do not require a law degree but are frequently filled by persons with such a degree. *Federal Law-Related Careers* defines a "law-related career" as one in which "a law degree, legal training, or knowledge of one or more areas of law is directly applicable to the work involved" and, in fact, "the job description [may require] the incumbent to utilize certain legal skills." *Federal Law-Related Careers* currently lists more than 150 law-related positions. However, as the issues of the day change and new areas become increasingly important, additional opportunities are created.

This publication also contains an excellent topical index showing federal law-related careers according to legal fields of interest. A job seeker can use this index to identify positions closely related to a particular legal background or interest. For example, a job seeker interested in international trade would be directed to seven different law-related positions, while the applicant interested in civil rights would find that there are six different types of law-related positions.

Law-related positions, unlike lawyer positions, do not have 905 occupational codes; each law-related position has a different code. Lawyers working in law-related positions have frequently sought to have their positions reclassified. Reclassifying a position, particularly attempting to have a law-related position designated as a 905 classification, is an extremely difficult task even when the job draws directly upon legal skills. Job seekers should not accept a law-related position with the expectation that, once in the job, they may be able to arrange for such a reclassification.

Unlike lawyer, attorney-advisor, or law clerk jobs, law-related positions are not part of the Excepted Service; they are part of the competitive OPM process and thus, in order to qualify, applicants must be listed on the appropriate register. For law-related positions, the SF 171 form becomes an extremely important factor. And as stated earlier about legislative positions, every word and description used can help to make an applicant more competitive.

In addition, the inclusion of law-related positions in the OPM rating process does offer the advantage of centralized job vacancy information sources. Job seekers can find advertised openings in the biweekly publication *Federal Career Opportunities Bulletin*. Additionally, a wide range of recorded federal job information, including current employment opportunities and special programs, is available by calling (202) 606-2700 in the Washington DC area or (912) 757-3000 in all other areas of the country. In Washington, a telephone device for the deaf (TDD) can be accessed at (202) 606-0591. Contact local state employment services for the TDD numbers in other regions of the country.

A sampling of positions are listed below to give you an idea of the variety and types of positions that are classified as law-related:

- Civil rights analyst
- Contract termination specialist
- Copyright examiner
- Court administrator
- Criminal investigator
- Employee relations specialist
- Estate tax examiner
- Hearings and appeals officer
- International trade specialist
- Labor-management relations examiner
- Mediator
- Procurement analyst
- Veterans claims examiner
- Wage and hour compliance specialist

For a complete listing of law-related positions, use *Federal Law-Related Careers* and *The Paralegal's Guide to U.S. Government Jobs*.

Where the Jobs Are and Will Be

Generally, agency opportunities exist for two reasons. First, openings occur because of normal attrition—lawyers leave and need to be replaced—and second, because the current economic conditions may make experience gained in particular agencies extraordinarily marketable. Thus, lawyers leave for higher salaries. Federal lawyer turnover is a function of how much private sector work exists. If a great deal of work is done in the private sector in a specific practice area, turnover in that area is greater and lawyers leave for private practice. Turnover may also be a function of how much funding Congress provides to a certain agency. Normally, the more funding an agency receives, the less turnover it experiences.

As a job hunter, it is important to recognize and be aware of market trends. Federal lawyer hiring fluctuates dramatically, as noted earlier, and is directly related to the vagaries of the economy. What are the current issues, hot new areas, and trends affecting American business and, therefore, federal lawyer hiring? Where is legal work growing and where is deregulation causing it to diminish? Two good sources are the front page of the monthly *National and Federal Legal Employment Report,* which occasionally chronicles current trends, and the regular "Federal Diary" column in the *Washington Post,* which often points out events that affect federal legal hiring. Regularly reading business periodicals such as the *Wall Street Journal, The Kiplinger Washington Letter,* which is published weekly, or scanning the *Index to Business Periodicals* will help you keep current.

In recent years, specialties that have been growing and showing evidence of continued activity are telecommunications, intellectual property, financial services, and law enforcement—including immigration and drug enforcement. How does this translate into federal hiring possibilities? Although an opening may not exist at any given moment, agencies involved in these areas are likely to be experiencing growth over the long term, and they are good choices for those seeking legal employment with the federal government. As one issue is resolved, another surfaces, and with it the need for more personnel to staff, direct, and implement programs, the law, and its regulations. Predicting where the jobs are likely to be is a matter of understanding current national priorities. Nonetheless, opportunities for experienced lawyers interested in federal employment always appear greater in agencies that recruit litigators as well as in those agencies whose staff consists of a high percentage of lawyers.

Federal Employment and Future Marketability

Although individuals who come to the federal government as laterals (those who have previously practiced) are more likely to remain in government employment, nevertheless, it is worth making career decisions with an eye toward flexibility. It is easier to move from private practice to agency practice because there is virtually no aspect of the private sector that does not exist in the federal government—although the opposite is not true. Agencies with private practice counterparts are more likely to have a continuous need for applicants as people move in and out. Therefore, to increase your long-term marketability when seeking government employment, do so with the prospect that you may eventually leave and go to the private sector. Keep several issues in mind as you consider the multitude of federal legal opportunities. Know which substantive areas have a counterpart in the private sector and thus are more marketable. Know which of the divisions within various agencies provide that experience because the division frequently plays a greater role in future transferability than the agency itself.

Individuals practicing in a particular specialty field, whether inside or outside the federal government, will know which federal agencies and which divisions within those agencies, provide sought-after experience. Seek their counsel. Recognize that some agencies, for example, the Internal Revenue Service (IRS) in the tax area, the Department of Justice in the litigation field, and the Comptroller of the Currency in the banking area, are recognized "training grounds" for the private bar. Mobility is afforded to those who practice with those agencies whether they begin there directly after law school or later in their career.

Many agencies are engaged in fields that are not practiced by the private bar. Although these areas of specialization can be extremely interesting, evaluate the future prospects of transferability ahead of time and make decisions regarding employment with all available information. Do not find out after the fact that your assumptions were inaccurate. You may expect that experience gained in a particular division is highly valued outside the government when indeed your views may not be shared by the private bar. Also, most agencies have lawyers handling "housekeeping matters" such as equal employment opportunity, contracts, conflicts of interest, Freedom of Information Act (FOIA), torts, property, work related to the Federal Advisory Commission's Act, the Sunshine Act, and the Administrative Procedures Act. Although the name of the office handling these matters varies and the content areas may be pursued in any agency, job seekers should recognize that experience in these areas is not easily transferable to the private sector.

The Job of Getting a Job in the Federal Government

In many agencies, lawyer hiring occurs through the general counsel's office; occasionally, lawyer hiring may be through the personnel office. To determine which of these patterns exists, and therefore to whom to send a resume, use *Now Hiring*. This publication designates by agency a lawyer, general counsel, personnel officer, or a lawyer recruitment coordinator as the contact person for applicants. Where a title is listed without a name, make a telephone call to the general counsel's office or the personnel office or use *The Federal Yellow Book* to obtain the correct name rather than addressing your correspondence to an unspecified person. When you have identified the correct person, send a resume and a well-written cover letter to the office listed in *Now Hiring* whether or not a job has been advertised.

Since each agency handles recruitment in its own manner, it is very difficult to describe the general process in great detail. When resumes are received, they may be automatically circulated to the division requested by the applicant or the one deemed appropriate by the reviewer, or they may be kept on file until a division requests resumes. Agencies keep resumes on file for varying lengths of time—generally three months to one year although a few, like the National Labor Relations Board, keep resumes in an active file for two years. After that time, if you wish to remain an active applicant, it is necessary to inform the agency in writing and to send another resume with a written request.

At the time you apply, it generally is not necessary to submit a Standard Form (SF) 171. Lawyers, and those who hire lawyers, usually rely on a resume; however, an SF 171 is generally completed after the fact to conform with government regulations. Since it is rarely necessary to begin the process with the SF 171, do not wait until that form is complete to apply for an opening. Those agencies which have their own forms or SF 171 supplements routinely send those forms to applicants from whom they received a resume.

An Aggressive Approach

It is critically important that you do not stop with a resume sent to a single, central location. It is imperative that you send a resume to each of the legal divisions in which you have an interest or, if you are uncertain about which division or have no preference, send the resume to all of the divisions within the agency staffed by lawyers. Call the unit and find out who is in charge of hiring and to whom you should direct your resume. Remember—it is appropriate to send multiple resumes to different divisions of a single agency. A breakdown of divisions is provided in the table of contents of *Federal Careers for Attorneys* and *Now Hiring*.

Whether your resume is received in response to an actual job listing or as part of your prospecting strategy, your job search has only just begun. Too many job seekers send a resume and then wait. The longer one is out of law school, the less likely this approach will work. If you are serious about finding a position with a federal agency, you cannot afford to stop after the resume is in the mail. Each agency receives an overwhelming number of applications. The personnel officer in an agency with a small legal staff says that they receive approximately 50–150 unsolicited resumes each month from experienced lawyers. If that is the case in agencies with small legal staffs, imagine the number of resumes received by the large agencies, and you will understand why you cannot afford to sit back and wait.

Another reason to avoid a passive approach is the tendency of everyone who has an opening to aggressively spread the word among professional colleagues involved in the same specialty area. "My top-notch litigator is accepting a position in private practice. Do you know anyone with a few years of litigation experience?" Additionally, everyone who receives a continuous flow of resumes realizes that there is no systematic, guaranteed way to find the best employee, nor is there a way to interview all of the applicants with promise. Consequently, for those individuals doing the actual hiring, the personal recommendation route has huge advantages. The hiring person's easiest venue is to hire someone they know or have recently gotten to know.

It is not surprising, therefore, that people coming into the government, as well as people leaving the government, continue relationships with their private sector counterparts and serve as unofficial hiring sources for one another. A Federal Communications Commission (FCC) lawyer mentioned that former colleagues, now in private practice, call him whenever their firm needs a communications lawyer. This process cuts across agencies, is unrelated to specialties, and takes place on a regular and continuing basis. Even when there is no direct private practice counterpart, hiring lawyers prefer to use recommendations from colleagues as a way to screen the pool of applicants they will interview. One young government lawyer indicated that when an opening occurred in his division, he solicited candidate recommendations from both a judge he had appeared before and a law school professor with whom he had worked. The position was advertised, but those who were actually interviewed were more likely to be candidates recommended by the judge, the professor, or other professional colleagues.

In addition to their private practice counterparts and professional colleagues, government-hiring people recruit experienced lawyers from client agencies. It is not unusual for applicants, for example, in the Environment and Natural Resources Division of the Department of Justice, to come from the Environmental Protection Agency and the Department of Interior, or for Comptroller of the Currency applicants to be sought from the Federal Reserve or from the Federal Deposit Insurance Corporation (FDIC). As an experienced lawyer, it is important to understand these "feeder" relationships and to plan a realistic strategy accordingly. You cannot rely on being at the right place at the right time or being selected from a huge pool of applicants based upon your paper credentials. A small percentage of job seekers find opportunities in that way; the majority do not. You must be willing to conduct an aggressive campaign.

If you do have contacts in an agency of interest, call the individual you know, even if it has been many years since you have seen or spoken to each other. You might say something like, "It has been a long time since I have seen you, and I understand that you have been at Housing and Urban Development [HUD] for five years. Currently, I'm at a crossroads in my career. I am contemplating seeking a position in the government [or switching agencies], but I have not yet made any decisions. I'm calling you now because you obviously know a great deal about the agency, and I would value your opinion. Would you be willing to spend fifteen or twenty minutes with me?"

If you do not know anyone in the agency of interest, it is important that you take on the time-consuming task of finding lawyers within each of the divisions of interest to whom you can direct another resume. These "insider" lawyers should be individuals to whom you have been referred through a mutual friend or acquaintance. There are several items of importance to remember. First, the insider lawyer is unlikely to be involved in hiring and may not be aware of openings within the division or agency as a whole. Second, the lawyers to whom you are referred by the intermediary friend or acquaintance do not have to be branch or section chiefs or even lawyers in the same department. If they practice law with the agency, if they are staff lawyers, they can still provide insider information and direct you to the appropriate sources, albeit less directly. Assume that this insider may be willing to be of some assistance based upon the positive impression that you make during your face-to-face meeting and based upon your having a mutual friend. He or she will know the power structure within the division, can provide the name of an individual with whom you should get in contact, or may be willing to personally direct your resume and possibly even put in a good word for you.

Once you have found people who know lawyers working for an agency in which you are interested, get started by using the name of your acquaintance. You might say, "Hello, Mr. Smith. My name is John Tailor. I'm a friend of Chris Potter, and I got your name from him. I am at a crossroads in my career and am contemplating several possible career moves. One possibility is to move into the federal sector or to transfer agencies. Based upon what I've learned about you from Chris, I would value your experience. Would you be willing to meet with me for fifteen or twenty minutes?" (See Chapter 7 for a discussion of informational interviewing.)

Frequently, job hunters are hesitant about using their contacts. They assume that their own contacts, and those to whom they have been referred, can do nothing to help because they are not (a) responsible for hiring, (b) high enough in the pecking order, (c) in the right division, or (d) likely to put themselves out for another applicant. Making such assumptions will have a detrimental effect on the job-search process. Regardless of the size of the agency's legal staff and the turnover, personal contacts are not just important; they are absolutely necessary. A dozen or more federal lawyers, interviewed for this chapter, made the following comments: "Networking is the only thing that works;" "I have worked for several different agencies, and it is clear that it makes a difference if you know someone;" "You will be more likely to get an interview if your resume is delivered by a colleague;" and "People who have obtained positions in federal legal offices have done so by making themselves known." A comment from a lawyer that he or she has met you and that you seem bright, articulate, and well qualified, can be extraordinarily helpful in giving you an edge over faceless applicants whose resumes sit piled on an interviewer's desk.

Once you have been helped by an insider and are under consideration for a position, obtaining the job requires that you demonstrate independence—evidence of your ability to work on your own. Also, you must be able to assume responsibility and to use the words of one Department of Justice practitioner, to "lawyer over your head." That is, as a government lawyer, you will be up against high-powered private lawyers who have been practicing for more than thirty years. You need to show confidence that you are able and willing to play over your head. Often, lawyers joining a federal agency from a private firm are surprised at how much greater responsibility and independence they have in the government. Good judgment is critical, as government lawyers are calling the shots, whereas clients typically dictate the shots in private firm practice. Consequently, whether you are networking or actually being interviewed for an opening, you will need to show evidence of your ability to work independently, to handle responsibility beyond your experience, and to exercise good judgment.

Timing Issues

Be prepared for the job search to take six to nine months or longer. The actual length of time, of course, depends upon many factors. Some of these factors are out of your control, such as the economy and the hiring goals of the agencies you have targeted. For example, the congressional appropriations process affects an agency's hiring needs for the following fiscal year because lawyer hiring is related to the agency's budget. In addition, your qualifications, level of job-seeking activity, and luck affects the time it will take.

While the largest percentage of experienced lawyers seeking government employment do so with two to six years of experience, seasoned lawyer applicants cover the whole spectrum in terms of years in practice and in background. They come with one to more than twenty years of experience from all legal settings including private law firms, corporate counsel, local government, solo practice, and even academe. These varying levels and types of experience also impact the amount of time it can take to obtain a federal legal position. Even job seekers with exceedingly strong credentials report that it takes many months to obtain a federal position.

In addition to being realistic about the amount of time it is likely to take to obtain a federal legal position, job seekers need to understand that there is no hiring season for experienced lawyers, although some agencies indicate that spring may be a good time for lawyers moving in laterally. Would-be government lawyers should recognize that hiring officials in those agencies that annually seek out large numbers of new law school graduates could be busy with new recruits from August through December. At those agencies, the process for experienced lawyer hiring may be slow in the fall. Also, if the target agency has a peak season, as the Internal Revenue Service does, recruiting and hiring will not be a top priority for a period of several weeks or months. Other agencies may have their own informal scheduling issues related to seasonally heavy workloads.

The New Lateral Lawyer Recruitment Program, Department of Justice

For several years, under the leadership of Linda A. Cinciotta, the Office of Attorney Personnel Management of the Department of Justice has surveyed government agencies regarding their hiring needs. In their most current survey, completed in April 1998, the Office of Attorney Personnel Management found little encouraging information regarding experienced lawyer hiring. Most of the agencies were noncommittal and indicated that they were "uncertain," "some hiring anticipated," or were "replacement hiring only." Of the twenty-six agencies surveyed, only two mentioned actual numbers of any consequence—the Department of Air Force (Judge Advocate General, or JAG), expecting to hire forty-five experienced lawyers for 1999 and the SEC anticipating hiring 150 for the same time period.

During the last several years, only a small percentage of lawyers have been hired for full-time permanent positions. Most others have been hired as contract lawyers for a year or two. An FCC lawyer mentioned that to his knowledge, "No position since 1996 has been permanent, but none of the [temporary lawyers] have been riffed either." These contract positions carry no benefits and individual lawyers do not accrue preferences if they later reapply.

However, the Department of Justice itself (DOJ), the largest legal employer in the world, has created a new and far-reaching pilot recruitment program known as the Lateral Attorney Recruitment Program, or LARP, in order to enhance experienced lawyer recruiting. Historically, the DOJ, including the United States Attorneys' Offices, has hired approximately 500 to 1,200 experienced lawyers annually and currently employs over 9,000 lawyers. The goal of LARP is to professionalize experienced lawyer recruitment through focused marketing, expanded outreach, enhanced technology, and more efficient systems. The implementation of LARP will greatly enhance the availability and accessibility of up-to-date information on lawyer employment opportunities for those interested in working for the department.

LARP advertises many of the DOJ's lawyer vacancies in one central location (http://www.usdoj.gov/careers/oapm/). *The Legal Activities Book* (*LAB;* see http://www.usdoj.gov/careers/oapm/lab/ or your law school career services office) describes the legal responsibilities of the DOJ and the work of each of its organizations. The *LAB* includes a directory of organizational contacts (including the name, telephone number, and mailing address) that can be used for submission of resumes.

However, there are always additional vacancies that for any number of reasons may not be advertised. Therefore, a lawyer interested in a particular organization within the DOJ may apply directly to that organization even if the Web page does not show current vacancies.

Compensation

Experienced lawyers generally begin federal service at the GS-13 level ($55,004), although this varies not only with the agency, but occasionally with the division (the Enforcement Division of the SEC begins lawyers at a GS-12 level) and also with the number of years and type of experience. Some laterals come in as GS-14 ($64,998) or GS-15 ($76,456), but this is certainly not the norm.

Salary has long been a factor for those considering federal government positions. The dramatic gap between private and public salaries is often compounded by the high cost of living in Washington, D.C., where most federal lawyers are based. Within grades, however, there is some flexibility if an agency can justify that the potential hire's expertise or credentials warrant a special circumstance. Some agencies have fairly rapid grade promotion ladders, so that salary can increase significantly in a short period of time. Nonetheless, regardless of in-grade flexibility and promotion schedules, the monetary differential has been a factor to consider. This extends beyond the General Schedule (GS) level into the Senior Executive Service (SES) where the pay cap is approximately $125,900. For new lawyers, there are real advantages to the GS system because the first couple of steps are almost automatic. Generally, in one year's time, an individual will earn a GS-12 salary and after another year will earn a GS-13 salary. Nonetheless, there is talk of changing the GS system and experimenting with one that is more merit-based, as in the private sector. Currently, the Pentagon is engaged in such an experiment and, depending upon its success, may pave the way for other agencies.

During the summer of 1998, private practice salaries escalated and compensation became an issue of even greater concern among those charged with finding bright legal talent for the federal government. However, lawyers' increasingly vocal commitment to a balanced lifestyle has reduced some concerns about salary differentials.

Career Advancement

Moving from a GS-13, where most experienced lawyers begin, to a GS-14 is a matter of time in the pay grade. In many agencies, the number of GS-15 positions are limited, and most require supervisory or management duties. A lawyer who wants to be a traditional practitioner and not handle the administrative matters may have difficulty securing a nonsupervisory GS-15 position.

The pyramid is clearly very wide at the bottom and narrow at the top. If you are in an office with more qualified people than top slots, you may get stymied at the GS-14 nonmanagement level. If that happens, what can you do? Very little, except for being patient and making your commitment to the agency known. A lateral move to a regional office is not the solution; it is difficult to transfer into those offices at high grades. Nor is a move to another office within the agency a viable option since they too have their own people in line. In many agencies there are a limited number of GS-15 positions, and the branch chief and section chiefs in these positions are generally career people not likely to be moving on. Nonetheless, although there are ceilings on the number of positions, ambitious individuals who plan to stay with the federal government and who make that known, do eventually get into supervisory positions.

Beyond the GS-15 level are the SES positions, which are compensated at levels above the grade schedules. Each agency establishes the technical qualifications for its SES positions, and there are government-wide managerial qualifications, known as "executive competency review factors," which are listed in each issue of the *National and Federal Legal Employment Report*. SES positions, such as technical advisor, division director, and so on, are extremely competitive, and many people find that leaving the government and then returning makes them more competitive for these prestigious appointments.

Advantages of Federal Legal Practice

There are numerous advantages to practicing law for the federal government. In addition to having the opportunity to be involved in making national policy decisions, government lawyers are given responsibility at a very early stage. As a result, those lawyers coming into the federal government having practiced for just a few years, have immediate opportunities to work on significant issues and to litigate. Often, they are dealing with law firm counterparts at the partnership level.

Private practitioners must continuously compete for new clients. This constant pressure to get and then to keep clients is not for everyone. Practicing law for a federal agency where there is a "captive client" frees lawyers of this concern and allows them to concentrate on solving legal issues rather than on wooing prospects.

Because government lawyers are not competing for clients or attempting to make a profit for the organization, they are also freed of billable hour pressures and the extraordinarily long days that often result. There is great variation from agency to agency but, as a general rule, government lawyers work more reasonable hours—another advantage of federal employment. An individual who wants to pursue outside interests will find government practice more in tune with personal needs.

Another advantage of federal practice is the marketability of the experience. Those who leave the federal practice go not only to private law firms but also to financial institutions, associations, Capitol Hill, and academia. Career mobility from the government, however, depends upon how much experience one has and by which agency or agencies one has been employed. Some agencies are clearly revolving doors, while others provide little transferability. Lawyers who enter the government having already practiced for a number of years are less likely to move around; they often stay and become the career lawyers. However, those who want to leave government should do so before they have practiced in that setting for too many years; otherwise it may be difficult to move because government lawyers will not have portable clients.

Often experienced lawyers change jobs to move into a different specialty. Changing specialties is not easy to do under any circumstances, but many lawyers have found federal agencies far more receptive than private employers. For those who want to move out of a particular content area that they dislike or one that is defunct, or for those who want to move into the private sector but whose credentials are lacking, the federal government often provides a credible interim move from which they are able to achieve their ultimate goal. One government lawyer with five years of experience wanted to achieve two goals—to change from energy to another specialty area and also to move into the private sector. She was unsuccessful in finding a private sector nonenergy position. However, although she was unable to achieve both goals simultaneously, she did find an agency that was willing to hire her in a totally different content area. If she later decides to leave the second agency, her new specialty is very marketable and could provide the opportunity to move into the private sector—having then achieved both her goals.

Interim moves into the federal sector as a way to change content specialities or as a way to fill a content gap before moving into private practice, while not without risk, has worked for many ambitious lawyers. The federal government provides the credibility and the opportunity that is otherwise difficult to attain.

Last, if a lawyer's career gets off track for some reason, accepting a position with the federal government can be a face-saving way to get back on track. Occasionally, lawyers who have been denied partnership in a private firm will take this route.

The advantage of federal employment, and thus the motivation of experienced lawyers to find a government position or to switch agencies, is most often related to the aforementioned advantages—a desire to change content specialties, get a career back on track, have time for other interests, or to escape the intense pressures of private practice.

The major disadvantage to being a government lawyer is perhaps compensation. Another issue that concerns many experienced lawyers is the time commitment required by a number of federal agencies. Those commitments, which ask that new hires remain with the agency for three or four years, are considered necessary because of the magnitude of the cases and the need to rely on experienced counsel. Some agencies require that new hires sign a commitment agreement, and other agencies appear to treat the issues more informally. Before accepting an offer with a federal agency, applicants should know whether a commitment is required and for how long.

In addition to this commitment to remain with an agency for a specified time period, there is now another time issue—the five-year rule, which does not permit an individual to appear before an agency with which he was previously associated. This ruling keeps many excellent lawyers from accepting high-ranking government appointments. Such individuals are anxious to make a contribution within the administration, but when they leave after four or five years, they do not want to wait another five years to pursue their personal and professional goals.

Other disadvantages are the negative perception of a "government lawyer," the lack of support staff and services which make the practice of law easier, and the levels of bureaucracy and "red tape," which cause everything to move very slowly. In spite of these drawbacks, career government lawyers experience a very high degree of career satisfaction, camaraderie, and work autonomy.

As mentioned at the outset, the process of obtaining a legal position in the federal sector can be an overwhelming and frustrating experience. However, armed with the information provided in this chapter (including the lists in Tables 24.1–24.3), knowledge of the agencies likely to be hiring experienced lawyers, recognition of the need to conduct an aggressive campaign, and a sense of humor, you are ready to begin the search. Career satisfaction awaits you!

Capitol Hill

Lawyers are found in many different positions on Capitol Hill but generally are employed either as House or Senate committee staff or on the personal staff of a member of Congress. Lawyers also work for the Democratic or Republican National Committees and the Congressional Research Service. Although lawyers occupy myriad different positions on the Hill, there are no standard criteria or written guidelines that make a law degree a requirement for obtaining a position. Nonetheless, those who have a law degree find it very helpful during the job search and a definite advantage once in the job. They are able to better understand the legislative language, recognize essential issues, write effectively, and develop persuasive arguments. While in theory a J.D. is not a requirement, in practice it has become essential, especially on a committee staff.

TABLE 24.1

Federal Government Agencies Employing over One Hundred Lawyers*

Agency	Number of Lawyers
Department of Justice	9,168
Defense agencies (military personnel)	6,689
Department of the Army	1,500
Department of the Air Force	1,335
Department of the Navy	834
Marine Corps (civilian personnel)	800
Department of the Army	832
Department of the Air Force	307
Department of the Navy	593
Civilian Agencies	463
Department of Treasury	1,873
Social Security Administration	1,513
Securities and Exchange Commission	1,079
Environmental Protection Agency	799
National Labor Relations Board	700
Department of Transportation	622
Department of Labor	605
Department of Commerce	567
Federal Deposit Insurance Corporation	529
Federal Communications Commission	522
Equal Opportunity Employment Commission	458
Federal Trade Commission	455
Department of Energy	316
Department of Housing and Urban Development	309
Department of Health and Human Services	307
Department of Interior	295
Small Business Administration	280
Department of Agriculture	240
Department of Education	225
Postal Service	191
Commodity Futures Trading Commission	173
Merit Systems Protection Board	134
General Accounting Office	126
General Services Administration	118
Department of State	110

*Information provided in the 1998 issue of "Government Employment Opportunities" prepared annually by the Office of Attorney Personnel Management, Department of Justice.

Lawyer Positions on the Hill

Responsibilities differ for personal staff lawyers, usually called legislative directors or assistants, and committee staff lawyers who most frequently are called legislative counsel, or associate/assistant counsel. What these positions have in common is that they do not involve practicing law in the traditional sense; rather, Hill lawyers draft and then negotiate final provisions of the law.

The legislative director generally has responsibility for several issue areas while also coordinating the work of the legislative assistants and legislative

TABLE 24.2

Change in Size of Departments between 1993 and 1998*

Departments That Grew	Department That Shrunk
Department of Justice	Commodity Futures Trading Commission
Defense Agencies	Department of Agriculture
Department of Commerce	Department of the Treasury
Department of Energy	Department of State
Department of Housing and Urban Development	Environmental Protection Agency
Department of the Interior	Federal Deposit Insurance Corporation
Department of Labor	Federal Trade Commission
Department of Transportation	Department of Health and Human Services
Equal Opportunity Employment Commission	General Accounting Office
Federal Communications Commission	
Merit Systems Protection Board	
National Labor Relations Board	
Postal Service	
Securities and Exchange Commission	

*Information compiled from a comparison of the February 1993 and April 1998 publication of "Government Employment Opportunities," prepared annually by the Office of Personnel Management, Department of Justice.

TABLE 24.3

Web Sites for Federal Agencies and Departments

Agency of Department	Web Site Address (begin with *http://*)
Bureau of Alcohol, Tobacco, and Firearms	www.atf.treas.gov/
Central Intelligence Agency	www.odci.gov/cia/
Commodity Futures Trading Co.	www.cftc.gov/
Department of Agriculture	www.usda.gov/
Department of Commerce	www.doc.gov/
DOC: Patent and Trademark Office	www.uspto.gov/
Department of Defense	www.dtic.mil/defenselink
Department of Education	www.ed.gov/
Department of Energy	www.doe.gov/
Department of Health and Human Services	www.dhhs.gov/
Department of Housing and Urban Development	www.hud.gov/
Department of the Interior	www.doi.gov/
Department of Justice	www.usdoj.gov/
Department of Labor	www.dol.gov/
Department of State	www.state.gov/
Department of Transportation	www.dot.gov/
Department of the Treasury	www.ustreas.gov/
Department of Veteran Affairs	www.va.gov/
Environmental Protection Agency	www.epa.gov/
Equal Employment Opportunity Comm.	www.eeoc.gov/
Farm Credit Administration	www.fca.gov/
Federal Bureau of Investigation	www.fbi.gov/
Federal Communications Commission	www.fcc.gov/

(Continued)

TABLE 24.3   (Continued)

Agency of Department	Web Site Address (begin with *http://*)
Federal Deposit Insurance Company	www.fdic.gov/
Federal Election Commission	www.fec.gov/
Federal Trade Commission	www.ftc.gov/
Food and Drug Administration	www.fda.gov/
Internal Revenue Service	www.irs.ustreas.gov/
International Trade Commission	www.usitc.gov/
NASA	www.nasa.gov/
National Endowment of the Arts	www.arts.endow.gov/
National Security Council	www.whitehouse.gov/WH/EOP/NSC
Office of Management and Budget	www.whitehouse.gov/WH/EOP/OMB
Office of Personnel Management	www.opm.gov/; www.usajobs.gov/
Pension Benefit Guaranty Company	www.pbgc.gov/
Postal Service	www.usps.gov/
Securities and Exchange Commission	www.sec.gov/
Small Business Administration	www.sbaonline.sba.gov/
Smithsonian Institution	www.si.edu/
Social Security Administration	www.ssa.gov/
U.S. Information Agency	www.usia.gov/

correspondents. For legislative assistants, typical duties involve advising members on legislative proposals, preparing memos on particular matters, developing policy positions and legislative initiatives, writing position papers and speeches, negotiating contested provisions, overseeing agency activities, dealing with constituents and the press, and handling a variety of administrative matters.

Personal staff lawyers are generalists and focus on a wide variety of issues. They regularly work with local politics and constituents. Their duties vary depending not only on the position and level of activity of the particular Congress person with whom they work, but also on that individual's issues of interest. Since these positions are usually less well-defined, the quality of experience of a personal staff lawyer varies widely and is dependent upon the chemistry that develops between the lawyer and the member.

Unlike personal staff lawyers, those on a committee staff need substantive knowledge in a particular issue area. As a result, lawyer graduates who are successful in obtaining a committee staff position are often individuals who developed a content expertise prior to attending law school. Otherwise, lawyer graduates whose goal is to obtain a committee position often go first to another employer (i.e., a federal agency), develop an expertise, and then pursue Hill employment. Committee staff lawyers are more autonomous and more involved in policy work and getting legislation passed than are their personal staff lawyer colleagues.

The administrative assistant (AA) position, the highest position in a member's office, often requires extensive experience. These individuals, as the title implies, handle major administrative matters such as developing annual operating goals, hiring staff, and preparing budgets. As such, these positions may hold less interest for lawyer applicants, although there are certainly many Hill AAs who have law degrees. The legislative director coordinates the work of the legislative assistants and counsel and may also be responsible for several different issue areas.

Due to the political nature of Hill work, certain personality characteristics and skills are valuable. Staff members must act vigorously to accomplish their agendas while simultaneously reacting to the agendas of others. Consequently, those who are successful possess an extraordinary combination of interpersonal skills that make them good negotiators and consensus builders. And while it sounds contradictory, the most successful Hill professionals also tend to be aggressive and tenacious. The environment is fast-paced and demanding; therefore, lawyers work quickly and often at a hectic pace with little time to attend to details. Those who enjoy Hill work and find the pace energizing have a genuine fondness for strategy and policy.

Job-Search Techniques

There is no central placement authority or formal structure in the hiring of committee staff and even less structure to hiring for the personal staffs of members of Congress. Rather, each office, committee, or subcommittee has individual hiring authority. Each can set its own hiring requirements, salary, and conditions of employment and does not have to justify selections or adhere to equal opportunity dicta. As a result, obtaining a position on the Hill not only requires a great deal of effort and persistence, but often seems overwhelming to even the most sophisticated job hunters.

It is very unusual to get an interview on Capitol Hill through the passive resume mailing approach, and while many job hunters are adverse to developing contacts and networking, it is an indispensable part of securing a position on the Hill. Networking is not only the most effective way of finding a Hill job, it may actually be the only way to be successful. Job hunters must use whatever contacts they have or can develop. For this reason, campaign work has long been a favored method for making initial contacts because it frequently puts workers in contact with individuals who know the ins and outs of obtaining Hill positions.

The most valuable contacts are with individuals who have political connections, those who currently are employed on the Hill, or with those who recently worked on the Hill. However, beyond these direct contacts, job hunters must be willing to start the networking process on a more remote level—with non-Hill contacts, like members of various interest groups who are likely to be able to connect them with someone on the Hill. It is necessary to utilize every professional, educational, social, and political contact available including one's own congressional representative. Additionally, Hill job seekers should contact both their law school and undergraduate school alumni offices for names of graduates on the Hill. Remember to ask each individual with whom you are meeting to suggest another contact because the more contacts you make, the greater your chances are of obtaining a position.

Committee staff positions go to those with previously established content knowledge. Prior to beginning the search, job seekers with a developed expertise should target the committee staffs where that knowledge could be useful. This can be accomplished by checking the *Congressional Directory* to determine the content specialty of the various committees. Often the scope of a committee's work is not evident from the name, and therefore, it is very important to look beyond the title when using the directory. It is also worth remembering that most committees have both a majority and a minority staff, organized by political party affiliation.

Although many of the committees hire lawyers, certain staffs are considered to be among the most likely to employ legal personnel. In the House of Representatives, Armed Services, Judiciary, Education and Labor, Energy and Commerce, Interior and Insular Affairs, and Ways and Means committees hire lawyers. In the Senate, Judiciary, Labor and Human Resources, and Select Committee on Ethics also hire lawyers.

Job candidates who may be seeking a position on a member's personal staff should target specific members. The targets would be those individuals with whom the job seeker shares some common interest or background. Thus, the targeting criteria may be based upon party affiliation or mutual interests as noted by the member's committee assignments. Additionally, consider geography when creating a target group. Individuals in a position to make hiring decisions frequently seek out applicants who have geographic ties to the member's state or district. Undoubtedly, such applicants have an inherent advantage in the Capitol Hill job market.

Those interested in a member's personal staff can develop their target group by checking the *Almanac of American Politics* and *Politics in America* to learn about the members, how they vote on key issues, and their states or districts. Just as one might have done as a prospective judicial clerk, it is worth checking into a member's style and reputation. The working relationship between the member and the personal staff lawyer greatly influences how enjoyable the term of employment will be and how much the lawyer will learn while on the Hill. Choosing to work for someone who takes a visible position on issues and who is actively involved in the legislative process might increase both job satisfaction and personal growth.

When the appropriate committees or members have been targeted, applicants should then identify the staff members who would be involved in the hiring process. The situation varies between offices, but generally it is appropriate to contact the chief counsel or minority counsel on senate committees, the chief counsel, minority counsel, or staff director on house committees, and the administrative assistant or legislative director on the personal staffs of members. The names and titles of staff may be found in *The Congressional Yellow Book* and *The Congressional Staff Directory*. Since job seekers should leave no stone unturned, the resume and other application materials should be directed to these traditional hiring officials. Simultaneously, the job-seeking applicant should also be heavily involved in the networking process and identifying connections to the Members of committees they have targeted.

Although one is unlikely to find a Hill position without networking, there are several publications that contain Capitol Hill job listings and are recommended to job seekers. They are *Roll Call* and *The Hill,* which many Hill staffers have mentioned as valuable sources. Occasionally, positions are advertised in *The National and Federal Legal Employment Report,* in *Opportunities in Public Affairs,* and in law school placement offices.

There is both a House and a Senate Placement Office, and these act as employment referral services for members, committees, and administrative offices. Job seekers may complete application forms that will be sent to those offices that have requested assistance in filling positions matching their qualifications.

The Senate Placement Office can be reached at (202) 224-9167 and also offers a telephone job line that is updated each Friday that can be accessed by calling (202) 228-5627. Another source of information for job vacancies is the special employment office established for new Senate members every two years, when a large number of positions change on Capitol Hill. This temporary employment office receives resumes for new members and functions alongside of, but independently from, the traditional Senate Placement Office.

In the House of Representatives, job seekers can increase their chances of obtaining a position by participating in a resume bank or referral service. The House of Representatives Office of Human Resources can be contacted at (202) 225-2450. The office maintains a Resume Referral Service, which is updated every three months, and a telephone job line at (202) 226-6731, which lists current vacancies. In addition, the Republican Majority Whip Office coordinates a resume bank, which can be accessed by calling (202) 225-0197. When Republican members have openings in their offices, they can contact the resume bank. Resumes of individuals whose qualifications match the job requirements are forwarded to the appropriate office. This resume bank is also updated every three months, thus job seekers must recontact the office after that time period in order to keep their resume in the bank.

Resume job banks are also available at the Democratic Policy Committee, the Republican Policy Committee, the Senate Republican Conference, the House Republican Conference, the Congressional Black Caucus, the Congressional Hispanic Caucus, the Democratic National Committee, and the Republican National Committee. However, lawyer job seekers should recognize that a large percentage of the positions listed with these placement offices are administrative or clerical.

The *House Action Report* (formally known as the *Democratic Study Group Newsletter*) is another source of information about job vacancies on Capitol Hill. Although this publication was formally sponsored by the Democratic Party, it is now nonpartisan and includes information about job vacancies. The *House Action Report* is available only on the Internet (http://www.cq.com) through its publisher, *Congressional Quarterly.* Once on the Web site, users should use the "Staff Bulletin" subdirectory, which provides more than just employment listings but can be a source of insider information about positions. For example, Hill staffers may post messages and members of Congress can post job openings on this site, which may not be advertised in other places. In order to access the *House Action Report,* users must subscribe to the Web site. However, free trials are available by sending an e-mail to clientservices@cq.com and including your name, address, phone number, and e-mail address.

It is important to understand that these job listing services do not include every vacancy available on Capitol Hill; they list only those openings in offices that have requested publication. Since most vacancies on Capitol Hill are never advertised, it is helpful for job seekers to review such publications regularly, even if the majority of these listings are for support positions. Furthermore, in utilizing all of these resources, it is important not to assume that the listed positions are no longer available and to pursue every lead. In addition, lawyers seeking to make a transition to the Hill cannot view these tools as a substitute for networking or for making direct contact with the administrative assistants in hundreds of elected representatives' offices, with the staff directors of the full committee and subcommittees, and with other staffers to whom they personally have been referred.

Once you have secured an interview, be prepared to convey your interest and enthusiasm to the interviewer. To ensure that you are well informed the day of the interview, consider the following ideas. Read the *Almanac of the Unelected* to learn about the backgrounds of select committee staff members. Be familiar with the jurisdiction of the committee or subcommittee and knowledgeable about the member's state or district. As stated above, this information can be found in the *Congressional Directory* and the *Almanac of American Politics*. Second, learn about the issues currently before the committee, subcommittee, or member. Both the *National Journal* and the *Congressional Quarterly Weekly Report* contain well-written reports on the key legislation currently facing Congress.

It would be helpful for applicants interviewing for committee positions to learn about the member who chairs that committee. Similarly, those who are seeking positions on a personal staff should investigate that member's committee assignments.

Locating Hill employment is time-consuming and requires a great deal of legwork and persistence, all of which makes long-distance job hunting extremely difficult. In fact, since most congressional offices receive thousands of resumes, it is unlikely for an out-of-town job seeker, unless well connected, to obtain a Hill position without coming to Washington for an extended stay. Not only does getting a job on the Hill require continuous effort, but it can be frustrating to novices because of the all-too-familiar catch-22 that applicants with previous Hill experience are preferred. Some job-seeking lawyers have gained Hill experience during their undergraduate summers, others worked on the Hill during law school, and still others worked with a Hill staffer on a pro bono case or other matter. It is unclear why such short-term experience is so sought after; perhaps it is merely a screening device, given the volume of applications received. Regardless of the rationale, because Hill experience is so important, job seekers frequently take whatever low-level job is available and set out to prove their value to the organization.

Specific times to anticipate vacancies on the Hill include the period directly following an election when new members are building their staffs or possibly in September when the congressional session begins. Frequently, there is staff turnover in August, and, since Congress is not in session, staffers often are more willing to take time to talk and be a source of information and advice. When Congress is in recess, job seekers have a better chance of getting Hill staffers to meet with them. For practical reasons, if one networks with staffers while Congress is in session, the best days to contact them are reportedly Mondays and Fridays.

Advantages and Disadvantages

Working on the Hill is generally very exciting, and one certainly has the opportunity to impact national decisions and influence the direction of legislation. Hill staffers are called upon to develop new ideas to implement a member's goals, translate those ideas into legislation, and build the political support necessary to implement the ideas. Hill positions offer a great deal of variety, independence, and the opportunity to work with extremely interesting people.

Another advantage is the marketability afforded Hill lawyers. When staffers decide to leave, there are a number of different places where those with law degrees find employment. However, just as was true of federal agency employment, a lawyer's particular marketability depends greatly upon the type of work done while on the Hill. Law firms hire Hill-experienced lawyers when they are interested both in the applicant's contacts and Hill "know-how" as well as in the specific content expertise. Also, lawyer-trained staffers find positions with the White House administration, public interest organizations, and trade associations. This marketability, however, is generally limited to the greater Washington area and may not be as valued in other locales.

On the other hand, two of the most frequently mentioned disadvantages are long hours and low pay. Salaries for individuals with a J.D. cover an amazingly wide range. Since there are no guidelines, some members pay whatever the market will bear; therefore, it is not unheard of for a Hill lawyer to earn as little as $25,000. Capitol Hill employees earn less and have fewer guaranteed benefits than federal executive branch employees. In fact, in the executive branch pay and benefits are standardized by law, whereas congressional staff pay and benefits vary according to the individual member.

On the House side, committee members can make $100,000, especially those on the committees that pay the highest salaries, including Appropriations, Energy, Commerce, and Ways and Means. Personal staff lawyers without much experience could earn about $30,000. Committee positions, which require some Hill experience, usually pay more. Previous agency or law firm experience is helpful, and allowances may also be made for special expertise. On the Senate side, committee staff lawyers may earn between $90,000 and $100,000.

Two publications enable the public to locate precise salary information for the staffs of particular members or committees. The *Chief Administrative Officer's Statement of Disbursements*, published quarterly, and *The Report of the Secretary of the Senate*, published semiannually, itemize personnel expense accounts in each office. Salary figures are identified both by the staff person's name and title. In order to find these publications, contact libraries that have government document collections or call the House or Senate Document Rooms through the congressional switchboard at (202) 224-3121.

Furthermore, lack of job security is another disadvantage associated with Hill positions. Jobs are at the whim of the committee chair or the election process. The highly charged political atmosphere can be another frustrating reality when it leads to "politics over substance." One can work exhaustively on an issue and lose because of unrelated political issues that have nothing to do with the merits of a particular case. Additionally, although the daily pace may be fast, actual bills, legislation, and preliminary negotiations tend to move very slowly because of the bureaucracy and red tape associated with government practice. As one staffer describes it, work on the Hill moves in "fits and starts."

Finally, working on the Hill requires the ability to work under pressure. The process of getting a bill on the floor and having it reflect your member's interest or a committee's goals can be very stressful. You are expected to know everything in the bill plus every amendment on the floor. In meetings, you will be responsible for having all of the appropriate documents ready. When something happens on the floor, you will need to know about it and to make a quick decision about whether to notify the member of what took place on the floor or whether to get him or her onto the floor as soon as possible. This often requires having a television monitor on at all times, even when trying to concentrate on drafting other documents.

These disadvantages, while real, are clearly overshadowed by the positive aspects of being employed on the Hill. There are many more qualified job seekers than available openings, and there are always lawyers who are willing to give up very large salaries to be involved on Capitol Hill.

Job-seeking lawyers who want the challenge, excitement, and enjoyment of a career on Capitol Hill and who are determined to achieve their goal succeed in finding a position. It requires an unrelenting commitment to the job of finding a job; it takes persistence, persistence, and yet more persistence; however, those who do persevere are likely to be successful. Now, it is your turn.

Federal Agencies and Capitol Hill—Resource List

Print Publications

171 Reference Book. 1991. Washington, DC: Workbooks, Inc.

Almanac of American Politics. 1998. Washington, DC: National Journal.

The Almanac of the Unelected. 1998. Washington, DC: Almanac Publishing, Inc.

Congressional Directory (biannual). Washington, DC: Government Printing Office.

Congressional Staff Directory (quarterly). Alexandria, VA: Congressional Quarterly Directories, Inc.

Congressional Yellow Book (quarterly). Washington, DC: Leadership Directories, Inc.

Directory of Federal Jobs and Employers. 1996. Manassas Park, VA: Impact Publishers.

Federal Career Opportunities (subscription series). Vienna, VA: Federal Research Service, Inc. P.O. Box 1059 Vienna, VA 22180 (703) 281-0200.

Federal Careers for Attorneys. 1991. Washington, DC: Federal Reports, Inc.

Federal Law-Related Careers. 1994. Washington, DC: Federal Reports, Inc.

Federal Legal Directory. 1990. Phoenix, AZ: Oryx Press.

Federal Regional Yellow Book (quarterly). Washington, DC: Leadership Directories, Inc.

Federal Regulatory Directory. 1997. Washington, DC: Congressional Quarterly, Inc.

Federal Yellow Book (quarterly). Washington, DC: Leadership Directories, Inc.

The Harvard College Guide to Careers in Government and Politics. 1992. Cambridge, MA: Harvard University Press.

Judicial Staff Directory (quarterly). Mt. Vernon, VA: Staff Directories, Ltd.

Kiplinger Washington Letter (subscription series). Washington, DC: Kiplinger Washington Editors. 1729 H Street NW, Washington, DC 20006 (800) 544-0155.

National Directory of State Agencies. 1989. Bethesda, MD: Cambridge Information Group Directories, Inc.

National and Federal Legal Employment Report (subscription series). Washington, DC: Federal Reports, Inc. 1010 Vermont Avenue, NW, Suite 408, Washington, DC 20005 (202) 393-3311.

Now Hiring: Government Jobs for Lawyers. 1995–1996. Chicago, IL: American Bar Association.

Opportunities in Public Affairs (subscription series). Bethesda, MD: Brubach Enterprises, Inc. P.O. Box 34949 Bethesda, MD 20827 (301) 571-0102.

Paralegal's Guide to U.S. Government Jobs. 1993. Washington, DC: Federal Reports, Inc.

State Elective Officials and the Legislatures. 1993–1994. Lexington, KY: Council of State Governments.

State Yellow Book (quarterly). Washington, DC: Leadership Directories, Inc.

U.S. Government Manual. 1997–1998. Washington, DC: Office of the Federal Register, National Archives and Records Administration.

Washington Information Directory. 1997–1998. Washington, DC: Congressional Quarterly, Inc.

Internet Publications

Congressional Quarterly, http://www.cq.com/

Department of Justice Attorney Vacancies, http://www.usdoj.gov/careers/oapm/

Department of Justice Legal Activities Book, http://www.usdoj.gov/careers/oapm/lab/

Federal Bar Association (Lawyer's Job Bulletin Board), http://www.fedbar.org/
Federal Research Service, Inc., http://www.fedjobs.com/
Kiplinger Washington Letter, http://www.kiplinger.com/
Lexis-Nexis, http://www.lexis-nexis.com/research/
Westlaw, http://www.westgroup.com/

Note

Marilyn Tucker wishes to express her gratitude to Máriam A. Nawabi, a 1999 graduate of Georgetown University Law Center, for her invaluable assistance in preparing this chapter.

CHAPTER 25

Judgeships

Honorable Rebecca Albrecht

From time to time, almost every law student and lawyer considers the possibility of a career on the bench. But is that really a calling for you? And if it is, what should you do to best assure success in seeking and maintaining the office? The purpose of this chapter is to give you some answers to these questions.

What Skills Should a Judge Have?

At the trial level, most judges come from the ranks of lawyers who have practiced in that court. The appellate courts attract some judges from the trial bench, law professors, and other lawyers who have developed their legal writing skills. However, the skills necessary to be an effective advocate and those necessary for an effective judge are fundamentally different.

The basic requirement for an effective judge is the ability to make decisions. This requirement does not seem to be a difficult one to meet, but for many lawyers it is not an easy thing to do. A judge must be able to make a decision and move on. As a judge, you are responsible for making decisions about other people's lives and property. This responsibility is awesome, but one that a judge may exercise four, five, or more times a day. If you are a person who makes a decision and revisits that decision for weeks, serving as a judge will be very stressful for you.

A judge's role is not to frame the issues of the case, but, based on the presentation of the issues by lawyers, to analyze the pleadings and to challenge the law cited when necessary. Having spent an entire career presenting one side of the issue, the new judge suddenly finds that he or she is called upon to review impartially a set of facts and to apply those facts to the broad base of law applicable to the facts. A new judge must learn to sit quietly during a lawyer's presentation of the case. A few thoughtful questions from a judge may help clarify an issue or move a case forward, but a judge cannot become the examiner. Many judges find it very difficult to set aside their former roles. If your blood still rises when an objection is not made, the key line

241

of questioning is overlooked, or a witness is dancing around a question, perhaps you need a few more years at the bar before you take on the quieter courtroom role on the bench.

In many jurisdictions, the trial judge is called upon to be an active participant in the movement of cases through the courts. Through trial management and pretrial conferences, the "managerial" judge is expected to take control of the pace of litigation.

With the increasing costs of litigation, the courts and their judges are being called upon to participate in alternative means of dispute resolution. Judges, acting in the capacities of arbitrators or mediators, are adding innovative settlement techniques, including minitrials and advisory jury trials, to traditional judicial skills.

What Are the "Costs" of a Judicial Career?

In many states, the courts are chronically underfunded. The reasons for underfunding of state courts vary, but the effects on the courts are similar nationwide. Court staff and judges are being asked to do more and more with less and less. As a result, courts are turning trailers into courtrooms, trimming budgets, even cutting the number of or time allotted to certain types of trials.

For a lawyer from a successful law practice, the reality of working for an underfunded bureaucracy may pose a difficult adjustment. Nationwide, judges generally earn less per year than do associates entering large law firms. An individual considering becoming a judge must carefully consider the needs and expectations of his or her family. Some judges find that the demands of a growing family cannot be met on current judicial salaries and, for that reason alone, leave the bench. Staff salaries lag even further behind that of the judges, so finding and keeping qualified personnel is another problem for the judiciary.

The opportunity to interact with peers and clients is an important outlet for many lawyers. A judge must act to ensure his or her ability to remain impartial and, even more difficult, to maintain the appearance of impartiality. Participation in certain partisan or agenda-based organizations may have to be limited or terminated. This does not mean that a judge must live in isolation; many judges are active in a variety of organizations. However, the judge always must be aware of the effect that his or her participation may have on the appearance of impartiality.

Advantages of Being a Judge

With so many negatives, why would anyone want this job?

In the judiciary, a person has the opportunity to make a difference. For a child in a dependency case, the judge can help assure a bright and promising future. For a partner in an unhappy marriage, the judge can offer hope and a new life. In his or her rulings, the judge can ensure that justice is served. Not often, but on occasion, long after the case is concluded, the judge will hear from one of the parties that the judge's decision made a positive difference.

There is, for a judge, a sense of control and independence that cannot be achieved in other areas of the law. Judges are not subject to the challenges of the billing process. If you choose to write an opinion in a particular case, the time you spend on that opinion is up to you. You are not limited in your research and writing to those cases and articles that support a client's particular requirements. You are granted the power—indeed, have the duty—to look at an issue impartially and make decisions for other people when they cannot or will not.

The practice of law for most lawyers is limited to a few areas of law. As a judge, you have the opportunity to learn and apply areas of law about which you had little or no knowledge before you took the bench. This opportunity to learn and to apply that learning to real life problems can be among the most satisfying and challenging rewards of a career on the bench.

For those judges who leave the bench, the experience can be an aid to greater success in a legal career or as a stepping-stone to "higher" political office.

The Judicial Selection Process in the State Court System

Judges in the state court systems are selected in a number of ways. They may be selected through contested elections, appointed by the chief executive, or first appointed and than retained through an election process. You will need to determine which system is in place in your jurisdiction.

The merit selection/retention process used in some states is often referred to as the Missouri Plan after the first state to utilize the system for selection of judges. Although the process will vary somewhat from state to state, in general, when a vacancy is announced, all qualified persons are invited by public notice to apply. The application may inquire into political affiliation. After a review of the applications, a commission composed of lawyers and nonlawyers will interview some or all of the applicants. The commissioners then recommend persons to the governor. The governor may also interview the candidates. Judges, once appointed, are subject to a retention election.

In a number of states, the governor appoints judges, again subject to retention, but without the intervening step of a commission recommendation. In those states party affiliation, political connections, and name recognition, as well as professional competence, will help assure an appointment to the court.

And, of course, in some states, judges are selected through the partisan contested election process. This process requires that the candidate raise funds and campaign in the community.

Most state courts have quasi-judicial positions that are filled by the courts themselves. These positions frequently are seen as first steps toward judicial office. The commissioners, referees, or special masters, as they are variously called, preside over a limited range of matters, generally uncontested or referred by the judges. You should contact your local court to determine the process used to select persons for these positions.

Administrative law judges may be found in a number of state agencies. These judges usually are not a part of the judicial branch, but are attached to an agency in the executive branch of government. A lawyer who specialized in administrative practice may find the position of an administrative law judge open to him or her. These positions generally are not seen as avenues to positions on a general jurisdiction bench. If you have decided that you want to remain in a specialty area of law, the administrative law judge position is a good one to consider.

Not a part of the state court system are the municipal courts. These judges usually are appointed by the city council and mayor. Municipal courts generally are not seen as avenues to the general jurisdiction court.

Generally, jurisdictions have certain minimum requirements that must be met before one can become a candidate for judicial office. With the exception of some limited jurisdiction courts, most courts require that their judges be lawyers. Most jurisdictions include minimum age and years-in-practice requirements. While it would certainly be necessary to live within the state in which one seeks office, some jurisdictions may have further residency requirements.

In most states a judge's continued service on the bench is subject to periodic review, either through a retention election, contested election, or review by the legislative branch. In only a few jurisdictions is a state court judge granted life tenure and usually that comes after the judge has successfully defended his or her position in some type of review process.

The Federal Court System

Judges of the district courts, circuit courts of appeals, and the Supreme Court (or Article III judges) are nominated by the president of the United States and confirmed by the Senate. Article III judges, once appointed, have life tenure. Names of persons to consider as judges of the district courts are submitted to the president by the senior senator of the state of the president's political party. The recommendations of the senators for district court appointments are given great weight. It is up to each senator how he or she obtains names of potential appointees. Many senators have their own judicial screening committee that seeks out potential nominees. The process from the screening committee to the nomination is political in nature. Qualifications are not irrelevant; a good reputation in the community is important. But once it is determined that a candidate meets the minimum requirements, political considerations take over.

At the circuit court and Supreme Court levels, the preference of the president's staff generally is given greater weight than in the district court process.

Bankruptcy judges are appointed by the circuit courts of appeals. These judges are Article I judges and are appointed for fourteen years. They may be reappointed for an additional fourteen-year term. Bankruptcy judges are considered a part of the district courts in which they serve. A strong background in all areas of bankruptcy practice is considered an excellent factor in the appointment of a bankruptcy judge. The appointments are merit appointments. An extensive application is required. Each application is screened by a bench/bar committee in the circuit, and the top candidates' names are sent to the circuit court for the final selection.

Magistrates in the federal system are appointed by the district judges for the district in which they serve. As in state government, the federal government uses administrative law judges to adjudicate matters in many of its agencies. These vacancies are advertised in the legal press or in the Federal Register.

Becoming a Judge

The route every person takes to the bench is different. There are some things that you can do, however, to help yourself along the way. A strong academic background and a clerkship with a judge will certainly be pluses. If you are interested in becoming an administrative law judge or in a bankruptcy court position, specialization in those areas will be invaluable.

A reputation for fairness is probably the most important asset you can bring to the pursuit of a judicial appointment. Service as a judge pro tem or as an arbitrator or mediator not only can help you decide if the judiciary is a career for you, but can help you develop the reputation for fair, thoughtful decision making. Involvement in your community is also an important asset: a recognized community leader will have the advantage of name recognition as well as an acknowledged commitment to community service.

Every judicial selection process has an element of politics in it. You, and the persons supporting you, must have strong, positive connections with whoever is making the selection decisions. Strong letters of support from well-respected members of the legal and civil community can be extremely helpful in an appointment process, and their vocal support will help in an elective process.

Finally, you have to be in the right place at the right time. Do not be discouraged if you are not successful on your first attempt or attempts in the selection process. If you are convinced that you should be a judge, and that you will be a good judge, eventually you will succeed in achieving your goal.

CHAPTER 26

Judicial Administration, Staff Lawyers, and Law Clerks

The judicial branch offers other opportunities besides judgeships as described in Chapter 25. Your job hunting should not rule out evaluating these other options posed by the court system, including judicial administration, staff lawyers, and law clerks. Further pointers on securing staff lawyer or law clerk positions are set forth below.

If you are more interested in administration duties, yet keeping your hand in the legal field, you may want to consider a job in the Clerk of Court's office. To determine what opportunities are available, your best bet is to contact the Clerk of Court for your local, state and federal court system. While such positions do not necessarily require a law degree, legal background and training certainly may be helpful and also assist in getting your foot in the door. Additionally, many clerks for state court systems are elected, so a little politicking may be required if you aspire to that post.

A. Appellate Staff Lawyers

Daniel P. Schaack

Why did you become a lawyer? Do you want to help clients get out of a jam? Do you dream of the glory of head-to-head courtroom battle? Do you revel in being the star of your organization? Do you want or need to make a six-figure income? If so, then turn to another chapter; being a staff lawyer is probably not for you.

On the other hand, if these things do not appeal to you at this stage in your career, but being a member of a team doing high-level and important legal work attracts you, read on.

What Staff Lawyers Do

Although most people are aware that appellate judges have law clerks who help them make and explain their rulings, most have never heard of a staff lawyer. A staff lawyer is similar to a law clerk, but with important differences.

Like law clerks, staff lawyers assist judges in ruling on issues facing the court. Staff lawyers often perform the first neutral evaluation of a case. The evaluation entails (1) reading the briefs, (2) reviewing the case record, (3) writing up a recommended disposition, and (4) presenting that recommendation to the court. Staff lawyers work in various practice areas, including civil, criminal, juvenile, tax, and workers' compensation.

The job description varies with the different appellate courts. In some, staff lawyers prepare bench memoranda, which the judges may use to prepare for oral argument and as rough outlines for their decisions. In others, staff lawyers actually prepare draft decisions—writing as if they were the authoring judge. The draft is the starting point for the judges when they discuss the case at conference. The judge assigned to write the decision may then make use of the draft when preparing his or her own final product.

In some courts, staff lawyers present cases orally to the court at conference. This is the staff lawyer's opportunity to exercise his or her oral advocacy skills.

Unlike law clerks, staff lawyers generally are semiautonomous: they are not attached to a particular judge but work for the entire court. And while law clerks are often fresh out of law school, staff lawyers have generally practiced law for several years. Appellate courts require this experience because they expect the staff lawyer to evaluate the issues independently, while the law clerk usually works hand in hand with, and at the direction of, the judge.

Pros and Cons of the Job

Pros: The working conditions can be quite good. The courts tend to have excellent legal resources at hand or nearby. If you need a copy of some obscure turn-of-the-century statute, chances are good the law library has it. Computerized research is also available.

Staff lawyers have the opportunity to work on exciting cases, helping decide important legal issues. Amid the everyday appeals are sprinkled important political and social issues and interesting cases of first impression. In them, the staff lawyer gets his or her chance to have some influence on some of society's powerful decision makers.

Coworkers are generally bright, dedicated, and interested in their work. They are willing to discuss weighty legal issues and are generous with their time because they do not have to bill hours, another big plus. The atmosphere is more relaxed than a hectic law office. The judges tend to be bright and interesting people.

Staff lawyers mostly do not have to advocate positions they do not believe in. Unlike most lawyers, who take their clients as they see them, staff lawyers decide which side is correct and then attempt to convince the judges to rule that way.

Another big attraction is time. Staff lawyers tend to work saner hours than many lawyers in private practice. Some courts offer flextime and job sharing.

Finally, the job is excellent preparation for the lawyer who plans to return to active practice. A staff lawyer becomes quite familiar with his or her practice area and gains an excellent working knowledge of the courts, at both the trial and appellate levels. These assets can be a big advantage in the legal job market.

Cons: Government pay is significantly lower than that in the private market. And the staff lawyer does not have a single boss, but many. Trying to satisfy numerous judges of different judicial persuasions with varying styles can be maddening.

Many parts of the job are mundane. Reviewing case records can be tedious and does not provide an enjoyable mental challenge. It is work a paralegal could do, but the courts do not have paralegals.

Staff lawyers frequently must make sense of appeals that have been handled by persons unfamiliar with good appellate practice. The briefs may fail to cite to the record or legal authority, and the arguments may be incomprehensible. The staff lawyer must nevertheless divine the pertinent issues, perform the necessary research, and recommend the appropriate result.

Finally, consider the milieu. Staff lawyers labor in anonymity; they are essentially ghostwriters for judges. Theirs is a small community with little room for advancement.

Getting a Staff Lawyer Position

First, determine whether you are suited for the position. The staff lawyer job is a scholarly position: you should enjoy working with the intellectual and theoretical aspects of the law. You should have practice experience and be familiar with the litigation process. You must be strong in legal research and analysis, and you must be able to write clearly and persuasively.

Getting a staff lawyer position is difficult, partly because openings are infrequent. Do not wait for an opening; contact the chief staff lawyer of the court you are interested in and send a resume along with a well-thought-out cover letter. If you have the credentials, the court will probably keep your name on file for the next opening.

The court will want to see a writing sample, so have one ready. It should be your own writing and should demonstrate your ability to analyze complex legal issues and to write clearly and persuasively about them.

Strong references are important. They should be able to attest to both your strong legal abilities and solid character.

As with any lawyer job, the interview is critical. You should show confidence. You must demonstrate ease with judges—persons of no small authority—and the ability to get along with co-workers.

Being a staff lawyer is rewarding if you enjoy the more intellectual aspects of the law and want to develop your skills and knowledge as a lawyer. It is a position worth considering, either in its own right or as preparation for further advancement in your career.

B. Law Clerks

Sylvia J. Lett

In many respects, clerking is intellectually more rewarding than working at a law firm. Although law clerks do no advocating on behalf of clients, the appellate court is the arena in which laws are upheld or overruled. For law clerks, the Constitution and all of the theoretical issues of law that seem remote in the real world come alive.

Trial court clerkships and appellate court clerkships are available at state and federal courts. The types of cases a law clerk handles depend upon whether a clerkship is for a federal or a state judge.

Federal courts are courts of limited jurisdiction, and cases heard in federal courts include those involving disputes between the states, bankruptcy matters, Social Security benefits, federal laws, stock fraud, and protections of the Bill of Rights, to name a few. In the federal court system, a district court is the trial court; a circuit court is the intermediate appellate court; and the Supreme Court is the court that accepts appeals from circuit courts upon its own discretion. There are currently ninety-four federal district courts and eleven Circuit Courts of Appeals. Also, there are two additional circuit courts: the United States Court of Appeals for the Federal Circuit, which handles patents and contract claims against the United States, and the United States Court of Appeals for the District of Columbia.

State courts, in contrast, are courts of general jurisdiction and handle a wide range of cases including personal injury claims, contract disputes, domestic relations matters, and criminal offenses.

Although job responsibilities may vary considerably from court to court, chamber by chamber, most law clerks are responsible for legal research and first drafts of case dispositions such as orders, memoranda decisions, or opinions. Both the appellant and the appellee provide briefs to the court setting forth their arguments. This provides, at the very least, an important springboard from which legal research can begin. A judge may disagree with a majority's analysis of a particular case and may ask a law clerk to assist in drafting a dissent.

Another important aspect of the law clerk job is to check legal citations and the substance of drafts from other judges. This double-checking ensures that a factually or legally incorrect decision will not be published. Also, a judge often relies on a law clerk as a fresh set of eyes to review the record of the case and spot any legal issues that the parties' briefs might have missed. In a sense, a clerkship marries the intellectual "hypothetical" thinking of law school with the sometimes tedious attention to detail of editorial work.

Which Court Is Right for You?

In general, trial court clerkships move at a faster pace than appellate court clerkships and offer many opportunities to see and participate in all aspects of trials, including last-minute motions. A law clerk may even be asked to perform bailiff duties while the court is in session.

An appellate-level clerkship, on the other hand, is generally slower paced, allowing for plenty of reflection on the appellate briefs, which frequently contain complicated legal issues in often unsettled areas of the law. While an appellate clerkship may not provide the excitement of witnessing a trial, clerks are encouraged and often required to listen to and take notes on oral arguments for cases.

State court clerkships rarely, if ever, require travel. Federal court clerkships such as circuit court clerkships, however, do require travel. On average, a clerk for a circuit court judge can expect to travel between three days to one week per month for nine months of a year. This travel is often a boon to people wishing to see other cities, as all travel expenses are reimbursed and the workload during these weeks of hearing oral arguments is somewhat light.

Most clerkships run twelve to twenty-four months. However, some judges prefer to have "permanent" clerks who work for them indefinitely. Always find out the anticipated time requirement before applying so that your time and the judge's time are not wasted. Although most state and federal judges observe national holidays, flexible work hours and vacations are entirely up to the personal discretion of each particular judge.

The Application Process

Before sending out applications, it is always wise to check with the placement office of your alma mater or nearby law school for information on available clerkships. Applications should be sent to judges one to two years before the intended clerkship. For federal clerkships, applicants should submit their applications at least twenty-four months in advance. However, while rare, occasionally clerkship positions open up in the late summer or early fall due to last-minute cancellations.

Law school placement offices often have copies of "evaluations" of judges filled out by former law clerks. Also, the offices may be able to provide invaluable information as to the type of candidate a particular judge is seeking, as well as the qualifications and background experience necessary. Martindale-Hubbell is also a good resource to use to locate past law clerks who may be able to provide information as to a particular judge's hiring practices. Finally, it is wise to keep your ear to the ground about the personalities of judges because, after all, you may be working very closely with one in a small office for twelve to twenty-four months.

Any clerkship application should include (1) a concise cover letter, (2) a resume, (3) a writing sample, (4) a law school transcript, and (5) two or three letters of recommendation.

- *Cover letter:* The cover letter should not be a lengthy rehash of your resume. Instead, the letter should express your interest in a clerkship, explain the supporting documentation you submit with the letter, let the judge know your availability for an interview, and most important, list a number where you can be reached at all times. Clerkship positions sometimes become available on a last-minute basis when, for example, a new judge is appointed to the bench. When an unexpected opening occurs, the judge's secretary spends an afternoon going through filed resumes, trying to reach applicants to schedule interviews. If you move or start a new job at a new number but are still interested in a clerkship should an opening unexpectedly arise, notify the judge's office.

- *Resume:* Your resume should reflect all academic honors and emphasize legal research and writing experience. Many judges seem to enjoy seeing a Hobbies or Interests section on a resume because, in addition to academic qualifications, a judge is looking for someone whose personality and interests will mesh well with the other law clerks and staff in an office.

- *Writing sample:* Do not worry if the sample is not from an award-winning published law review article. Judges just want to make sure that an applicant can organize thoughts coherently, analyze legal issues competently, and spell and use grammar correctly. Use a sample that reflects your ability and style instead of one that has been so heavily edited that it is no longer representative of your writing.

- *Law school transcript:* Although law school grades (especially first year) are not true arbiters of future success in the field of law, submitting your transcript is a necessary evil, especially if you have never worked as law clerk before. If the law school that you attended has an unusual grading system, or if you have an extraordinary excuse for poor grades, attach an addendum to explain.

- *Letters of recommendation:* It is always better to submit a stellar recommendation from a professor or work supervisor who is not known worldwide then a tepid, informal recommendation from a legal "superstar." If possible, provide information about yourself, such as "I worked forty hours per week to defray law-school costs while taking your class," to prospective recommendation writers. Also, do not overlook supervisors or co-workers at pro bono or volunteer jobs as potential recommendation letter writers if they can comment on your writing and organizational skills.

The Interview Process

- *Preinterview:* Do some homework. Familiarize yourself with the judge's political leanings and writing style by researching opinions authored by him or her from online legal services providers. Familiarity with opinions shows your level of interest. Also, encourage people whom the judge holds in high regard to put in a good word on your behalf. If you have not been to the court building where the judge's chambers are located, call ahead for advice on public transportation or parking, and get there early.
- *At the interview:* Introduce yourself to the judge's assistant and law clerks. The judge's staff may have input into the hiring decision. Make a good impression by being approachable. Use the poise and maturity years of practice have cultivated but avoid being a "know-it-all." The judge may hold their impressions of prospective law clerks in high regard when making hiring decisions. At the conclusion of the interview, ask when a hiring decision will be made.
- *Attitude:* Let your "true" self shine through during the interview. Keep in mind that almost everyone applying for clerkship positions looks great on paper. More important to a judge is your personality and how it will mesh with others in the office.
- *Postinterview:* Send the judge a thank-you letter for the opportunity to interview. Even if you are not hired, judges will remember your courtesy and may recommend you to another judge looking for a law clerk. If you have not heard from the judge more than three weeks after your interview, call his or her secretary and politely ask when the judge is expected to make a hiring decision.

Some Final Thoughts

As with any job in the law, there are advantages and disadvantages to clerking. The advantages to clerking extend far beyond boosting credentials. As a law clerk, you will gain immeasurable knowledge about and respect for our legal system. Many of the theoretical issues of law school will become real as you read appellate briefs, listen to oral arguments, and research the law. Further, your legal writing ability will increase tremendously because you will learn exactly what courts are looking for in a legal brief or motion.

Another advantage of clerking is the opportunity to develop a relationship with a judge who has years of invaluable legal experience. Your judge could become an important mentor for you.

In addition, the hours that law clerks work are generally very reasonable. Unless there is a heavy workload due to an upcoming calendar or deadline, a normal day begins around 8 A.M. and ends at 5 P.M. Also, all the major holidays are observed, and some judges (especially for clerkships longer than a year in duration) grant vacation time. Clerking is a very attractive option for those wishing to spend more time with their families and in social activities.

The only real disadvantage to clerking is that the pay is usually lower than the pay at law firms. Most state and federal clerkships range from $20,000 to $50,000 per year. In certain circumstances, if you leave a law firm to accept a federal clerkship, the federal government will match your previous salary. Also, lawyers carrying heavy student loan debt should not despair, because repayment of most loans can be deferred for a year or two during the clerkship. One bonus is that many law firms will count clerkship experience as a year at a firm so that a lawyer returning to a law firm will receive credit for the clerkship. For example, a newly graduated lawyer, upon completion of a clerkship, would begin work at a firm not as a first-year associate, but as a second-year associate with the commensurate salary.

Whether you are a recent law school graduate or an established lawyer looking for a fresh change, a clerkship is an attractive proposition. The rewards of a clerkship are invaluable, the time commitment is manageable, and participation in the legal process of interpreting and clarifying law is intellectually rewarding.

CHAPTER 27

The Public Interest Market

Alexa Shabecoff
C. A. Webb

Every year, Harvard Law School's Office of Public Interest Advising receives hundreds of phone calls from experienced lawyers looking for a new job in the public interest world. Sometimes the calls are from lawyers already in a public interest job looking for a new position within the public interest realm. More often, the calls are from lawyers in the private sector seeking to move into the public interest sector. What motivates these lawyers to change paths, often at some financial cost, are the many benefits that public interest work offers.

The Benefits of Public Interest Work

While the rewards of public interest practice are many, some of the most notable are listed below.

A confluence of professional work and public service values: While in the private sector, many lawyers struggle to fulfill their public service aspirations through extracurricular activities. Lawyers who move to the public interest world are finally able to blend their personal values with their professional lives. Public sector lawyers believe that they are now in a position to make a difference: to the public, to their clients, or to a cause. They are proud to be using their law degrees in the way they envisioned they would when they entered law school. Working on the cutting edge of the day's big issues, public interest lawyers enjoy the feeling that their work centers on the very topics that fill headlines: mounting major civil rights challenges, lobbying on behalf of low-income families as welfare laws change, fighting for school choice, prosecuting corrupt politicians.

Rewarding, challenging work: Public interest jobs expand beyond traditional lawyering to community organizing, fund-raising, and press relations.

Often, public interest lawyers find they have to win not only in a court of law but also in the court of public opinion. For people who like the spotlight, there are plenty of opportunities to engage in public speaking, press conferences, television, and op-ed page debates.

Greater responsibility: Since public interest organizations are often leanly staffed, they typically rely upon the lawyer handling the case to make decisions alone. This level of responsibility can be daunting, especially to lawyers who have been trained to run everything past several layers of senior colleagues. But in time, the lawyers come to cherish this independence. Even when a team works on a case, their decisions are usually made democratically, not dictated by a superior.

Time for family and personal life: Lawyers in public interest often find they have relatively reasonable hours, generally working from 9:00 AM to 6:30 PM with occasional nights and weekends. While some lawyers work comparable hours to their counterparts in private practice, they find that outside of court filings and appearances, they can set their own deadlines. This greater control over workload enables public interest lawyers to preserve time for a life outside of work.

On the whole, public interest employers are more flexible about family leave and part-time work. Some employers allow lawyers to work four-day weeks or to set up alternative and flextime schedules that give them the freedom to pursue outside interests. Other lawyers arrange to work at home part of the time. Particularly for parents who have primary childcare responsibilities, relatively predictable hours and few travel demands may be critical.

Collegial work environment: Public interest lawyers frequently work as part of a team, either as co-counsel on cases or, more informally, as sources of advice and support. Laboring toward a common goal as they work together on cases or trade ideas, public interest lawyers develop strong bonds.

More time in court: In public interest organizations, even fairly junior lawyers are given their own caseloads. Often, they are solely responsible for a case, from start to finish. Even while working as co-counsel with more-experienced lawyers, public interest lawyers are allowed into the courtroom, starting with simpler matters, such as motions, and quickly assuming responsibility for more significant court appearances.

Financial Considerations

If you are contemplating a switch from the private sector to the public interest world, you will most likely face a pay cut. According to a National Association for Law Placement (NALP) survey, in 1997 the mean level public interest salary was $31,175 compared to the mean of $48,986 for all law school graduates; the median salary for that year for graduates going into public interest work was $30,000, while the median for all entry level jobs was $40,000. The salary disparity often widens over the years. If you are going to be facing a pay cut, the more prepared you are, the better. Ideally, that means saving and investing a portion of your current salary, paying down debt, and avoiding expensive spending habits. It also means making sure your family understands that change in spending. To keep a positive outlook about a lower-paying job, consider your reasons for moving to that type of job in the first place. When calculating how your future wages will shrink your budget, factor in the ways that your new job might improve your lifestyle. A financial sacrifice is often outweighed by substantial nonmonetary benefits, such as job fulfillment or time for a personal life.

The Public Interest World: Finding Your Niche

Figuring out just what type of public interest law you want to practice can be one of the toughest steps in your quest to change jobs. What type of work will suit your personality, let you put your energy and talent to use, fulfill your professional expectations, and make you eager to get to your job each morning?

The range of public interest opportunities for lawyers is broad, leaving you no shortage of career options. However, the public interest market may seem difficult to master at first. There is no centralized information on employment opportunities and hiring trends are unpredictable. To get you started, we have provided you with general information (responsibilities, salary trends, hiring preferences) about the major areas of public interest law. Many jobs do not fall neatly within any of these categories. To learn more about the practice settings described here and the wider range of opportunities in the public interest world, read some of the other publications listed in the Resource List at the end of this book. You should also get back in touch with your law school's career services office or public interest advising office. Your law school may have directories of public interest organizations in different locales and may receive job announcements from public interest employers looking for experienced lawyers. Bar associations also frequently have directories of nonprofit organizations in their jurisdiction.

In addition to examining written materials, you should also set up informational meetings with lawyers who have experience in practice areas that have sparked your interest; visit the offices or courtrooms where they work (see Chapter 8 on networking). Networking does not come naturally to everyone, but it is critical in the public interest market. Talking to lawyers working in areas that interest you will not only give you a clearer sense of the options ahead of you, but will also introduce you to contacts who can eventually help you land the job. Since no headhunters exist for the public interest world, and because public interest job positions are often not widely advertised, word of mouth is often the only way to learn about job openings. Your new contacts may also know someone in the organization you want to join and may be able to put in a good word for you. You will have to be persistent in your attempt to navigate the public interest world, but your efforts will pay off. You will discover an eclectic universe of exciting possibilities, one that might be just right for you.

Public Defenders

Public defenders serve as court-appointed counsel to indigent men and women facing criminal charges on the federal and state level. Federal public defender offices represent indigent defendants charged with federal crimes. Typical federal criminal cases involve white-collar crime, interstate kidnaping, large-scale drag trafficking, bank robberies, or violations of federal property laws. State and county public defender offices represent individuals charged with state and local misdemeanors and felonies, such as assault, burglary, drunk driving, and murder. Working as a public defender offers one of the best means of gaining trial experience. Public defenders quickly assume extensive responsibility for all phases of their cases and appear frequently in court. Their work includes interviewing clients and witnesses, developing case strategies, filing motions and briefs, performing legal research, and preparing for and conducting numerous trials. On the federal level, defenders handle fewer, more-complex, cases.

Some public defender offices are organized on a model of vertical representation, in which lawyers handle all stages of their own cases, from pretrial investigation through appeals. Other public defender offices have horizontal representation, where trial lawyers conduct trials and appeals go to an appellate division. Some offices handle only appellate work, with an emphasis on research, writing, and appellate argument. Some public defender offices have specialized programs. For example, a number of public defender offices now take on death penalty cases because Congress has stopped funding the death penalty resource centers throughout the country. Juvenile advocacy is another area in which specialized services are often offered.

Public defenders represent low-income individuals; some clients may be emotionally troubled or mentally disabled, and many clients will have serious problems in their lives beyond those presented by their involvement in the criminal justice system. The challenges of this work do not suit everyone. Heavy caseloads, offices that seem primitive by firm standards, and a lack of administrative support are a constant part of a public defender's work life. However, many public defenders enjoy seeing the immediate results of their client-intensive work and find tremendous satisfaction in helping individuals who are among the most disadvantaged and disenfranchised in our society. A good starting point for locating public defender offices around the country is the *Directory of Legal Aid and Defender Offices in the United States and Territories* published by the National Legal Aid and Defender Association (NLADA).

You probably will start out in an entry-level position if you lack substantial trial experience. Federal defender offices may demand a greater level of experience in their hires than a state defender's office and usually take only lawyers with extensive litigation experience either at a state defender's office or a private firm. Salaries for state public defenders vary quite a bit from state to state. In many states, starting salaries are between $30,000 and $40,000 per year with incremental raises based on years of experience. Federal public defenders receive higher salaries generally based on the federal government pay scale.

Nonprofit Public Interest Organizations

Nonprofit organizations that focus on particular causes or the problems of a particular group offer lawyers an array of advocacy agendas and practice styles. Each organization is unique in terms of the clients it represents, the issues it addresses, and the methods it uses. Nonprofit advocacy organizations do, however, tend to fall into one of two categories: client-oriented or direct-service organizations and policy-oriented organizations.

Client-Oriented/Direct-Service Organizations

Client-oriented or direct-service public interest organizations focus on the representation of individuals. These organizations are private, nonprofit law offices that assist underserved communities. Often these organizations focus on representing a particular segment of underrepresented clients, such as immigrant groups or children. Lawyers in these public interest agencies have a substantial amount of client contact. Such offices, which are usually community-based and located near the client groups they serve, are generally small, and the staff is limited. Client-centered organizations rely on individual donors, foundations, lawyer's fees, and occasionally some government support as their preliminary funding sources.

The lawyers in these offices take cases that are significant to their clients, regardless of whether they have any national importance. Their practice often involves a wide range of casework, from writing demand letters, to litigating on the clients' behalf in administrative hearings or state or federal court. Sometimes these organizations lobby and work on legislation when policies affect their client populations directly.

A career in client-oriented public interest also has potential drawbacks. Lawyers often must handle a high volume of cases, many of which are time sensitive. Locating private funding for a small community-based organization can be frustrating, as many funders are attracted to larger, more glamorous national nonprofits. Due to limited funds, the pay scale for client-centered nonprofit lawyers is quite low, with typical starting salaries in the $25,000–$30,000 range.

Client-oriented public interest organizations look for lawyers with knowledge of foreign languages as well as public service experience. Applicants should have a passion for the core issues to which the organization responds, even if they have not gained experience in that area in a professional legal capacity.

Policy-Oriented Organizations

Policy-oriented organizations use impact litigation and other forms of advocacy to bring about systemic change centered on particular issues. Such organizations aim to protect the legal rights of a client group or effect a policy change through broad class action litigation or through significant cases of first impression. Many of these organizations seek to bring about public policy and legal reform through means other than, or in addition to, litigation, such as lobbying, community organization, policy analysis, and education.

Policy-oriented organizations, especially the ones that litigate, frequently hire only experienced lawyers. These positions are extremely competitive, and applicants must demonstrate a commitment to both public service generally and the organization's specific goals. Doing some pro bono work for a policy-oriented organization will provide you with essential experience and may even lead to employment with the organization itself. Writing and legal analysis skills are essential, and policy advocacy or lobbying experience is helpful. Applicants often must also have strong academic credentials.

It is difficult to generalize about pay rates for nonprofits. Each organization's pay scale depends on its funding sources and its affiliations. Better-known national organizations tend to pay the most, while smaller, grassroots offices pay very little, often in the low $20,000s for young lawyers. Entry-level salaries at some of the more prominent urban nonprofits range from $30,000 to $40,000.

Private Public Interest Firms

A small but growing number of private firms engage in public interest practices similar to those conducted by public interest organizations. Private public interest firms work on a wide range of issues, including landlord-tenant cases, immigration matters, criminal defense, consumer protection, civil rights issues, municipal law, labor law, and employment discrimination.

Like traditional nonprofit public interest organizations, public interest law firms have a particular social, political, or economic vision that includes helping underrepresented groups or promoting change. But unlike traditional nonprofits, public interest firms operate as for-profit businesses. Public interest firms rely on the fees generated by their cases, rather than foundation grants or tax dollars, to pay the rent and their lawyers' salaries. Thus, a public interest firm looks not only at the merits, but also at the potential profitability, of a case in deciding whether to take it on.

Private public interest firms do not always advertise job announcements, so, as with other public interest positions, informational interviewing and word of mouth are very important. Private public interest firms look for lawyers with a superior academic record, research, writing, and organizational skills, an ability to lure clients, and a commitment to public interest work that can be demonstrated throughout law school and professional practice. Salaries at private public interest law firms vary dramatically based on the firm's geographic location and type of practice, but most firms offer starting salaries in the mid-$30,000s, with the mid-$50,000s being a typical salary for a lateral hire. Top salaries at private public interest firms are often far higher than in nonprofit organizations.

International

International public interest law is a broad and fast-growing field. Although the variety of careers for qualified lawyers is great, the very diversity of public international law can make locating opportunities challenging. Many international nonprofit organizations, known as nongovernmental organizations (NGOs), have lawyers on staff. NGOs tend to specialize in a particular aspect of international law, such as human rights, development, environmental, or immigration and refugee issues. The type of work lawyers do within NGOs varies dramatically, depending upon the specialty of that organization. At human rights organizations, for example, lawyers may investigate, document, and report on human rights abuses and sometimes litigate. Development NGOs, on the other hand, tend to have lawyers serve as legal counsel to economic development and relief projects where they may assist in developing the project strategy, provide technical assistance, review contracts, and otherwise provide advice on transactional matters.

The market for public international jobs is competitive. Most public international employers require proficiency in at least one foreign language, prior experience in the field, travel in a foreign country, and often knowledge of economics and finance. Salary ranges for international nonprofits vary dramatically based on the nonprofit's location and type of work.

Legal Services/Legal Aid

Legal services programs, often called "legal aid societies," provide direct civil representation, at reduced cost or for free, to low-income and elderly clients throughout the United States. They handle diverse issues, which range from housing to domestic violence to government benefits. Many legal services offices are organized by subject matter, and the staff lawyers specialize in one area of practice. In some offices, lawyers are generalists, handling the spectrum of cases that fall within their program's mandate.

Lawyers working in legal services have intensive client contact, significant autonomy and responsibility, a varied workload, a casual and often non-hierarchical environment, and a great deal of time in court or before administrative law judges. They often manage as many as forty to sixty active cases at one time. Legal services lawyers frequently collaborate on larger projects, such as community education or complex cases. On the downside, some lawyers find the large caseloads and quick turnover of cases stressful. Others feel that their work does not have enough of a global effect; they feel that the individual client approach often treats the symptom instead of the disease. Many, however, find the mix of client contact, responsibility, and a hospitable working environment an attractive combination.

Traditionally almost all legal services programs have relied heavily on funding from the federal Legal Services Corporation and were vulnerable to political funding decisions. (An exception to this is the Legal Aid Society in New York City, which has both criminal and civil divisions and has historically been funded by the private bar and state and local government.) However, in recent years, in response to funding cuts and further restrictions on the type of cases they can take, programs have increasingly turned to other sources of funding, such as support from state legislatures, the private bar, foundations, and income from IOLTA (Interest on Lawyer Trust Accounts). In some areas entire programs have chosen to give up their federal funding entirely so that they can continue to take on the activities that recipients of federal funding are prohibited from engaging in, such as class action litigation and legislative advocacy. In other locales some programs have spun-off separate offices to handle prohibited types of advocacy. As a result, there are now legal services programs that handle almost exclusively individual direct service cases and other programs that, without any federal funding, handle law reform cases.

As legal services programs have adjusted to the earlier funding cuts, hiring at legal services programs has recently increased. Legal services employers prefer lawyers who have hands-on experience with indigent clients and an abiding commitment to public service. Legal services employers also seek out lawyers with litigation or other advocacy experience. To find legal services that receive federal funding, consult the annual program directory published by the Legal Services Corporation. The NLADA directory also lists legal services offices, both federally funded and those receiving alternative funding, around the country.

Legal services salaries tend to fill at the lower end of the public interest spectrum; starting salaries range from $20,000 to $30,000 per year, depending on geographic location. Generally, legal services lawyers receive a $1,000 to $2,000 pay increase each year. Managers and directors in legal services programs earn more than staff lawyers, with the highest salaries reaching $100,000 for a legal services director in a major metropolitan area. To offset their relatively low salaries, legal services programs often offer generous leave and other benefits.

Creating Your Own Job: Fellowships and Entrepreneurial Grants

Because of the great personal satisfaction that comes from public interest work, even low paying jobs draw many applicants. Low turnover or tight funding may leave organizations with no openings for long periods. Fellowships and entrepreneurial grants are increasingly becoming a way in which lawyers are creating public interest positions for themselves. With a fellowship or entrepreneurial grant, you can create the job of your dreams. There are two ways to do this: you can create a new position in an existing organization, or you can start your own organization.

Most public interest employers, desperate for help, enthusiastically welcome staff who bring their own funding. Many organizations will "sponsor" an individual who wants to work with them and is applying for funding from outside sources such as foundations. Having the sponsorship of an existing organization, especially one that is well known and has a good reputation, is helpful in gaining the trust of potential funders. For information on fellowships you can consult Harvard Law School's *Public Interest Job Search Guide,* which contains a lengthy list of organizations that grant law-related fellowships, or Yale Law School's *Directory of Public Interest Fellowships.* Be aware, however, that some are limited to applicants currently in law school or in a judicial clerkship; other fellowships are available to lawyers a specified number of years out of law school or will have no limitations whatsoever.

Entrepreneurial grants allow you to create your own public interest project, either attached to an existing organization or as a completely new, independent organization. If you wish to pursue this route, you will have to educate yourself about drafting a project proposal and a working budget. In looking for advice about how to create a project and obtain grant money, you should check the guides listed above and also contact the Foundation Center, a nonprofit with branch offices in several cities, which has an abundance of information on locating potential funding sources.

Making Yourself Marketable

Acquiring the appropriate public interest credentials can be a challenge, especially if you do not already have public interest experience. Proving that you have what a public interest employer is looking for may just be a matter of how you present the skills you already have. It may require, however, that you take additional steps to gain relevant experience or show your commitment.

If you do not have relevant public interest credentials, or they are very rusty, you need to think strategically about how to add public interest experience to your resume. Below are some of the ways you can build a public interest track record.

Taking on pro bono work.   Taking targeted pro bono cases allows you to build credentials while working on issues that you care about. If you would like to move into family law, for example, helping battered women obtain temporary restraining orders through a local shelter may bring you closer to the issues that interest you.

Join a law-related not-for-profit organization that interests you.   Becoming part of an organization will put you in closer contact with job sources and help demonstrate your commitment to that area of public interest. Organizations such as the NAACP, Sierra Club, National Organization for Women, and National Lawyer's Guild have large memberships that consist largely of professionals who meet at night or on weekends.

Publish.   Write articles in an area of interest for any publication, whether for law review journals or the op-ed page of a newspaper. This allows you to identify yourself as an expert to a larger audience.

Learn the field.   Reading journals, key cases, and other publications in your field of interest will help you stay up-to-date on current issues and developments in that area. You may also find it helpful to take continuing legal education classes in order to learn some necessary skills or gain familiarity with substantive practice areas.

Conclusion

Understanding the public interest market, finding the right type of position, and making yourself marketable for a job change into that position may seem like a daunting task. However, with careful research, networking, and focused credential building, it can be done. Your persistence will be rewarded with a job that suits your unique personality and where you will make a difference in people's lives.

CHAPTER 28

Teaching Law

Gary A. Munneke

The teaching profession offers unique opportunities and rewards for many lawyers. Virtually every lawyer retains in his or her mind images of law professors and law school. Individually and collectively, law school teachers have a profound effect on their students' perceptions of the legal system, approaches to analytical problems, and attitudes about clients, the law, and life. Whether they terrorized, bored, challenged, or nurtured their students, law school teachers certainly molded them.

Given the powerful influence that law school teachers can exert on their students, those who choose this career path assume a weighty responsibility. They bear the burden of instilling professional values and imparting legal knowledge to succeeding generations of lawyers. In a changing and uncertain professional environment, this responsibility is even heavier.

A law school is in one sense a highly specialized law firm. The tenured faculty are the partners; the nontenured faculty, the associates. The dean is the managing partner who oversees a large support staff. A law school engages in a very specialized type of practice: education. Its clients are the students, and fees are collected in the form of tuition. Because of the school's specialized mission, its offices contain unusually large conference rooms called classrooms and an extremely large library. This analogy may be helpful to someone from practice considering a career in teaching.

Opportunities in Teaching

Traditional tenure track positions are the most desirable and sought-after opportunities in legal education. A tenured faculty member is somewhat like a federal judge who sits for life unless impeached or retired. The tenure system ensures contract renewal to professors who have passed successfully through a period of review, generally from three to six years. Unlike an employee at will or even a law firm partner, a tenured professor cannot be dismissed without cause.

At most schools, the tenure review process is designed to weed out those who just want an easy job; the emphasis is on identifying lawyers who have a long-term commitment to scholarship, teaching, and academic service. To attain tenure, a candidate must demonstrate excellence in writing, in service to the school, community, and profession, and in the classroom. Professors considered for tenure are evaluated with the same kind of rigorous scrutiny that is applied to associates being considered for law firm partnership.

In addition to teaching in substantive fields of law—for example, torts—a large number of law school faculty members teach in clinical education or practice skills programs.

All law schools provide some form of clinical education program, and clinical and other skills courses have evolved over the years in response to charges that the traditional Socratic legal education was incomplete. Experience in practice may prove to be an important qualification for clinical and skills teaching, where knowing how to do something is more important than substantive legal knowledge.

In recent years, an increasing number of law schools have applied their resources to hiring full-time, tenure track teachers in other skill areas, such as legal research and writing, trial and appellate advocacy, client interviewing and counseling, negotiation, law practice management, and mediation. In the past, skills courses, if taught at all, were assigned to part-time teachers.

Law schools also offer administrative opportunities that may or may not include a teaching role. These nonteaching positions include assistant and associate deans, placement services and admissions directors, financial-aid officers, comptrollers, recruiters, development officers, registrars, and assistant librarians.

Such administrative positions typically do not lead to teaching opportunities. The better career path for the lawyer/administrator is to advance through the ranks of university administration or laterally to other law schools into more responsible administrative positions. A few career administrators have become successful deans, although most deans come from the academic ranks.

One exception to this rule involves head librarians at law schools, who also are tenured faculty members. Librarians often carry a teaching load in addition to their administrative responsibilities. Thus, the field of law librarianship may prove to be an avenue to teaching status of individuals qualified in both law and library science.

Many women who want both career and family are attracted to law teaching because of the flexibility of scheduling, liberal sabbatical policies, and open attitudes about working mothers. Consequently, the number of women entering the law teaching profession has risen dramatically since 1970.

On the other hand, the number of minorities engaged in law school teaching is very small. Despite an increase in the percentage of minority law students and lawyers, racial and ethnic diversity remains an issue for many law school faculties.

For anyone who is determined to teach but unable to find a job because of the competition, many opportunities exist outside law school. Universities, colleges, community colleges, and even secondary schools often hire lawyers to teach certain law-related courses, such as business law, legal history, legal philosophy, criminal justice, real estate, and tax. Positions also are available in such places as paralegal programs and law enforcement training institutes.

Adjunct or part-time teaching positions also provide excellent opportunities for many practitioners, although these are unlikely to lead to full-time employment in a law school. Adjunct professors usually are respected practitioners who teach one course at a law school in an area of special expertise. Compensation for adjunct positions, however, may be one-tenth of full-time salaries or less.

Work

Lawyers who simply want to teach regardless of the venue should consider lecturing in continuing legal education (CLE) programs, public education, or client seminars. These activities may provide an outlet for some inner desire to teach without necessitating a career change.

Lawyers teaching in a law school typically carry a class load of two or three courses per semester, depending on such factors as number of hours per week the class meets, class size, level of individual student contact, number of sections of the same course, and whether the course is a new one under development. A teacher carrying a six-hour load must spend considerably more time than that in preparation, particularly if this is the first time that he or she has taught the class. At the end of the term, the teacher must spend a significant amount of time grading exams or papers. Most law professors consider this task the most onerous aspect of teaching.

Obviously, the work of a law professor includes more than just teaching classes. In addition to teaching, faculty members are expected to engage in research and writing in areas related to their professional expertise. In fact, at almost all law schools, there is a publication requirement for tenure. Anyone considering a career in law teaching should be admonished: The adage "publish or perish" is not an empty phrase. If you do not enjoy research and do not like to write, do not choose this career path. While some schools may be liberal in what they consider acceptable scholarly writing, most expect untenured professors to produce a series of traditional law review articles during their probationary period. After tenure, professors are expected to demonstrate continued productivity, and failure to do so may be reflected in raises, assignments, and status in the law school.

Effective professors spend a large portion of their time working with students outside of class. With the advent of e-mail, professors may find themselves communicating daily with students and colleagues. Following almost every class, some students come by their teacher's office with questions. Faculty members direct students' research for papers; they help students clerking with law firms to handle cases; they advise moot court teams, law journals, and other student organizations; they attend banquets, receptions, picnics, and social events when invited. This aspect of teaching can be rewarding and fun, but it cuts into the time available for pursuits such as research and writing.

Every faculty member assumes various administrative responsibilities, such as law school and university committees. Just as a lawyer in a law firm may be required to serve on administrative committees, law professors frequently are expected to participate in the governance of the institution.

Moreover, law professors are expected to engage in work outside of the law school. Such external activities not only increase the visibility and reputation of the law school itself, but keep the academician in touch with realities and trends in the real world. Some professors handle pro bono cases in their areas of expertise. Some work with law firms on a consulting basis. Others become active in local, state, and national bar association activities and CLE programs. Still others participate in the political process in a variety of ways.

Qualifications

Law professors tend to be drawn from a narrow range of candidates. The typical law professor studied law at a prestigious national law school, where he or she ranked at the top of the class and often served as a law review editor. After graduation, this future professor clerked for a high-ranking judge and perhaps worked in a large law firm for a couple of years.

The traditional teaching career path from law review to law clerk to teacher demanded that candidates have strong academic credentials, either good grades from a leading school or superior grades from a good school. Even the best students from less-prestigious institutions often found few doors open to them. One survey showed that 50 percent of all law teachers graduated from seven law schools and many of the rest from a handful of others. Thus, the law school attended may present an insurmountable barrier for many aspiring law school teachers.

Although the range of schools from which law teachers are recruited seems to be broadening, and practice experience is becoming more important than a judicial clerkship, the emphasis on grades has not waned but has increased with the level of competition for available positions. If you are thinking about law teaching, you should discuss candidly with one or more law professors whom you know what your prospects for getting a job will be.

Some aspiring teachers, who discover that their paper qualifications do not give them the appeal that they need to land a position, may earn a graduate law degree, a master of laws (LL.M.), from a school more prestigious than the one where they received their J.D. Some of these LL.M. programs are promoted as preparation for teaching, while others may be associated with a particular field of law. Generally, schools place their LL.M. students in teaching positions at a success rate commensurate with the prestige of the school.

Many schools utilize LL.M. candidates or practicing lawyers as first-year writing instructors. Although some law schools may hire tenure-track faculty from the ranks of these instructors, such a bootstrap approach is frequently not a realistic one. On the other hand, schools that maintain permanent writing faculty may recruit writing teachers from the ranks of such programs.

Another career path is to attain recognition as a leading practitioner in a specialized area of law. Many law schools have begun to seek out teachers with practice experience. These schools conclude that three to six years of practice with a good firm not only gives candidates substantial expertise but also establishes solid work values and habits. Those who follow this path frequently have developed a specialty or expertise that proves to be marketable to law schools.

Judicial clerkships, particularly at the federal appellate level, remain an important training ground for law teachers. Even though many law schools today expect teaching applicants to have some practice experience, clerking is almost never a detriment and many significantly improve the candidate's marketability. Many law graduates these days go to work for a firm after clerking and before applying for teaching positions. Some individuals are doing the reverse, clerking for a judge after a stint at a law firm.

Pay and Benefits

No one goes into teaching for the money. Most individuals with the credentials to be hired by a law school could make more money in the private practice of law. Starting salaries for law teachers, while above the national median of $40,000 for law school graduates, are significantly below the $100,000 paid to new associates in large New York firms. Although salaries for teachers vary according to the location and resources of the school, as well as the academic rank of the professor, the SALT survey reported a range of median salaries (by school) between $39,796 and $81,450 for assistant professors, $41,900 and $87,550 for associate professors, and $54,300 and $122,500 for full professors. Salary increases are typically 3 to 6 percent per year. These figures may be competitive with lawyers' incomes generally, but they certainly are far below the seven figure incomes that top the profession or the high six-figures earned by many law firm partners.

Low salaries are ameliorated in several ways. First, there are nonmonetary rewards associated with ego gratification and personal satisfaction. Law schools frequently offer liberal leave and sabbatical policies that simply do not exist in private practice. In addition, schools generally have long holiday breaks during the school year.

More important, base salaries can be somewhat deceiving; most law professors supplement their base salaries in a variety of ways. Teaching contracts are normally for ten months, giving teachers two months during which they can vacation, teach summer school, or write. Law schools usually offer supplemental pay for summer teaching or research. Many schools have chairs and professorships—trust funds donated by alumni and other benefactors—that supplement the salary of professors to whom they are awarded. As a rule, the more prestigious schools have more such endowed positions. Most schools also have a good benefit package, including a tax-deferred annuity/retirement program.

Opportunities to earn outside income are not to be ignored. Because many professors write casebooks and other publications, the prospect of receiving royalty income is very real. It also may be possible to handle a small number of fee-generating cases while teaching or to engage in consulting on a part-time basis.

In short, while it is unlikely that an individual will get rich teaching in a law school, it is possible to attain a very comfortable standard of living. The nonmonetary rewards combine with real income to provide a quality of life difficult to match in any other area of practice.

Finding a Job

Full-time law school teaching openings are limited. Of 177 ABA-approved law schools, there may be as few as one or two openings per school each year. Academic appointments run for an academic year beginning in August or September, so the heaviest interviewing season is typically from January through March or April. Some positions may be filled before or after this time, depending on the needs of the school, but most offers are made during the spring.

Every school has a hiring or appointments committee charged with soliciting and reviewing resumes, conducting interviews, and evaluating candidates. Hiring decisions normally are made by the entire faculty, although the dean may be empowered to make one-year appointments or visitorships. Schools frequently advertise in the *Chronicle of Higher Education,* a weekly educational paper, the *New York Times* classified advertisements, local newspapers, and other journals. Schools usually do not use headhunters.

The Association of American Law Schools (AALS) maintains a register of candidates and conducts an annual recruiting fair attended by most schools that is held around December 1 in Washington, D.C. Anyone interested in teaching should utilize these AALS services (AALS, 1201 Connecticut Ave. NW, Suite 800, Washington, DC, 20036-2605). Many applicants also write directly to an appointments committee, dean, or faculty member whom they know. Some may schedule informal meetings outside the formal hiring process. Those who are fortunate enough to have attended a law school with a substantial number of graduates engaged in law school teaching may be able to utilize that network. Some may get a better audience at their own law school than elsewhere, although schools differ widely regarding their willingness to hire their own graduates.

Competition for positions will remain fierce through 2010. Practitioners seeking to enter the teaching field will compete with recent graduates for available positions. As a result, most schools will find themselves in a buyer's market for the foreseeable future. Some law schools have discussed reducing the size of their student bodies, which would limit opportunities further. And because most law school teachers suggest they are happy where they are and not contemplating retirement any time soon, openings related to attrition will not increase appreciably for a number of years.

Conclusion

Law school teachers lead comfortable lives. They maintain status and respect in the community and enjoy a highly flexible schedule with very little supervision or external control. Institutional politics can be bitter and petty, but probably no more so than in any other organization of thirty to fifty lawyers.

On balance, for those who possess the qualifications, determination, and good luck to find a position in legal education, a career in teaching can be highly satisfying.

Who among us has not speculated about what we would do if given the opportunity to step up to the podium and teach a law school class? For some of us, that fantasy comes true. For those who do enter law teaching, the questions should be: How can I be like the teacher I admired most? How do I avoid becoming the one I enjoyed least? And how do I give my students the type of legal education they deserve?

CHAPTER 29

Part-Time, Temporary, and Contract Employment

Shelley Wallace

The industry that spawned part-time, temporary, and contract employment in the late 1980s continues to proliferate. This phenomenon has created a myriad of opportunities for alternate legal employment. Reflecting firmly established trends in workforce demographics and sweeping changes in corporate philosophy, the number of these opportunities has continued to expand throughout the 1990s. This trend will continue into the next millennium. By the year 2000, most lawyers will have considered the pursuit of such an option or will have found themselves in a position to offer such an opportunity to others.

Overview

Economic and societal forces converged in the late 1980s to create many different groups of lawyers who would form a highly qualified and experienced applicant pool for temporary and part-time work. Simultaneously, market forces influenced law firms and corporate law departments to explore alternatives to more traditional hiring retention methods. This candidate pool includes the following:

- *Corporate counsel* in firms that were caught in the frenzy of merger, acquisition, relocation, or dissolution found it difficult in some cases to find comparable positions within the corporate community.
- *Associates and partners,* in the wake of a recession that reduced the number of paying clients at the firm, were quietly asked to leave their law firms for economic reasons.
- *Women lawyers* formed the next largest class of qualified candidates seeking part-time or temporary work arrangements. By the end of the 1980s, law schools had graduated record numbers of women into the workforce; some found the traditional legal career path at odds with child rearing.

Part-Time, Temporary, and Contract Employment

Not coincidentally, during the middle to late 1980s, a new commercial enterprise also emerged to match the needs of able and deserving candidates with those of legal organizations: the temporary lawyer placement agency. Emerging in different regions of the country, and with different motivations and perspectives, the agencies' message found an eager audience, especially among prospective applicants. Gradually, the advocacy of alternative working arrangements by these temporary services encouraged trial of the concept by a growing number of corporations and law firms and served to move such options into the mainstream of legal staffing.

Alternative Working Arrangements Defined

Encompassing many different work arrangements in a variety of legal settings, these temporary and part-time opportunities are characterized by a unique employee-employer relationship. Thus, the lawyer acts as an independent provider, serving at the will of the client in an attorney-client relationship while receiving benefits, bonuses, sick pay, vacation pay, or personal days from most employment agencies. There are some temporary attorney arrangements that maintain independent contractor status; however, all lawyers in temporary arrangements are paid a set fee for hours worked. Frequently, this remuneration is greater than a comparably experienced lawyer receives in a full-time permanent position.

A law firm or corporation—the "client"—may engage the lawyer's services directly or through an agency that specializes in these types of arrangements. The client can decide to pay hourly fees directly or have them paid by the agency. Assignments can last for any length of time—from a few hours to a few years—and can entail any area of the law, from the most routine to the most complex. Most clients usually prefer to hire through the agency and have the agency act as the employer of the attorney or legal professional. The client can require that the work be conducted on its own premises, at the lawyer's home or office, at some distant location, or at any combination of these locations.

The length of a temporary assignment is determined exclusively by the client. Although clients usually provide a general estimate of the time required for the job's completion, they retain the right to terminate the project and position at any time and for any reason. Similarly, the client can stipulate both the number of days to be worked per week and the number of hours to be worked per day. These standards, and the fees to be paid, are negotiated by the candidate or by an agency acting as an intermediary for that purpose before the assignment begins.

Temporary and part-time assignments also can include job sharing when two lawyers work together closely to fulfill the responsibilities of one full-time position. Job-sharing arrangements often evolve into permanent part-time positions for one or both of the job sharers. In such an event, hourly payment is usually abandoned in favor of fixed salaries and is set to reflect the anticipated number of hours or days to be worked. These positions frequently entitle their holders to certain company or firm-paid benefits.

Contract employment implies that the terms and conditions of the assignment are agreed to and affirmed in writing before the assignment begins. At the end of the term, at their mutual consent, the parties can renegotiate these terms and conditions.

Corporate Law Departments

With no end in sight to the fierce competition throughout the global marketplace corporations have been compelled to rethink virtually every aspect of their operation. Responsiveness is the modern imperative. Success will derive from the ability to turn on a dime, to pursue emerging opportunities, and to get to the market faster with products and services that anticipate rather than react to buyers' needs. To accomplish this, the organization must be structured to allow rapid response to every contingency. A small group of highly competent managers and task specialists will be found at its core. Each member of this "nucleus" will be charged with the responsibility of building, training, sizing, and deploying staff as conditions dictate. To the extent that such conditions change, so, too, will the character and composition of staff. As a consequence of this new corporate profile, a worker's livelihood and security will reside in his or her abilities and distinctive competence. These workers will be employed with increasing frequency by specialized leased labor pools to which corporate management will turn to meet current staffing requirements.

Legal departments within these "nucleus" organizations will face a very specific challenge. On the one hand, fewer permanent staff resources will be available to deal with an ever-expanding workload. On the other hand, departments will be pressed by senior management to hold the line on outside counsel fees. As elsewhere throughout the corporation, when significant gaps emerge between varying work demands and the capacity of permanent staff resources to meet those demands, general counsel will have to resort to new and creative approaches to hiring and utilizing legal professionals.

For the able and experienced lawyers open to these new conditions, flexibility will be key. Today, in one company, the premium may be on lawyers with extensive environmental or employment expertise; in another company, the needs may center on health care or finance. Opportunities will be arising constantly for qualified candidates willing to get the job done and move on to the next challenge. In some cases, this may mean assignments measured in weeks. In others, terms may stretch to several months and even years.

Law Firms

As mentioned previously, the influx of women lawyers has served to expand and legitimize part-time alternatives within the law firm sector. Recognizing the value of retaining women lawyers who had been trained by the departments and now were producing an excellent work product, most major law firms established policies addressing part-time partnership, full-time requirements prior to partnership consideration, the amount of part-time work that can be allocated toward partnership track, and so forth. Different tiers of partnership, permanent associates, and job sharing of files all may be seen as products of women advocating change within their law firms.

In the fledgling days of the temporary legal staffing industry, concerns about quality work product, conflicts of interest, and confidentiality have tended to discourage the practice of hiring temporary staff, especially in large firms. In 1988, however, some of those concerns were swept away by the opinion of the Ethics Committee of the ABA. The ABA stated in Formal Opinion 88-356, December 16, 1988, that the use of temporary lawyers was "an efficient and cost-effective way" for law firms and corporations to "manage their work flow and deployment of resources." Careers of the early 1990s supported the use of temporary lawyers.

In the early 1990s, downsizing left some firms either with a lack of depth and substance in certain specialized areas or without the staff to handle large, unexpected projects. Here, the high caliber of the temporary lawyer applicant pool has played a part in reassuring partners of the quality of their work product and encouraged partners to look much more carefully at the temporary employment alternative.

Smaller law firms, which typically do not have the resources to maintain a permanent staff to cope with peak work periods, present the greatest number of opportunities for temporary and part-time assignments. This is especially true given their client base, which usually is less corporate and more focused on a general practice—personal injury, negligence, family, and real estate law, and so on. These law firms tend to be less demanding about the credentials and experience required of the temporary lawyer. At the same time, many of these firms are employing temporary lawyers as a means of serving those client needs that fall outside the expertise of the partners and full-time associates. The end result is improved service and an enhanced client relationship.

Alternative Work Arrangements: Circumstances and Opportunities

After a decade, this marketplace is still adapting to the changing demographics and work environment of the legal community. Many ground rules have evolved for buyers and sellers alike that are likely to prevail for some time. The following conveys the alternative working arrangement options that currently address a variety of legal career situations.

Newly graduated lawyers.   With the growth of law firm usage of temporaries, law school graduates have found work in large document production projects, from due diligence to litigation support. This work may be perceived by seasoned attorneys as repetitive, but it offers the inexperienced attorney an opportunity to gain exposure and to build legal skills that are valuable for advancement. Moreover, this arrangement presents an opportunity to learn from more experienced lawyers. This on-the-job legal training is a direct result of the growth of the legal staffing industry and the consequences of corporate legal departments constantly searching for ways to reduce bottom line costs, coupled with their reluctance to add full-time, permanent corporate legal staff.

Newly graduated or junior lawyers will find that the sources of those prospects that do exist will most likely be found in smaller law firms. Resumes from new lawyers are most often rejected by these firms on the assumption that the new lawyer is seeking only a permanent position. To counter this, the cover letter and resume should reflect a desire for an alternative work arrangement. A personal presentation showing what can be provided to the firm at any level and an eager desire to work on a trial basis may be appealing to the overworked practitioner.

Top-performing senior associates just turned down for partnership.   In the face of a dwindling number of clients, and with increased pressure on logging more billable hours, law firms strive to maintain steady income by not adding to their partnership ranks. Over a decade ago, associates expected that diligent work habits would be rewarded by an offer to become a principal of the firm. Today, the years to achieving partnership status have been extended and associates are more sophisticated in exploring other opportunities. Besides being stunned by the announcement, these senior associates now are facing career decisions of great importance. Faith in the law firm environment is shaken, and there is curiosity about opportunities in corporate legal departments. Most associates also are aware that there are few permanent opportunities within this segment, and, frankly, unsure whether this is the career path to follow. A temporary position within a corporate setting will allow a lawyer to assess his or her aptitude for such a career path and may even engender an offer of permanent employment.

Associates who do not want to pursue a full-time law career or who have decided to open their own practices.   Evaluations at the law firm by the partners indicate that these associates are excellent lawyers; however, they have decided that they do not want to become a partner at a large law firm because they want to have their own solo practices or they have too many outside interests to devote and dedicate themselves to full-time careers. With years of experience behind them, these associates have decided that this is the time to take the plunge and pursue opportunities as legislative assistant, lobbyist, author, real estate developer, musician, entrepreneur, or talk show host.

In any event, these lawyers still need income to meet mortgage payments while new careers are taking off or wish to keep their legal skills sharp in case their entrepreneurial dreams do not come true. Temporary assignments in specific areas of expertise probably will be available in both the law firm and corporate sectors.

Senior corporate counsel (eight or more years) displaced by merger, acquisition, or reorganization.   The hierarchical nature of the law firm makes it very difficult for senior corporate lawyers to move to a new larger law firm environment in a permanent position. Although a senior counsel may be willing to assume an associate's position, the other associates may feel threatened by his or her greater experience and maturity. Partners do not want to create an uncomfortable situation for their associates who expect to advance each year toward partnership. Partners also prefer to work with associates who have recently graduated from law school, believing that their way of training is the best. These days, the only senior lawyers of interest to law firms are those who can bring business to the firm. For those who do not fit within this category, temporary assignments may offer a number of benefits. Besides providing a substantial hourly wage, the law firm and its partners may well present a route of access to corporate clients who are seeking to build or enlarge in-house legal departments.

Women associates at major law firms or within corporate legal departments. These women lawyers would like to remain at the firm or within the legal department but also would like more time with their families. If other women associates at the firm or department are currently working on a part-time basis, inquire about their situation to determine whether that is a viable option. Before approaching the partners or supervising counsel, have a clear idea about the number of days per week and hours per day to be worked. Options include working a few full days or only part of the day five days a week. Some women with school-age children prefer working daily until the children come home from school in the late afternoon. Some firms consider a working schedule of nine to five, five days a week, a part-time position within the firm. If there are no other women working part-time, a woman lawyer may want to make a more formal presentation to the partnership or department by gathering articles and information to support an economic argument for the part-time position. Local women's bar organizations may know whether surveys have been issued to the various firms or departments within their areas. Most salary arrangements are a prorated portion of the full-time salary, and benefits often are negotiated as part of the arrangement.

Bear in mind that it is much easier to secure a permanent part-time position with the current employer where the partners or counsel are familiar with your work. If your evaluations have been good and you are held in high regard by the firm or department, there is a better chance of being retained. Also understand that there are both advantages and disadvantages to a prospective part-time status. On the negative side, many associates find themselves in the position of being expected to discharge full-time responsibilities for part-time salary. By and large, though, the permanent part-time option offers an optimum solution: ongoing compensation and benefits, the potential for entering the partnership or advancing up the corporate ladder, and a more balanced lifestyle.

Retired, "golden handshake" lawyers. These lawyers have the most knowledge and experience, but as a group are very difficult to place. Most law firm and corporate clients prefer junior associates or those in the ten- to fifteen-year range for temporary assignment. Unfortunately, there is an industry bias against senior lawyers on the part of supervising lawyers who suspect that the senior lawyers will be reluctant to take orders and directions from young, less-experienced superiors. Similarly, they imagine that senior lawyers will not do "grunt" work. Unless an agency or other referral source is acting on their behalf, and serving to dispel these stereotypes, chances of these senior lawyers landing temporary assignments will be meager.

Pursuing the Opportunity

As with any career decision, the pursuit of a temporary assignment should be grounded in an honest assessment of each lawyer's situation and prospects in light of the credentials, experience, and performance. Take the time to define the ideal situation: the setting, the hours to be worked, and the experience the lawyer wishes to gain. If that ideal is not dramatically different than the current reality, and there is strong evidence that the lawyer will be retained and advanced in the current position, a change may not be in his or her best interests. If, on the other hand, such security is lacking, or if the lawyer's working conditions are incompatible with certain personal needs or aspirations, an alternative arrangement may be in order.

The approaches available in the pursuit of temporary or other alternative employment opportunities are much the same as one might employ in a permanent job search: do it yourself or do it with the help of an agency. In fact, enterprising applicants who are willing and able to do the extensive brainwork and legwork that are required to uncover needs can land assignments. The truth is that very few corporations and law firms advertise temporary openings. Those that do tend to be barraged by resumes, the overwhelming majority of which are either wholly inappropriate to the need or come from permanent job seekers who see it as a means of getting their foot in the door. With barely enough time to fulfill the professional responsibilities of their jobs, most corporate counsel and hiring partners quickly tire of the burdensome and usually unproductive interviewing process. Such assignments reflect immediate needs and, in the absence of an immediately acceptable candidate, in most cases the search is abandoned.

The "immediate need" factor works just as strongly against the practice of distributing unsolicited resumes as part of a job search strategy. Yes, it is conceivable that the receipt of one's resume could coincide with the identification of an appropriate project or task. Unfortunately, most such resumes never reach the right decision maker at the right time and are rarely retained for future reference.

As a practical matter, most lawyers who currently are employed do not have the time or resources to explore the job market for continuing opportunities. Today's temporary legal placement agencies, which are typically managed and staffed by lawyers, are in the day-to-day business of finding and filling temporary job openings through routine interaction with the area's hiring partners and administrative general counsel. The best are equipped with sophisticated computerized systems to match prospective employers and applicants. They provide ongoing access to the marketplace and the expertise to help applicants translate access into employment.

For information on agencies within local markets, check local legal trade publications, bar magazines and journals, or the classified sections of major daily newspapers. Friends and fellow staff members can be good sources of insight into the local agency's capabilities, professionalism, and customer service. Every lawyer has the right to expect the utmost in confidentiality and the certainty that his or her resume will be sent to prospective employers only with expressed permission. These qualities and operating policies may best be assessed through inquiries into the experience of others. Several long-established agencies do have very similar standards, but with new firms emerging with great frequency it is only prudent to know as much about the people an applicant will be dealing with before beginning the process.

When working with most agencies, the lawyer applicant will be required to send a resume and a cover letter before any communication is received. If the resume is selected, the lawyer will be called for an interview. During the interview process, the applicant will be asked to fill out a variety of forms regarding legal experience, references, type of work hours and setting desired, financial needs in terms of hourly rate, travel preferences and so on. References will be checked, as well as facts pertaining to admission to the bar, graduation, and law school attendance.

Permission will be requested to send the resume to the client. If the client is interested in meeting the applicant, the agency will assist in arranging interviews. Sometimes the agency will have the lawyer report to the client immediately to begin work. The temporary lawyer will be responsible for sending a time card, signed by the client, to the agency before receiving payment by the agency.

Positions for independent contractors are available at a lower premium. The lawyer who meets the criteria as an independent contractor is generally responsible for his or her own tax payments, health insurance, and other benefits. Malpractice coverage is sometimes provided by the agency, the law firm, or the corporation. Most lawyers, however, do not seek this insurance if they are working under the supervision of other lawyers within a law department or firm. Temporary lawyers who are litigating on behalf of the client or those temporary lawyers involved in complex securities work are advised to seek their own coverage.

In terms of compensation, hourly rates vary by geographic region and tend to reflect a combination of the lawyer's experience, area of specialization, and the complexity of the assignment. At present, lawyers are receiving from $30 per hour for routine work to upward of $125 per hour for highly specialized and sophisticated assignments. Even a brief stint as a temporary lawyer can be highly lucrative.

The Alternative Career Path

The following list of practical "dos and don'ts" can be very helpful in assisting a lawyer during this career transition:

1. *Dealing with the agency.* To get the most from a temporary agency, understand that the agency is dealing with a large, changing roster of candidates and the constantly changing needs of its clients. As a result, qualifications or expertise not in demand today may be just what is required tomorrow. Keep your profile high and take every opportunity to make an impression that will differentiate you from your counterparts:
   - Call the agency periodically to update your resume or discuss upcoming opportunities.

- Ask to meet all of the lawyer personnel who may be involved in your placement, or establish a relationship with one recruiter who will be your contact for all opportunities.
- Be forthcoming about references and reasons for job changes. The more the agency knows about you, the more information it will have at its disposal to argue on your behalf to the client.
- Request that your resume remain on active status regardless of how long the job search continues. (A rule of thumb in this business is that it could take a minimum of one month for each $10,000 of salary before a position of choice is secured; in recessionary periods you could double that time comfortably).

2. *Maintaining flexibility.* Be flexible and open to new situations. Your idea about part-time work may be very different from the client's notion of temporary or part-time work. A great opportunity could be two full days a week with a prestigious company. You should actively consider this position if there may appear to be possibilities of further employment. Also, a short-term assignment often is better than no assignment and can lead to other opportunities. Some lawyers were offered permanent placement positions while on short-term or menial assignments. One lawyer accepted a temporary paralegal position and did such a great job that the company offered her a permanent counsel position within the company. Be flexible:

- Work part-time for two clients at the same time, thus maximizing your opportunities from one or both of them.
- Rearrange your schedule if you are a solo practitioner to accommodate one big corporate client.
- Be realistic about your pride. So many lawyers do not register for temporary positions or accept them because they think that the positions are beneath them. You should be informed about all opportunities and then make a decision. You cannot assess what you do not know.
- Rewrite your resume, if requested by the agency, to emphasize your experience in a particular area of law or to highlight a particular credential.

3. *Listening to your placement director or counselor.* You might be the most knowledgeable, substantive lawyer on earth, but you probably know precious little about the placement process, particularly within the temporary employment field. If you are told to spend more time onsite by the lawyer placement director, do so. Visibility is important to future work opportunities. If the placement director tells you to mingle and mix if possible with the other lawyers, listen to this advice. Relationships and friendships are great sources for learning about opportunities within the company, so make a sincere effort to learn about your colleagues. Come out of your office, make lunch dates, and take time to smile and be cordial to everyone you come in contact with, especially the support staff; one of the best supporters on your behalf could be a well-regarded secretary, clerk, or paralegal.

4. *Fulfilling the assignment.* First and foremost, clients are interested in your completing the task as accurately and quickly as possible. If they believe you are lobbying for a permanent position among the other counsel, you will be perceived as not focused on the task at hand. You also run the risk of becoming embroiled in a political situation by crossing departmental lines. In one incident, a temporary lawyer was dismissed when he asked another department head for additional work. It so happened that the "client" was an underling to the other department head, and he was affronted that the temporary lawyer would go over his head. Now, this is not always the case, and there are times when bringing up your availability will lead to new assignments, but you must first assess your work environment regarding alliances, departmental lines, and hierarchical positions. Always include your agency in your planned actions. Often, the agency's knowledge of the department or experience in this area is invaluable.

5. *Working "temp" but wanting "perm".* If you are concerned that a temporary assignment may limit your ability to accept a permanent position should it arise while you are on assignment, there are tips you should know that could permit you to accept both opportunities:
   - First, be realistic about your permanent "irons in the fire." If you are on a third interview and selected as one of the finalists for a permanent position, do not accept a temporary position. If you back out at the last minute after you have been put forward for the temporary spot, the agency and the client will not think very highly of your character. Although you may not care, you must remember what a small world this is becoming and what appears secure and guaranteed one moment is subject to dissolution and acquisition the next.
   - Be candid at every step of the process with the temporary agency. Together you can assess the course of action to undertake. The agency can request an initial time commitment from the client. If you are just beginning a job search, a two-month assignment will hardly interfere and could present other opportunities. Also, if an unexpected offer does arise, the agency can arrange for you to train your replacement, minimizing the lag time and the client's ire.

6. *Making the most of every assignment.* Regardless of your long-term expectations or aspirations, your interests always will be best served by approaching even the most humble assignment with the utmost in energy, interest, and professionalism. Here are some rules to live by:
   - Treat the opportunity of the temporary assignment as you would any other permanent offer.
   - Send thank-you notes after the interview process, but make sure you proofread them. A client was all set to hire a temporary lawyer until a thank-you note arrived with typographical errors.
   - Act professionally at all times while on an assignment.

- Minimize personal calls and absences.
- Keep the confidences of every lawyer within the department and certainly those of your immediate supervisor.
- Stay away from all politics and do not take sides.
- Analyze the working environment and conform. If the client is an early riser and starts work at 7:30, you should be there.

Always search for ways to create a great impression. Attitude is key. If the client does not want a dissertation paper on every issue, but wants you to approach the caseload more like a business lawyer than a fourth-year associate, do so. Learn to handle the matter in the client's manner.

CHAPTER 30

Creating an Ideal Law Practice in Conjunction with Your Home[1]

Diane L. Drain

The master in the art of living draws no sharp distinction between his labor and his leisure, his mind and his body, his work and his play, his education and his recreation. He hardly knows which.

He simply pursues his vision of excellence through whatever he is doing and leaves others to determine whether he is working or playing.

To himself, he is always doing both.

Michael Scott Karpovich

For the last thirty-plus years the general perception of the practice of law has been that it is conducted from high-rise buildings with marble column entries, richly clad floors, and cherry wood paneling. Lawyers dress in expensive three-piece suits that would cost the average client two to five months' wages. Ironically, most lawyers wonder why they feel isolated from their clients, family, and community.

This isolation problem is not unique to the 1990s. On September 9, 1861, Abraham Lincoln relieved General John C. Fremont of his command, stating that the General's cardinal mistake was that he had isolated himself and allowed nobody to see him. Consequently, Lincoln found that "he did not know what was going on in the very matter he is dealing with." Mr. Lincoln fired General Fremont because of this isolation from those that he was responsible to and for his troops.[2]

Abraham Lincoln would be appalled if he visited most modern law firms. We have removed our practices from the physical and financial reach of the people that Lincoln so greatly cherished—the common person. In segregating ourselves from the rest of society we have become argumentative, self-serving, and lonely. We have come to accept that a bold display of ego-based anger is admirable. We have held deception and manipulation of facts and the law as the proper way to represent our clients. In truth, our bad manners and lack of civility appall most of our clients, as they would President Lincoln.

Many of us begrudge the lack of respect that the general public currently has for most lawyers. Yet few of us are willing to challenge the existing hierarchy in an attempt to bring the practice of law back to the honorable position that it held in Lincoln's day. There is no magic to returning to the grace of a past style of practice, other than for every lawyer to decide that it is his or her responsibility to change their own behavior. This chapter identifies the steps I have taken to bring honor, pride, civility, and a community purpose back into my life and, in a small way, my profession.

Eight years ago, I decided to reevaluate the basic principles I was using in practicing law. During that evaluation period I realized that I had adopted a style of practice that I did not respect. Also I realized that I had long ago abandoned my family and community. I worked long hours for clients I never met, mass-produced documents for land developers I did not respect, and was responsible for multimillion dollar construction projects that I never saw. I was responsible for overseeing other lawyers and staff members—people that I really did not know. I knew very little about their personal life, and I did not know whether they liked their work. Firm rules strictly prohibited mingling with staff and other attorneys not on the same floor or the same department. The firm's method of billing for services (the billable hour) had created so much in-house competition that the office atmosphere was similar to a series of small, warring camps, rather than a large, unified body focused on producing the best legal work for the firm's clients. I talked to others from my law school class and found that most were having similar problems no matter the size of their firm. Therefore, I was left with the realization that these problems had invaded the mindset of most of the legal community, not just my small part of the world.

For a brief time I wondered if I could be a lawyer, at least as the legal community then defined that term (remember it was 1990). This brief self-deprecating period lasted just a few weeks. During that reevaluation period I came to the conclusion that I was a good lawyer, but that the conflict was that I honestly cared how my clients were treated. I saw bill padding or billing for unnecessary work as theft. I also felt that unnecessary litigation or the unending flow of documents for the sole sake of producing documents contributed to the backlog in our courts at a huge cost to all taxpayers. I believed that I could not make a difference in my firm's philosophy because the problem had spread throughout the profession. Instead, I decided to carve a path for myself that reflected my respect for my profession and my honest caring for my clients, my family, and myself.

What was the answer? The best one was to open my own practice. That was a very expensive and frightening prospect. I had several practical issues to address: (1) Would my large corporate clients come with me? (2) Would they feel that a solo lawyer could provide the type of service that they had come to expect? The supervising agent for my main corporate client summed it up: "Diane, we sent the work to you, we do not care where you practice, just so long as the quality that you have always given us continues." That locked my decision to go solo.

Once I made the decision to open my own practice, my next decision was where to locate the office. Another important part of life that had been negatively affected by the marble tower philosophy was my family. In order to be the conforming big-firm lawyer, I had succeeded in missing my daughter's first soccer goal, thirteenth birthday party, and first dance. I had permitted things to get so bad that my sister had to help my daughter pick out her high school graduation dress. Fortunately, or perhaps unfortunately, my family was very understanding. Perhaps if they had been more demanding, I would have been forced to take a critical look at my lifestyle much earlier. In their eyes I was just taking the same dedicated path chosen by my father. This is the father who missed almost every class play, social event, or athletic activity that any of his children were involved in. How special that Diane was following in her very successful father's footsteps!

My family became a very important part of my decision to set up the office in my home. I had just married a wonderful man with three very confused and angry girls. None of these new members to my home had been raised with the absent parent principal. If this marriage was to be a success, and if I was to help these children through the most difficult time in their young lives, then I would have to reprioritize my life. My work could not be all-consuming; somehow I had to balance it with my family's needs. How can both groups be given equal time when it appears that the needs of both are in direct conflict? After a great deal of soul-searching my new husband and I decided that we could handle the challenge, but the only answer was to move my work to our home, which would then remove the physical barriers I had accepted for so many years. This breaking of the physical barriers allowed me to be a valuable contributing force to everyone–family and professional.

When I first decided to set up an office in my home I did so without much fanfare; I was not sure my clients and peers would respect a lawyer practicing out of the home. Was I ever wrong! From the first day my office opened I realized that I was able to provide more efficient and cheaper service for all of my clients. Those clients referred other clients, who referred other clients, and so on and so on. No one cared whether or not I was housed in an elaborate, marble-embossed castle. My clients wanted to be able to communicate with me, to be involved in the management of their case, to know the status of their files, and to feel that their money was being well spent. I provided all this and more.

Originally I told myself I would only be at home until my family situation had stabilized, which I believed would be one to two years. That was almost eight years ago. The family situation stabilized long ago. I adore being a lawyer and my career has skyrocketed. Each year has been more financially, professionally, and emotionally rewarding. Removing the physical barriers added hours to each day. Time that was originally spent commuting or waiting for documents from the word processing department is now used to work or play. Despite the challenges, I have never regretted making the move.

I refer to my office as an office that is "on-site" or "in conjunction" with my home. By that I mean that my office is a full-time, completely self-sustained, law office that just happens to adjoin my home. I have never looked at my practice as a part-time job. However, the suggestions in this chapter will fit any alternative style, including part-time practice. The business of practicing law and making decisions about technology and client relationships applies equally to home offices and traditional offices. This chapter is unique because it discusses the philosophical issues relative to blending the practice of law with your home and family, along with some very practical tips to survive this transition.

This chapter is designed to help you analyze whether or not a home office is a practical solution for you and your situation. What you are considering is similar to merging several different companies: your profession, your clients, your family, your extended family, your neighbors, your community, and your personal goals and needs. Any corporate attorney will tell you that the merger of multiple companies is not an easy task and can only be accomplished successfully with a great deal of advance planning.

Is an Office in or Near Your Home Possible?

According to *Link Resources,* 37 million people work at home. Of that number, 10 million work full-time at home. The average age of these workers is 41.2 years, with an income of $58,400. Workers with postgraduate degrees total 34 percent, and 54 percent are male and 46 percent female. AT&T employs approximately 35,000 telecommuters, and IBM estimates a savings of approximately $35 million in overhead costs as a result of their telecommuting program.

Goals

In deciding whether you want to change your current situation, you must first clearly understand your own goals. These goals may be best defined by recalling some of your past dreams that depicted your future. First define the following four terms: success, respect, security, and responsibility. Put these definitions in writing and make sure to use your own interpretations, not those of your family or friends. Next, analyze your long-term needs and those of your family and your business relations. The following questions may help you in defining your goals and analyzing the style of practice that will be best suited for you. Be completely honest.

1. Break your definition of success into specific terms. Draw a pie chart using these terms: money, power, reputation, family relationship, community involvement, or something else. Place each of these terms into a separate area, making the size of each area proportionate to its importance. How does each item rate in relationship to the way that you are currently living?
2. What are your own specific needs: time, money, emotional commitment to family, and work?

3. What are the specific needs of your family: time, money, emotional commitment?
4. How do you picture your future? Examine the next five, ten, twenty, thirty, and fifty years. Create a picture in your mind of your surroundings and your involvement in your family, profession, and community. Build on that picture so that each successive time period adds additional pieces of the puzzle until the ultimate picture is complete. (Hint: It is usually easier to begin by visualizing one of the later periods and then work backward.)
5. Determine what you need to accomplish each year in order to create the picture you have for these various stages in your life. Never reject an option just because it does not fit one of your other goals. Some of the wildest ideas become the mainstay of your future life. Also, be willing to reanalyze your long-term goals to determine whether you have changed your ultimate picture. Do not be so flexible that your goals have no chance of becoming reality.
6. Answer these questions if one of your goals is to open up your own:
   - Are you able to motivate yourself? Where are your deficiencies in being your own boss? Is it possible to supplement those deficiencies with other resources? For example, can you hire a bookkeeper if you cannot or will not balance your checkbook or bill your clients efficiently?
   - How much staff assistance do you and your area of practice require?
   - How much peer interaction do you and your area of practice require?
   - How will your clients view a move to a solo office?
   - What resources do you and clients deem necessary? Which of those resources are merely luxuries that could be supplemented with alternative resources? Can you afford to purchase the resources that you and your clients deem necessary?
   - Do you believe that you can produce quality work on your own?
   - Do you need the environmental stress inherent within the traditional law firm environment (the adrenaline rush from all the hustle and bustle)?
   - Are you capable of handling a multitude of tasks at one time?
   - Are you challenged by and do you take pride in managing multiple tasks?
   - Are you willing to compromise billable time for management time? (Most solos will tell you that they spend at least 50 percent of their time managing their practice.)
   - Are you willing and able to keep up with technology, including taking the time to learn how to use whatever you have invested in?

Look closely at your answers to determine whether or not a solo practice, whether in your home or elsewhere, is the best option.

Special Issues Related to On-Site Offices

An on-site or home-based office can either be an extension to a traditional downtown office or it can be your only office. In addition to those issues discussed above, consider the following:

- *Your family situation.* Will your family tolerate your invasion of their privacy? What are their expectations of a normal home?
- *The geographical location.* Will your new office be convenient for your clients? How far is it from the courts or other necessary services?
- *The physical layout.* Is your home, with its existing floor plan, practical for an office, or will you need to remodel, add on or move? What can you afford?
- *The balance of work and home.* Will you be able to balance the invasion of work into home and vice versa? Do you have the ability to mentally separate each so that you have a home and not a bed within your office?
- *Security and privacy.* Typically two issues that are often overlooked in setting up an on-site office, determine what you can do to provide you family and your clients with secure and private environments.
- *Zoning.* Check the zoning restrictions for your property before investing in adding a new office. Some areas limit or prohibit businesses in the home that will "substantially increase traffic" in the neighborhood. Some of the newer residential developments have absolute prohibitions for any home-based offices. In the future, home-based businesses will become the norm and there will be increased demand that these limitations be relaxed or eliminated. For now, be sure that you are fully informed on current restrictions and be willing to make necessary changes.

Setting Up a Small Office in Conjunction with Your Home

The considerations in setting up a small office in conjunction with your home are the same as setting up a multiple-lawyer firm, except that you are the sole decision maker. All equipment, file setup, and staffing requirements must be determined. Your choices will be influenced by the physical size of the office, monetary constraints, the client's requirements, and the particular demands controlled by your type of practice. The following issues relate specifically to an on-site office.

Office Requirements

It is necessary that your office be a separate room dedicated to only office equipment, furniture, and files. Not only will this satisfy most with requirements of the Internal Revenue Service, but it will also assist you in practicing more efficiently and in creating a professional image.

Design a layout for your desk and other work surfaces that satisfy your needs based on the available space. Take into consideration equipment that needs to be easily accessible, the necessary file space, and whether or not you are your own secretary. In addition, you need at least two client chairs (assuming you will be seeing clients in your on-site office).

To ensure privacy, it is essential to have a door that separates your office from the rest of the house. The only exception to this requirement would be if you are the only occupant of your home and do not have pets. If you have a family then they have the right to a normal home environment. The separation between the two worlds—office and home—will give them that normal environment.

The perception of a home is in conflict with our current perception of the typical office environment. Giggling children, barking dogs, and washing machines are the sounds of a normal home, but are not acceptable for an office. These sounds will disturb your meetings with clients and inhibit your ability to work efficiently. Most importantly, these distractions reduce the professional image you wish to create.

You have an obligation to protect and secure client confidentiality. This includes protecting client files from the peeping eyes of others. Your office is not a place for personal visitors or children at play. It is essential that you educate each member of your family to honor the confidences of your work and to respect your clients' information and documents. Receive personal visitors in your home, not your office. Meet with your clients in your office, not your home.

In addition to a security alarm system on both the house and office, and in order to enhance the security of my office, I have built a lattice patio as part of the entrance to the office. This adds a wonderful atrium and provides me a conference room in a lovely garden setting. The patio adds privacy to the entry of the office and limits visibility from the street. Curious passersby cannot see into the office nor can they see the expensive electronic equipment.

Adequate file storage is a necessary evil. If storage in your home is limited, then rent space in a convenient, air-conditioned facility. That rent will be additional overhead but is usually inexpensive. As technology becomes more reasonably priced, you will be able to convert all files to computer images through scanning. Storage can then be on a small disk, which will eliminate most storage problems.

Clients

Your choice of location or style of practice may be dictated in large part by your current or prospective clients. Many of my clients are large, commercial, out-of-state lenders. Historically, I met these clients at their local office, if they had one, or we limited our meetings to the telephone, e-mail, or fax. For these clients, an on-site office was extremely convenient. In fact, most of them have come to prefer it because they can make arrangements for me to be available during hours that a traditional law office is closed. In a profession where our clients are spread throughout the world, this more-flexible work schedule is very appealing to clients who work in different time zones.

The majority of my individual clients are professionals or referrals from other professionals. These people are typically self-employed and many have their own home-based offices. They enjoy the low-stress environment offered by my on-site office. I can pull computer court dockets, make necessary copies, and direct my runner/process server, all while my client is in the office to help with the instructions. Evening and weekend hours are easily arranged. The client's travel time is greatly reduced, with little or no traffic or parking problems.

Client Management

It is very important to lay the ground rules for your on-site office. It is not permissible for clients to drop by. Explain to them that each client has assigned times for meetings, thereby assuring that their meetings are uninterrupted. Locate a pickup and delivery box outside the entrance to your office and invite your clients to use it at any time. Explain that the office phone is only answered during normal business hours, but that the fax machine is left on twenty-four hours. Let your clients know that in special situations you can be available during nonbusiness hours.

Equipment

In addition to the normal computer and electronic equipment for a small office there are a few other items that are specific to an on-site office.

Telephones and telephone lines: There are as many different choices for telephones as there are long-distance providers. It is advisable to stay with a manufacturer of your phone equipment that has a good reputation. At a minimum, you will want a two- or three-line phone with speaker, hold, conferencing, mute, and "do not disturb" features.

One line is dedicated as your main office line. This number should be listed as a business line and will be included in the Yellow Pages under your specific area of practice. There will be an additional charge for this business line, but it is worth the few extra dollars to have a presence in the business section of the telephone book. You may also elect to have caller ID on this line. Include voice messaging, or some similar service, that will answer all incoming calls after a predetermined number of rings or in the event that the line is busy. Do not use call waiting on your office line. It is far too distracting for you and your callers, and it does not give the professional image that you are trying to create. Establish a habit of turning off the ringer on the phone during nonbusiness hours unless you have made special arrangements to receive late or weekend calls.

The second line should be used for the fax/modem and as a second outgoing line. This separate line will permit leaving the fax machine on twenty-four hours, seven days a week. This allows clients, worldwide, to fax at their leisure and not be dictated to by office hours. Of course e-mail will replace this need in the very near future. If you are frequently on the Internet, or you have an excessive amount of faxes coming to your office, then take a look at US West Never Busy Fax. This system will retain faxes and send them once the fax/modem is no longer busy. Contact US West Small Business (or a similar service if you have a different local provider) for assistance in setting up your phone system.

Use a third line as your home line. Do not give this phone number to any of your clients. All incoming and outgoing personal calls should be restricted to the home line, not your business lines. You may decide not to have your personal phone number included in the personal section of the telephone book. That is an individual choice. I have retained my maiden name, therefore can list our home number under my married name and still retain our privacy.

Your preference may be to use a speaker phone. Personally, I find speaker phones objectionable, and I believe that most clients have the same opinion. If you are too busy to pick up the phone to talk directly to your clients, then your clients may decide to find another lawyer who has more time or is willing to treat them with more respect. Also some older clients have a difficult time understanding someone using a speakerphone; the echo distorts the voice. There is also an issue about confidentiality with the use of a speakerphone.

To reduce your chiropractic bills, invest in an ear loop attachment as a replacement for the handset. This device is extremely helpful in eliminating the stiff neck suffered while holding the phone between your chin and shoulder. It also frees your hands in order to type or write comfortably. The person on the other end of the phone can rarely tell whether you are using an ear loop or the regular handset.

Personnel

Even if you are working from an on-site office, you will still find it necessary to consider hiring employees or outside labor.

Employees: Factors to consider are: (1) the training and supervision that will be necessary in order for these employees to be self-sufficient and profitable, (2) whether you have the space to accommodate them, (3) whether they can work full- or part-time from their homes, and (4) whether part-time employees will accommodate your needs. The possibilities are limited only by your imagination.

Do not forget the additional legal obligations you have as an employer, such as making payroll, paying taxes, and providing a safe work environment.

Contract labor: Contract lawyers, research assistants, legal assistants, and secretaries can be used on a one-time or ongoing basis, depending on your needs. Be very careful whom you allow to gain access to your computer via modem.

Even if you decide not to hire office staff, contract with a delivery and process servicing company. Learn to consolidate deliveries and other errands by using your delivery service.

Miscellaneous

There are several basic issues related to the operation of any small office: mail, library, and supplies. In addition to establishing office policies related to each of these there are also unique issues for the on-site office.

Mail: Do not use your home address on your correspondence or business cards. This will make privacy and security more difficult.

One option for an address other than your on-site office is to rent "virtual" space from an existing law firm and use their address for your mail and deliveries. This rental may be limited to no physical use of the offices or it may be expanded to hourly use of the conference room and a per-use charge for their copier, fax, and other equipment. Some of these offices will even offer reception services so that you can forward your phone calls if you are going to be out of your office.

Library: The Internet has become a very popular place for research. The Arizona Revised Statutes are online for no charge (see *http://www.azleg.state. az.us*), and access to U.S. Supreme Court cases and the federal code is available through the Web site at Cornell University Law School (see http://www.law.cornell.edu). There are hundreds of other sites for free research. All of this information can be accessed through a private Internet provider for approximately $20 a month. In addition to the legal resources, there is access to an international e-mail service. I have reduced my long distance bills by approximately $100 to $150 per month by using e-mail rather than my long distance carrier. For sites of interest to lawyers, I recommend an ABA publication, *Law Law Law on the Internet,* by Erik J. Heels and Richard P. Klau.

Office Management

Additional office management policies you will need to establish include the handling of mail, docketing, files, timekeeping, and accounting. Each of these items could be an entire chapter of their own (for more information on these subjects see "How to Set Up a Small Efficient Law Practice: Going Solo in the '90s," by Diane L. Drain in *Life, Law and the Pursuit of Balance: A Lawyer's Guide to Quality of Life).*

Final Thoughts

As I stated above, these are steps I have taken to bring honor, pride, civility, and a community purpose back into my life and my profession. They have worked for me and can work for you. If you dream of having control over your daily life and including your family as part of your day, then an on-site office may be the answer. I guarantee your clients will appreciate the lower hourly rate, the more timely response, and the ease of accessing their lawyer without maneuvering through several layers of staff.

Remember—image is everything. As long as you believe that you are a professional, as long as you look, act, and talk like a professional—then you are a professional no matter where your office is located. Trust in yourself.

Notes

1. An earlier version of this article was first published in *Life, Law and the Pursuit of Balance,* edited by Jeffrey R. Simmons, State Bar of Arizona Young Lawyers Divisions and American Bar Association, 1996.

2. See Donald T. Phillips, *Lincoln on Leadership: Executive Strategies for Tough Times* (New York: Warner, 1992).

CHAPTER 31

Telecommuting

Nicole Belson Goluboff

Telecommuting: When Going the Distance Means Staying at Home

Telecommuting, simply defined, is about thinking before you choose a work site. It is about going to the office on Tuesday, not because it is Tuesday, but because there are tasks you can accomplish most efficiently and effectively in that place on that day. It is about forgoing a trip to the office on Wednesday, if you can better meet your goals for that day somewhere else.

Ideally, telecommuting, or teleworking, is a management strategy in which all lawyers at a firm are authorized to telecommute at least some of the time. Firms offering this ideal strategy do not perceive telecommuting as an accommodation or privilege awarded a few individuals whose personal circumstances seem to merit special consideration. Rather, they consider the reasons lawyers may elect to telecommute irrelevant, focusing on telework's ability to improve client service and the firm's profitability.

Lawyers have long worked outside the office, in courthouses, clients' offices, and (especially at night and on weekends) at home. A telework program simply formalizes the routine practice of remote working, acknowledging that the technology is now available to make working inside and outside the office completely fungible.

The Advantages of Telework

The principal reasons firms should develop telecommuting programs are that telework increases productivity, enables firms to attract and retain better lawyers less expensively, and reduces overhead expenses.

These three features, among others, result in the improved marketability of teleworking firms.

Increased Productivity

Telecommuting increases the productivity of telecommuters, whether they are working off-site or in the office. Moreover, telecommuting also increases the productivity of lawyers whose work remains based in the office, as well as the productivity of teleworkers. Telework increases productivity by improving efficiency, improving the quality of the firm's work product, and increasing the hours available to lawyers to work.

Greater Efficiency

Among the reasons telecommuting lawyers become more efficient is that at home they have fewer disruptions. For example, colleagues are not constantly stopping by their offices to chat. While some telecommuters receive telephone calls and other communications at home with the same frequency they do in the office, others elect to take a block of time to focus on a problem, retrieving messages only when they are ready to address them. "The ability to work without distractions is a big advantage to my firm and clients, as well as me," said Celia Leber, a patent prosecutor with Fish & Richardson. Leber telecommutes full-time to the firm's Boston office from her home in Maine. According to Jennifer Downs-O'Shaughnessy, an environmental litigator, who telecommutes full-time from Chicago to the Kansas City office of Spencer, Fane, Britt & Browne, "I get the same amount of work done without being in the office until nine P.M."

With telework, office-based lawyers also enjoy a greater ability to focus. This is due partially to the fact that both office-based and remote lawyers must become more reliant on e-mail and voice mail. "Telecommuting allows lawyers—both inside and outside the office—to control work flow. The ability to communicate by e-mail and voice mail puts a buffer between a lawyer concentrating on a particular matter and the demands of the office environment," observed Scott Beach, a business lawyer with Day, Berry & Howard, LLP, in Connecticut. Beach telecommutes periodically during the week and frequently at night and on weekends.

Another advantage to the increased use of e-mail and voice mail is that such communications can be sent more frequently than in-person communications can occur. Thus, lawyers at teleworking firms become accustomed to keeping each other and clients continuously updated.

The quality of communications may improve, as well. For example, according to Molly Mosley-Goren, who also telecommutes to the Boston office of Fish & Richardson, "Whether I use voice mail or e-mail, and even when I have a phone conversation, my communications are very focused, now. I get to the point a lot faster." In-person meetings, which remain important in teleworking firms, also improve. In that lawyers are in the office less often, face-to-face meetings must be scheduled in advance. People tend to come better prepared to planned meetings. As a result, such meetings can be shorter and more productive.

The ability to quickly transfer documents back and forth also makes lawyers more efficient. "I can send documents to clients by e-mail. They can make changes or supply fill-ins and e-mail it back. With the old system, they might have to retype entire documents and return them by fax. [Telework] has made clients happier," said Christopher Rizik, a business law member with Dickinson Wright, PLLC, in Detroit. Rizik telecommutes two days a week from one of his client's offices and periodically from home. He anticipates more frequent home-based telecommuting as the firm further enhances its remote access.

Better Work Product

Lawyers in teleworking firms report that a primary advantage to telecommuting is simply that the quality of the work product improves. There are a host of reasons. One is that lawyers can handle emergencies anytime they occur regardless of where the lawyers are. "I handle emergencies when I telecommute all the time," said Rizik. "A client will call and say, 'I need this document in ten minutes.' This is possible now."

"When a client has a problem over the weekend or late at night, he or she can page me and fax me the relevant documents at home. I can fax comments back almost immediately," said Beach, who relies more on fax than e-mail because clients will often send him papers received in hard copy from third parties. "If I didn't have the pager and home office fax machine, the client would send the material to the office, and it would just sit there, or I would have to go in," he said.

Further, "if something comes up at the end of the day, I can plan for it. I don't have to wait around the office for documents to arrive. I can make sure it will be sent to my home office when it is ready, and I can go home and have dinner with my family," Beach explained. "Clients don't typically ask anymore, 'How late will you be there tonight?' They try me at the office, and, if they don't reach me there, they just page me. The capacity to telecommute gives me more flexibility, while making me more accessible to clients."

Work product also improves because telecommuting enables more parties to participate effectively in the product's development. "We have a very strong national tax expert in our D.C. office, as well as experts in other specialties who work in remote offices," said Rizik. "If I couldn't reach these experts when I needed to, the result for clients wouldn't be as good."

Further, home offices tend to be more relaxed than traditional offices, and the work product improves when you are more relaxed. Similarly, lawyers spared a daily stressful commute have more energy for their work. Teleworkers also have the flexibility to work when they are most productive (perhaps before sunrise or in the middle of the night) and to take more rejuvenating breaks when they are not.

Increased Available Work Time

The hours available for work increase when lawyers telecommute. One reason is that lawyers can use time they previously spent commuting as work time. For example, if your one-way commute is just twenty minutes and you use that time to work instead, you will increase your work hours by about 160 hours a year (see Lis Fleming, *The One-Minute Commuter* [Fleming, 1988], citing Paul Edwards and Sarah Edwards, *Working from Home*).

Another reason for increased work time is that telecommuters tend to use fewer personal days and sick days. Rather than taking a whole day off to meet a personal obligation, a telecommuter can attend the nonprofessional event and still build a full work day around it. Similarly, "In Michigan, we have lots of snow advisories. The ability to telecommute means I won't lose the day," said Rizik.

Further, work time can be increased simply because the telecommuters may always have their tools available. They can work during early morning, late night, and weekend hours and may take their tools with them on nonprofessional trips. Said Beach, "Because telecommuting allows lawyers to work during hours they wouldn't ordinarily be able to work," it is cost-effective for the firm.

A Better and Cheaper Recruitment Process and Lower Turnover Costs

Teleworking firms can recruit better lawyers. They can attract top recent graduates seeking technologically sophisticated or flexible work environments. According to Bob Hillman, managing principal at Fish & Richardson, "Most new lawyers are familiar with computers and the Internet. The fact that we are also familiar with these tools and use them makes us a more attractive firm to young lawyers." Teleworking firms can also attract highly skilled laterals that are looking for such environments and have been trained at the competitor's expense. They can attract uniquely credentialed lawyers living in outlying regions who would not otherwise consider distant firms. Once the word is out that the firm uses telework as a management strategy, there may be much less cost associated with recruiting lawyers (see Nicole Belson Goluboff, *Telecommuting for Lawyers* [LPM, 1998], 20).

Further, teleworking firms may be better able than their competitors to retain lawyers. For example, according to a spring 1998 *National Law Journal* article, many lawyers are leaving law firms for investment banking. One reason is that they cannot tolerate the billing requirements of law firms and, according to a legal consultant, they wish to gain " 'more control over their lives.' " The "crossovers" are reportedly the best of the firms' midlevel associates—those " 'not easily replaced,'" and whose defections are "bound to have an impact on the bottom line," according to a partner at one large New York firm (see Lisa Brennan, "They're Leaving for Wall Street" *National Law Journal* [May 25, 1998] A01).

Law firms implementing telework have helped lawyers achieve control without leaving the firm. In the meantime, the firms are able to secure the substantial investment they made in recruiting and training such lawyers. They are also able to save the costs of recruiting and training replacements and the otherwise chargeable time necessary to make clients comfortable with those replacements. Indeed, because large firms may lose as much as $1 million per defecting associate (Ed Good, "Retain Lawyers," *Empire Law*

Source: New York Edition [May 1997], 12), the savings teleworking firms enjoy can be dramatic.

Reduced Overhead Potential

Two large expense categories law firms face that telecommuting can reduce are support staff and occupancy expenses. Teleworking firms report that their timekeeper-to-secretary ratios increase as a result of telecommuting, principally because lawyers become more familiar with computers and telecommunications. According to Downs-O'Shaughnessy, the firm has been able to assign an additional paralegal to her secretary, because she gives less work to her secretary now that she telecommutes. Similarly, according to Rizik, "We used to have two secretaries for three lawyers. Now, we have one secretary for two lawyers and, in some instances, one secretary for three lawyers. I expect the 1:3 ratio will become more common over time."

In addition, the services support staff continue to provide become more cost effective. Secretaries may assume different responsibilities, including more communications with clients and, in some firms, nonlegal research. "The work of our assistants involves more analytic and organizational skills; they take a more proprietary interest in the work of the office," said Rizik. "For example, I prepare the annual minutes of about 100 companies. My assistant keeps track of the data I need for these minutes and when I need it by, and she collects it. She performs more of the role of a paralegal than a secretary," he said. "The role of secretary and legal assistant will merge over time, and in the long run, lawyers probably won't need as many traditional secretaries or legal assistants."

If lawyers are routinely out of the office, even if each lawyer only telecommutes part-time, the firm may be able to realize significant occupancy savings. It may be able to maintain its current space even though it is growing, or it may be able to reduce the space it currently uses. According to Downs-O'Shaughnessy, since 1996, when she began telecommuting on a full-time basis, Spencer, Fane has hired at least twenty new lawyers. When the firm "maxed out on space, it assigned my old office to another lawyer," she said.

Costs will go down if telecommuters use alternative offices when they do work at the firm. For example, telecommuters may share offices, use "visiting lawyer offices," or use such common space as conference rooms on office-bound days. (The more frequently lawyers are authorized to telecommute, the more receptive they are likely to be to alternative officing.) Reducing support staff can also save occupancy costs, as can putting large volumes of reference materials on CD-ROM, rather than using costly real estate to store books.

Dispelling Concerns

The evidence to the contrary notwithstanding, a common concern among supervisors is that telecommuters will not be available when on-site lawyers or clients need them.

Although trusting lawyers to work outside the office may seem like a new idea, that trust has long been in place. Just because a lawyer commutes to the firm everyday does not mean colleagues or clients can always find the lawyer at his or her desk. Lawyers leave their offices all the time without suspicion. The firm simply expects them to retrieve their messages and respond as promptly as possible. Further, many communications among lawyers sitting at their desks are by phone and e-mail.

Similarly, many clients communicate with their lawyers primarily by phone, fax, and computer. According to Downs-O'Shaughnessy, who works for many national companies, "I am used to distance-working with clients. For example, I work with a client in Denver. Because we communicate mostly by telephone, fax, and [courier], it makes no difference whether I am in Chicago or Missouri."

According to Beach, "Many of my clients are telecommunications and other high-tech companies. They demand that we use voice mail, e-mail, and cell phones. They do much of their work outside the office, they expect to be just as efficient on the road as in the office, and they expect the same from us." In short, responsible lawyers who are properly equipped and trained for remote work will be available whenever necessary.

Another concern expressed by partners who bill by the hour is that greater efficiency may lead to less revenue. The opposite is true. Clients seeking more predictable costs will choose lawyers—and refer other clients to lawyers—whose increased efficiency results in lower fees. According to Hillman at Fish & Richardson, "Clients no longer pay for inefficiency."

Lawyers can also use their newfound time to develop business. The increase in business justifies the fee reduction. Further, the improved work product that results from increased efficiency can actually command *higher* fees (see Goluboff, 13). In any event, the firm can save money. "Say I draft a contract under the hourly billing method, and I bill $1000 for the job," Rizik illustrated. With telework, "I'm more efficient. The value of the document to my client may still be $1,000, but it takes me less time. We recoup the cost of technology in our savings, and our clients are better assured of a direct relationship between the value of the product they receive and its cost."

Among the concerns some junior lawyers express is that, if they are physically absent, they may miss the political interaction that can be crucial for advancement in a firm. For this reason junior lawyers may need to spend at least some of their time in the office. However, the concern of these lawyers stems from the fact that neither they nor their firms are ready for telework.

Lawyers seeking to introduce the idea of telework to their firms must first research the viability of this management approach for their particular firm. To learn in detail how to do this, how to pitch a proposal for firmwide telework, and how a firm can implement a program, including a guide to topics a telecommuting policy should cover, see *Telecommuting for Lawyers*. Once telecommuting becomes commonplace, the mechanics of politicking will change, too. Further, when telecommuters, nontelecommuting lawyers, and support staff are all properly trained for remote work—as they should be—off-site workers will not be considered outsiders. Out-of-sight will not mean out of mind. It will mean *outstanding*.

CHAPTER 32

Nontraditional Careers for Lawyers[1]

Deborah Arron

What else can we as lawyers do with our extensive education and professional experience besides practicing law? The short, honest answer is: Anything we want to do. Our choices are as vast as our imagination and perseverance can make them.

"Come on. Be realistic," I hear you saying. "What companies consider a law degree an attractive credential? What jobs do we qualify for that pay as much as practicing law?"

Having assisted lawyers and law students with their career development for over ten years, I have learned that those are the wrong questions to ask. Making a list of the realistic options for someone with a law degree is—without qualification—an ineffective way to build a career. Success stories are seldom motivated by realism.

Take Dace, for example. She did not become the first underwater diver planner for the Grand Cayman Islands by looking at a list of realistic options. She converted her passion for scuba diving and her experience as counsel for the Seattle City Council into a position where she examines the coastal waters, figures out what needs to be protected, and drafts and enforces new environmental legislation.

Then there is Barrie, a Vanderbilt Law School student who became executive director of the Tennessee Bar Foundation immediately upon graduation from law school. The job was not posted on a list at her school; it was not her law school education that impressed her new employer. She succeeded by acknowledging her love of administrative work rather than the practice of law and by concentrating her job search on those types of opportunities in the legal profession.

Although there are hundreds of fields for which your legal background might be helpful, that background alone will not get you employed outside the legal profession. Not anymore. The competition is just too fierce. Nowadays, you also have to demonstrate a deep, personal connection to the work you seek. Anything less and you are just another faceless resume.

Here is my challenge to all of you: Whether you are unemployed, underemployed, or unhappily employed, the most effective way to capitalize on your legal education and experience is to ask the more provocative, and ultimately more practical, question: "What do I *want* to do next with my law degree?"

Why Change Careers?

Each of us could pinpoint a different reason for wanting to leave the profession. We may be frustrated by the limited opportunities for entry-level lawyers or by the high cost of running an office and the growing pressure to get and keep clients. We may be tired of the overly adversarial posture of our opponents, or we may be losing the struggle to balance the demands of our personal and professional lives. For some of us, a desire to express ourselves creatively, or a need to contribute to society in a more positive way, is the stimulus. Others simply yearn for a change of environment or pace.

But consider whether one of these statements is motivating your thoughts of escape:

- I cannot find a job practicing law.
- I am not earning enough money.
- I am looking for less demanding work.
- I am burned out.
- I want new challenges.

None of these are good foundations for a career change. If you can identify with any of them, first take steps to meet your needs within the profession.

A transition is also better delayed if any of these circumstances apply:

- You have been disenchanted with law less than three years and are not strongly drawn to an alternative career.
- You are not sure what type of field attracts you, and you are holding a job that provides enough flexibility or financial security to concentrate on self-assessment.
- You have not explored how to generate greater satisfaction in the legal profession, or you have not tried to implement the solutions you have identified.
- You do not have sufficient financial resources to support yourself (and your family) for the six months to two years it can take to switch from law into another field.
- You are undergoing a marital separation or divorce, grieving a recent death, experiencing serious health problems, frustrated in your efforts to start a family, or feeling great strain from some other personal matter.

If you have done all you can to find satisfaction within the law, and you are prepared for the emotional and financial trauma career transition can bring, then evaluate whether your desire to leave the law is grounded in one of four sound reasons to change careers:

- You are dissatisfied with the practice of law and strongly drawn to a new career.
- You have reached the end of your career path in law and are unlikely to experience any further growth in the profession.
- You never had the opportunity to pursue another career, and you now wish to act on that long-suppressed desire.
- You have experienced a significant shift in your life interests, goals, or values that has ended your interest or belief in the law, and you wish to express your newfound ideals and objectives in another field.

Keys to Success in Making a Career Change

Although a law degree is a valuable credential and earning one tells the world you are worthy of consideration, it is not an automatic entrée to any job or career. Putting your legal background to work for you requires serious effort and a well thought out plan.

In the first step, self-assessment, you focus on what is right for you—not on what opportunities might be out there—by analyzing your preferences and figuring out what motivates you in the workplace. Once you have identified your preferences through self-assessment, you move to the second step: researching the employment scene to determine where you best fit in. After you identify a suitable target, you can move to the third step, implementation, the process of actually getting the job. This is the stage at which you begin fine-tuning your resume and cover letter, and mining job leads.

The three steps to career transition work best when you add one more skill to your toolbox: You need to involve others in your efforts. "What helped me the most was a lot of support, but I wouldn't have thought that when I started," says human services consultant and former law firm partner Nancy Ashley. "I think of myself as a very independent person. I had gotten through law school on my own. Why would I need all these other people? But I'm certain I never would have accomplished my career change without all the support I received."

Some of you worry that you will jeopardize your security if you confide your plans to others. "I kept waiting for my clients to notice what a great job I was doing for them and invite me in-house or tell their business associates that I was a guy who should be working for them," says one lawyer who eventually left private practice for Nike's marketing department. "But they didn't know I was dissatisfied and I was caught in the vicious cycle of feeling like I couldn't tell them I was because then they'd want to find another lawyer. On the other hand, I was always aware that they couldn't read my desires on my face."

Unless you convey messages to the contrary, the people around you will assume you are happy doing what you are doing. If you cannot take the risk of telling other people about your goals, they will not be able to help you with job leads and contacts.

If your family thinks you are crazy and you are afraid to trust your friends, you can seek moral support from private career counselors and coaches, your law school career services office or perhaps your bar association's lawyer assistance program. You might also form your own support group, take career development classes, join forces with friends in a similar situation or contact nonprofit organizations in your area that provide support to job seekers.

Should You Be Leaving the Law?

Every person is born with, and develops in life, a unique employment profile—a combination of interests, skills, values, and people and environmental preferences. Being employed in an area that does not suit your profile is like trying to write your name with the hand you do not ordinarily use. Sure, you can do it; sometimes you can even write legibly that way. Yet the process always feels awkward and uncomfortable. If forced to use your nondominant hand whenever you sign your name, you will try to avoid situations that require your signature. In terms of job or career dissatisfaction, the equivalent tendency is to avoid certain projects and tasks—or even getting out of bed on mornings you have to face them.

The work of a lawyer involves an extraordinarily wide range of skills. You might procrastinate when facing some tasks but feel great energy to accomplish others. For example, you might love meeting and communicating with clients but hate having to research a brief. So you will gladly take phone calls and schedule emergency conferences with clients, but never seem to find the time to draft a summary judgment motion.

Many lawyers find their skills misapplied in this way. Young lawyers with good people skills apprentice by spending solitary years in the library; lawyers who loved the legal analysis, research and writing they did in their early years are expected to switch to a rainmaking (or client development) role as they mature.

Lawyers who dislike *what they do* as lawyers, as opposed to *how much time* they spend or *with whom* they spend it—and who are certain that there is no other place in law where they can use the skills they do enjoy—are good candidates for a career switch.

How your values mesh with those of law practice is also significant. If your work clashes with your values, you may produce easily enough, but you will not feel good about it. You will experience a gut conflict, an unsettling doubt that you are doing the right thing. If your work is consistent with your values, on the other hand, you will feel motivated to do more, even if the work itself is difficult. You will want to accomplish your goals in order to express that value.

Occasional clashes in values tend to be manifested in personality conflicts with opposing counsel, judges, clients or coworkers. On the other hand, clashes with the essential values of the legal profession—competition, structure, power and conformity among others—will trigger persistent and escalating feelings of conflict or anxiety.

One way to determine whether your work is compatible with your skills and values is to pay attention to your emotional responses. If the practice of law is right for you:

- When faced with a new project, you feel stimulated to learn rather than tempted to procrastinate.
- When you have finished a task, you feel proud of the accomplishment rather than relieved that you are done.
- You tend to initiate work rather than avoid it.
- You generally approach your work with enthusiasm and high energy—not anger, boredom, or lethargy.

The most reliable way to identify your preferences is to analyze your good and bad past experiences and define the qualities that tie them together. This type of analysis will often be more accurate than what you have learned about yourself from family and friends, or from experiences in past employment. For example, you may think of yourself as liking to write, but when you study your most enjoyable experiences, you discover that you were actually doing more talking than writing during the best times. The only reason you are now focusing on writing is because you have had more opportunity recently to write than to converse and you find the writing more enjoyable than the legal research and document organization that have been an even greater part of your responsibilities.

Transferable Skills Analysis

Our work as lawyers helps us develop and perfect a wide variety of skills used and valued in other environments: for example, negotiation and persuasion; gathering, organizing and analyzing data; simplifying complex concepts; oral and written communication; and interviewing. Many of us, however, get so used to thinking in technical terms—taking depositions, writing briefs, filing motions, drafting contracts—that we are unable to see the relationship between our legal experience and the demands of other fields. When we try to market ourselves to nonlegal employers as former civil litigators, or we describe our extensive "discovery" experience, nonlegal employers have no idea what skills we used in our work.

Some of us figure the solution is to try to find employers who already recognize the relationship between our legal backgrounds and their nonlegal positions. We ask which employers like to hire lawyers in nonlegal positions or better yet, which headhunters are able to market lawyers into alternative careers. There are no such employers or headhunters. It is our responsibility, and our responsibility alone, to understand and communicate the transferability of our background and experience.

The application of skills from field to field is a fundamental building block of successful career change. It is only after you have invested time in a thorough assessment of your skills and strengths, and researched the field that interests you, that you will be able to articulate your qualifications in terms a nonlegal employer will understand.

For help in coming up with names of transferable skills, see the listings in *What Can You Do with a Law Degree?* and *What Color Is Your Parachute?*

Representative Alternative Career Choices

What *can* you do with your law degree and practice experience besides practicing law? Truly, the options are almost unlimited. In the last ten years, I have discovered nearly a thousand types of positions that actual law school graduates have secured. For inspiration, here are some of the more common nontraditional ways lawyers and recent graduates make use of their legal backgrounds *without* practicing law. Please keep in mind that just knowing what positions other lawyers have found or created will not lead you into a new career.

Servicing the Legal Profession
Let's start with law firms themselves. Former practitioners happily serve as firm managers or administrators, or as directors of practice development, client services, professional development and associate recruiting.

You can also work for one of the thousands of service providers to the profession, many of which were founded by former practicing lawyers. Any edition of the *National Law Journal* or the *ABA Journal* will offer dozens of examples: computer software vendors, contract lawyer placement agencies, litigation management and legal research services, and jury, marketing or management consultants.

And do not forget the publishers of legal books, magazines, newsletters and newspapers, as well as the increasing number of online services. All of them hire law school graduates in departments as diverse as editorial, sales, management, acquisitions, and training.

Regulation or Enforcement Specialist
In general, corporations and government agencies are interested in lawyers with knowledge relevant to compliance and enforcement functions. Examples include the Americans with Disabilities Act (ADA), affirmative action and equal employment opportunity (EEO), the environment, employee benefits, internal ethics, labor relations, and legislative or community affairs. Purchasing agent and contract administration positions are also prevalent.

Educational Administration
Most law schools these days prefer to hire law school graduates for positions in career services, alumni relations, fund-raising, and continuing legal education (CLE). Colleges and universities also hire lawyers to work as ADA and EEO investigators, to monitor risk management, human resources, or technology transfer, or to work in contract negotiation and administration.

Nonprofit Management
Every bar association provides opportunities for law school graduates to manage or supervise operations. Lawyers frequently handle discipline, CLE, attorney assistance, mentoring, public affairs and lobbying functions.

Nonprofit organizations outside the legal profession often look to their volunteers—many of whom are lawyers—to fill new positions as directors or project managers, or specialists in development or planned giving.

High Technology Companies

Lately, more lawyers are moving into the high-tech business sector. With shortages across the country of skilled computer technicians, more and more companies are turning to prospective candidates with good problem-solving and analytical skills and a passion for, if not a deep understanding of, technology. Positions that former practicing lawyers have filled include compensation specialist, software engineer, systems analyst and systems sales representative.

Leaving the Law Behind

It is hard to imagine a career that would not use any of the background we develop as lawyers. Those who return to school to become high school teachers make use of the insight, self-discipline, and knowledge they developed as lawyers. Even a couple of Pacific Northwest entrepreneurs who decided to lead mountain treks using llamas called upon their legal experience to navigate the licensing process.

Those lawyers who move the farthest from the profession, though, seem to gravitate toward the following fields and positions:

- *Entrepreneurial ventures,* ranging from restaurants like the California Pizza Kitchen chain developed by two lawyers in Southern California, to retail operations like the Sharper Image, founded by former practicing lawyer Richard Thalheimer, to publishing successes like Nolo Press and the Zagat (restaurant rating) guides
- *Communications,* using such skills as editing, writing, and reporting, for newspapers, magazines, television, radio and public relations companies, not to speak of well known successes like John Grisham and David E. Kelley
- *Real estate,* including development, property management, construction, remodeling, and interior decoration
- *Teaching,* in both public and private schools and at all levels, from elementary school through graduate level work
- *Counseling,* with or without an advanced degree and focusing on individual psychotherapy, family, or career issues

As I said at the outset, these opportunities are only a starting point. The possibilities are almost limitless if you let your preferences guide you into the marketplace and use your skill and sophistication to get ahead.

Getting the Job

Almost half of those surveyed in a Minnesota study of law school graduates who chose nontraditional careers said they faced employer resistance. For some, the objection stemmed from a prejudice against lawyers; for others it was simply the employer's inability to recognize the transferability of their skills and background. As a result, the graduates understood it was up to them to explain the value of their degree and legal experience. They could not expect an employer to make the connection for them.

The first step in countering any objections to your application is intensive self-study and preparation. Why are you moving into this field? What are your strengths and what "life credits" and experiences demonstrate them? You are going to have a hard time overcoming objections to your background and experience if your only reason for switching to a new career is that it seems better than what you are doing now.

The next step is research: ask contacts in the new field what stereotypes or objections they anticipate someone with your background will face. Then honestly evaluate whether those objections apply to you. If they do, figure out why the objectionable qualities might be an advantage to the employer. If the objections are not true for you, be prepared with examples from your past that prove they are not.

Take a look at some of the objections the career-changing lawyer can expect to encounter.

Would Only a Loser Lawyer Want a Job Outside the Profession?

No matter how well we craft our cover letters and resumes, no matter how sincere our enthusiasm and commitment to a new endeavor, as law school graduates or practicing lawyers we must expect the inevitable: Why do you want to leave the profession?

First, we ought to be flattered. It suggests the interviewer holds our profession in high regard. It is possible the interviewer wanted to be a lawyer and cannot understand why anyone in our position would be dissatisfied. Many members of the general public regard law as a glamorous field they might have pursued if only they had the talent and persistence. To some, anyone who would leave the profession is suspect.

If you cannot find a job practicing law, or if you have not come to terms with leaving the legal profession, the question—Why do you want to leave?—will hit you like a brick wall. In fact, you might be asking yourself the same question and wondering if you are a failure.

Such feelings may cause you to behave as though you have failed. One former lawyer was complimented by an interviewer for having a "very, very great" background. The lawyer's response was, "I do?" The interviewer replied, "Yes, but you still think there's something wrong with not wanting to practice law anymore." She had not mentioned her feelings, but her body language somehow signaled "failure" to him. People want to hire successes. Present yourself as somebody who has made a conscious, well-considered decision to do what you are doing.

You Cannot Afford to Take This Job

The subtext here may be the same as the objection we just covered: "Why would someone as well educated as you consider taking a job that pays so little money? Something must be wrong." It could also be that the employer is worried you will quit as soon as you find a job in law that pays better; that subtext is handled later in this chapter. Usually though, this objection is raised when the employer assumes your salary demands will be excessive. Alison Cooper anticipated that objection when she lobbied for a position as director of career services at a Texas law school.

At the time Alison began her job search in university administration, she was earning $75,000 annually as a third-year associate in a large Dallas law firm. In preparation for what she knew would be a huge cut in pay, she had paid off her credit card debt and rented an inexpensive apartment in a less desirable part of town. When she heard about the opening as director of career services, paying $25,000 per year, she immediately applied. The review committee, however, assumed she was not aware of the salary and discarded her resume. Undaunted, Alison obtained an interview by contacting several employees of the law school and describing to them the steps she had already taken, thereby assuring them of her willingness to accept a substantial pay cut. She was hired. Within two years, she was promoted to assistant dean for alumni relations, and her salary doubled. She is now the marketing director of a large law firm.

We Do Not Want a Lawyer in This Job

According to a story in the *New York Times*, "Lawyers trying to switch careers say they are often typecast as narrow-minded, confrontational, and unimaginative." Career consultants agree that your best strategy is to deal with those stereotypes head-on. One tactic is to take the high ground by explaining that you just did not have "the killer instinct." That bit of humor answers the anti-lawyer objection before the interviewer has a chance to say, "We do not want to hire a lawyer because you'll be too argumentative and competitive."

If you think the interviewer holds but is not voicing some prejudices against lawyers, bring them up yourself and explain why they do not apply to you. One non-threatening way to bring up the subject is to acknowledge your awareness of lawyer stereotypes and tell the interviewer that you have done a lot of thinking about how you would present yourself to fellow employees or potential clients to overcome their prejudices.

On the other hand, if any of these stereotypes *do* apply to you, do not argue that they do not. (If you are accused of being contentious and confrontational, you will only prove the point!) Instead, show how that characteristic strengthens your credentials. For example, "Sometimes being confrontational is an advantage in a management position. You need to have the courage to deal with difficult people, to confront them and get the issues resolved. My legal training has taught me not to fear conflict and to hit problems head on."

You Will Quit as Soon as You Find a Job in the Law

If it is true, play fair. Admit that you will continue your search for legal employment and point out what you will be able to contribute to their operation in the meantime. Also assure them that you will provide whatever length of notice they require. But do not expect this argument to sell very well, except for temporary or project assignments.

That raises one last point: showing employers that their objections are unfounded does not mean you will overcome those objections, or that you will get the job. The employer's prejudice may be intractable and, of course, you are often competing with others who are more qualified than you. But you will never get anywhere if you cannot at least address the employer's concerns.

Repeatedly running into the same objections may mean that you need to get some educational, volunteer or internship credits behind you. It may also mean that you ought to target different employers. A small entrepreneurial venture may appreciate a jack-of-all-trades more than a large company where functions are sharply defined and separated. A history of providing good results but remaining in jobs for only a short time will make you an appealing candidate in temporary, project-driven, consulting, or contract work situations.

Stepping Out of the Profession

Many lawyers have moved from law into another career. They came from widely different backgrounds and chose equally diverse second careers, but they approached their transitions in the same way:

- They first figured out what they wanted to do and then researched the market to find a place to do it.
- They overcame their fear of the unknown and took the risk of failing.
- They developed the courage to follow their footsteps and to find their own answer to the question: *What do I want to do next with my law degree?*

Note

1. This chapter is excerpted and adapted from the fourth edition of *What Can You Do with a Law Degree?* by Deborah Arron (Niche Press, 1999).

RESOURCE LIST

Career-Planning Information

Altman, Mary Ann, *Life After Law—Second Careers for Lawyers*. Washington, DC: The Wayne Smith Company, Inc., 1991.

Anderson, Evelyn, and Elaine Dushoff, *Legal Careers—Choices and Options*, Vol. II. Washington, DC: NALP, 1984.

Anderson, Nancy, *Work with Passion*. New York: Carroll & Graf, 1984.

Arron, Deborah L., *Running from the Law: Why Good Lawyers Are Getting Out of the Legal Profession*. Berkeley, CA: Ten Speed Press, 1992.

Arron, Deborah L., *What Can You Do with a Law Degree?: A Lawyer's Guide to Career Alternatives Inside, Outside, and Around the Law*, 4th Ed. Seattle, WA: Niche Press, 1999.

Barber, Professor David H., *Surviving Your Role as a Lawyer*. Dillon, CO: Spectra Publishing Co., Inc., 1987.

Bell, Susan J., *Full Disclosure: Do You Really Want to Be a Lawyer?* Princeton, NJ: Peterson's Guides, 1989.

Bellon, Lee Ann, "Coping with Job-Loss Trauma," *The National Law Journal* (November, 1990).

Bellon, Lee Ann, "Recruiting Requires Joint Effort," The National Law Journal (March 26, 1990).

Bellon, Lee Ann, and Kathryn C. Alexander, "Scaling Down—Need Seen for Project Attorneys," *The National Law Journal* (December 31, 1990).

Bellon, Lee Ann, and Tamara Hampton, "Minimizing Trauma of Terminations," *The National Law Journal* (August 27, 1990).

Bennett, Hal Z., and Susan J. Sparrow, *Follow Your Bliss*. New York: Avon Books, 1990.

Bodner, Joanne, and Venda Raye-Johnson, *Staying Up When Your Job Pulls You Down*. New York: Perigee Books, Division of The Putnam Publishing Group, 1991.

Bolles, Richard N., *How to Find Your Mission in Life*. Berkeley, CA: Ten Speed Press, 1991.

Bolles, Richard N., *The Three Boxes of Life and How to Get Out of Them*. Berkeley, CA: Ten Speed Press, 1987.

Bolles, Richard N., *What Color is Your Parachute?* Berkeley, CA: Ten Speed Press, 1987.

Bridges, William, *Transitions: Making Sense of Life's Changes*. Reading, MA: Addison-Wesley, 1980.

Byers, Samuelson, and Gordon Williamson, *Lawyers in Transition: Planning a Life in the Law*. Natick, MA: The Barkley Company, Inc., 1988.

Cabrera, James, and Charles Albrecht, Jr., The Lifetime Career Manager. Holbrook, MN: Adams Media Corporation, 1995.

Cain, George H., *Turning Points: New Paths and Second Careers for Lawyers*. Chicago: American Bar Association, Senior Lawyers Division, 1994.

Camenson, Blyth, *Careers for Legal Eagles & Other Law and Order Types*. Chicago: VGM Career Horizons, 1998.

Camenson, Blythe, *Real People Working in Law (On the Job Series)*. Chicago: VGM Career Horizons, 1997.

Caple, John, *Careercycles*. Englewood Cliffs, NJ: Prentice Hall, Inc., 1983.

Career Associates, *Career Choices for Undergraduates Considering Law*. New York: Walker and Company, 1985.

Couric, Emily, *Women Lawyers' Perspectives on Success*. Clifton, NJ: Prentice Hall Law & Business, 1984.

Crystal, John C., and Richard N. Bolles, *Where Do I Go From Here with the Rest of My Life?* Berkeley, CA: Ten Speed Press, 1974.

Csikszentmihalyi, Mihaly, *Flow: The Psychology of Optimal Experience*. New York: Harper Perennial, 1990.

Curran, Barbara A., *The Lawyer Statistical Report: A Statistical Profile of the United States Legal Profession in the 1980s*. Chicago: American Bar Foundation, 1985.

Dail, Hilda Lee, *The Lotus and the Pool: How to Create Your Own Career*. Boston, MA: Shambhala, 1983.

DeBold, Elizabeth, Ed., *Legal Career Planning Strategies to Plan and Live a Life in the Law*. Chicago, IL: Samuelson Associates, 1989.

Elwork, Amiram, *Stress Management for Lawyers: How to Increase Personal & Professional Satisfaction in the Law,* 2nd Ed. PA: The Vorkell Group, 1997.

Figler, Howard, *The Complete Job-Search Handbook*. New York: Holt, Rinehart & Winston, 1979.

Flood, John A., *The Legal Profession in the United States,* 3rd Ed. Chicago: American Bar Foundation, 1985.

Ford, George, and Gordon Lippit, *Creating Your Future: A Guide to Personal Goal Setting*. San Diego, CA: University Associates, 1988.

Frank, Steven J., *Learning the Law—Success in Law School and Beyond*. New York: Citadel Press, 1992.

Freund, James C., *Lawyering—A Realistic Approach to Legal Practice*. New York: Law Journal Seminars Press Inc., 1979.

Gibaldi, Carmine, and Thom McCarthy, *Self-Directed Career Planning Workbook*. New York: McGraw-Hill, 1993.

Glasser, Robert, *Control Theory: A New Explanation of How We Control Our Lives*. New York: Harper & Row, 1984.

Granfield, Robert, *Making Elite Lawyers—Visions of Law at Harvard and Beyond*. New York: Routledge, 1992.

Haldane, Bernard, *Career Satisfaction and Success—How to Know and Manage Your Strengths*. Seattle, WA: Wellness Behavior, 1988.

Hirsch, Ronald L. "Are You on Target?", *Barrister* (Winter 1985), 17–20.

Hirsch, Sandra, and Jean Kummerow, *Life Types*. New York: Warner Books, 1989.

Hollander, Dory, *Doom Loop System: A Step-by-Step Guide to Career Mastery*. New York: Viking Penguin, 1991.

Jackson, Tom, *Guerilla Tactics in the New Job Market*. New York: Bantam, 1991.

JD Preferred! Legal Career Alternatives. Washington, DC: Federal Reports, Inc., 1996.

John-Roger and Peter McWilliams, *Do It! Let's Get Off Our Buts*. Los Angeles, CA: Prelude Press, 1991.

Killoughey, D.M., Ed., *Breaking Traditions: Work Alternatives for Lawyers*. Chicago: Section of Law Practice Management, American Bar Association, 1993.

Kroeger, Otto, and Janet Thuesen, *Type Talk*. New York: Delacorte Press, 1988.

Lawrence, Gordon D., *People Types and Tiger Stripes*, 2nd Ed. Gainesville, FL: CAPT, Inc., 1982.

The Lawyer's Almanac, 8th Ed. New York: Prentice Hall Law & Business, 1988.

Lipman, Burton E., *Professional Job Search Program: How to Market Yourself*. New York: John Wiley & Sons, 1983.

Magness, Michael K., with Howard I. Bernstein, "How to Build Your Career," *Barrister* (Spring 1984), 35.

McCormack, Mark H., *What I Should Have Learned at Yale Law School—The Terrible Truth About Lawyers*. New York: Aron Books, 1987.

Moll, Richard W., *The Lure of the Law—Why People Become Lawyers, and What the Profession Does to Them*. New York: Penguin Books, 1990.

Munneke, Gary, *Careers in Law*, 2nd Ed. Chicago: VGM Career Horizons, 1997.

Munneke, Gary, *Opportunities in Law Careers*. Chicago: National Textbook Co., 1986.

Myers, Isabel B., with Peter B. Myers, *Gifts Differing*. Palo Alto, CA: Consulting Psychologists Press, Inc., 1980.

National Association for Law Placement, *Employment Report and Salary Survey*. Washington DC: NALP, published annually.

Pearson, Carol S., *Awakening the Heroes Within: Twelve Archetypes to Help Us Find Ourselves and Transform Our World*. New York: HarperCollins, 1991.

Pearson, Carol S. *The Hero Within*. New York: HarperCollins, 1986.

Peck, M. Scott, M.D., *The Road Less Traveled*. New York: A Touchstone Book, Division of Simon & Schuster Trade, 1978.

Pilder, Richard J., and William F. Pilder, *How to Find Your Life's Work*. New York: Prentice Hall, 1981.

Raelin, Joseph, A., *The Salaried Professional: How to Make the Most of Your Career*. New York: Praeger Publishers, 1984.

Richard, L.R., "Lawyer Dissatisfaction Rising, But Many Alternatives Exist," *Pennsylvania Law Journal-Reporter* (November 5, 1990), 4, 8.

Richard, L.R., "Personality Styles of U.S. Lawyers: New Findings," *ABA Journal* (July 1993), 4–14.

Richard, L.R., "Resolving for New Year to Effectively Plan Career," *Pennsylvania Law Journal-Reporter* (January 21, 1991), 4.

Richard, L.R., "Understanding Lawyers' Personalities," *The Pennsylvania Lawyer* (1992; 14:2), 22–26, 32.

Robinson, David A., *Practicing Law without Clients: Making a Living as a Free-lance Lawyer.* Chicago: American Bar Association, Law Practice Management Section, 1996.

Rodin, Robert J., *Full Potential: Your Career and Life Planning Workbook.* New York: McGraw-Hill, 1983.

Scheele, Adele, *Skills for Success.* New York: Ballantine, 1979.

Schein, Edgar H., *Career Anchors: Discover Your Real Values.* San Diego, CA: University Associates, 1985.

Schwartz, Laurens, R., *What You Aren't Supposed to Know About the Legal Profession—An Exposé of Lawyers, Law Schools, Judges, and More.* New York: Shapolsky Publishers, Inc., 1991.

Sells, Benjamin, *The Soul of the Law: Understanding Lawyers and the Law.* Element Books, 1995.

Sher, Barbara, *Wishcraft: How to Get What You Really Want.* New York: Ballantine Books, Division of Random House, 1979.

Simmons, Jeffrey R., Ed. *Life, Law and the Pursuit of Balance: A Lawyer's Guide to Quality of Life,* 2nd Ed. Phoenix, AZ: Maricopa County Bar Association, 1997.

Sinetar, Marsha, *Do What You Love, the Money Will Follow.* Mahwah, NJ: Paulist Press, 1987.

Sinetar, Marsha, *Living Happily Ever After.* New York: Dell Doubleday, 1990.

Snelling, Robert O., *The Right Job: How to Get the Job That's Right for You.* New York: Penguin, 1993.

Stephan, Naomi, *Finding Your Life Mission.* Walpole, NH: Stillpoint Publisher, 1989.

Strausser, Jeffrey, *Judgment Reversed: Alternative Careers for Lawyers.* Hauppauge, NY: Barron's, 1997.

Studner, Peter K., *Super Job Search: The Complete Manual for Job Seekers and Career Changers.* Los Angeles: Jamenair, 1993.

Sturman, Gerald M., *If You Knew Who You Were, You Could be Who You Are!* Woodstock, NY: Bierman House, 1989.

Tieger, Paul D. and Barbara Barron-Tieger, *Do What You Are: Discover the Perfect Career for You Through the Secrets of Personality Type.* Boston: Little Brown and Company, 1992.

Utley, Frances, and Gary Munneke, *From Law Student to Lawyer.* Chicago: Career Series, American Bar Association, 1984.

Vogt, Leona M., *From Law School to Career: Where Do Graduates Go and What Do They Do?* Cambridge, MA: Harvard Law School, 1986.

Wasserman, Steven, and J.W. O'Brien, Eds., *Law and Legal Information Directory,* 4th Ed. Detroit, MI: Gale Research Co., 1986.

Wayne, Ellen, and Betsy McCombs, *Legal Careers—Choices and Options,* Vol. I. Washington, DC: NALP, 1983.

Wendleton, Kate, *Through the Brick Wall: How to Job Hunt in a Tight Market.* New York: Villard, 1992.

Woodman, Marion, *Addiction to Perfection.* Toronto, Ontario: Inner City Books, 1982.

Zemans, Frances Kahn, and Victor G. Rosenblum, *The Making of a Public Profession.* Chicago: American Bar Foundation, 1981.

Job Finding Information

Arron, Deborah L., and Deborah Guyol, *The Complete Guide to Contract Lawyering: What Every Lawyer and Law Firm Should Know About Temporary Legal Services*, 2nd Ed. Seattle, WA: Niche Press, 1999.

Brennan, Lawrence D., Stanley Strand, and Edward Gruber, *Resumes for Better Jobs*. New York: Monarch Press, 1981.

Carey, Williams T., *Law Students: How to Get a Job When There Aren't Any*. Durham, NC: Carolina Academic Press, 1986.

Dickhut, Harold W., *Professional Resume & Job Search Guide*. Englewood Cliffs, NJ: Prentice Hall, 1981.

Feferman, Richard N. *Building Your Firm with Associates: A Guide for Hiring and Managing New Attorneys*. Chicago: Section of Economics of Law Practice, American Bar Association, 1988.

Good, C. Edward, *Does Your Resume Wear Blue Jeans? The Book on Resume Preparation*. Charlottesville, VA: Word Store, 1985.

Kanter, Arnold B., *Kanter on Hiring: A Lawyer's Guide to Lawyer Hiring*. Chicago: Lawletters, Inc. 1983.

Komar, John K. *Resume Builder*. Chicago: Follett Publishing Company, 1980.

Lathrop, Richard, *Who's Hiring Who*. Berkeley, CA: Ten Speed Press, 1977.

Law Firms Yellow Book. Washington, DC: Monitor Publishing Co., published semiannually.

Lewis, Adele, *How to Write Better Resumes*. Woodbury, NY: Barron's Educational Series, Inc., 1983.

Magness, Michael K., "The Art of Effective Interviewing," *National Law Journal* (October 11, 1982), 15.

Mantis, Hillary Jane, and Kathleen Brady, *Jobs for Lawyers: Effective Techniques for Getting Hired in Today's Legal Marketplace*. Manassas Park, VA: Impact Publications, 1996.

Medley, Anthony H., *Sweaty Palms: The Neglected Art of Being Interviewed*. Belmont, CA: Lifetime Learning Publications, 1978.

Miller, Saul, *After Law School? Finding a Job in a Tight Market*. Boston: Little, Brown and Company, 1978.

Pell, Arthur R., *How to Sell Yourself on an Interview*. New York: Monarch Press, 1982.

Provost, Maureen, *Charting Your Course: Identifying Your Success Patterns and Career Preferences*. New York: Fordham University School of Law, 1987.

Resumes for Law Careers. Chicago: VGM Career Horizons, 1995.

Ryan, Joseph, *Stating Your Case: How to Interview for a Job as a Lawyer*. St Paul, MN: West Publishing Co., 1982.

Student Lawyer. Chicago: American Bar Association, Law Student Division, published monthly (nine times a year).

Turnicky, Ann D., *How to Get the Job You Want in a Law Firm*. New York: John Wiley & Sons, Inc., 1997.

Walton, Kimm Alayne, *Guerrilla Tactics for Getting the Legal Job of Your Dreams*. Chicago: Harcourt Brace Legal and Professional Publications, Inc., 1995.

White, Christine, and Abbie Willard Thorner, *Managing the Recruitment Process.* New York: Law of Business, Inc., 1982.

Career Choice Information

Private Practice (General)

American Lawyer. New York: American Lawyer Media, published monthly.

American Lawyer Guide to Leading Law Firms. New York: Am-Law Publishing Corp., 1983.

Arron, Deborah, *Full Disclosure: Do You Really Want to Be a Lawyer?* Chicago: American Bar Association, 1989.

Directory of Legal Employers. Washington, DC: National Association of Law Placement, published annually.

Flying Solo, A Survival Guide for the Solo Lawyer, 2nd Ed. Chicago: Section of Law Practice Management, American Bar Association, 1994.

Foonberg, Jay, *How to Start and Build a Law Practice,* Millennium Fourth Edition. Chicago: American Bar Association, Law Practice Management Section, 1999.

Guide to Law Specialties. Cleveland, OH: Law Placement Association of Cleveland, 1990.

J.D. Preferred: 400+ Things You Can Do with a Law Degree. Washington, DC: Federal Reports, Inc., 1994.

Law Practice Management. Chicago: American Bar Association, Law Practice Management Section, published monthly (eight times a year).

Martindale-Hubbell Law Directory. Summit, NJ: Martindale-Hubbell, Inc., published annually.

The National Law Journal. New York: New York Law Publishing Co., published weekly.

O'Neill, Suzanne, and Catherine Gerhauser, *From Law School to Law Practice,* 2d Ed. Philadelphia, PA: American Law Institute—American Bar Association, 1998.

Profiles of Minority Attorneys in Specialty Practices. Washington, DC: National Association for Law Placement, 1995.

Samuelson, Don, et al., *Lawyers in Transition: Planning a Life in the Law.* Berkeley Company, Inc., 1988.

Singer, Gerald M., *How to Go Directly into Solo Practice (Without Missing a Byte).* New York: Lawyers Co-operative Publishing Co., 1986.

Smith, Janet, *Beyond L.A. Law.* Washington, DC: Harcourt Brace Legal & Professional Publications.

Stevens, Mark, *Power of Attorney: The Rise of the Giant Law Firms.* New York: McGraw-Hill Book Co., 1987.

Government Agency Information

Almanac of American Politics. Washington, DC: National Law Journal, 1998.

The Almanac of the Unelected. Washington, DC: The Almanac of the Unelected, 1998.

Braddock's Federal-State-Local Government Directory. Washington, DC: Braddock's Publications, Inc., 1984.

Braddock's Federal-State-Local Government Directory. Alexandria, VA: Braddock Communications, 1990.

Brownson, Anna L., *Congressional Staff Directory.* Mt. Vernon, VA: Staff Directories, Ltd., 1999.

Brownson, Anna L., *Judicial Staff Directory.* Mt. Vernon, VA: Staff Directories, Ltd., 1999.

Congressional Directory. Washington, DC: Joint Committee on Printing (Congress), 1998.

Congressional Yellow Book. Washington, DC: Monitor Publishing Company, 1999.

DumBaugh, Kerry and Gary Serota, *Capitol Jobs: An Insider's Guide to Finding a Job in Congress.* Washington, DC: Tilden Press, 1986.

DuChez, Jo-Anne, Ed., *The National Directory of State Agencies.* Bethesda, MD: NSA Directories, 1987.

DuChez, Jo-Anne, Ed., *The National Directory of State Agencies.* Bethesda, MD: Cambridge Information Group Directories, Inc., 1989.

Directory. Washington, DC: Federal Reports, Inc., 1989.

Federal and State Judicial Clerkship Directory. Washington, DC: NALP, 1987.

Federal Careers for Attorneys. Washington, DC: Federal Reports, Inc., 1991.

Federal Judiciary Almanac. New York: John Wiley & Sons, 1999.

Federal Law-Related Careers. Washington, DC: Federal Reports, Inc., 1991.

Federal Legal Directory. Phoenix, AZ: The Oryx Press, 1999.

Federal Personnel Office Directory. Washington, DC: Federal Reports, Inc., 1990–1991.

Federal Regional Yellow Book. Washington, DC: Monitor Publishing Company, 1999.

Federal Regulatory Directory. Washington, DC: Congressional Quarterly, Inc., 1990.

Federal Reports, Inc. *The National and Federal Legal Employment Report.* Washington, DC: Monthly newsletter.

Federal Research Service, Inc., Federal Career Opportunities. Vienna, VA: bi-weekly.

Federal-State Court Directory. Washington, DC: Want Publishing Company, 1999.

Federal Yellow Book. Washington, DC: Monitor Publishing Company, 1999.

Hermann, Richard L., and Linda P. Sutherland, *110 Biggest Mistakes Job Hunters Make (And How to Avoid Them).* Washington, DC: Federal Reports, Inc., 1993.

Krannich, Ronald L., and Caryl Rae Krannich, *The Directory of Federal Jobs & Employers.* Manassas Park, VA: Impact Publications, 1996.

Lawyer's Job Bulletin Board. Federal Bar Association, 1815 H. Street, N.W., Suite 408, Washington, DC (subscription series).

National and Federal Legal Employment Report, *Landing a Legal Job,* Revised Ed. Washington, DC: Federal Reports, Inc., 1987.

National and Federal Legal Employment Report, *1988–89 Federal Personnel Office.*

National Directory of Prosecuting Attorneys. Alexandria, VA: National District Attorneys Association, 1999.

The National Directory of State Agencies. Bethesda, MD: National Standards Association, 1999.

Now Hiring: Government Jobs for Lawyers, 1997–98. Chicago: American Bar Association, 1997.

171 Reference Book. Washington, DC: Workbooks, Inc., 1991.

Opportunities in Public Affairs. Washington, DC: The Brubach Corporation (subscription series).

The Paralegal's Guide to U.S. Government Jobs, 7th Edition. Washington, DC: Federal Reports, Inc., 1996.

Politics in America. Washington, DC: Congressional Quarterly, Inc., 1999.

Shapiro, Norman H., *How to Find a Job on Capitol Hill.* Chicago: University of Chicago Law School Record, 1981.

State Elective Officials and the Legislatures. Washington, DC: The Council of State Governments, 1995.

State Elective Officials and the Legislatures. Lexington, KY: The Council of State Governments, 1991–1992.

State Information Book. Washington, DC: Potomac Books, 1998.

State Yellow Book. Washington, DC: Monitor Publishing Co.

Thorner, Abbie, *Now Hiring: Government Jobs for Lawyers.* Chicago: Law Student Division, American Bar Association, 1987, 1990.

U.S. Court Directory. Washington, DC: The Administrative Office of the U.S. Courts, 1987.

U.S. Government Manual. Washington, DC: U.S. Government Printing Office, 1998.

Washington Information Directory, Washington, DC: Congressional Quarterly, 1999–2000.

Public Interest

Anzalone, Joan, Ed., *Good Works: A Guide to Careers in Social Change,* 3rd Ed. New York: Dembner Books, 1985.

Balancing the Scales of Justice: Financing Public Interest Law in America. Washington, DC: The Council for Public Interest Law, 1976.

Bergner, Douglas J., *Public Interest Profiles,* 5th Ed. Washington, DC: Foundation for Public Affairs, 1992–1993.

Brown, Burnett, Lolita Plank, and Lynne Plank, *Annotated Bibliography of Public Interest Placement Resources.* Washington, DC: National Association for Public Interest Law (NAPIL), 1988.

Clearinghouse Review. Chicago, IL: National Clearinghouse for Legal Services, Inc., published monthly.

Conservation Directory. Washington, DC: National Wildlife Federation, 1999.

DeBroff, Stacy M., *The Public Interest Job Search Guide: Harvard Law School's Handbook Employer Directory.* Cambridge, MA: Harvard Law School, 1992.

The Directory of Legal Aid and Defender Offices in the United States. Washington, DC: National Legal Aid and Defender Association, 1999.

Fox, Ronald, *Lawful Pursuit: Careers in Public Interest Law.*

Fox, Ronald, W., Ed., *The Public Interest Directory, A Law Student's Guide on How and Where to Find Public Interest/Human Service Jobs.* Cambridge, MA: Harvard Law School, Placement Office, 1986.

Fellowship Opportunities Guide 1993–1994. New Haven, CT: Yale Law School Career Development Office, July, 1993.

Hughes, Kathleen, *Good Works: A Guide to Social Change Careers.* Washington DC: Center for Study of Responsive Law, 1983.

Kaiser, Geoffrey, and Barbara Mule, *The Public Interest Handbook: A Guide to Legal Careers in Public Interest.* West Cornwall, CT: Locust Hill Press, 1987.

Konen, James S., *How Can You Defend Those People? The Making of a Criminal Lawyer.* New York: McGraw-Hill, 1983.

Law Firms & Pro Bono 1992/1993. Washington, DC: National Association for Public Interest Law, 1992–1993.

Legal Services Corporation Program Directory. Washington, DC: Legal Services Corporation, 1984.

McAdams, Terry W., *Careers in the Nonprofit Sector: Doing Well by Doing Good.* Washington, DC: The Tact Group, 1986.

Mental and Developmental Disabilities Directory of Legal Advocates. Chicago: Commission on the Mental Disabled, American Bar Association, 1983.

The NAPIL Connection. Washington, DC: National Association for Public Interest Law, July, 1992.

The NAPIL Guide to Public Interest Career Resources 1992/1993. Washington, DC: National Association for Public Interest Law, 1992–1993.

The NAPIL Post-Graduate Fellowships Guide 1992–1993. Washington, DC: National Association for Public Interest Law, 1992–1993.

NAPIL Public Interest Career Resources Guide. Washington, DC: National Association for Public Interest Law.

National Lawyers Guild National Referral Directory. New York: National Lawyers Guild National Office, 1986.

The Public Interest Employer Directory. Legal Support Systems, Inc.

Public Interest Private Practice—A Directory of Progressive Private Law Firms in Northern California. San Francisco, CA: Public Interest Clearinghouse, 1993.

Public Interest Profiles, 5th Ed. Washington, DC: Foundation for Public Affairs, 1992–1993.

Renz, Loren, Ed., *The Foundation Directory,* 11th Ed., New York: The Foundation Center, 1999.

Wiseberg, Laurie S., and Hazel Sirett, *North American Human Rights Directory,* 3rd Ed. Cambridge, MA: Human Rights Internet, 1984.

Corporations

ACCA Docket. Washington, DC: American Corporate Counsel Association, published quarterly.

American Bank Directory, Vols. I and II. Norcross, GA: McFadden Business Publications, 1987.

The Corporate Counsellor. New York: Leader Publications (The New York Law Publishing Co.)

Directory of Corporate Counsel. Clifton, NJ: Law & Business, Inc., Prentice Hall Law & Business, 1988–1989.

Ennico, Clifford, *Business Lawyer's Handbook.* Fairfield, Conn.: Biennix Corporation, 1992.

Law and Business Directory of Corporate Counsel, Vols. I and II. Aspen Law and Business.

Parker, Penny, Ed., *Legal Careers in Business,* Vol. III. Washington, DC: National Association for Law Placement, 1984.

Standard and Poor's Register of Corporations. New York: Standard and Poor, 1999.

Stevens, Mark, *The Big Eight.* New York: Collier Books, Macmillian Publishing Co., 1981.

Specific Areas of Practice (Legal and Nonlegal)

Altman & Weil, Inc., *Compensation Plans for Lawyers and Their Staffs—Salaries, Bonuses, and Profit-Sharing.* Chicago: Section of Economics of Law Practice, American Bar Association, 1986.

Arts Law in Theory and Practice. Washington, DC: Washington Area Lawyers for the Arts, Inc., 1985.

Attorneys & Agents Registered to Practice Before the U.S. Patent and Trademark Office. Washington, DC: U.S. Department of Commerce, 1996.

Bailey, F. Lee, *To Be a Trial Lawyer,* 1994.

Bay, Monica, *Careers in Civil Litigation.* Chicago: American Bar Association, 1990.

Berry, C.S. "Temporary Lawyers: The Do's and Don'ts." Special Section: Law Office Management, *New York Law Journal* (April 17, 1989), 201.

Best's Directory of Recommended Insurance Attorneys and Adjusters. Oldwick, NJ: A.M. Best Company, 1999.

Careers in Patent Law. Chicago: American Bar Association, 1971.

Careers in Trademark Law. U.S. Trademark Association, 1990.

Cherovsky, E., "The Use of Temporary Lawyers Is on the Rise in Many Firms," Special Section on Recruitment, *New York Law Journal* (March 4, 1991), 205.

Cook, John R., *The New Complete Guide to Environmental Careers.* Washington, D.C.: CEIP Fund, 1993.

Couric, E., "Contract Attorneys," *Student Lawyer* (September 1988), 21–27.

Davis, Anthony E., and Jeffrey Glen, *The Law and Ethics of Partner Movement: An Overview.* Washington, DC: NALSC, 1992.

Directory of Entertainment and Sports Attorneys. Aspen Law and Business, 1994.

Directory of Intellectual Property Attorneys. Aspen Law and Business, 1994.

Directory of Law Teachers. Washington, DC: Association of American Law Schools, 1999.

Directory of Opportunities in International Law. John Basset Moore Society of International Law.

Echo, Glen, M.D., *Environmental Career Opportunities.* Washington, DC: The Brubach Corporation.

Evans, Daniel B., *How to Build and Manage an Estates Practice.* Chicago: American Bar Association, Law Practice Management Section, 1999.

Evers, M., "A Non-Traditional View on Job Search Strategies," *Chicago Bar Association Record* (January 1993), 30.

Farber, Mindy, *How to Build and Manage an Employment Law Practice.* Chicago: American Bar Association, Law Practice Management Section, 1997.

Fleming, P.E. and L. Friedman, "Evaluating Temporary Lawyers; Careful Screening Yields Rewards," *New York Law Journal* (April 15, 1991), 13:18(2).

Gibson, K. William, *How to Build and Manage a Personal Injury Practice.* Chicago: American Bar Association, Law Practice Management Section, 1997.

Gottschalk, Jack A., and Robert J. Small, *Managing a Law Firm for Survival.* Philadelphia, PA: American Law Institute-American Bar Association, 1992.

Green, Jonathan, et al., Eds., *ILSA Guide to Education and Career Development in International Law,* 1991.

Greene, Robert Michael, *Making Partner—A Guide for Law Firm Associates.* Chicago: Section of Law Practice Management, American Bar Association, 1992.

Gruber, Katherine, Ed., *Encyclopedia of Associations,* 21st Ed. Detroit, MI: Gale Research, Co., 1999.

Guiley, Rosemary, *Career Opportunities for Writers.* New York: Facts on File Publications, 1985.

Heintz, Bruce D., and Nancy Markham-Bugbee, *Two-Tier Partnerships and Other Alternatives: Five Approaches.* Chicago: Section of Economics of Law Practice, American Bar Association, 1986.

Henslee, William, *Careers in Entertainment Law.* Chicago: American Bar Association, 1990.

Janis, Mark, *Careers in International Law.* Chicago: American Bar Association, 1993.

Jessup, Deborah H., *Guide to State Environmental Programs.* Washington, D.C.: BNA Books, 1994.

Katz, Judith A., *The Ad Game.* New York: Barnes & Noble Books, 1984.

Kelly, Robert E., *Consulting: The Complete Guide to a Profitable Career.* New York: Charles Scribner's Sons, 1981.

Knowles, D., and P.S. Knowles, "One Family's Experience," *Oregon State Bar Bulletin* (February/March 1993), 31–33.

Kocher, Eric, *International Jobs: Where They Are, How to Get Them.* Boston: Addison-Wesley Publishing Co., 1984.

Kutler, Robert, *Resource Careers: Options and Opportunities in Environmental and Natural Resources Law.* Chicago: American Bar Association, 1979.

Lavins, D.L., "Staffing Document Productions with Temporary Assistants," *New York Law Journal* (November 3, 1986).

Law & Business Directory of Bankruptcy Attorneys. Englewood Cliffs, NJ: Prentice Hall Law & Business, 1999.

Law & Business Directory of Entertainment and Sports Attorneys/Agents. Englewood Cliffs, NJ: Prentice Hall Law & Business, 1999.

Law & Business Directory of Environmental Attorneys. Englewood Cliffs, NJ: Prentice Hall Law & Business, 1999.

Law & Business Directory of Intellectual Property Attorneys. Englewood Cliffs, NJ: Prentice Hall Law & Business, 1999.

Law & Business Directory of Litigation Attorneys. Englewood Cliffs, NJ: Prentice Hall Law & Business, 1995.

Law and Legal Information Directory, 9th Ed. Gale Research, 1996.

Law Practice Management. Chicago: American Bar Association, Law Practice Management Magazine, published monthly (eight times a year).

LoPucki, Lynn M., *Directory of Bankruptcy Attorneys.* Englewood Cliffs, NJ: Prentice Hall, 1999.

Lubofsky, M. "The Pros and Cons of Temporary Work," *Massachusetts Lawyers Weekly* (June 22, 1992).

Lubofsky, M. "Time to Kiss Hourly Rates Goodbye" (Special Supplement), *Massachusetts Lawyers Weekly* (December 14, 1992).

Luney, Percy R. Jr., *Careers in Natural Resources and Environmental Law.* Chicago: American Bar Association, Career Series, 1987.

Magness, Michael K., and Carolyn M. Wehmann, Eds., *Your New Lawyer—the Legal Employer's Complete Guide to Recruitment, Development, and Management,* 2nd Ed. Chicago: Section of Law Practice Management, American Bar Association, 1992.

Malone, Gerry, and Howard Mudrick, *Anatomy of a Law Firm Merger—How to Make or Break the Deal.* Chicago: Section of Law Practice Management, American Bar Association, 1992.

Marcotte, P., "Temporary Lawyer Firms Get O.K.," *ABA Journal* (March 1989).

Moberly, R. B., "Temporary, Part-Time, and Other Atypical Employment Relationships in the United States," *Labor Law Journal* (November 1987), 38.

The National Job Bank, 4th Ed. Boston: Bob Adams, Inc. 1987.

Opeschowski, Charles, *A Guide to Environmental Law in Washington,* D.C. Washington, D.C.: Environmental Law Institute, 1990.

Pashker, Marti, and S. Peter Valiunas, *Money Jobs.* New York: Crown Publishing Inc., 1984.

Powell, K., "Alternative Work Schedules," *Oregon State Bar Bulletin* February/March 1992).

Russell, John J., Ed., *Directory of National Trade and Professional Associations of the United States,* 23rd Ed., Washington, DC: Columbia Books, 1988.

Scheffey, T., "In House," *The Connecticut Law Tribune* (November 2, 1992).

Scogland, W.L., and K.P. Hacket, "Employee Leasing Comes to the Legal Profession," *Illinois Bar Journal* (November 1991), 80:577(2).

Shropshire, Kenneth, *Careers in Sports Law.* Chicago: American Bar Association, 1990.

Utley, Frances, with Gary A. Munneke, *Nonlegal Careers for Lawyers in the Private Sector,* 2nd Ed. Chicago: American Bar Association, Career Series, 1984.

Walker, E., and R. Webster, "Contract Attorneys Can Be Useful in Many Situations," *Los Angeles Daily Journal* (May 11, 1992), 105:12(1).

Wayne, Ellen, *Careers in Labor Law.* Chicago: American Bar Association, Career Series, 1985.

Wayne, Ellen, and Betsy McCombs, *Graduate Law Study Programs.* Boston: Joint Committee on Law Study Programs, 1986.

Williams, John W., *Career Preparation and Opportunities in International Law.* Chicago: Section of International Law Practice, American Bar Association, 1984.

Miscellaneous

Brown, Ronald L., *Juris-Jacular: An Anthology of Modern American Legal Humor.* Littleton, CO: Fred B. Rothman, & Co., 1988.

Goluboff, Nicole Belson, *Telecommuting for Lawyers.* Chicago: American Bar Association, Law Practice Management Section, 1998.

Hay, Peter, *The Book of Legal Anecdotes.* New York: Facts on File Publications, 1989.

James, Simon, and Stebbings, Chantal, *A Dictionary of Legal Quotations.* New York: Macmillan Publishing Company, 1987.

Kanter, Arnold B., *Advanced Law Firm Mismanagement from the Offices of Fairweather, Winters & Sommers.* North Haven, CT: Catbird Press, 1993.

Kaufman, George W., *The Lawyer's Guide to Balancing Life and Work.* Chicago: American Bar Association, Law Practice Management Section, 1999.

Magness, Michael K., "Bullet-Proofing Your Firm: Why You Should Integrate Associates," *Lawyer Hiring and Training Report* (April 1989), 2.

Magness, Michael K., "Dealing with Dog Days: Staying in the Law Business is Serious Business," *Lawyer Hiring and Training Report* (August 1991), 2.

Magness, Michael K., "Reaping What They've Sown: Firms Struggle with Yesterday's Mistakes," *Lawyer Hiring and Training Report* (March 1993), 2.

Magness, Michael K. "The Problem with Recruiting," *National Law Journal* (August 23, 1982,) 14.

Magness, Michael K. and Carolyn M. Wehmann, "Extending Effective Interviewing Beyond Campus: Tips on Conducting Callbacks," *National Law Journal* (September 1, 1986), 14.

Magness, Michael K. and Carolyn M. Wehmann, Eds., *Your New Lawyer: The Legal Employer's Complete Guide to Recruitment, Development and Management.* Chicago: American Bar Association, August, 1992.

Magness, Michael K., with Peter N. Kutulakis, "A Guide to Lawyer Recruiting," *The Pennsylvania Lawyer* (December 1987), 26.

Magness, Michael K., with Peter N. Kutulakis, "Campus Recruiting by Non-Attorneys," *National Law Journal* (April 28, 1986), 16.

Magness, Michael K., with Peter N. Kutulakis, "Getting Value from Campus Visits," *National Law Journal* (December 23, 1985), 14.

Magness, Michael K. and Carolyn M. Wehmann, *Attracting Law Students You Want to Hire.* New York: Magness and Wehmann Management Consultants, Seminar handbook, March, 1989.

Magness, Michael K. and Carolyn W. Wehmann, *Boosting Your Sign-Ups on Campus: Marketing and Summer Program Strategies.* New York: Magness & Wehmann Management Consultants, Seminar handbook, February, 1990.

Magness, Michael K. and Carolyn M. Wehmann, *Interviewing Skills for Lawyers.* New York: Magness & Wehmann Management Consultants, Seminar handbook, 1990.

Magness, Michael K. and Carolyn M. Wehmann, *Marketing Your Firm to Law Students More Effectively.* New York: Magness & Wehmann Management Consultants, Seminar handbook, March, 1988.

Magness, Michael K. and Carolyn M. Wehmann, *Maximizing the Return from Your Summer Program*. New York: Magness & Wehmann Management Consultants, Seminar handbook, March 1988.

Magness, Michael K. and Carolyn M. Wehmann, *Reducing the High Costs of Lateral Hiring*. New York: Magness & Wehmann Management Consultants, Seminar handbook, March 1989.

Schrager, David and Elizabeth Frost, *The Quotable Lawyer*. New York: Facts on File Publications, 1986.

Simmons, Jeffrey R., Ed., *Life, Law and the Pursuit of Balance: A Lawyer's Guide to Quality of Life*. Published by the Maricopa County Bar Association in partnership with the State Bar of Arizona Young Lawyers Division and the American Bar Association Young Lawyers Division, 1996.

Tamminen, Julie M., Ed., *Living with the Law: Strategies to Avoid Burnout and Create Balance*. Chicago: American Bar Association, Law Practice Management Section, 1997.

Wehmann, Carolyn M., "Beating the Odds with First-Years," *National Law Journal* (August 24, 1992), 27–29.

Wehmann, Carolyn M., "Better Preparation Helps a Firm Take the Guesswork Out of Recruiting," *New York Law Journal* (September 12, 1992), S9–S10.

Wehmann, Carolyn M., "Downsized Firms May Still Recruit Inefficiently," *New York Law Journal* (November 23, 1992), 7.

Wehmann, Carolyn M., "Evaluation Checklist Helps Rate Candidates," *New York Law Journal* (November 13, 1989), 35.

Wehmann, Carolyn M., "Getting the Best—In a Buyer's Market," *Lawyer Hiring and Training Report* (June 1992), 2.

Wehmann, Carolyn M., "How Does a Firm Change an Apathetic Attitude Toward Recruiting?" *Lawyer Hiring and Training Report* (May 1989), 4.

Wehmann, Carolyn M., "In Slow Economy, Firms Use 'Down-Time' to Reshape Goals," *New York Law Journal* (April 15, 1991), 42.

Wehmann, Carolyn M., "Planning Ahead Pays Off for Interviewers," *National Law Journal* (December 16, 1991), S4–S5.

Wehmann, Carolyn M., "Recruiting More Effectively," *National Law Journal* (January 25, 1988), 21.

Wehmann, Carolyn M., "Welcome to the 1990s—And the Lifestyle Generation," *Lawyer Hiring and Training Report* (April 1990), 2.

White, Daniel R., *Trials & Tribulations—Appeal Legal Humor*. Highland Park, NJ: Catbird Press, 1989.

Web sites

American Bar Association,
   www.abanet.org/
ABA Law Practice Management Section Website:
   www.abanet.org/lpm/
Attorneys @Work, **www.attorneys @work.com**
Cal Law, **www.callaw.com/classifieds/index.shtml**
Career Services for Attorneys, Alumnae Resources. **www.ar.org**

Center for Professional Development in the Law, **www.findlaw.com**
CompLaw, the Computer Law Resource, **www.complaw.com/joblist.html**
Emplawyernet, **www.emplawyernet.com**
Find Satisfaction in Law, **www.findlaw.com/satisfaction**
Hieros Gamos Legal Employment Classifieds, **www.hg.org/**
    employment.html or contract lawyer openings listed at
    www.hg.org/temp-serv.html
Law Guru.com, **www.lawguru.com/classifieds/jobresources.html**
Law Info, **www.lawinfo.com/employment**
Law Jobs WWW, **http://lawlib.wuacc.edu/postlaw/html**
Lawjobs-L. An e-mail discussion group for job hunters in the legal profes-
    sion. Job announcements sent directly to your e-mail box. To subscribe,
    send an e-mail message to listserv@lawlib.wuacc.edu. In the body of the
    message write: subscribe lawjobs-L, followed by your name. Cancel
    your membership by sending an e-mail message to the same address
    with the message unsubscribe lawjobs-L.
Law Journal Extra!—Law Employment Center, **www.lawjobs.com**
LawMatch, **www.lawmatch.com**
Lawyers in Transition, The Association of the Bar of the City of New York,
    www.abcny.org/joblisth.stm
Lawyers Weekly Classifieds, **www.lweekly.com/class.html**
Legal Employment Search Site, **www.legalemploy.com**
Legal Employment Report, **www.attorneyjobs.com**
Legal Researcher's Desk Reference, Infosources Publishing,
    www.infosourcespub.com
Seamless Legal Job Center, **www.seamless.com/jobs/**

CONTRIBUTORS

Bradley Abbas is a sole practitioner in Scottsdale, Arizona. He practices in general litigation, emphasizing personal injury, wrongful death, and products liability matters. He received a B.A. in Architecture from Iowa State University in 1987 and a J.D. with honors from Drake University in 1993. He was elected a member of the Order of the Coif and was an Associate Editor of the *Drake Law Review.* He currently serves on several committees within the Maricopa County Bar Association and the State Bar of Arizona. He also serves on the Board of Directors of the Sunflower Foundation, Inc., a nonprofit foundation dedicated to providing educational scholarships and career training to victims of domestic violence.

Hon. Rebecca Albrecht was appointed to the Arizona bench in 1985. Since that time she has served in the criminal, civil, domestic relations, juvenile, and special assignment departments; as the presiding judge of the domestic relations department; and as the associate presiding judge of the court. She is an active member of the American Bar Association, serving on the Delivery of Legal Services Committee, the IOLTA Commission, in the House of Delegates, and as the chair of the Lawyers Conference of the Judicial Division. Judge Albrecht was the first woman president of the Maricopa County Bar Association and is a member of the Arizona Women Lawyers Association. She is a founding master of the Horace Rumpole Inn of Court and served as its president. Judge Albrecht has also been an AYSO soccer coach, a Cub Scout den leader, and the president of the Mesa Symphony Board.

Deborah Arron is the author of three popular career books for lawyers, *What Can You Do with a Law Degree?*, *Running from the Law,* and *The Complete Guide to Contract Lawyering.* Over 10,000 lawyers and law students nationwide have attended her career development seminar, *What Do You Want to Do Next with Your Law Degree?* A 1975 graduate of UCLA Law School, Arron worked as a civil litigator and bar association leader in Seattle from 1976 to 1986. She has made her living as a public speaker, writer, and career consultant since 1988.

Suzanne Baer is president of Baer Diversity Resources, a firm that specializes in gender, race, and ethnic diversity consulting and research. From 1992 to 1996, Baer served as the diversity consultant to thirty-five corporate law firm members of the Association of the Bar of the City of New York (ABCNY) Committee to Enhance Opportunities for Minorities in the Profession chaired by Cyrus R. Vance. In addition to her consulting practice, Baer is a Ph.D. candidate at the Fielding Institute (University of California, Santa Barbara) in Human and Organization Development.

Donna M. Ballman is an AV-rated solo practitioner in North Miami Beach, Florida. Her practice includes employment litigation, discrimination litigation (including sexual harassment, employment discrimination, housing discrimination, and Voting Rights), and election law. Her writings have been published in the *Florida Bar Journal, Barrister Magazine,* ABA's *Full Disclosure— Do You Really Want to Be a Lawyer?,* the *University of Miami Law Review, The Miami Herald Almanac of Florida Politics,* and the *Miami Daily Business Review.* She no longer flies except as a passenger.

Brion A. Bickerton is the founder and a principal of the Boston-based, legal recruiting firm, Bickerton & Gordon LLC. Bickerton & Gordon LLC recruits lawyers and other legal professionals for law firm and in-house positions in New England, the East Coast, and overseas. Mr. Bickerton has been recruiting for lawyers for over twelve years and is a contributor to many seminars and presentations concerning legal careers. He is a former corporate and international lawyer, having practiced in the Boston and London offices of Bingham & Dana LLP. He is the former general counsel of an international development company and was a law clerk for the Federal District Court in Boston.

Kathleen Brady has written two books: *What Lawyers Earn* (Harcourt Brace) and *Jobs for Lawyers: Effective Techniques for Getting Hired in Today's Legal Marketplace* (Impact Publications). She has also published several articles related to the career development of lawyers. She is the former assistant dean of Fordham University School of Law's Career Planning Center and past president for the National Association for Law Placement. Currently, Brady is a communication consultant with Exec I Com and working on her third book about enhancing professional development through effective communication skills.

H. Ward Classen has been general counsel of CSC Intelicom, Inc., with responsibility for all legal activities, since December 1990 and assistant general counsel of Computer Sciences Corporation since November 1996. He was previously associate general counsel and assistant secretary for International Mobile Machines Corporation (now Interdigital Corporation) from 1987 to 1990, and an associate with Weinberg & Green from 1985 to 1987. He has a B.A. in economics from Trinity College (Connecticut), a J.D. from Catholic University; and an MBA from the Wharton School of the University of Pennsylvania. Classen serves on a number of business, professional, and civic boards, including the board of advisors of *The Intellectual Property Counsel,* a publication addressing intellectual property issues, as well as *The Commercial Law Advisor.* He is an adjunct professor at the University of Baltimore Law School.

Vanessa Davila is the director of minority affairs of the State Bar of Texas, where she seeks to increase the participation of minority and women lawyers in the bar and to develop programs to enhance employment and economic opportunities for minority and women lawyers in Texas. She has a B.A. from Harvard-Radcliffe College, and an MBA from the University of Texas at Austin. She has worked in association management in the areas of business development, membership, and race and gender issues since 1992, when she came to the law from a career in corporate human resources.

Diane L. Drain graduated from the University of Arizona Law School in 1985. In 1990 Drain left the large firm practice and established one of the first woman-owned "boutique" firms in Arizona, marketing itself as a "referral firm" focusing in the areas of real property and bankruptcy. She also established a consulting service to assist other lawyers in law office setup, administration, and computerization. Drain is past president of the Maricopa Chapter of the Arizona Women Lawyer's Association, past chair of the Solo Practitioner's Section of the Arizona State Bar, and was appointed by the Arizona Supreme Court to the Commission on Judicial Review. She received the Arizona State Bar Member of the Year Award in 1996.

Tracy S. Essig has been an Assistant Attorney General with the State of Arizona, Civil Division, Tax Section since 1992. He is the Unit Chief of the Arizona Collection Enforcement Revolving Fund. Essig graduated with high distinction from the University of Arizona Law School and received a B.A. in both Economics and Political Science from the University of Arizona. He is a past president of the Young Lawyer's Division for the State of Arizona, Maricopa County Representative to the Public Lawyer Section Executive Council, and a former member of the board of governors for the Arizona State Bar.

Nicole Belson Goluboff is a lawyer in New York City who writes, lectures, and develops programs to educate lawyers about telecommuting and other alternative work arrangements. She is the author of *Telecommuting for Lawyers* (ABA Law Practice Management Section, 1998), which details why and how lawyers should telework, from the perspective of both law firms and individual lawyers. She is a member of the New York State Bar Association Committee on Citizenship Education, the Association of the Bar of the City of New York Standing Committee on Lawyers in Transition, and the LAAWS Network (Lawyers Advancing Alternative Work Solutions). She graduated summa cum laude and Junior Phi Beta Kappa from Columbia College of Columbia University in the college's first coed class, and is a 1990 graduate of the Columbia University School of Law.

Laura Hagen received her B.A. in 1972 and her J.D. with honors in 1976 from the University of Texas at Austin, where she was a staff member of the *Texas Law Review*. She also received an LL.M. from Harvard Law School. From 1978 to 1983, she was an associate with Paul, Weiss, Rifkind, Wharton & Garrison in New York and Washington, D.C. After moving to Chicago in 1983, she was first affiliated with Coffield Ungaretti Harris & Slavin and then with Bell, Boyd & Lloyd, where she was a partner in the corporate and securities department before establishing the Chicago office of Major, Hagen & Africa in 1988.

Toya Cook Haley is an assistant county attorney with the Travis County Attorney's Office in Austin, Texas. As a member of the Civil Litigation Division, her practice focuses on all aspects of employment law and civil appellate practice. In addition, she serves as adjunct faculty at the University of Texas School of Law. Haley earned her B.A. from Rice University in 1983 and her J.D. from the College of William and Mary in 1990. She is past president of the Austin Young Lawyers Association and has served in leadership positions in the Texas Young Lawyers Association. Haley is an officer of the ABA Young Lawyers Division, currently serving as assembly clerk.

Erik J. Heels is a legal technologist and a patent lawyer. His book *The Legal List: Law-Related Resources on the Internet and Elsewhere* is in its seventh edition and is published by Lawyers Cooperative Publishing. He writes the "nothing.but.net" column for the ABA's *Law Practice Management* magazine and regularly speaks about issues related to law and technology. He earned his B.S. in electrical engineering from MIT and his J.D. from the University of Maine School of Law. With Rick Klau, Heels cowrote *Law Law Law on the Internet: The Best Legal Web Sites and More,* published by the ABA in 1998. He is a partner with Red Street Consulting, a marketing consulting company focused on helping law firms use the Internet.

Deborah Howard is the director of career services at New York Law School. She received her B.A. from Harvard University in 1979 and her J.D. from Northeastern University School of Law in 1982. After a number of years working as a litigator, Howard left the practice of law to join a legal recruitment firm before joining the administration of New York Law School. Howard is also a consultant in the areas of staff development and diversity.

Timothy R. Hyland is a shareholder in the law firm of Bess Kunz in Phoenix, Arizona. His practice emphasizes insurance defense, insurance coverage, commercial litigation, and homeowners association matters. Hyland received his undergraduate degree from Grand Canyon College (B.A. 1982, with high honors) and his law degree from the University of Arizona College of Law (J.D. 1985, with high honors). Following his law school graduation, Hyland was a judicial law clerk for the Honorable James Duke Cameron, Justice, Arizona Supreme Court. He is currently a member of the Maricopa County Bar Association Board of Directors and the chair of the State Bar of Arizona and Maricopa County Bar Associations joint committee on Quality of Life. He is past president of the Young Lawyers Division of both the Maricopa County Bar Association and the State Bar of Arizona.

Carol M. Kanarek specializes in providing career-related services to lawyers and law firms. She holds B.A. and M.A. degrees in anthropology and received her J.D. from the University of Michigan Law School. Kanarek served as chairperson of the Career Issues Committee of the ABA's Young Lawyers Division from 1986 to 1988 and conceived and edited the first edition of *Changing Jobs: A Handbook for Lawyers,* which was published in 1989. Kanarek is a vice chair of the Careers Task Force of the ABA's Law Practice Management Section, a member of the board of editors of *Law Firm Partnership and Benefits Report,* and a member of the Lawyers in Transition Committee of the Association of the Bar of the City of New York.

Maureen P. Kane is an attorney with Jackson, White, Gardner, Weech and Walker, P.C., a Mesa, Arizona, law firm where she represents plaintiffs in personal injury actions and employment disputes. She clerked in the Arizona Court of Appeals for three judges after graduating from the Arizona State University College of Law in 1994. During law school, Kane helped two professors write book chapters on children's legal issues and factors influencing courts in AIDS decisions. A former art teacher and writer/producer of corporate videos, Kane spends her free time pursuing photography, video, and art projects and writing for local legal publications.

Richard P. Klau is a graduate of the University of Richmond School of Law. While in law school, he founded the *Richmond Journal of Law and Technology,* the first student-edited law journal in the world to publish exclusively online. A regular presenter on law-related Internet topics at trade shows, CLE seminars, and bar associations around the country, Klau coauthors "Online," a monthly column for the ABA's *Student Lawyer* magazine. He is an active member of the ABA Law Practice Management Section and serves on the LPM Publications Board. He coauthored *Law Law Law on the Internet: The Best Legal Web Sites and More* (ABA, 1998) with Erik Heels, and is a partner with Red Street Consulting, a marketing consulting company focused on helping law firms use the Internet.

Janina C. Latack, Ph.D., is a career management consultant with Right Management Consultants, an outplacement and organizational consulting services firm. She has been an adjunct faculty member in the University of Arizona Department of Management and Policy for five years; prior to that she was a faculty member in the Ohio State University College of Business for thirteen years. In her career management practice, she works one-on-one with professionals, managers, and executives to assess strengths and create development plans for maximum career effectiveness. Latack also conducts management and executive development seminars on managing during organizational transitions, career resilience, and effective managerial communication. She is certified as a career counselor by the National Board for Certified Counselors (NBCC) and by the state of Arizona.

Sylvia J. Lett received her B.A. in 1990 from Harvard University and her J.D. in 1994 from New York University School of Law. After law school, she worked as an associate at Anderson, Kill & Olick, P.C., in New York City. Thereafter, Lett clerked for Hon. Susan A. Ehrlich, Arizona State Court of Appeals (1995–1996), and then worked at the law firm of Mariscal, Weeks, McIntyre & Friedlander, P.A., in Phoenix. While on sabbatical from that firm, she clerked for Hon. Barry G. Silverman, United States Court of Appeals for the Ninth Circuit (1998–1999), during his first term on that court.

Robert A. Major received his B.A. in 1973 from Stanford University and his J.D. in 1976 from the University of Texas at Austin, where he served as an Editor of the *Texas Law Review*. From 1976 to 1981 he was an associate with Wilmer, Cutler & Pickering in Washington, D.C. After a year as counsel to Saga Corporation in Menlo Park, California, he established Robert A. Major & Associates in 1982 as the predecessor firm to Major, Hagen & Africa. Major is a former director and cochair of the ethics committee of the National Association of Legal Search Consultants. Since 1998, he has served as an advisor to the Board of Directors of the National Association of Legal Search Consultants.

David Machlowitz is associate general counsel of Siemens Corporation in New York City. He supervises all of the lawyers who provide specialized legal advice in such areas as mergers and acquisitions, litigation, and antitrust to all Siemens companies in the United States, which have annual revenues in excess of $12 billion. He is also the company's compliance officer. A 1977 graduate of Yale Law School, Machlowitz has lectured and written extensively about law department management, compliance programs, litigation tactics and employment issues. Machlowitz has also edited a book on working with environmental consultants. He was president of the New Jersey chapter of the American Corporate Counsel Association from 1995 to 1997 and was honored by the New York Chapter as the 1993 In-House Lawyer of the Year.

Michael K. Magness has twenty-seven years of experience advising law firms and businesses across the country on matters relating to communication and public relations, marketing, professional development, recruitment, and training. He assists clients in conducting management audits, marketing themselves more effectively, training lawyers in interviewing skills, designing in-house management programs, and conducting management seminars and retreats. Magness spent the earlier part of his career as an assistant dean at Case Western Reserve University School of Law and at New York University School of Law as Director of Career Planning and Placement. He holds undergraduate and law degrees from Case Western Reserve University.

Hillary Mantis is Director of Alumni and LL.M. Career Services at Fordham University of Law and a career counselor in private practice in New York City. She specializes in working with lawyers who are making career transitions or seeking alternative careers. Mantis is the author of two career books for lawyers: *Alternative Careers for Lawyers* (Random House, 1997) and *Jobs for Lawyers: Effective Techniques for Getting Hired in Today's Legal Marketplace* (Impact Press, 1996). She is a former chair of the ABA Young Lawyers Division Career Issues Committee.

Londell McMillan is a lawyer in New York City.

Gary A. Munneke is a professor of law at Pace University School of Law, in White Plains, New York, where he teaches courses in professional responsibility, torts, and law practice management. He is active in ABA leadership, serving as 1998–1999 chair of the Law Practice Management Section and as a member of the ABA Standing Committee on Publishing Oversight. Munneke is the author of numerous books and articles about the legal profession, legal careers, and the practice of law. A 1973 graduate of the University of Texas School of Law, Munneke is a member of the Texas and Pennsylvania bars and is a fellow of the American Bar Foundation and the College of Law Practice Management.

Sandra O'Briant has an M.A. in education and was the assistant director of a tutorial program at Arizona State University before relocating to California and beginning work at an executive search firm in Beverly Hills. As a principal in her own firms since 1979 (Keogh, O'Briant & Brown, 1979–1984, and Ziskind, Greene & O'Briant, 1984–1987), she has placed both partners and associates. Her client base includes law firms ranging in size from three to over a thousand lawyers and corporations in the Fortune 200, as well as closely held businesses. O'Briant has participated in the National Association of Legal Search Consultants (NALSC), a professional organization that has drafted a code of ethics governing the legal search industry, since its founding in 1984.

Consuelo M. Ohanesian is an assistant attorney general of Arizona, where she works in the Criminal Appeals Section. She is the author or editor of several books on federal tax, securities, and criminal law. She has served as a research assistant for the International Criminal Tribunal on the Former Yugoslavia, is a Certified Securities Arbitrator, and a frequent lecturer on criminal law. She is currently on the boards of directors of the Public Lawyers Division of the Maricopa County Bar Association and Arizona Women Lawyers Association. She received her B.A. from the University of Southern California and her law degree from Arizona State University, where she was executive editor of the law review.

Larry Richard, Ph.D., is a principal with Altman Weil, a nationally known consulting firm headquartered in Newtown Square, Pennsylvania, that specializes in the legal profession. Richard's practice focuses on organizational improvement, communication, motivation, and leadership issues in law firms. Richard earned his J.D. degree from the University of Pennsylvania Law School and his Ph.D. in psychology from Temple University. His doctoral research examined the relationship between personality differences (as measured by the Myers-Briggs Type Indicator) and job satisfaction among U.S. lawyers.

Maureen Provost Ryan has been working with lawyers in career transition since 1979 as a career planning professional in three law schools, a career counselor in private practice, and as an associate development professional for a large New York firm. Provost Ryan has been active in the National Association for Law Placement since 1980, serving as president of the organization during 1988–1989. She holds an M.S./Ed.S. in counseling psychology from SUNY Albany and a B.A. in English from SUNY Geneseo.

Daniel P. Schaack received his B.A. in Spanish from the University of Iowa in 1981, and his J.D. from the University of Michigan Law School in 1984. After law school he became an associate with the Phoenix law firm of Warner, Angle, Roper & Hallam. He then became a staff attorney at the Arizona Court of Appeals, Division One, a position he held for nine years. He is now an associate with the Phoenix firm of Logan & Geotas. He is on the editorial board of the *Maricopa Lawyer,* for which he writes the "CourtWatch" column.

Michael J. K. Schiumo is the assistant dean for Career Development at Fordham University School of Law. He is a 1989 graduate of the University of Virginia School of Law and a 1984 graduate of Cornell University. He practiced corporate law in Philadelphia with the firm of Dechert, Price & Rhoads prior to leaving practice to join the career planning staff of Boston University School of Law in 1993.

Alexa Shabecoff is the director of the Office of Public Interest Advising (OPIA), the first office of its kind in the nation, dedicated to advising Harvard Law School students and alumni about public service careers. As director of OPIA, Shabecoff oversees a staff of attorney advisers with expertise in public service, runs OPIA's extensive programming schedule, oversees OPIA's publications and visiting fellows programs, and counsels numerous Harvard Law students about public service opportunities. Shabecoff was a Wasserstein Fellow-in-Residence during fall 1993 before joining OPIA as a member of its staff. Shabecoff currently serves on the board of directors of Project Parents, Inc., and is a participant in the Lead Boston program of the National Conference for Community and Justice. Before joining OPIA, Shabecoff was a legal services lawyer in St. Louis and Framingham, Massachusetts. Shabecoff graduated from New York University School of Law in 1986, where she was a Root Tilden Scholar.

Marcia Pennington Shannon is a principal in the Washington, D.C., legal consulting firm of Shannon & Manch, L.L.P., which specializes in attorney personnel management issues, including retention, evaluation, recruitment, mentoring, coaching, and outplacement counseling. Shannon's previous experience includes nine years as the Assistant Director and Public Interest Counselor of Career Services for Georgetown University Law Center. She holds degrees from Emory University and the University of Cincinnati.

Jeffrey R. Simmons is a litigation attorney in the Phoenix office of DeConcini, McDonald, Yetwin & Lacy, P.C., with significant experience in commercial, employment, and transportation-related cases. He received his A.B. in 1983 from Georgetown University and a J.D. in 1986 from the University of Arizona College of Law. He is past president of the State Bar of Arizona Young Lawyers Division and a former member of the State Bar of Arizona Board of Governors. He currently serves as the ABA Young Lawyers Division Liaison to the ABA's Standing Committee on Professionalism. Simmons served as Editor of *Life, Law and the Pursuit of Balance: A Lawyer's Guide to Quality of Life* (2d ed., 1997; published by the Maricopa County Bar Association in partnership with the ABA Young Lawyers Division and the State Bar of Arizona Young Lawyers Division).

Heidi McNeil Staudenmaier is a partner with the Phoenix, Arizona, law firm of Snell & Wilmer, where her practice emphasizes commercial litigation, Indian law, and gaming law. She received her B.A. from the University of Iowa in 1981 and her law degree from the University of Iowa in 1985. Before law school, she worked as a sportswriter for two midwestern newspapers. Currently, she is the president of the Maricopa County Bar Association. She is a past Young Lawyers Division Delegate to the ABA House of Delegates and is a past member of the ABA Commission on Domestic Violence. She also is a past chair of the State Bar of Arizona Indian Law Section. She is currently a judge pro tem for both the Arizona Court of Appeals and the Superior Court of Maricopa County, Arizona.

Brenda M. Thomas is the executive director of the Maricopa County Bar Association in Phoenix, Arizona. She obtained a B.A. in English from Yale University in 1983 and a J.D. from Yale Law School in 1989. She practiced corporate law with Cooley Godward Castro Huddleston & Tatum in Palo Alto, California, for approximately one year before moving to Washington, D.C., to work as an extern for Congressman Major Owens. In 1992 she clerked for Federal District Judge Edward Dean Price in Fresno, California. She came to Phoenix in 1993 to practice with the Urban Indian Law Project of Community Legal Services before joining Moore McCoy & Payne as an associate in 1995.

Pat Bowers Thomas is the owner of BowersThomas, a Los Angeles–based legal search firm working globally to address the lawyer search and consulting needs of corporate and law firm clients. Practicing since 1983, Thomas is regularly called upon as an expert in her field including professional and eleemosynary speaking and writing engagements.

Marilyn Tucker, after serving as the director of the Office of Career Services at Georgetown University Law Center from 1986 to 1995, assumed a new role as director of Alumni Career Services at the Law Center. During the 1998 American Bar Association convention, Tucker received the *Law Practice Management* magazine's Distinguished Writer's Award, 1997–1998, for "Will

Women Lawyers Ever Be Happy?" which appeared in the January 1998 issue. In 1994, Tucker, in collaboration with Georgia Niedzielko of the Catholic University School of Law, won the National Association for Law Placement's (NALP) Mark of Distinction Award for a review of available research into the career paths of women lawyers for the ABA Commission on Women in the Profession.

Bruce Tulgan is the author of several books, most recently *Work This Way: How 1,000 Young People Designed Their Own Careers in the New Workplace and How You Can Too* (Hyperion, 1998). He is also the founder of Rainmaker Thinking, Inc., a research and consulting firm in New Haven, Connecticut. His work has been the subject of more than a thousand news stories.

David E. Vieweg is an attorney with the Phoenix, Arizona, law firm of Fennemore Craig. He has an M.A. (with honors) from the University of St. Andrews, Scotland, and is a graduate of Stanford Law School. His principal practice areas include commercial leasing, real estate, acquisition and finance transactions, development and construction projects, and loan restructuring and workouts. He is an editor of the second edition of the *Commercial Real Estate Transactions Practice Manual* published by the State Bar of Arizona, and he has recently served as chair of the State Bar of Arizona's Real Property Section. He is a member of the International Council of Shopping Centers and has hosted numerous roundtable discussion groups at the annual law conferences.

Shelley Wallace is founder of the Wallace Law Registry, the nation's preeminent legal staffing firm for the placement of temporary and permanent attorneys and paralegals. During her tenure, the Wallace Law Registry grew to fifteen offices from coast to coast and had gathered the most number of preferred provider and exclusive staffing relationships among Fortune 100 companies. A member of the New York and Connecticut State Bars, Wallace currently resides in West Hartford, Connecticut.

C. A. Webb, OPIA's associate, helps advise Harvard students and alumni seeking public service legal careers. Webb oversees the daily administration of the office, helps organize the office's programs, and assists with office publications. Webb graduated cum laude from Wellesley College in 1997. While working for Wellesley's College's Center for Work and Service, Webb coauthored a student guide to experiential education and helped develop faculty and student programs to enhance experiential learning opportunities. Webb has worked for President Carter's Atlanta Project and has designed and taught classes in gender psychology to junior high school students.

Carolyn M. Wehmann has twenty-two years of experience working with legal employers and law schools: nine years as a law firm administrator in New York City and thirteen years as a management consultant in the United States and Canada. Her expertise is in targeting, recruiting, and retaining lawyers, behavioral interviewing, and developing innovative marketing strategies and materials. Before forming Carolyn Wehmann Consulting, Inc. (founded in 1987 as Magness & Wehmann), she held positions as director of professional development, legal personnel administrator, and recruitment programs coordinator for a 250-lawyer firm in New York. Wehmann is a 1975 graduate of Smith College.

Abbie F. Willard, Ph.D., is assistant dean of Career Services and Publications for the Georgetown University Law Center. Before joining Georgetown, she served as the Director of Student Affairs and Placement at the University of Georgia School of Law and was employed as the recruitment administrator for the Washington, D.C., law firm of Hogan & Hartson. She also taught courses and seminars in the development of writing and communication skills at the University of Illinois. Dean Willard has served as a reporter and editorial consultant to organizations such as the ABA and the Georgia State Department of Vocational Education and as a management and recruitment consultant at large, medium, and small law firms throughout the country.

INDEX

Numbers in italics denote figures.

A

ABA Division for Bar Services, 87
ABA Network, 86
ABA. *See* American Bar Association
ABA State and Local Bar Directory, 87
Abbas, Bradley, 311
Academic history, 109
ACCA Docket (American Corporate
    Counsel), 207
Accomplishments lists, 10
Acquisitions, 30
Active listening, 146–147
Adding value, 6, 7
Administrative law judges, 243–244,
    245, 260
Advisory jury trials, 242
Affirmative action programs, 96
Age Wave (Dychtwald), 171
Aging population, 40
Albrecht, Honorable Rebecca, "The
    Judgeships," 241–245, 325
ALI-ABA. *See* American Law Institute-
    American Bar Association
Allison, G. Burgess, *The Lawyer's Guide to
    the Internet*, 290
Allocation of time in job searching, 52–54
Almanac of American Politics, 234, 236
Almanac of the Unelected, 236
Alternative career choices. *See*
    Nontraditional careers for lawyers
Alternative Careers for Lawyers (Mantis), 330
Alternative work arrangements, 270–280
    for associates not wanting full-time
        career or have opened own
        practices, 274
    candidate pools for, 270
    circumstances and opportunities of,
        273–275
    corporate law departments, 272
    dealing with agencies, 277–278
    definition of, 271–272
    dos and don'ts for, 277–280
    fulfilling assignments, 279

    for laid-off senior corporate counsel,
        274–275
    law firms, 272–273
    listening to placement directors and
        counselors, 278
    maintaining flexibility, 278
    making the most of every assignment,
        279–280
    for newly graduated lawyers, 273–274
    overview, 270–271
    pursuing opportunities, 276–277
    for retired workers, 275
    salaries and benefits, 271–272
    for top-performing senior associates
        turned down for partnership, 274
    for women, 270, 275
    working temporary but wanting
        permanent, 279
Alumni job newsletters, 73
Alumni reunions, 57
American Indian Bar Association, 101
American Bar Association (ABA), 86
American Bar Association Commission on
    Opportunities for Minorities in the
    Profession, 100
American Bar Association Division for Bar
    Services, 86
American Corporate Counsel Association,
    207, 329
American Law Institute-American Bar
    Association (ALI-ABA), 86
American Lawyer, 79, 163
Analysis paralysis, 34
Analytical thinking, 134
"Anchors," 12
Annual Directory of Legal Employers, 99
"Annual Survey of America's 100 Highest
    Grossing Firms" (*American
    Lawyer*), 167
Antitrust law, 169–170
Appellate court clerkships, 249, 250
Appellate staff lawyers, 246–249
    duties of, 247
    job searching, 248–249
    pros and cons of the job, 247–248

"Appellate Staff Lawyers" (Schaak), 246–249, 331
Appellate courts, 241
Arao, Maki, 27
Arbitrators, 242, 245
Arizona Women Lawyers Association, 316
Arron, Deborah and Guyol, Deborah, *The Complete Guide to Contract Lawyering*, 31
Arron, Deborah, "Nontraditional Careers for Lawyers," 298–307, 325
Arron, Deborah, *What Can You Do with a Law Degree*, 303, *Running from the Law, The Complete Guide to Contract Lawyering*, 325
Arron, Deborah, *What Do You Want to Do Next with Your Law Degree?* (career development seminar), 325
Article III judges, 244
Assessment types, 16
AT&T, 284
Atlanta Project, 333
Attachments to e-mail, 65–66

B
Baby boom generation, 170–171
Bad-mouthing current employer, 79
Baer Diversity Resources, 325
Baer, Suzanne, McMillan, Londell and Davila, Vanessa, "Career Opportunities for Minorities," 96–100, 325, 326, 330
Bait and switch tactics, 79
Balance, 30–33
    strategies to achieve, 31–33
Ballman, Donna M., "Flying Solo," 200–205, 325–326
Bankruptcy judges, 244
Bar association programs, 73
Bar associations, 34, 84–95
    American Bar Association Division for Bar Services, 87
    bar web sites, 86
    international bar associations and websites, 94
    jobs for bar staffs, 87–88
    legal placement services and job banks, 85–86
    local bar associations and websites, 90–92
    membership directories, 85
    newsletters and periodicals, 84–85
    specialty bar and other legal organizations and their websites, 92–94
    state bar associations and websites, 88–90
Bar memberships, 110
Bar staff jobs, 87–88

Barrister Magazine, 326
Beach, Scott, 293, 294, 297
Belonging needs, 29
Benefits. *See* Salary and benefits negotiations
Berra, Yogi, 173
Bess Kunz, 328
"Best Places to Live in America" (*Money Magazine*), 175
Bickerton & Gordon LLC, 326
Bickerton, Brion A., "Practice Areas," 167–170, 326
Bill padding, 45
Billable hours, 34, 153, 194
Billing records, 12
Bingham & Dana LLP, 326
Blue chip work, 197
Bolles, Richard, *How to Create a Picture of Your Ideal Job or Next Career*, 33
Bolles, Richard, *The Quick Job Hunt Map*, 9
Bolles, Richard, *What Color Is Your Parachute?*, 9, 75, 303
Book of business, 155–156
    See also Salary and benefits negotiations
Boston Globe, 69
Boutiques, 197
Brady, Kathleen, "Networking," 56–62, 326
Brady, Kathleen, *What Lawyers Earn* and *Jobs for Lawyers: Effective Techniques for Getting Hired in Today's Legal Marketplace*, 326
Brain physiology, 27
Bull market, 167
Bulletin (Computer Law Association), 207
Burning bridges, 43
Burnout, 6

C
California Lawyer, The, 26
California Pizza Kitchen, 304
Capitol Hill. *See* Federal agencies
Card-sort processes, 9
Career Center, 215
Career changing, 3–7
    changes in economy, 3–4
    entrepreneurial options, 7
    forces shaping the workplace of the future, 4–6
    new career paradigm, 6
    reinventing present job, 7
    thinking "outside the box," 6–7
"Career Changing in the New Millennium" (Tulgan), 3–7, 333
Career consultants, 9

Career counselors, 19, 72, 80–82
   guidance provided, 80
   versus search firms, 80
Career decisions, 159–164
   colleagues, 161–162
   factors affecting goal attainment,
     162–163
   geography, 161
   long-term goals, 160–162
   making job selection comport with
     goals, 164
   partnership or equivalent, 160–161
   research, 163–164
   short-term goals, 159–160
Career dissatisfaction reasons, 29–30
Career identity elements, 19
Career interests, 19
Career investment, 26
Career objective statement, 17
"Career Opportunities for Minorities"
  (Baer, McMillan, Davila), 96–100, 325,
  326, 330
Career paradigm, 6
Career planning steps, 144
Career satisfaction
   definition of, 28
   factors of, 33–34
Career self-assessment, 8–17, 51
   exercises for, 10–15
   goals and benefits of, 8–9
   Holland code, 16
   how to, 9
   results from, 8–9
   skills identification, 9–10
   synthesizing results of, 16–17
"Career Self-Assessment" (Ryan), 8–17, 331
Career testing, 9
Career transition trauma, 299
CareerPath, 70
Carolyn Wehmann Consulting, 333
Cash flow, 7
CEELI. *See* Central and East European
  Law Initiative
Center for Applications of Psychological
  Type, Inc., 19
Central and East European Law Initiative
  (CEELI), 181
Certified Securities Arbitrator, 330
Chambers of Commerce, 175
Changes since early 1990s, xvii–xviii
Chaotic markets, 3
Checklist for long-distance job search,
  178–179
*Chief Administrative Officer's Statement of
  Disbursements*, 237
Chronicle of Higher Education, 268
Cinciotta, Linda A., 213
Circuit court clerkships, 250

Circuit courts of appeals, 244, 249
Class standing, 109
Classen, H. Ward, "Corporations,"
  206–212, 326
CLE. *See* Continuing legal education
Clerk of Court's office, 246
Clerkships, 98, 245
   See also Law clerks
Client billings, 78
Client contacts, 196–197
Client culture, 108
Client preferences, 9
Client-oriented nonprofit advocacy
  organizations, 258
Climate, 178
Code-based practice, 22
Cold cover letters, 141
Commercial Law Advisor, The, 326
*Commercial Real Estate Transactions Practice
  Manual* (Vieweg, editor), 333
Commission on Domestic Violence, 332
Committee on Continuing Legal
  Education, 86
Communicating priorities, 31–32
Communication style, 19
Communications, 304
Community activities, 110
Community organizations, 98
Community service, 34
Compensation committees, 155
   See also Salary and benefits
     negotiations
Compensation packages. *See* Salary and
  benefits negotiations
Compensation survey, 87
Complete Guide to Contract Lawyering, The
  (Arron and Guyol), 31, 325
Computer Law Association, 207
Conciliators, 163
Congressional Black Caucus, 235
Congressional Directory, 234
Congressional Hispanic Caucus, 235
Congressional Quarterly, 235
Congressional switchboard, 237
Congressional Yellow Book, The, 234
Constitution, The, 249
Contact follow-up, 61–62
Contingencies to job offers, 158
   See also Salary and benefits negotiations
Continuing education materials, 86
Continuing legal education (CLE), 5, 97,
  100, 177, 182, 265
Contract partners, 154
Contract work, 31, 85, 179, 195, 289
   See also Alternative work
     arrangements
*Control Theory: A New Explanation of How
  We Control Our Lives* (Glasser), 29

Cooper, Alison, 306
Corporate resumes. *See* Resume writing
"Corporations" (Classen), 206–212, 326
Cost of living, 177–178, 182
Cost-effective services, 174
Costs of litigation, 242
Counseling, 304
Court-appointed counsel, 257
    See also Public defenders
"CourtWatch," 331
"Cover Letter, The" (Howard),
   138–143, 328
Cover letters, 56, 81–82, 106, 138–143
    for clerkships, 251
    closing paragraph, 143
    crossover applications, 142–143
    customizing each letter, 141
    drafting the letter, 139
    opening paragraph, 139
    out-of-town employers, 141–142
    preparation, 138
    research on employers, 139
    sample format, *140*
    self-inventory, 138–139
    selling yourself, 142
    target lists, 139
    what to leave out, 143
    writing skills, 143
"Creating an Ideal Law Practice in
   Conjunction with Your Home" (Drain),
   281–290, 326–327
Creative processes, 34
Criminal Appeals Section of Arizona, 330
Criminal law, 23, 24, 330
Criminal Tribunal on the Former
   Yugoslavia, 330
Criticizing resumes. *See* Resume writing
Crossover applications, 142–143
CSC Intelicom, Inc., 326
Cultural fit, 110
Cultural flavor, 182

D
Deans, 264
Death penalty cases, 257
Default law careers, 26–27
Democratic National Committee, 235
Democratic Policy Committee, 235
Demographic information, 87
Demographic map, 5
Department of Justice, 213, 216, 225–226
Dilenschneider, Robert, 33
Direct-service nonprofit advocacy
   organizations, 258
Directory of Corporate Counsel, 47, 152
Directory of Legal Aid and Defender Offices in
   the United States and Territories
   (NLADA), 257, 261

Directory of Public Interest Fellowships (Yale
   Law School), 261
District courts, 244
Diversity in workforce, 5, 100, 110
Doom Loop System, The (Hollander), 10
Downs-O'Shaughnessy, Jennifer, 293,
   296, 297
Downsizing, 4, 30, 273
Drain, Diane L., "Creating an Ideal Law
   Practice in Conjunction with Your
   Home," 281–290, 326–327; "How to Set
   Up a Small Efficient Law Practice, 290
Drake Law Review, 325
Draws, 154
Dual-career families, 30
Dunn & Bradstreet, 208
Dychtwald, Ken, *Age Wave*, 171

E
E-mail addresses, 64
    See also Internet
Eastern Europe, 5
Economic climate of geographic areas. *See*
   Geographic areas
Economic downturn, 175
Economic trends in geographic areas. *See*
   Geographic areas
Educational administrations, 303
"Effective Job-Search Techniques and
   Strategies" (Schiumo), 51–56, 331
Ego-based anger, 281
Elder care law, 171
Electronic resumes, 136
    See also Web sites ·
EmplawyerNet, 67
Employment law, 171
Encryption, 66
Endowed positions, 267
Enforcement specialists, 303
Entrepreneurial grants, 261–262
Entrepreneurial ventures, 304
Entrepreneurship, 3, 7, 200–205,
   281–290, 304
    See also Solo practice; Home practice
Equity partnership position, 78
Essig, Tracy S., 327
Ethics Committee of the ABA, 273
Euthanasia issues, 171
Excepted Service, 214, 219
Exchange programs, 181–182
Extracurricular activities, 109
Extraversion versus introversion, 20–21

F
Family-friendly environment, 178
Fastest growing forms of work, 3
FBA. *See* Federal Bar Association

Federal agencies, 213–240
   advantages and disadvantages of
      federal legal practice, 227–229
   advantages and disadvantages of
      working on Capitol Hill, 237–238
   advertising of positions, 214–216
   agencies with regional or satellite
      offices, 217
   career advancement in, 227
   change in size of departments
      between 1993 and, 1998, *231–232*
   compensation, 226–227
   federal employment and future
      marketability, 220–221
   highest salaries on Capitol Hill, 237
   how to obtain a job in, 221–224
   Internet publications, 239–240
   and interviewing, 236
   job availability, 219–220
   job-search techniques for Capitol Hill,
      233–237
   Lateral Attorney Recruitment
      Program (LARP), Department of
      Justice, 225–226
   law-related positions, 218–219
   legislative/policy positions, 218
   and long-distance job hunting, 236
   phone numbers, 219
   print publications, 238–239
   statistics of law jobs, 213–214
   targeting job search, 216–218
   those employing over 100
      lawyers, *230*
   time it takes to job hunt, 224–225
   Web sites for, 215–216, *231*
   working on Capitol Hill, 229–230,
      232–238
"Federal Agencies" (Tucker), 213–238,
   332–333
Federal Bar Association, 215
Federal Career Opportunities Bulletin,
   215, 219
Federal Careers for Attorneys, 216, 217, 222
Federal court clerkships, 250
Federal district courts, 249
Federal Law-Related Careers, 218
Federal Regional Yellow Book, The, 217, 221
Federal Register, 245
Federal Research Service, Inc., 215
Feedback, 56, 196
Feeling versus thinking, 22–23
Fellowships, 261–262
FindLaw Legal Classifieds, 68, 70
Fleming, Lis, *The One-Minute
   Commuter,* 295
Flex-time, 7
Flexibility, 278
Flexibility in job search, 162

Flexible schedules, 6
Flextime, 28
Florida Bar Journal, 326
"Flying Solo" (Ballman), 200–205, 325–326
Follow-up interview questions, 148
Forbes, 171
Formal Opinion 88–356 (ABA), 273
Formal personality, 9
Fortune, 171, 172
Free agents, 6
Freedom needs, 29
*Full Disclosure-Do You Really Want to be a
   Lawyer?* (ABA), 326
Fun needs, 29
Future designing, 9

G

Gaming law, 332
GATT. *See* General Agreement on Tariff
   and Trade
General Agreement on Tariff and Trade
   (GATT), 5
General Job Sites CareerWeb, 68
General Schedule (GS), 226–227
Generalists, 40
Geographic areas, 173–193, 194
   assessing motivations, 173–174
   checklist for long-distance job search,
      178–179
   climate considerations, 178
   cultural activities, 178
   current economic trends, 176–177
   economic climate of, 175–177
   and federal agencies, 236
   and federal jobs, 217
   international job search, 180–182
   marketability of practice area, 174–175
   Midwest, 175, 176
   Northeast and Middle Atlantic,
      174, 176
   and opportunities for professional
      development, 177
   and personal considerations, 177–178
   practice development plan, 179,
      192–193
   Rocky Mountain and Southwest,
      175, 177
   Southeast, 176, 177
   state bar admissions and reciprocity,
      182–192
   and temporary or contract
      positions, 179
   transportation issues, 178
   West, 175, 177
   worksheet for move, 182
"Geographic Areas" (Shannon), 173–192,
   331–332
Geopolitical changes, 5

Glasser, Robert, *Control Theory: A New Explanation of How We Control Our Lives,* 29
Global competition, 30
Global marketplace, 39
Globalization, 3, 5, 39
Goal clarification process, 9
Goal identification, 159
Goluboff, Nicole Belson, "Telecommuting," 292–296, 327
Goluboff, Nicole Belson, *Telecommuting for Lawyers,* 295, 327
GS. *See* General Schedule
Guide to Corporate Counsel (Prentice Hall), 208

H

Hagen, Laura J., "Negotiating Salary and Benefits," 152–158, 327
Haley, Toya Cook, 327
Hard copy resume, 105
Harvard Career Paths Study, 11
Harvard Law School public service opportunities, 331
Harvard Law School's Office of Public Interest Advising, 254
Headhunters, 44–46, 75, 77–80, 164, 256
    See also Search firms
Health care law, 171–172
Health care reform bill, 172
Hearsay, 145
Heels, Erik J. and Klau, Richard P., "Using the Internet," 63–71, 327–328, 328–329
    and *Law Law Law on the Internet: The Best Legal Web Sites and More,* 328
Heels, Erik J., *Legal List: Law-Related Resources on the Internet and Elsewhere,* 324
Hidden agendas, 57
Hierarchy, 6
Hill, The, 235
Hillman, Bob, 295
Hispanic National Bar Association, 101
Holland code, 16
Hollander, Dory, *The Doom Loop System,* 10
Home page, 66
Home practice, 281–291
    clients, 287–288
    equipment, 288–289
    goals and style of practice, 284–285
    the Internet, 290
    library, 290
    mail, 290
    office management, 290
    office requirements, 286–287
    personnel, 289
    See also Solo practice

special issues related to, 286
statistics for, 284
Horizontal representation, 257
"Hoteling," 6
House Action Report, The, 235
House Placement Office, 235
House of Representatives, 235
House Republican Conference, 235
"How to Change Jobs If You Want To or Have To" (Machlowitz), 42–47, 329
How to Create a Picture of Your Ideal Job or Next Career (Bolles), 33
"How to Set Up a Small Efficient Law Practice: Going Solo in the '90s" (Drain), 290
How to Switch Careers: The Professional Step-by-Step Guide, 26
"How to Use the Bar Association as a Career Resource" (Thomas), 84–88, 332
"How to Use Your Law School's Office of Career Services" (Mantis), 72–76, 330
Howard, Deborah, "The Cover Letter," 138–143, 328
Hunter, Scott, 36
Hyland, Timothy R., 328
Hyperlinks, 66–67
"Hypothetical" compensation packages, 153–154
    See also Salary and benefits negotiations

I

IBM, 284
Ideal job, 15
In-house compensation, 156
    See also Salary and benefits negotiations
In-House Lawyer of the Year, 329
In-house practice, 4, 16, 44, 46–47, 160, 206–212
    advantages of, 206–207
    beginning at, 211
    finding a position, 206
    identifying job opportunities, 207–208
    interviewing for, 208–209
    job bank Web site, 207
    mapping careers, 211–212
    nature of, 206–207
    offers and negotiating, 209–211
    researching the corporation, 208
Inappropriate questioning in interviews, 150
Index to Business Periodicals, 220
Indian law, 318
Indices of commitment to workforce diversity, 100
Industrial Revolution, 3

Informational interviews, 52, 53, 59–61, 81
　issues to cover during, 60
　See also Networking
Informational meetings, 256
Innuendo, 145
Intellectual Property Counsel, The
　(board), 326
Intellectual property law, 171
Interdisciplinary cooperation, 39
Interest Inventory, 81
Interesting work, 159–160
Internal clients, 156
　See also In-house practice
Internal Revenue Service (IRS), 216, 286
International corporations, 181
International job search, 180–182
　differing regulations, 181
　exchange programs, 181–182
　resume preparation, 180–181
　See also Geographic areas;
　　Resume writing
　volunteering, 182
International law, 39, 171
International public interest law, 259–260
International trade, 5
Internet, 26, 53, 63–71, 163, 175
　discussion sites, 70
　e-mail addresses, 64
　encryption, 66
　law firm Web sites, 69–70
　law-specific online resources, 67–69
　message body in e-mail, 64–65
　posting on the Web, 66–67
　See also Web sites
　sending a resume e-mail, 65–66
　subject line in e-mail, 64
　topic-specific lists, 71
Internet law, 67, 171
Interpersonal issues, 161–162
Interview-skills workshops, 73
Interviewing, 144–151
　dos and don'ts of, 150–151
　and federal agencies, 236
　follow-ups: selection, 147–149
　formulating questions for, 145
　for in-house counsel, 208–209
　inappropriate questions, 150
　initial: screening, 146–147
　pitfalls to avoid, 147
　preparing for, 144–145
　tips for, 149–150
　what interviewer will ask, 145
"Interviewing Techniques" (Magness and
　Wehmann), 144–150, 330, 333
Interviews, 9
Introspection, 8
Introversion versus extraversion, 20–21
Intuition versus sensing, 21–22

Involuntary job changes, 43–47
　consequences of layoffs, 46–47
　preparing for, 45
　See also Voluntary job changes
　warning signs of layoffs, 44–45
IRS. *See* Internal Revenue Service
Isolation problem of lawyers, 281

J
Job banks, 85–86
Job Descriptions for Bar Association Staff, 87
"Job hopper," 6
Job Hunter's Spiritual Companion, The, 28
Job opportunity exercise, 164
Job satisfaction, 18
Job satisfaction factors, 12–13
Job stability, 109
Job-Person Fit Theory, 18–19
Job-search package, 41
Job-search paradox, 17
Job-search steps, 55
Job-search support groups, 72
Job-search techniques and strategies, 51–55
　allocating time, 52–54
　developing support network, 55
　devoting full effort, 54–55
　focusing and planning, 51
　informational interviews, 52
　mass mailings, 54
　personal contact base, 53
　published notices, 53–54
　search firms, 54
Job-sharing, 31, 248, 271
Jobs for Lawyers: Effective Techniques for
　Getting Hired in Today's Legal Marketplace
　(Brady and Mantis), 326, 330
Judge pro tem, 245
Judgeships, 241–245
　advantages and disadvantages of,
　　242–243
　appointments, 243–245
　becoming a judge, 245
　costs of, 242
　process selection in the federal court
　　system, 244–245
　process selection in state court
　　systems, 243–244
　salaries, 242
　skills required for, 241–242
"Judgeships," (Albrecht), 241–245, 311
Judging versus perceiving, 23–25
"Judicial Administration, Staff Lawyers,
　and Law Clerks" (Schaak and Lett), 329,
　331, 246–252
Judicial clerkships, 267
Jung's Theory of Psychological Types,
　19–25

extraversion versus introversion, 20–21

judging versus perceiving, 23–25
See also Personality factors and career choice

sensing versus intuition, 21–22

thinking versus feeling, 22–23

Junior lawyers, 159–160

Juvenile advocacy, 157

K

Kanarek, Carol M., "Using Third-Party Intermediaries," 77–83, 327 and Changing Jobs: A Handbook for Lawyers (editor of first edition), 327

Karpovich, Michael Scott, 281

Kaufman, Judge Irving, 44

Keeping the Keepers: Strategies for Associate Retention in Times of Attrition (study), 37–38

King & Spaulding, 70

Kiplinger Washington Letter, The, 220

Knowledge areas, 11–12

Knowledge work, 4–5

L

Language skills, 98, 111, 160, 180, 258

LARP. See Lateral Attorney Recruitment Program

Latack, Dr. Janina C., 26–36, 34, 329

Lateral Attorney Recruitment Program (LARP), 225–226

Lateral hires, 63, 152–158, 194, 199
and federal jobs, 220, 225–226
See also Salary and benefits negotiation

Lateral hiring, xvii–xviii

Law clerks, 249–253
advantages and disadvantages of clerking, 252–253
application process, 250–252
courts, 250
interviewing process, 252
responsibilities of, 249–250
salaries of, 253

"Law Clerks" (Lett), 249–252, 329

Law firm brochures, 163

Law firm career choice, 194–199
advantages of moving from a bigger firm to a smaller, 198
advantages of moving from a smaller firm to a larger, 198
law firm culture in the new millennium, 198–199
marketability, 195–197
size of law firms and mergers, 197–198

Law firm compensation, 153–154
See also Salary and benefits negotiations

Law Firm Partnership and Benefits Report, 329

Law firm resumes. See Resume writing

Law firm Web sites, 69–70
See also Web sites

Law firm/law school analogy, 263

"Law Firms" (O'Briant), 194–198, 330

Law Jobs, 70

Law Law Law on the Internet: The Best Legal Web Sites and More (Heels and Klau), 314

Law librarians, 264

Law Practice Management (periodical by ABA), 328, 332

Law Practice Management Section (ABA), 328

Law Review experience, 98, 109

Law school career services, 9, 72–76, 144, 331
books and periodicals, 75
handouts and regional law firm lists, 75
job listings, 74
newsletters, 74
online services, 75
programs, 73–74
resources, 74
services, 72–73
technology, 74
what they do not offer, 75

Law school transcripts, 251

Law school/law firm analogy, 263

Lawyer skills, 11–12

Lawyer stereotypes, 306

Lawyer's Guide to the Internet, The (Allison), 290

Lawyer's Job Bulletin Board, 215

Lawyer's Jungle Book, The (Messinger), 31

Lawyers in Transition Committee of the Association of the Bar of the City of New York, 314

Layoffs, 43–47, 270, 274–275
facing consequences of, 46–47
preparing for, 45
reasons for, 44
See also Involuntary job changes
warning signs, 44–45

Leased work, 3

Leber, Celia, 293

Left-brain approach to career satisfaction, 27–34
See also Right-brain approach to career satisfaction; Whole brain approach to career satisfaction

Legal aid, 23, 24, 260–261
See also Public interest work

Legal List: Law-Related Resources on the Internet and Elsewhere, The (Heels), 313
Legal placement services, 85–86
Legal Services Corporation, 260, 261
Legal services/legal aid, 260–261
Legal Times, 215
LegalMinds, 70, 71
Leisure activities, 110
Lett, Sylvia J., "Law Clerks," 249–252, 315
Letters of recommendation, 251–252
Letters to contacts, 58
Lexis-Nexis, 5, 75, 208, 215
Library research for contacts, 57
Lieutenants, 154
Life key events, 10
Life, Law and the Pursuit of Balance: A Lawyer's Guide to Quality of Life (Maricopa County Bar Association publication), 33, 290, 332
Lifestyle needs, 8
Link Resources, 284
Liquid investments, 45
Listening, 146–147, 148–149
Litigation-intensive companies, 78
Litigator resumes. *See* Resume writing
LL.M. *See* Master of laws
Lockstep system of compensation, 153
    See also Salary and
        benefits negotiations
Long-distance job search. *See* Geographic areas; Out-of-town employers
Long-term goals, 160–162
"Looking for More Career Satisfaction? Use Your Whole Brain" (Latack), 26–36, 329
Los Angeles Times, 69
LSAT scores, 109

M
Machlowitz, David S., "How to Change Jobs If You Want To or Have To," 42–47, 329
McKenna & Cuneo, 69
Magistrates, 245
Magness, Michael K., and Wehmann, Carolyn M., "Interviewing Techniques," 144–150, 330, 333
Maintenance behaviors, 23
Major, Hagen and Africa, 329
Major, Jr., Robert A., "Making the "Right" Career Decision," 159–164, 329
"Making the "Right" Career Decision" (Major), 159–164, 329
Malaise, 28
Management committees, 160
Mantis, Hillary, *Alternative Careers for Lawyers; Jobs for Lawyers: Effective Techniques for Getting Hired in Today's Legal Marketplace*, 330
Mantis, Hillary, "How to Use Your Law School's Office of Career Services," 72–76, 330
Maricopa Bar Association, 332
Maricopa County Bar Association's Quality of Life Committee, xviii
Maricopa Lawyer, 331
"Market Assessment: Translating Your Skills to the Changing Profession" (Willard), 37–40, 334
Market assessment, 37–41, 51, 81
    career changes in law, 37–39
    focus group findings, 38
    translating skills to the changing profession, 40–41
    trends in the market, 39–40
Marketability of practice area, 174, 195–197
Martindale-Hubbell directory, 75, 163, 164, 208
Mass mailings, 54
Master of laws (LL.M), 266
Matrimonial law, 23
MBTI (Myers-Briggs Type Indicator), 19–20, 24, 25, 81
Mediators, 242, 245
Meditation, 28, 35
Megatrends (Nesbitt), 170
Membership directories of bar associations, 85
Mentors, 55, 61, 196
    for minority lawyers, 96–97, 99
Merge mailings, 141
Mergers, 30, 197–198
Merit appointments, 244
Merit selection/retention process, 243
Messinger, Thane, *The Lawyer's Jungle Book*, 31
Miami Daily Business Review, 326
Miami Herald Almanac of Florida Politics, The, 326
Microsoft Outlook, 66
Midcareer analysis, 9
Midsize firms, 197
Midwest. *See* Geographic areas
Military law, 22
Millennium lawyer opportunities, 168–169, 170–172
    See also Practice areas;
        Geographic areas
Minitrials, 242
Minorities in the Profession Committee, 100
Minority career opportunities, 96–102
    advice from minority lawyers, 98–99
    bar associations and city and state groups of law firms which have

signed Statements of Goals to increase minority representation, 102
choosing a place of employment, 99–100
dealing with a highly competitive work environment, 97–98
networks and mentors, 96–97
recruitment opportunities and professional networks, 100–102
Minority faculties, 98
Missouri Plan, 243
Mobility, 7, 195
Mobility model, 99
Mock interviews, 73
Money Magazine, 175
Monster Board, 68
Moot Court, 10
Moral support, 56
Morale, 8
Mosley-Goren, Molly, 293
Motivated skills, 19
Motivations for interest in geographical locations. *See* Geographic areas
Multinationalism, 5, 39
Munneke, Gary A., "Teaching Law," 263–268, 330
Mutual fund industry, 170
Myers-Briggs Type Indicator. *See* MBTI
Myths, 144

N

NABE Membership Directory, 87
NABE. *See* National Association of Bar Executives
NAFTA. *See* North American Free Trade Agreement
NALSC. *See* National Association of Legal Search Consultants
Name dropping, 79
NAPL. *See* National Association for Law Placement
National Asian Pacific American Bar Association, 101
National Association of Bar Executives of the American Bar Association, 87
National Association for Law Placement Foundation for Research and Education, 37
National Association for Law Placement (NAPL), 75, 76, 101, 161, 163, 255, 331
National Association of Legal Search Consultants (NALSC), 329, 330
National Association of Bar Executives (NABE), 87
National Bar Association, 101
National Board for Certified Counselors (NBCC), 329

National and Federal Legal Employment Report, 215, 220, 235
National Journal, 236
National Labor Relations Board, 221
National Law Journal, 163, 215, 295
NBCC. *See* National Board for Certified Counselors
Needs, 29
"Negotiating Salary and Benefits" (Hagen), 152–158, 327
Negotiating status for compensation, 154
   See also Salary and benefits negotiations
Nesbitt, John, *Megatrends*, 170
Net-Lawyers, 70
Netscape Communicator, 66
Networking, 45, 46, 53, 56–62
   at bar-sponsored events, 85
   contacts, 57–62
   and federal jobs, 222–224, 233–234
   follow-up, 61–62
   informational interviews, 59–61
   letter to contacts, 58
   for minority lawyers, 96–97
   and nontraditional careers for lawyers, 300
   and public interest work, 256, 262
   and target lists, 141
   teaching law, 268
   telephone calls to contacts, 58–59
   what to expect from, 56
"Networking" (Brady), 56–62, 326
Networking conferences, 97
New York Times, 26, 69, 268, 306
Newsletters, 53, 74, 84–85
NLADA. *See* Directory of Legal Aid and Defender Offices in the United States and Territories
Nolo Press, 304
Nonbillable legal responsibilities, 110
Nonequity partnerships, 32
Nonlegal business concept, 7
Nonlegal positions, 78, 142
Nonmonetary benefits of teaching law, 267
Nonpartnership, 32
Nonprofit management, 303–304
Nonprofit organizations, 256
Nonprofit public interest organizations, 258
Nontraditional careers for lawyers, 98, 298–307
   educational administrations, 303
   high technology companies, 304
   leaving the law, 301–302, 304
   monetary considerations, 305–306
   nonprofit management, 303–304
   obtaining a job, 304–305

potential employers' objections to, 305–307
regulation or enforcement specialists, 303
servicing legal professions, 303
sound reasons to change careers, 300
steps for career transition, 300–301
transferable skills analysis, 302–303
unsound reasons to change careers, 299
"Nontraditional Careers for Lawyers" (Arron), 298–307, 325
North American Free Trade Agreement (NAFTA), 5
Northeast and Middle Atlantic. *See* Geographic areas
Now Hiring: Government Jobs for Lawyers, 216, 221, 222
Number of lawyers in U.S., 167
Nursing homes and abuse, 171

O

O'Briant, Sandra, "Law Firms," 194–198, 330
Obsolescence, 6
OCC. *See* Online Career Center
Occupational 905 code, 214, 218–219
Offer letters, 158
Office of Human Resources, 235
Office of Personnel Management (OPM), 213–214, 219
Office of Public Interest Advising (OPIA), 331
Ohanesian, Consuelo M., 330–331
Old-fashioned jobs, 3
One-Minute Commuter, The (Fleming), 295
Online Career Center (OCC), 69
Online resources for lawyers, 67–69
See also Web sites; Internet
OPIA. *See* Office of Public Interest Advising
OPM. *See* Office of Personnel Management
Opportunities in Public Affairs, 235
Oral skills, 107, 247
Order of the Coif, 109, 325
Organizational behavior theorists, 28
Organizational climate, 9
Out-of-town employers, 141–142
See also Geographic areas
Outplacement consultants, 46, 82–83
"Outside the box" thinking, 6–7
Outsourced work, 3
Overhead, 31
Overworked American: The Unexpected Decline of Leisure, The (Schor), 30

P

Paper-and-pencil exercises, 9
Paralegals, 248, 278
Part-time employment, 7, 31, 47, 267
See also Alternative work arrangements
"Part-Time, Temporary, and Contract Employment" (Wallace), 270–277
Partner compensation, 154–155, 160–161
See also Salary and benefits negotiations
Peace Corps, 181
"Peer breeding grounds," 109
Pensions, 157, 170
Perceiving versus judging, 23–25
Performance-based compensation, 153
See also Salary and benefits negotiations
Periodicals, 84–85
Personal career identity, 18
Personal contact base, 53
See also Networking
Personal mission, 35
Personality factors and career choice, 18–25
extraversion versus introversion, 20–21
judging versus perceiving, 23–25
Jung's theory of psychological types, 19–25
MBTI, 19–20
sensing versus intuition, 21–22
thinking versus feeling, 22–23
"Personality Factors and Career Choice" (Richard), 18–25, 331
PGP. *See* Pretty Good Privacy
Pictorial directories, 85
Pigeonholed, 7
Pitfalls in interviewing, 147
Points, 154
Policy-oriented organizations, 258–259
Political changes, 170
Politics in America, 234
Portable practice, 174, 194
Post-information revolution economy, 5
Poverty law, 22
See also Public interest market
Power needs, 29
Practicality in job search, 162
Practice areas, 40, 167–172
of the 1980s and early 1990s, 169–170
current, 168–169
emerging, 168–169
marketability of, 174
for the new millennium, 170–172
"Practice Areas" (Bickerton), 167–170, 312
Practice breaks, 106
Practice development plans, 192–193

Prelaw, 26
Press reports, 164
Pretty Good Privacy (PGP), 66
Private practice career moves study, 37–39
Private public interest firms, 259
Pro bono work, 16, 262, 266
Productivity requirements, 107
Professional association meetings, 57
Professional development, 177
Professionalism, 32
Profit-sharing, 153, 157
    See also Salary and
        benefits negotiations
Programs of the ABA Commission on
    Opportunities for Minorities in the
    Profession, 101
Programs for alumni in job market,
    73–74
Project Parents, Inc., 331
Proxy statements, 208
Psychological comfort, 19
Psychological impact of layoffs, 43
Psychological needs, 19
Public defenders, 23, 24, 257
        salaries, 257
        See also Public interest market;
            Poverty law
Public Interest Job Search Guide (Harvard
    Law School), 261
Public interest market, 254–262
        benefits of, 254–255
        client-oriented/direct-service
            organizations, 258
        creating marketability, 262
        fellowships and entrepreneurial
            grants, 261–262
        financial considerations, 255–256
        international, 259–260
        legal services/legal aid, 260–261
        nonprofit public interest
            organizations, 258
        policy-oriented organizations,
            258–259
        private public interest firms, 259
        public defenders, 257
"Public Interest Market, The" (Shabecoff
    and Webb), 254–262, 331, 333
Public Lawyers Division of the Maricopa
    County Bar Association, 330
Public school systems, 178
Publication of the ABA Judicial Division,
    Task Force on Opportunities for
    Minorities, 101
Publications of the ABA Commission on
    Opportunities for Minorities in the
    Profession, 101
Published notices, 53–54
Publishing, 262

Q
Quasi-judicial positions, 243
Quick Job Hunt Map, The (Bolles), 9

R
Race dynamics, 97
Rainmaker Thinking, Inc., 333
Rainmakers, 20, 44, 73, 128, 156, 163, 194,
    199, 301
Real estate, 304
Real estate investment trusts (REITs),
    169, 170
Recession of the early 1990s, 167, 194
Reciprocity, 110, 179, 182–192
Recommendations, 134
        See also Resume writing
Recruiting pitches, 159
Recruitment opportunities and
    professional networks, 72, 100–102
Red Street Consulting (helps law firms use
    Internet), 329
Reengineering, 4
References, 46, 107, 134
        and job offers, 158
        See also Resume writing
Referrals, 56
        See also Networking
Reflection, 40
Regulation specialists, 303
Regulatory practice, 22
REITs. *See* Real estate investment trusts
Report of the Secretary of the Senate, The, 237
Republican Majority Whip Office, 235
Republican National Committee, 235
Republican Policy Committee, 235
Researching employers, 139
Restructuring, 4
Resume Referral Service, 235
Resume writing, 105–137
        appearance of resumes, 111
        for clerkships, 251
        comprehensive addenda and the
            resume package, 133–134
        corporate (corporate resume)
            example, 119, *120–122*, 123
        corporate (law firm resume) example,
            116, *117–118*, 119
        delivering resumes, 135–136
        description resumes, 105
        different uses of resumes, 105–106
        education, 109
        employment experience, 109–111
        evaluating experiences, 107
        first-draft components, 109–111
        general rules for, 108
        for international job searches, 180–182
        layout of resumes, 112

limitations of resumes, 106–107
litigator (corporate resume) example,
    129, *131–132*, 133
litigator (law firm resume) example,
    123, *124–127*, 128–129
memberships, certifications,
    affiliations, activities, 110–111
misconceptions, 106–107
organization of resumes, 112
preparation, 107–108
reviewing critically, 133
targeting audience, 107–108
technical example, 113, *114*, *115*
testing the audience, 134–135
updating, 136–137
visual effects, 111, 112
Resumes, 56
    e-mailing, 65–66, 135–136
    hard copy, 105
Retreats, 35
Richard, Dr. Larry
    doctoral research on Myers-Briggs
        Type Indicator (MBTI) and job
        satisfaction, 331
    See also Personality and career choice
Richard, Dr. Larry, "Personality Factors
    and Career Choice," 18–25, 331
Richmond Journal of Law and Technology, 314
Right-brain approach to career
    satisfaction, 27, 34–36
    See also Left-brain approach to career
        satisfaction; Whole brain approach
        to career satisfaction
Rizik, Christopher, 294–297
Rocky Mountain. *See* Geographic areas
Role models, 99
Roll Call, 235
Rolling Stones, 29
Root Tilden Scholar, 331
Rose, Jennifer, 30, 36
Royalty income, 267
Running from the Law (Arron), 325
Ryan, Maureen Provost, "Career Self-
    Assessment," 8–17, 331

S
Sabbaticals, 106, 167
Salary and benefits negotiations, 152–158,
    170–171
    basic compensation schemes, 152
    book of business, 155–156
    in-house compensation, 156
    for in-house counsel, 209–211
    law firm associates, 153–154
    negotiating status, 154
    overview, 152
    partner compensations, 154–155
    rules for, 157

Salary histories, 106–107, 157
Salary surveys, 157
Salary wars, 152
SAT scores, 109
Schaack, Daniel P. and Lett, Sylvia J.,
    "Judicial Administration, Staff, and Law
    Clerks," 246–252
Schaak, Daniel P., "Appellate Staff
    Lawyers," 247–249, 331
Schiumo, Michael J.K., "Effective Job-
    Search Techniques and Strategies,"
    51–56, 331
Schloss, Ernest, 34
School transcripts, 134
    See also Resume writing
Schor, Juliet, *The Overworked American: The
    Unexpected Decline of Leisure*, 30
Search firms, 46, 54, 77–80, 157, 158
    employers who use, 78
    and in-house practice, 207
    and international job searching, 181
    list of practices to avoid, 79–80
    list of things they should do, 80
    See also Headhunters
    states that use, 78
    versus career counselors, 80
Security, 6
Self-analysis, 37
Self-assessment, 138, 149, 162–163, 299–300
    See also Career self-assessment
Self-help books, 25
Self-inventory, 138–139
Seminars, 12
Senate Placement Office, 235
Senate Republican Conference, 235
Senior Executive Service (SES), 226–227
Seniority, 6, 155, 174
Sensing versus intuition, 21–22
Servicing the legal professions, 303
SES. *See* Senior Executive Service
Severance packages, 46, 82
SF 171 form, 219, 222
Shabecoff, Alexa and Webb, C.A., "The
    Public Interest Market," 254–262,
    331, 332
Shannon & Manch, LLP, 317–318
Shannon, Marcia Pennington,
    "Geographic Areas," 173–192, 331–332
Sharpter Image, 304
Short-term goals, 159–160
Sidley & Austin, 69–70
Siemens Corporation, 329
Simmons, Jeffrey R., 332
Skill clusters, 11–12
Skill-training seminars, 73
Skills courses, 264
Snell & Wilmer, 332
Snelling, Sr., Robert O., 8

Societal trends, 170
Socratic legal education, 264
Solo practice, 200–205, 278, 325
    See also Home practice
    what it's like, 203–204
Solo practice and solo flying analogy, 200–205
Southeast. *See* Geographic areas
Southwest. *See* Geographic areas
Speaking assignments, 47
Specialization, 31, 40, 45–46, 175, 220
Specialized educational courses, 98
"Spiders" (to attract surfers to Web sites), 136
Staff lawyers. *See* Appellate staff lawyers
Standard Form, 171, 214
State bar admission requirements, 177, 182–192
State Bar of Arizona, xviii
State Bar of Arizona Indian Law Section, 318
State court clerkships, 250
State court system judges. *See* Judgeships
Statements of Goals (to increase minority representation), 102
Statistical Analysis and Services Division of the Office of Personnel Management, 213–214
Staudenmaier, Heidi McNeil, xvii–xviii, 318
Stock options, 157, 160
Stress questions, 145
Strong Interest Inventory, 16
Student Lawyer (ABA periodical), 329
Substantive knowledge, 107, 174, 180, 220
Substantive practice experience, 156
Success pattern, 9–11
"Summary of Experience," 12
Superfund site cleanup activities, 170
Supply and demand of lawyers, 167
Support groups, 46
Support network, 55
Support staff, 24
Supreme Court judges, 244
Surfing the Web, 33
Survival and reproduction needs, 29

T
Talents use, 14–15
Target lists of potential employers, 139
Tax Reform Act of 1986, 169
Tax-deferred annuity/retirement program, 267
Teaching, 304
Teaching law, 263–269
    finding a job, 268
    opportunities, 263–265
    pay and benefits, 267–268
    qualifications for, 266–267
    tenure, 263–265
    work duties, 265–266
    working with students, 165
"Teaching Law" (Munneke), 263–268, 316
Technical resumes. *See* Resume writing
Technological changes, 4, 170
Technology, 40
Technology advances, 4
Telecommuting, xvii, xviii, 28, 292–297
    better work product advantage, 294
    dispelling concerns, 296–297
    for greater efficiency, 293–294
    increased available work time, 294–295
    increased productivity advantage, 293
    recruitment process and lower turnover costs, 295–296
    reduced overhead potential, 296
"Telecommuting" (Goluboff), 292–296, 327
Telecommuting for Lawyers (Goluboff), 295, 297, 327
Telephone calls to contacts, 58–59
Teleworking. *See* Telecommuting
Temporary legal placement agencies. *See* Alternative work arrangements
Temporary work, 3, 85, 179, 195
    See also Alternative work arrangements
Tenure, 263–265
    See also Teaching law
Texas Law Review, 326, 329
Text-only format, 65
Thalheimer, Richard, 304
Theoretical issues of law, 249
Thinking versus feeling, 22–23
Third-party intermediaries, 77–83
    career counselors, 80–82
    legal search firms, 77–80
    outplacement consultants, 82–83
Thomas, Brenda M., "How to Use the Bar Association as a Career Resource," 84–88, 332
Thomas, Pat Bowers, "Writing an Effective Resume," 105–137, 332
Toffler, Alvin, 170
Topic-specific discussion list, 71
Trade barriers, 5
Trade publication surveys, 157
Traditional associate's role, 16
Traditional law firms, 22
Training, 159, 194, 196
Transactional expertise, 78
Transferable skills, 8, 10, 27, 142–143
Transferable skills analysis, 302–303
Transition steps for job changes, 42–43
Trend in the market, 39–40
Trial court clerkships, 249, 250

True Work: The Sacred Dimension of Earning a Living, 28
Tucker, Marilyn, "Federal Agencies," 213–238, 332–333; "Will Women Lawyers Ever Be Happy?," 333
Tulgan, Bruce, "Career Changing in the New Millennium," 3–7, 333
Two-income families and layoffs, 43

U

Uniform resource locator. *See* URL
United Nations, 180
United States Court of Appeals for the Federal Circuit, 249
University of Miami Law Review, 326
URL (uniform resource locator), 66
U.S. Government Manual, 216
U.S. Patent & Trademark Office, 110
US West Never Busy Fax, 288
"Using the Internet" (Heels and Klau), 63–71, 327–328, 328–329
"Using Third-Party Intermediaries" (Kanarek), 77–78, 328

V

Values, 19, 301–302
Values assessment, 12–14
Vendor advertisements, 85
Vertical representation, 257
Vesting anniversary, 157
Videotaped mock interviews, 73
Vieweg, David E., *Commercial Real Estate Transactions Practice Manual* (editor), 333
Virtual workplace, 5–6
Visualization, 28, 34–36, 40
Voluntary job changes, 42–43
    See also Involuntary job changes

W

Wall Street Journal, 220
Wallace Law Registry, 333
Wallace, Shelley, "Part-Time, Temporary, and Contract Employment," 270–277
Warm cover letters, 141
Washington Post, 69, 215
Web sites, 32, 53, 74, 163, 290
    electronic resumes, 136
    for federal agencies, 215–216, 226, 231–232, 239–240
    in-house job bank, 207
    international bar associations, 94
    local bar associations, 90–92
    for relocation, 178
    specialty bar and other legal organizations, 92–94
    state bar associations, 88–90
Wehmann, Carolyn M., 333
West Legal Directory, 215
West. *See* Geographic areas
Westlaw, 5, 75, 215
What Can You Do with a Law Degree? (Arron), 303, 325
What Color Is Your Parachute? (Bolles), 9, 75, 303
What Do You Want to Do Next with Your Law Degree? (career development seminar by Deborah Arron), 325
What Lawyers Earn (Brady), 326
Whole brain approach for career satisfaction, 26–36
    factors for, 33–34
    job versus career, 29–30
    left brain, 27–34
    quest for balance, 30–33
    right-brain, 34–36
Willard, Dr. Abbie, "Market Assessment: Translating Your Skills to the Changing Profession," 37–40, 334
Within-class compensation distinctions, 153
    See also Salary and benefits negotiations
Work focus, 35
Work quality during job changes, 43
Work settings, 14–15
Work This Way: How 1,000 Young People Designed Their Own Careers in the New Workplace and How You Can Too (Tulgan), 333
Work values, 8
"Writing an Effective Resume" (Thomas), 105–137, 332
Writing instructors, 266
Writing portfolio, 99
Writing samples, 134, 251
    See also Resume writing
Writing skills, 99, 107, 143
    for judgeships, 241
    and staff lawyer positions, 248
Written reviews, 158

Y

Y2K disaster scenarios, 28
Young Lawyers Division Career Issues Committee (ABA), 316

Z

Zagat (restaurant rating guides), 304

Law Firm Partnership Guide: Strengthening Your Firm.
Addresses what to do after your firm is up and running, including
how to handle: change, financial problems, governance issues,
compensating firm owners, and leadership.

Law Law Law on the Internet. Presents the most influential law-
related Web sites. Features Web site reviews of the *National Law
Journal's 250*, so you can save time surfing the Net and quickly find
the information you need.

Law Office Policy and Procedures Manual, 3rd Ed. A model for
law office policies and procedures (includes diskette). Covers law
office organization, management, personnel policies, financial
management, technology, and communications systems.

Law Office Staff Manual for Solos and Small Firms. Use this
manual as is or customize it using the book's diskette. Includes
general office policies on confidentiality, employee compensation,
sick leave, sexual harassment, billing, and more.

The Lawyer's Guide to Creating Web Pages. A practical guide that
clearly explains HTML, covers how to design a Web site, and
introduces Web-authoring tools.

The Lawyer's Guide to the Internet. A guide to what the Internet
is (and isn't), how it applies to the legal profession, and the different
ways it can—and should—be used.

The Lawyer's Guide to Marketing on the Internet. This book
talks about the pluses and minuses of marketing on the Internet, as
well as how to develop an Internet marketing plan.

The Lawyer's Quick Guide to E-Mail. Covers basic and
intermediate topics, including setting up an e-mail program, sending
messages, managing received messages, using mailing lists, security,
and more.

**The Lawyer's Quick Guide to Microsoft® Internet Explorer; The
Lawyer's Quick Guide to Netscape® Navigator.** These two guides
de-mystify the most popular Internet browsers. Four quick and easy
lessons include: Basic Navigation, Setting a Bookmark, Browsing
with a Purpose, and Keeping What You Find.

The Lawyer's Quick Guide to Timeslips®. Filled with practical
examples, this guide uses three short, interactive lessons to show to
efficiently use Timeslips.

**The Lawyer's Quick Guide to WordPerfect® 7.0/8.0 for
Windows®.** Covers multitasking, entering and editing text,
formatting letters, creating briefs, and more. Includes a diskette with
practice exercises and word templates.

Leaders' Digest: A Review of the Best Books on Leadership. This
book will help you find the best books on leadership to help you
achieve extraordinary and exceptional leadership skills.

**Living with the Law: Strategies to Avoid Burnout and Create
Balance.** Examines ways to manage stress, make the practice of law
more satisfying, and improve client service.

Marketing Success Stories. This collection of anecdotes provides an
inside look at how successful lawyers market themselves, their
practice specialties, their firms, and their profession.

Microsoft® Word for Windows® in One Hour for Lawyers. Uses
four easy lessons to help you prepare, save, and edit a basic
document in Word.

**Practicing Law Without Clients: Making a Living as a Freelanc
Lawyer.** Describes freelance legal researching, writing, and
consulting opportunities that are available to lawyers.

Quicken® in One Hour for Lawyers. With quick, concise
instructions, this book explains the basics of Quicken and how to us
the program to detect and analyze financial problems.

Risk Management. Presents practical ways to asses your level of
risk, improve client services, and avoid mistakes that can lead to
costly malpractice claims, civil liability, or discipline. Includes Law
Firm Quality/In Control (QUIC) Surveys on diskette and other tools
to help you perform a self-audit.

Running a Law Practice on a Shoestring. Offers a crash course in
successful entrepreneurship. Features money-saving tips on office
space, computer equipment, travel, furniture, staffing, and more.

Successful Client Newsletters. Written for lawyers, editors, writers,
and marketers, this book can help you to start a newsletter from
scratch, redesign an existing one, or improve your current practices
in design, production, and marketing.

Survival Guide for Road Warriors. A guide to using a notebook
computer (laptop) and other technology to improve your productivit
in your office, on the road, in the courtroom, or at home.

Telecommuting for Lawyers. Discover methods for implementing
successful telecommuting program that can lead to increased
productivity, improved work product, higher revenues, lower
overhead costs, and better communications. Addressing both law
firms and telecommuters, this guide covers start-up, budgeting,
setting policies, selecting participants, training, and technology.

Through the Client's Eyes. Includes an overview of client relations
and sample letters, surveys, and self-assessment questions to gauge
your client relations acumen.

Time Matters® in One Hour for Lawyers. Employs quick, easy
lessons to show you how to: add contacts, cases, and notes to Time
Matters; work with events and the calendar; and integrate your data
into a case management system that suits your needs.

Wills, Trusts, and Technology. Reveals why you should automate
your estates practice; identifies what should be automated; explains
how to select the right software; and helps you get up and running
with the software you select.

Win-Win Billing Strategies. Prepared by a blue-ribbon ABA task
force of practicing lawyers, corporate counsel, and management
consultants, this book explores what constitutes "value" and how to
bill for it. You'll understand how to get fair compensation for your
work and communicate and justify fees to cost-conscious clients.

Women Rainmakers' 101+ Best Marketing Tips. A collection of
over 130 marketing from women rainmakers throughout the country.
Features tips on image, networking, public relations, and advertising.

Year 2000 Problem and the Legal Profession. In clear,
nontechnical terms, this book will help you identify, address, and
meet the challenges that Y2K poses to the legal industry.

**TO ORDER CALL TOLL-FREE:
1-800-285-2221**

Qty	Title	LPM Price	Regular Price	Total
____	ABA Guide to International Business Negotiations (5110331)	$ 74.95	$ 84.95	$_____
____	ABA Guide to Lawyer Trust Accounts (5110374)	69.95	79.95	$_____
____	ABA Guide to Legal Marketing (5110341)	69.95	79.95	$_____
____	ABA Guide to Prof. Managers in the Law Office (5110373)	69.95	79.95	$_____
____	Anatomy of a Law Firm Merger (5110310)	24.95	29.95	$_____
____	Billing Innovations (5110366)	124.95	144.95	$_____
____	Changing Jobs, 3rd Ed.	*please call for information*		$_____
____	Compensation Plans for Lawyers, 2nd Ed. (5110353)	69.95	79.95	$_____
____	Complete Internet Handbook for Lawyers (5110413)	39.95	49.95	$_____
____	Computer-Assisted Legal Research (5110388)	69.95	79.95	$_____
____	Computerized Case Management Systems (5110409)	39.95	49.95	$_____
____	Connecting with Your Client (5110378)	54.95	64.95	$_____
____	Do-It-Yourself Public Relations (5110352)	69.95	79.95	$_____
____	Easy Self Audits for the Busy Law Firm	*please call for information*		$_____
____	Finding the Right Lawyer (5110339)	14.95	14.95	$_____
____	Flying Solo, 2nd Ed. (5110328)	29.95	34.95	$_____
____	Handling Personnel Issues in the Law Office (5110381)	59.95	69.95	$_____
____	HotDocs® in One Hour for Lawyers (5110403)	29.95	34.95	$_____
____	How to Build and Manage an Employment Law Practice (5110389)	44.95	54.95	$_____
____	How to Build and Manage an Estates Law Practice	*please call for information*		$_____
____	How to Build and Manage a Personal Injury Practice (5110386)	44.95	54.95	$_____
____	How to Draft Bills Clients Rush to Pay (5110344)	39.95	49.95	$_____
____	How to Start & Build a Law Practice, Millennium Fourth Edition (5110415)	47.95	54.95	$_____
____	Internet Fact Finder for Lawyers (5110399)	34.95	39.95	$_____
____	Law Firm Partnership Guide: Getting Started (5110363)	64.95	74.95	$_____
____	Law Firm Partnership Guide: Strengthening Your Firm (5110391)	64.95	74.95	$_____
____	Law Law Law on the Internet (5110400)	34.95	39.95	$_____
____	Law Office Policy & Procedures Manual (5110375)	99.95	109.95	$_____
____	Law Office Staff Manual for Solos & Small Firms (5110361)	49.95	59.95	$_____
____	Lawyer's Guide to Creating Web Pages (5110383)	54.95	64.95	$_____
____	Lawyer's Guide to the Internet (5110343)	24.95	29.95	$_____
____	Lawyer's Guide to Marketing on the Internet (5110371)	54.95	64.95	$_____
____	Lawyer's Quick Guide to E-Mail (5110406)	34.95	39.95	$_____
____	Lawyer's Quick Guide to Microsoft Internet® Explorer (5110392)	24.95	29.95	$_____
____	Lawyer's Quick Guide to Netscape® Navigator (5110384)	24.95	29.95	$_____
____	Lawyer's Quick Guide to Timeslips® (5110405)	34.95	39.95	$_____
____	Lawyer's Quick Guide to WordPerfect® 7.0/8.0 (5110395)	34.95	39.95	$_____
____	Leaders' Digest (5110356)	49.95	59.95	$_____
____	Living with the Law (5110379)	59.95	69.95	$_____
____	Marketing Success Stories (5110382)	79.95	89.95	$_____
____	Microsoft® Word for Windows® in One Hour for Lawyers (5110358)	19.95	29.95	$_____
____	Practicing Law Without Clients (5110376)	49.95	59.95	$_____
____	Quicken® in One Hour for Lawyers (5110380)	19.95	29.95	$_____
____	Risk Management (5610123)	69.95	79.95	$_____
____	Running a Law Practice on a Shoestring (5110387)	39.95	49.95	$_____
____	Successful Client Newsletters (5110396)	39.95	44.95	$_____
____	Survival Guide for Road Warriors (5110362)	24.95	29.95	$_____
____	Telecommuting for Lawyers (5110401)	39.95	49.95	$_____
____	Through the Client's Eyes (5110337)	69.95	79.95	$_____
____	Time Matters® in One Hour for Lawyers (5110402)	29.95	34.95	$_____
____	Wills, Trusts, and Technology (5430377)	74.95	84.95	$_____
____	Win-Win Billing Strategies (5110304)	89.95	99.95	$_____
____	Women Rainmakers' 101+ Best Marketing Tips (5110336)	14.95	19.95	$_____
____	Year 2000 Problem and the Legal Profession (5110410)	24.95	29.95	$_____

*Handling
$10.00-$24.99......................$3.95
$25.00-$49.99......................$4.95
$50.00+ $5.95   MD residents add 5%

**Tax
DC residents add 5.75%
IL residents add 8.75%

Subtotal	$_____
*Handling	$_____
**Tax	$_____
TOTAL	$_____

PAYMENT
☐ Check enclosed (to the ABA) ☐ Bill Me
☐ Visa ☐ MasterCard ☐ American Express

Account Number   Exp. Date   Signature

Name   Firm

Address

City   State   Zip

Phone Number   E-Mail Address

Mail: ABA Publication Orders, P.O. Box 10892, Chicago, Illinois 60610-0892 ♦ **Phone:** (800) 285-2221 ♦ **FAX:** (312) 988-5568

E-Mail: abasvcctr@abanet.org ♦ **Internet:** http://www.abanet.org/lpm/catalog

Source Code: 22AEND499